European Collaboration in Research and
Development

European Collaboration in Research and Development

Business Strategy and Public Policy

Edited by

Yannis Caloghirou

Assistant Professor of Industrial Economics and Business Strategy, Laboratory of Industrial and Energy Economics, National Technical University of Athens, Greece

Nicholas S. Vonortas

Director, Center for International Science and Technology Policy, Elliott School of International Affairs, and Associate Professor of Economics and International Affairs, The George Washington University, Washington DC, USA

Stavros Ioannides

Associate Professor of Economics, Department of Political Science and History, Panteion University, Athens, Greece

Edward Elgar
Cheltenham, UK • Northampton, MA, USA

Published by
Edward Elgar Publishing Limited
Glensanda House
Montpellier Parade
Cheltenham
Glos GL50 1UA
UK

Edward Elgar Publishing, Inc.
136 West Street
Suite 202
Northampton
Massachusetts 01060
USA

A catalogue record for this book
is available from the British Library

Library of Congress Cataloguing in Publication Data

European collaboration in research and development : business strategy and
    public policy / edited by Yannis Caloghirou, Nicholas S. Vonortas, Stavros
    Ioannides.
        p. cm.
    Includes index.
    1. Research, Industrial–Europe–International cooperation.   2. Research and
development partnership–Europe–International cooperation.   3. Technology
and state–Europe–International cooperation.   I. Caloghirou, Yannis, 1952–
II. Vonortas, Nicholas S., 1958–   III. Ioannides, Stavros.

T177.E8E98   2003
338.94′07–dc22   2003049269

ISBN 1 84064 371 4

Printed and bound in Great Britain by MPG Books Ltd, Bodmin, Cornwall

Contents

PART II   POLICY

Figures

Tables

List of contributors

Katharine Barker   PREST, Manchester University, UK

Maria Rosa Battaggion   Università degli Studi di Bergamo, Bergamo, Italy and CESPRI, Università L. Bocconi, Milan, Italy

Patrizia Bussoli   Nextra Investment Management sgr, Milan, Italy

Yannis Caloghirou   Laboratory of Industrial and Energy Economics, National Technical University of Athens, Greece

Hugh Cameron   PREST, Manchester University, UK

Luke Georghiou   PREST, Manchester University, UK

Stavros Ioannides   Panteion University, Athens, Greece and Laboratory of Industrial and Energy Economics, National Technical University of Athens, Greece

Ioanna Kastelli   Laboratory of Industrial and Energy Economics, National Technical University of Athens, Greece

Pedro L. Marín   Universidad Carlos III de Madrid, and CEPR, Spain

Mireille Matt   Bureau d'Economie Théorique et Appliquée (BETA), Université de Strasbourg, France.

Georges Siotis Universidad Carlos III de Madrid, Spain

Aggelos Tsakanikas   Laboratory of Industrial and Energy Economics, National Technical University of Athens, Greece

Nicholas S. Vonortas   George Washington University, Washington DC, USA and Laboratory of Industrial and Energy Economics, National Technical University of Athens, Greece

Foreword

This book represents a timely initiative. In recent years, collaborations in research and development have gained enormous importance for innovation and technology diffusion, and have therefore gained the attention of managers, economists and policy makers. This new form of organization of research activity is a quite effective way to share knowledge, gain complementary assets and generate new technologies in most sectors where advancement is rapid. Therefore it has become the focus of European and national policies in support of innovation and technology diffusion.

The work by Yannis Caloghirou, Nicholas Vonortas and Stavros Ioannides and their co-authors addresses the relevant topic of collaborations in research and development at two complementary levels. First, it focuses on their determinants, performance and impact through a survey of more than 500 companies in seven European countries and through case studies on several research joint ventures. Second, it examines public policy in support of R&D cooperation in various European countries and by doing that it emphasizes similarities and differences.

Thus the book represents a very rich and insightful analysis of the characteristics of collaborations in research. It is very documentative and provides a useful evaluation for the researcher and the policy maker. In order to examine collaborations it not only combines successfully various complementary databases with survey and case studies. It also maintains a comparative perspective in looking at the ways firms collaborate and at the role of national innovation systems within Europe.

The conclusion that one can draw from this work is that research collaborations are now a pervasive and diffused way to get access to knowledge and generate innovation, but that firms differ widely in the motivations for collaborations and the benefits gained, and governments follow a wide variety of policies in this respect. All these differences have to be well known and understood by the researcher and the policy maker. No doubt this book greatly advances our understanding about the characteristics and policy aspects of collaborations in R&D. And this understanding becomes particularly relevant when the new Sixth Framework Programme moves Europe towards the creation of an integrated Research Area.

Franco Malerba
CESPRI – Bocconi University, Milan

Acknowledgements

The chapters of this book share a common background in the research project 'Science and Technology Policies towards Research Joint Ventures' funded by the Targeted Scio-Economic Research Programme (TSER) of the European Commission's Directorate General Research (Project SOE1-CT97-1075). This project was undertaken during 1998-2000. We are grateful to the Commission for generous support that made it possible. We would also like to express our gratitude to the programme officers assigned to this project, Steve Parker and Virginia Vitorino. They followed the work of the consortium members from close range, were present in all the meetings of the consortium and provided very useful advice. Needless to say, they share in the praise but not in the mistakes and any remaining misunderstandings, which are the exclusive responsibility of the editors and the chapter authors.

A consortium involving seven research teams from six European countries participated in that research project. While the names of some of the people involved in the research are reflected on the chapter titles of this book, the project benefited from the hard work and expertise of many others whom we would like to thank sincerely. The following academics and other experts participated at different stages of the project: Jacques Arlandis, Maria Rosa Battaggion, Assimina Christoforou, Olivier Dartois, George Hondroyannis, Ioanna Kastelli, Yannis Katsoulacos, Giorgio Barba Navaretti, Aggelos Tsakanikas, David Ulph, Patrizia Bussoli, Virginia Recchia, Alessandro Sembeneli, Salvatore Torrisi, Praveen Kujal, Elena Revilla, George Siotis, Pedro Marín, Roberto Hernan, Lars-Gunnar Mattsson, Dimitris Ioannidis, Eva Wikstrand, Kate Barker, Luke Georghiou, Hugh Cameron, Deborah Cox and Carole McKinlay. They all worked with diligence and with a lot of humour, both necessary ingredients of long-term working relationships.

Finally, we would like to acknowledge the very valuable contribution of external reviewers and participants at various seminars and conferences where material from this project was presented at different times. Equally, our graduate students have been exposed to this material and have offered very valuable ideas and suggestions. It is impossible to name them all here.

Abbreviations

AGRIRES 3C	Agricultural Research Programme
AIC	Associazione Italiana Calciatori
ANOVA	Analysis of variance
ANVAR	National Agency for the Valuation of Research (France)
ARPA	Advanced Research Projects Agency (USA)
ASI	Agenzia Spaziale Italiana
ASTER	Agenzia Scienza Technologia Emilia-Romagna
ATP	Advanced Technology Program (USA)
ATYCA	Iniciativa de Apoyo a laTecnología, la Seguridad y la Calidad Industrial (Supporting Actions for Industrial Technology, Safety and Quality – Spain)
BAP	Biotechnology Action Programme
BERD	Business expenditure on research and development
BRITE/ EURAM 3	Basic Research in Industrial Technologies for Europe / European Research on Advanced Materials
CAICYT	Scientific and Technical Research Advisory Commission (Spain)
CASE	Co-operative Awards in Science and Engineering
CATI	Cooperative Agreements and Technology Indicators
CDTI	Industrial Technological Development Centre (Spain)
CEA	Atomic Energy Commissariat (France)
CICYT	Comisión Interministerial de Ciencia y Tecnología (Science and Technology Inter-ministerial Commission – Spain)
CILEA	Consorzio Interuniversitario Lombardo per L'Elaborazione Automatica
CNES	National Space Research Centre (France)
CNR	Consiglio Nazionale delle Ricerche
CNRS	National Centre for Scientific Research (France)
CORDIS	Community Research and Development Information Service
CORE	Strategic alliance database compiled by Prof. Albert Link at the University of North Carolina

CRADA	Cooperative Research and Development Agreement (USA)
CRT	Technological Resource Centres (France)
DARPA	Defence Advanced Research Projects Agency (USA)
DECOM 2C	Decommissioning of Nuclear Installations Programme
DGFT	Director General of Fair Trading
DNRD	National research and development expenditure (France)
DTI	Department of Trade and Industry
EICTA	European Information and Communication Technologies Association
ENEA	Ente per la Nuove Tenologie, L'Energia e L'Ambiante
ENNONUC3C	Non-Nuclear Energy Programme
EPO	European Patent Office
EPSRC	Engineering and Physical Sciences Research Council
ERA	European Research Area
ESPRIT	European Strategic Programme of Research in Information Technologies
ETI	Environmental Technology Initiative (USA)
EU	European Union
EU-FWP	EU Framework Programmes
EURATOM	European Atomic Energy Commission
FCCSET	Federal Coordinating Council for Science, Engineering and Technology
FEEM	Fondazione Eni Enrico Mattei (Italy)
FNS	National Fund for Science (France)
FPST	Framework Programmes for Science and Technology
FRA	Fondo Speciale per la Ricerca Applicata (Italy)
FRT	Fund for Technological Research (Italy)
FWP	Framework Programmes for Research and Technological Development
GDP	Gross domestic product
GEIE	European Group of Economic Interest
GERD	Gross expenditure on research and development
GSM	Global System for Mobile telephony
ICT	Information and Communication Technologies
IDATE	Institut de l'Audiovisuel et des Telecommunications (France)
IEATP	Information Engineering Advanced Technology Programme
IMI	Istituto Mobiliare Italiano (Italy)
INFN	Instituto Nazionale de Fisica Nucleare

INRA	Institut National de la Recherche Agronomique (France)
INRETS	Institut National de la Recherche, sur les Transports et leur Sécurité (France)
INSERM	Institut National de la Santé et de la Recherche Médicale (France)
IP	Intellectual property
IPR	Intellectual property rights
IS&T	Italian Science and Technology
IT	Information technology
JESSI	Joint European Submicron Silicon Initiative
JRC	Joint Research Centre
LFCICT	Scientific and Technical Research Promotion and Coordination Act (Spain)
LIEE	Laboratory of Industrial and Energy Economics
LRU	University Reform Act (Spain)
MCYT	Ministerio de Ciencia y Tecnología (Ministry of Science and Technology – Spain)
MECUs	Million European Currency Units
MEDEA RJV	Microelectronics Development for European Applications Research Joint Venture
MENRT	Ministere de l'Education Nationale de la Recherche et de la Technologie
MEP	Manufacturing Extension Partnership (USA)
MERIT	Maastricht Economic Research Institute on Innovation and Technology
MINER	Ministry of Industry and Energy (Spain)
MITI	Ministry of Trade and Industry (Japan)
MMC	Monopolies and Mergers Commission
MURST	Ministry of University, Scientific and Technological Research (Italy)
NACE	Nomenclature Générale des Activités Economiques dans la Communauté Européenne
NBS	National Bureau of Standards (USA)
NCRA	National Cooperative Research Act, 1984 (USA)
NCRPA	National Cooperative Research and Production Act 1993 (USA)
NIC	Newly Industrial Country
NII	National Innovation Infrastructure (USA)
NIS	National innovation systems
NIST	National Institute of Standards and Technology (USA)
NP	National Plan (Spain)

NSI	National system of innovation
NTBF	New technology-based firms
OECD	Organisation for Economic Co-operation and Development
OFT	Office of Fair Trading
OLS	Ordinary Least Square
OSTP	Office of Science and Technology Policy (USA)
OTRI	Technology Transfer Office (Spain)
OTT	Oficina de Transferencia de Tecnología (Spain – Technology Transfer Office)
PACTI	Programme for the Promotion of the Science and Technological-Industrial System (Spain)
PATI	Plan de Actuación Tecnológica Industrial (Industrial and Technological Action Plan – Spain)
PETRI	Proyecto de Estímulo a la Transferencia de Resultados de Investigación
PF	Progetti Finalizzati (Italy)
PNGV	Partnership for a New Generation of Vehicles
PNR	National programmes of research
PREDIT	Programme National de Recherche et d'Innovation dans les Transports Terrestres (France)
PREST	Policy Research in Engineering, Science and Technology
PRO	Public Research Organization
PROFIT	Programa de Fomento de la Investigación (Spain)
RADWASTOM 3C	Radioactive Waste Storage and Management Programme
R&D	Research and development
R&D&I	Research and development and innovation
R&E	Research and Engineering
RJV	Research joint venture
RP	Research partnerships
RTD	Research and technological development
SBIR	Small Business Innovation and Research (USA)
SIRN	Strategic Industrial Research Networks
SME	Small and medium-sized enterprise
SMEs	Small and Medium Enterprises
SSE	Stockholm School of Economics
S&T	Science and technology
STEP TO RJV	Science and Technology Policies Towards Research Joint Ventures
TFP	Total factor productivity

TFTS	Terrestrial Flight Telephone Service
TRIPS	Trade-related aspects of intellectual property rights
TRP	Technology Reinvestment Program (USA)
TSER	Targeted Socio-Economic Research
U:Carlos III	Universidad Carlos III de Madrid
UKPO	UK Patent Office
VLSI	Very Large Scale Integration
WTO	World Trade Organization

1. General introduction

Yannis Caloghirou, Nicholas S. Vonortas and Stavros Ioannides

At the start of a new millennium, Europe finds itself at a crossroads. At Europe's core, the European Union (EU) has provided the continent with stable democratic institutions and is fulfilling long-held dreams of integration of the continent, divided for centuries by wars and languages but united by shared common cultures and traditions. With no fewer than ten new countries to add to its existing 15 member states and with an on-going debate on broadening versus deepening, the EU has launched unprecedented efforts to achieve monetary union among member states, to proceed with an orderly expansion to the east and south that may double membership in just a few years, and to reconsider its budgets, institutional organization and constitutional statutes.

In the midst of all this upheaval, the Union has embarked on a major reorganization of its famed Framework Programmes for Research and Technological Development (FWP). Officially initiated in 1984, the first five FWPs have been basic pillars of European scientific and technological development, integration and cohesion during the past couple of decades. They have supported all kinds of research and development (R&D) in high technology sectors, have forced European organizations to work together in cross-border partnerships, and have created a sense of European 'togetherness' in science and technology (S&T). The time of this writing coincides with the launch by the European Commission of the Sixth Framework Programme (FWP6).

The Sixth Framework Programme for Research and Technological Development (FWP6) has been touted as a new start and a major break on the previous five FWPs. Whereas they had imposed an R&D structure living and breathing in parallel with national S&T programmes and policies, FWP6 is the first expected to tackle yet another European dream: the creation of the European Research Area (ERA). The ERA is an institutional superstructure that will increasingly weave EU S&T programmes administered by the European Commission, EU-subsidized S&T programmes administered by national and regional governments, and national/regional

S&T programmes into a seamless web of a European-centered technical enterprise. In its abstraction, the ERA concept fits well with all other efforts for greater socio-economic integration.

On the eve of the introduction of FWP6, the European Union is taking stock of past S&T policies that have contributed to the Union's current levels of economic development, international competitiveness, and social cohesion. The success of FWP6 in spearheading a new era of scientific and technological achievement in Europe will critically depend on the clear understanding of the successes and shortcomings of past S&T policies both at the EU and member state levels.

A STUDY OF COOPERATIVE R&D IN EUROPE

This is the context of the present book. A single book cannot, of course, tackle all the important developments currently unfolding in Europe. It focuses on a small part of these developments, primarily relating to co-operative industrial research in the European Union in the last two decades. The book is itself a product of cooperative research, more specifically of research funded by the Targeted Socio-Economic Research Programme of FWP4.[1] The material presented herein builds on the collaborative work of seven capable European research teams, including senior researchers from:

- Laboratory of Industrial and Energy Economics (LIEE), National Technical University of Athens (coordinator) – Greece;
- Strategic Industrial Research Networks (SIRN) – United Kingdom;
- Fondazione Eni Enrico Mattei (FEEM) – Italy;
- Institut de l' Audiovisuel et des Telecommunications (IDATE) – France;
- Stockholm School of Economics (SSE) – Sweden;
- Universidad Carlos III de Madrid (U:Carlos III) – Spain;
- Policy Research in Engineering, Science and Technology, Victoria University of Manchester (PREST) – United Kingdom.

During a two-year period (1998 to 2000), this consortium undertook an in-depth theoretical, empirical, and policy analysis of cooperative R&D in Europe. This book recounts some of their important findings while paying particular attention to policy-related questions.

The research project dealt with various forms of cooperative research activity:

1. EU-funded cooperative R&D, primarily of a precompetitive nature, generated by a top-down procedure, activated by the Commission, and implemented through the FWP.
2. Cooperative R&D for the development of marketable products and services, generated by a bottom-up procedure, selected by EUREKA, and usually subsidized by national governments. Getting the 'Eureka label' for a project and granting public funding for its implementation differs between EU countries.
3. Nationally-funded cooperative R&D, generated by a top-down procedure, where part of the subsidies may be EU funds channelled through national agencies.

The partnerships in the first two categories involve partners based in two or more European countries. The majority of the partnerships in the third category involve partners based in the same country. An important characteristic of all examined partnerships is that at least one partner is an industrial firm. A significant number of these partnerships also include academic institutions and other public research organizations.

A very extensive data-collection enterprise was launched to support the multi-faceted analysis. The result was the creation of the STEP-TO-RJVs Databank, made of several different databases and a large number of case studies carried out by the partners of the consortium. Based on such data, the project explored the following issues:

- What is the scope and extent of subsidized R&D collaboration in Europe?
- Why do firms and other organizations collaborate?
- How do firms and other organizations collaborate in R&D activities?
- What is the outcome and the overall economic impact of R&D collaboration?
- How can R&D collaboration serve specific S&T policy objectives (and vice versa)?

The fundamental questions the research project dealt with include:

- To what extent does R&D cooperation promote technological progress?
- Do cooperative R&D agreements, considered as a strategic tool, assist firms to redefine industrial boundaries and create new market opportunities?
- Do the institutional set-up, the market organization and other structural factors facilitate cooperation in R&D?

- To what extent do cooperative R&D agreements promote the transfer and creation of knowledge across organizations?
- What type of policy initiatives may improve the effectiveness of R&D cooperative schemes?
- What is the importance of public funding in undertaking the R&D cooperation? In other words, what if public funding was not available?
- What has been the role of cooperative R&D in advancing the competitiveness of European industry and European socio-economic cohesion?

RESEARCH PARTNERSHIPS: SOME STYLIZED FACTS[2]

Inter-firm cooperation in R&D is neither a new phenomenon nor an exclusively European one. In fact, during the past couple of decades the number of cooperative agreements has increased dramatically world-wide, while their nature has changed from, primarily, agreements involving equity (formal equity joint ventures) to, primarily, non-equity agreements.

Research on the MERIT-CATI database has revealed a number of worldwide trends in technology partnerships (strategic technical alliances) during the last quarter century.[3] As announced in major technology and trade magazines and the popular press, the number of new partnerships set up annually has gradually increased from about 30–40 in the early 1970s, to 100–200 in the late 1970s, and then again to around 600 or more later in the 1980s and 1990s. During the early 1970s about 80 per cent of the announced research partnerships were equity joint ventures. Gradually this distribution changed. By the mid-1990s more than 85 per cent of technology partnerships did not involve equity investments.

The share of domestic inter-firm collaboration recorded in CATI as occurring during the 1970s and 1980s was only about 35 per cent of the total. The share of domestic partnerships has gradually risen to about 45 per cent during the 1990s. This change has largely been caused by the role of intra-US collaboration in two major fields, information technology and biotechnology, reflecting the very important role that United States firms have played in leading edge research in these two fields. That role not only makes them attractive partners for international collaboration, but also raises the probability of intra-US joint research at the scientific and technological frontier.

During most of the 1970s (when some current high-technology activities such as biotechnology and advanced materials research were almost non-existent), the share of high-technology sectors (OECD classification) was on average about 40 per cent of the total number of inter-firm partnerships. During the late 1970s and early 1980s, this share increased to between 50 per cent and 60 per cent. From the mid-1980s to the mid-1990s this share increased even further. According to the most recent data, about 80 per cent of the inter-firm research relationships are established in high-technology areas. Information technology has by far been the dominant technology area in partnerships, followed at some distance by biotechnology and new materials.

The majority of technology relationships have been established within the Triad – North America, the European Union and Japan. During the 1970s and 1980s the share of the Triad in all these partnerships was over 95 per cent. In the 1990s this dominance became less strong as the share of other combinations rose to about 20 per cent. The growth of inter-firm partnerships with partners from outside the Triad reflects the growth of the share of alliances with companies from South East Asian countries, such as South Korea, Taiwan, Singapore and Hong Kong (Freeman and Hagedoorn, 1994; Hagedoorn, Link and Vonortas, 2000).

The information on countries beyond the Triad is fragmented. Most of it shows an increase in the activity. Focusing on information technologies, Vonortas and Safioleas (1997) reported a number of interesting trends for alliances involving at least one participant from developing countries (including economies in transition) between 1984 and 1994. They found that the number of such alliances grew impressively during that period – faster in fact than alliances with participants from industrialized countries only. Transitional economies and NICs have dominated alliance activity. The vast majority of alliances have involved the creation, exchange, or transfer of technological knowledge. Telecommunications was found to have passed ahead of computers to dominate these alliances in the early 1990s. Contractual agreements tended to dominate alliances by developing country firms. Agreements involving R&D have been increasing.

There were clear indications that certain developing country firms have been able to extract significant benefits from alliances, not only in terms of accessing superior technology but also acquiring the capability to develop new technology on their own. The most active partners from industrialized countries have been large multinational enterprises in telecommunications, computers, electronic components and consumer electronics, reflecting their world-wide reach, indisputable technological strengths and significant financial resources.

These developments have been mirrored by a dramatic change in the way policy analysts and decision-makers perceive the advantages and disadvantages of inter-firm cooperation. Rather than organizational mechanisms to assist declining industries and weakened firms, inter-firm cooperative agreements to create and disseminate technological knowledge are now viewed as veritable competitive mechanisms, right at the strategy core of most companies in high technology industries (Vonortas, 1997). A voluminous economic and business literature has supported these views (see following sections).

Prompted by concerns over the lagging international competitiveness of high technology industries, both the United States and the European Union mobilized in the early 1980s to establish policies that both provided the necessary legal environment and actively promoted R&D cooperation. In a radical shift away from its earlier orientation, the US government made major policy steps in the past couple of decades to accommodate and actively promote government-university-industry partnerships (Vonortas, 2000). This system was further strengthened in the 1990s by a series of programmes actively promoting government-industry-university partnerships and efforts to 'channel' private sector R&D activity in technological areas with potentially widespread economic returns. Similar concerns over the international competitiveness of industry have also underlined the establishment of a formal science and technology policy in the European Union during the 1980s, very much based on the support of collaborative R&D through the FWP.

Such policy developments condoned collaboration in R&D and gave clear signals of the new policy orientation of the American and European leaderships. Industry has never looked back. The result has been a frenzy of 'deals', ranging from simple, long-term contractual agreements to share products, technologies and markets, all the way to complex mega mergers and acquisitions. The vast majority of these deals reflects the vision of corporate strategists of the shape of future business in an environment of rapid technological advance and increased technological and market uncertainty.

POLICY DEVELOPMENT BACKGROUND

In the 1980s, the debate about international economic competitiveness started focusing on what was considered to represent a new form of business self-organization for undertaking uncertain and complex business activities. Cooperation was considered to offer new capabilities to the private sector, especially in the form of allowing greater flexibility in an era of increasing international competition. Soon, economists and policy makers were proclaiming that cooperation allowed society to break free from the long recognized market failure in R&D by restoring (at least partly) the incentives of firms to engage in an activity that is uncertain, risky, increasingly expensive and whose results are usually only imperfectly appropriable by any single organization.

Everybody agreed that basic research is pretty close to a public good and that its funding is the obligation of the government. Almost everybody also agreed that development research, meaning the very applied part of the research activity leading to specific products and process, is largely the responsibility of the private sector. Where there was (and still is) disagreement is in the grey area between the two, a murky space that some say is small, some say is large, and many believe is of variable proportions that change with the characteristics of the industry and the technology. This area is sometimes called precompetitive, or generic, research (Nelson, 1989, 1990). This research was considered imperative for competitiveness but subject to serious market failures.

The debate was fairly clearly cast on the basis of competitiveness and market failure. It resulted in a series of very important policy changes on both sides of the Atlantic. In 1984, the European Union officially put in place what would become its main instrument of science, technology, and innovation policy: the 4-year FWPs. The cornerstone of these programmes has been support for cooperative R&D, since the beginning proclaimed to be focused on precompetitive R&D. A year later, the much-publicized EUREKA programme was set up in Europe in which all EU member states, the EU Commission, and other countries became members. Again, collaborative R&D was the objective, only this time the D was emphasised much more than the R. In contrast to the FWPs, EUREKA did not subsidize R&D. EUREKA selected worthy collaborative R&D projects – thus, raising their chances for getting funded at the national level or by the private sector. EUREKA projects were supposed to focus on the development of specific products and processes and, thus, be complementary to those funded by the Framework Programmes. Independently, national governments across Europe also increased their support of cooperative R&D.

Also in 1984, and exactly on the same conceptual grounds, the Congress of the United States passed the National Cooperative Research Act (NCRA) that provided antitrust protection to cooperative (generic) research. At the same time (early 1980s), the United States embarked on a serious effort to overhaul its competition system – trying to make it less punishing to cooperation that, even though somewhat suspect at present, alluded to greater innovation efficiency and better 'future markets'– and its intellectual property rights system, in terms of strengthening the protection of intellectual property ownership. Both changes facilitated inter-firm collaboration.

The basic policy changes have remained. Significant political and economic events during the intervening time period, however, have affected the raison d'être of these policies. On the one hand, the European Union already has five additional members and is currently (in 2003) preparing to accept several more. Economic cohesion between the 'centre' and the 'periphery' has thus become a larger issue in the Union than ever before. Moreover, several years of economic upturn have not managed to eliminate high rates of unemployment in Europe. Employment of Europeans has become a major policy concern. Overall, then, as competitiveness concerns receded somewhat in the European Union, concerns of employment and economic cohesion between member states have strengthened.

On the other hand, the United States has enjoyed the longest time period of continuous, strong economic growth in its history, achieving full employment for the largest part of the 1990s.[4] Meanwhile Japan, projecting the major competitive threat for both European and American industry in the late 1970s and throughout the 1980s, has reeled under prolonged economic recession during the 1990s. In other words, the 'competitiveness lobby' has lost ground in the United States without any other significant replacement.

The rationale for cooperative R&D has changed accordingly. In the European Union, the competitiveness and market failure rationales have been joined with the cohesion and employment rationales for supporting cooperative research. This has created some uneasiness among policy analysts who have argued that there may be a trade-off between competitiveness and cohesion, which may decrease the effectiveness of the FWP. Only the market failure rationale remains in the United States. Japan, a staunch supporter of cooperative R&D in its catch-up phase, has been distracted by its economic problems and has not paid much attention to the potential impact of cooperation on the needed structural change beyond facilitating the link between industry and universities and the strengthening of the latter.

This is actually a good time for taking stock. The study underlying the material in this book has tried to create a large source of data and use it to appraise the motives for, and effects of, cooperative R&D in the European Union and several of its member countries. In finalizing research hypotheses, the consortium partners took into consideration the main policy concerns above and the important questions raised in the economics and business literature.

ANALYTICAL APPROACH

We focus here on one kind of strategic technical alliance that we describe as Research Joint Ventures (RJVs). RJVs are defined as (temporary) organizations, jointly controlled by at least two participating entities, whose primary purpose is to engage in cooperative R&D. Equity investment may or may not be an issue and usually it is not. Most of the examined RJVs are essentially contract-based agreements between independent entities. Member entities may include firms, universities and other government organizations.

The study only dealt with RJVs involving at least one participant from the private sector. When more than one firm is involved, both horizontal RJVs (between competitors) and non-horizontal RJVs – vertical (upstream-downstream) and conglomerate (other combinations not vertically related) – were included. While this definition is broad enough to include both government-subsidized and private, non-subsidized cooperative R&D agreements, in practice our data sets include RJVs subsidized by government funds, at least in part.

The research methodology involved four kinds of activities.

- First, an extensive bibliographic analysis of policies regarding RJVs at the EU level, the seven represented EU-member countries, the United States and Japan. This analysis covered current policies as well as their recent historical development in three areas: science and technology policy, competition policy and intellectual property rights policy.
- Second, a very extensive data collection exercise was launched that resulted in what could be the largest and most detailed single source of information on subsidized RJVs in the world (see below).
- Third, this data was used for extensive empirical analysis, including (a) statistical analysis of RJVs and RJV participants' characteristics, objectives and strategies, and (b) econometric analysis of the determinants and impacts of RJVs. In addition, a large number of case studies of individual RJVs were carried out.
- Fourth, the results of the empirical analysis were used to assess the overall effectiveness of policies regarding RJVs in Europe and to draw lessons for future policies.

One of the most formidable undertakings in this study involved a multi-faceted data collection exercise, which, arguably, proved one of the project's most successful undertakings. The outcome is the STEP-TO-RJVs data-bank, which contains seven databases, three international and a set of four national databases.

EU RJV Database

This contains information on transnational RJVs established under the first four FWPs up to the end of 1996. It contains information on all RJVs with at least one participant from the private sector supported by 64 different programmes that include all commonly known programmes and many more. When all is told, the database includes 6,300 usable RJVs with 12,730 participating organizations from 42 countries. It also contains information for a large number of the identified private sector participants.

EUREKA RJV Database

The EUREKA RJV database includes all RJVs that have been chosen and promoted under the EUREKA label between 1985 and 1996. RJVs with a member from the private sector have been included in the database. They amount to 1,031 RJVs, which have been set up by 4,261 organizations from 36 countries.

National RJV Databases

Four national databases have been created with information on RJVs sponsored (fully or partially) by national sources since the mid-1980s in Greece, Spain, Sweden and the United Kingdom. Coverage of publicly funded RJVs in these countries is not exhaustive (with the possible exception of Greece), however, which limited the use for comparative purposes in this project. Nonetheless, the four national databases can be considered as a unique source of information on these countries.

RJV Survey Database

This database contains the results of a wide-ranging survey of firms that have engaged in one or more RJVs. The survey sample includes firms that have participated in a mixture of EU-funded, EUREKA, and nationally funded projects. It was conducted in the seven countries represented in this project – France, Greece, Ireland, Italy, Spain, Sweden and the United Kingdom. In all, completed responses were obtained from 504 firms relating to 636 RJVs. The available information relates to strategic motives to cooperate in R&D, factors that affect the choice of partners, the type of knowledge created, learned, and transferred between partners as well as the learning mechanisms, expected benefits from collaboration and the extent to which they were fulfilled.

An additional rich source of information used in this project came from 21 case studies of RJVs led by firms based in the seven countries represented in the consortium. The case studies provided important detailed information addressing the context of collaboration and the process and timing of events. In particular, case studies focused on the origins and objectives of the RJV and participating organizations, RJV organization and relationship to member firm strategy, working relationship among partners, RJV results and impact on participants, and commercial exploitation of cooperative R&D outcomes.

ORGANIZATION OF THE BOOK

The book is divided into two parts: an analytical part and a policy part. The chapters forming the analytical part deal with the theory on cooperative R&D and the empirical analysis of European RJVs. Chapter 2 concentrates on the theory of RJVs as it appears in the economics and business management literature. Chapter 3 recounts the main trends of European RJVs on the basis of the EU RJV and EUREKA RJV databases. Chapter 4 utilizes the responses of more than 500 companies in seven EU country members to illustrate the strategic considerations of European firms when forming RJVs and the expected tangible and intangible returns from this activity. Chapter 5 focuses on the qualitative evidence from the case studies of more than twenty RJVs exploring the factors that enable or constrain the formation and evolution of R&D cooperation, the effects of cooperation and the role of subsidies. Chapter 6 summarizes the results of empirical work undertaken by consortium partners on the determinants of RJV formation, RJV performance, and on the impact of RJVs on industries and regional economies.

Seven chapters form the policy part of the book. These chapters deal with the policies towards R&D cooperation of individual countries and one region. Three kinds of policy are discussed: science and technology policy, competition policy and intellectual property protection. Chapters seven to twelve, then, appraise the relevant policies of the European Union, the United Kingdom, France, Italy, Spain and the United States of America respectively. Policy chapters have been contributed by the consortium partners, with the exception of that on France, which has been prepared by an expert outside the consortium. Chapter 13 closes this part by tracing the common policy threads across countries.

Finally, Chapter 14 concludes the book by delineating the main policy lessons for Europe and by pointing out important avenues for future work.

NOTES

1. Y. Caloghirou and N. S. Vonortas, *Science and Technology Policy Towards Research Joint Ventures*, Final Report of the STEP-TO-RJVs Project SOE1–CT97–1075, Targeted

Socio-Economic Research Programme (TSER), European Commission, DG Research, March 2000.
2. This section draws extensively on Hagedoorn, Link and Vonortas (2000).
3. See Hagedoorn (1996, 2001), Hagedoorn and Schakenraad (1990, 1992), and Hagedoorn, Link and Vonortas (2000). Global alliance trends during the 1990s, including both technology-intensive and non-technology based agreements, have been described in Kang and Sakai (2000).
4. This remarkable achievement has been followed by a significant economic slowdown which, at the time of this writing, had yet to raise the competitiveness concerns of the 1980s.

REFERENCES

Caloghirou Y. and N. S. Vonortas (2000), *Science and Technology Policy Towards Research Joint Ventures*, final report of the STEP-TO-RJV's Project SOE1-CT97-1075, Targeted Socio-Economic Research Programme, European Commission, DG Research, March.

Freeman C. and J. Hagedoorn (1994), 'Catching up or falling behind: patterns in international interfirm technology partnering', *World Development*, **22**(5), 771–80.

Hagedoorn, J. (1996), 'Trends and patterns in strategic technology partnering since the early seventies', *Review of Industrial Organization*, **11**(5), 601–16.

Hagedoorn, J. (2001), 'Inter-firm R&D partnerships: an overview of major trends and patterns since 1960', in J. E. Jankowski, A. N. Link and N. S. Vonortas (eds), *Strategic Research Partnerships*, Arlington, VA: National Science Foundation, 63–89.

Hagedoorn, J. and J. Schakenraad (1990), 'Inter-firm partnerships and cooperative strategies in core technologies', in C. Freeman and L. Soete (eds), *New Explorations in the Economics of Technological Change*, London: Pinter Publishers, pp. 3–37.

Hagedoorn, J., A. N. Link and N. S. Vonortas (2000), 'Research partnerships', *Research Policy*, **29**(4–5), 567–86.

Kang, N.-H. and K. Sakai (2000), 'International strategic alliances: their role in industrial globalization', *STI* working paper 2000/5, Paris: OECD.

Nelson, R. R. (1989) 'What is private and what is public about technology?', *Science, Technology and Human Values*, **14**(3): 229–41.

Nelson, R. R. (1990) 'Capitalism as an engine of progress', *Research Policy*, **19**, 193–214.

Vonortas, N. S. (1997), '*Cooperation in Research and Development*', Boston, MA, Dordrecht, Netherlands: Kluwer Academic Publishers.

Vonortas, N. S. (2000), 'Technology policy in the United States and the European Union: Shifting orientation towards technology users', *Science and Public Policy*, **27**(2), 97–108.

Vonortas, N. S. and S. P. Safioleas (1997), 'Strategic alliances in information technology and developing country firms: recent evidence', *World Development*, **25**(5), 657–80.

PART I

Collaboration in research and development:
theory and practice

Introduction to Part I

The proliferation of a wide variety of inter-organizational cooperative agreements since the early 1980s has created the need for new definitions of cooperation (Hagedoorn and Schakenraad, 1990; Nooteboom, 1999). The term 'strategic alliance' was thus invented to encompass the multitude of forms these agreements have taken. According to one definition, a strategic alliance is a web of agreements whereby two or more partners share the commitment to reach a common goal by pooling their resources together and coordinating their activities (Teece, 1992). An alliance denotes some degree of strategic and operational coordination and may also include things such as technology exchanges, exclusionary market and manufacturing rights, and co-marketing agreements.

Collaborative arrangements can take many forms (Hagedoorn, Link and Vonortas, 2000; Littler, Leverick and Wilson, 1998): from formal collaboration, founded on an explicit, common purpose agreed by the parties and based on explicit contracts, to informal collaborations involving more tacit and casual relationships. It may take place between and among customers, suppliers, competitors, or even between organizations that just share some common expertise. An increase in the joint projects launched by companies with public research institutes and universities has been pointed out by many scholars (Caloghirou, Tsakanikas and Vonortas, 2001; Georghiou, 1998), along with a steady growth of interfirm alliances during the 1980s (Contractor and Lorange, 1988; Mytelka, 1991; Chesnais, 1988; Hagedoorn, 2001).

We focus in this book on collaboration on technological issues (Dodgson, 1993), and especially on Research Joint Ventures. RJVs are defined as organizations, jointly controlled by at least two participating entities, whose primary purpose is to engage in cooperative research and development (R&D). RJVs engage companies, universities and/or government agencies and laboratories in various combinations to pool resources in pursuit of a shared R&D objective. An alternative term for RJVs – the way we define them in this book – is research partnerships (RPs). We will use the terms RJV and RP interchangeably.

Collaboration in R&D is one of the most popular types of collaboration. The strategic choice of firms to perform common research activities either with other firms or other types of actors has attracted the attention not only of economists and business strategy scholars, but of policy analysts as well. Empirical analysis has shown that major objectives of firms when entering cooperative R&D agreements include cost and risk sharing, accessing complementary resources and skills, and exploiting research synergies along with keeping up with major technological developments (Caloghirou and Vonortas, 2000). An extensive literature has dealt with knowledge-based linkages. Among others, we can cite Hagedoorn's (1995) and Duysters & Hagedoorn's (1996) examination of private alliances focused on technological issues that have been created without any external source of funding. Vonortas (1997a) also provides information about RJVs that have been established in the US and registered under the National Cooperative Research Act (NCRA). *Strategic Research Partnerships* by Jankowski, Link and Vonortas (2001) includes several pieces addressing the question of RP indicators. There is also a voluminous body of literature focusing on specific subsets of linkages at the national or even at a sectoral level, examining the effectiveness of national or regional policies towards the promotion of cooperation among various types of actors (McFarlane, 1999; Miyata, 1996; Odagiri et al., 1997; Wang, 1994; Beecham and Cordey-Hayes, 1998; Staropoli, 1998; Aldrich and Sasak, 1994).

The book focuses on a special form of collaborative R&D: subsidised RJVs that have been established through project-based ventures in the European Research Area. The research partnerships that we examine are contractual agreements among independent entities, with at least one member of the consortium being a firm. Other member entities may include firms, universities, research institutes and other organizations.

The empirical analysis is firmly based on relevant economic, business and policy literature. This literature has indicated a long list of potential benefits and costs to cooperative R&D. Potential benefits to participating organizations include:

- R&D cost sharing;
- Reduction of R&D duplication;
- Risk sharing, uncertainty reduction;
- Spillover internalization;
- Continuity of R&D effort; access to finance;
- Access of complementary resources and skills;
- Research synergies;
- Effective deployment of extant resources; further development of resource base;
- Strategic flexibility, market access and the creation of investment 'options';
- Promotion of technical standards;

- Market power; co-opting competition;
- University and research institute research, better attuned with private sector interests.

Potential costs to RJV participants include:

- Actual resources devoted to the cooperative R&D activity;
- Incompatibility with company (or university) interests;
- Delay of technological advance (due to collusion);
- Loss of control to a vital technology.

Cooperative R&D also creates social benefits (and costs) that accrue to non-participating organizations and the rest of society. Social benefits may be the result of:

- Knowledge spillovers to non-participants;
- Increased industrial competitiveness;
- Increased levels of competition;
- Favourable changes in investment behaviour;
- More efficient establishment of technology standards;
- Broad socio-economic benefits as a result of structural adjustment, employment, and so on;
- Increased economic cohesion between European regions.

Potential social costs may be the result of:

- Anti-competitive behaviour;
- Limiting the number of R&D approaches to uncertain technological problems;
- Creating dependencies on public resources;
- Wasting taxpayers' money.

The insights of prior research were synthesized in five broad topical areas that this research project dealt with:

- Trends in RJV formation in Europe; characteristics of RJVs and participating organizations.
- Determinants of RJV formation.
- Performance of the RJV *per se*.
- Impact on firms participating in the RJV.
- Meso- and macro-economic level impacts for Europe, including competitiveness and cohesion.

- Development and comparison of policies promoting RJVs in Europe, the United States and Japan.

The chapters of Part I deal with the theory on cooperative R&D and the empirical analysis of European RJVs. While the underlying material in this section reflects the collaborative effort of all seven consortium partners in the TSER project, senior analysts of the project coordinator have written the individual chapters. Chapter 2 concentrates on the theory of RJVs. Chapter 3 recounts the main trends of publicly-funded, European-based RJVs. Chapter 4 illustrates the strategic considerations of European firms when forming RJVs and the expected tangible and intangible returns from this activity. Chapter 5 focuses on the qualitative evidence from the interview-based studies of more than twenty RJVs dealing with contextual issues and with issues related to the quality of the relationship among partners, information sharing in the RJVs, membership differences and limitations of collaboration. Chapter 6 summarizes the results of empirical work on the determinants of RJV formation, RJV performance and the impact of RJVs on industries and regional economies. Finally, a concluding section pulls together the main empirical findings.

REFERENCES

Aldrich, H. E. and T. Sasak (1994), 'R&D consortia in the United States and Japan', *Research Policy*, **24**(2), 301–16.

Beecham, M. A. and M. Cordey-Hayes (1998), 'Partnering and knowledge transfer in the UK motor industry', *Technovation*, **18**(3), 191–205.

Caloghirou, Y. and N. S. Vonortas (2000), 'Science and technology policies towards research joint ventures', final report to the commission, DGXII, TSER Programme, April.

Caloghirou, Y., A. Tsakanikas, and N. S. Vonortas (2001), 'University–industry cooperation in the context of the European Framework Programmes', *The Journal of Technology Transfer*, **26**(1–2), 153–61.

Chesnais, F. (1988), 'Technical cooperation agreements between firms', *STI Review*, 4.

Contractor, F. G. and P. Lorange (1988), 'Why should firms cooperate? The strategy and economic basis for cooperative ventures', in F. J. Contractor and P. Lorange (eds), *Cooperative Strategies in International Business*, Lexington: Lexington Books.

Dodgson, M. (1993), *Technological Collaboration in Industry*, London: Routledge.

Duysters, G. and J. Hagedoorn (1996), 'Internationalisation of corporate technology through strategic partnering: an empirical investigation', *Research Policy*, **25**(1), 1–12.

Georghiou, L. (1998), 'Global cooperation in research', *Research Policy*, **27**, 611–26.

Hagedoorn, J. (1995), 'Strategic technology partnering during the 1980s: trends, networks and corporate patterns in non core technologies', *Research Policy*, **24**(2), 207–31.

Hagedoorn, J. (2001), 'Research partnership trends 1960–1998', in J. Jankowski, A. N. Link and N. S. Vonortas (eds), *Strategic Research Partnerships*, Arlington, VA: National Science Foundation.

Hagedoorn, J. and J. Schakenraad (1990), 'Inter-firm partnerships and co-operative strategies in core technologies', in Christopher Freeman and Luc Soete (eds), *New Explorations in the Economics of Technical Change*, London: Pinter Publishers, pp. 3–37.

Hagedoorn, J. and J. Schakenraad (1992), 'Leading companies and networks of strategic alliances in information technologies', *Research Policy*, **21**, 163–90.

Hagedoorn, J., A. Link, and N. S. Vonortas (2000), 'Research partnerships', *Research Policy*, **29**(4–5), 567–86.

Jankowski, J., A. N. Link and N. S. Vonortas (eds) (2001), *Strategic Research Partnerships*, Arlington, VA: National Science Foundation.

Littler, D., F. Leverick, and D. Wilson (1998), 'Collaboration in new technology based product markets', *International Journal of Technology Management*, **15**(1–2), 139–59.

McFarlane, J. (1999), 'Collaborative research: the Australian experience', *International Journal of Technology Management*, **17**(4), 387–401.

Miyata, Y. (1996), 'An analysis of cooperative R&D in the United States', *Technovation*, **16**(3), 123–31.

Mytelka, L. (ed.) (1991), *Strategic Partnerships and the World Economy*, London: Pinter Publishers.

Nooteboom, B. (1999), *Inter-Firm Alliances: Analysis and Design*, London: Routledge.

Odagiri, H., Y. Nakamura, and M. Shibuya (1997), 'Research consortia as a vehicle for basic research: the case of fifth generation computer project in Japan', *Research Policy*, **26**(2), 191–207.

Staropoli, C. (1998), 'Cooperation in R&D in the pharmaceutical industry – the network as an organizational innovation governing technological innovation', *Technovation*, **18**(1), 13–23.

Teece, D. J. (1992), 'Competition, cooperation, and innovation: organizational arrangements for regimes of rapid technological progress,' *Journal of Economic Behavior and Organization*, **18**(1), 1–25.

Vonortas, N. S. (1997), *Cooperation in Research and Development*, Norwell, MA, Dordrecht, Netherlands: Kluwer Academic Publishers.

Wang, J. C. (1994), 'Cooperative research in a newly industrialized country: Taiwan', *Research Policy*, **23**(6), 697–711.

2. Research joint ventures: a survey of the theoretical literature

Yannis Caloghirou, Stavros Ioannides and Nicholas S. Vonortas

The phenomenon of cooperative R&D has attracted a great deal of both theoretical and empirical work in recent years, for a variety of reasons. Let us just mention two here. The first is that the growing willingness of firms to engage in cooperative R&D – thus sharing control over it – seems to contradict the long held conviction that R&D constitutes the absolute 'core' of the firm's essence. Thus cooperative R&D seems to raise questions that lie at the heart of the nature of the firm, as this is perceived by economic theory. Secondly, the explanation of the RJV phenomenon may have major implications for policy. If RJVs are viewed as efforts by participating firms to restrict competition, then policy should be directed against them, on the basis of well-established antitrust principles. If, on the other hand, RJVs are viewed as helping the cooperating firms to build competitive advantages while, at the same time, leaving the competitive market framework unchanged, they should be encouraged.

This chapter presents and discusses critically various theoretical approaches to RJVs and attempts to link these approaches to the underlying theories of the firm. We thus take heed of Ronald Coase's question 'What determines what a firm does?'; and of his response that 'To answer this question, it is necessary to understand why a firm exists at all . . .' (1972, p. 62). According to the logic of this statement, differing explanations of what the firm does may be attributable to differing explanations of its nature. The important implication for our task here is that we may link the various perspectives on RJV formation to corresponding ideas on the nature of the firm.

On these grounds, we divide the theoretical perspectives on RJVs into two broad strands,[1] each approaching the nature of the firm as an organization with a unique set of tools. The first strand approaches the firm with the tools of cost-benefit calculus of standard neoclassical analysis. Two theoretical perspectives on RJVs fall into this category: mainstream industrial organization, and transaction costs and incomplete contracts. The second strand stems from the theories of the firm that view this form of organization as a bundle of resources, and which are especially popular in strategic management literature. We discuss these perspectives in turn and we conclude this chapter with a brief discussion on the implications of the various theoretical perspectives for the design of empirical research on RJVs.

MAINSTREAM INDUSTRIAL ORGANIZATION LITERATURE

Economists have traditionally understood the theory of the firm to refer to the standard neoclassical theory of production, as we still find it in most introductory microeconomics textbooks. In that context, the firm is viewed as entirely describable by its production function, which summarizes the most cost-efficient transformations of inputs into outputs, given the appropriate technologies. Importantly for our concern here, the fact that technologies are given means that the 'entrepreneur'[2] does not have to 'discover' or, more importantly, to create technologies through innovation. In fact, all that this agent must decide is the combination of inputs and the scale of production that maximize profits. The fact that this analysis is cast in a general equilibrium framework ensures that input and output prices convey to the entrepreneur all relevant knowledge for his/her action. Therefore, the analysis can account for the behaviour of the firm as a unitary actor in input and output markets but it cannot address information asymmetries, uncertainty and costs associated with the negotiation and enforcement of contracts. It is for this reason that this view of the firm is usually described as approaching the firm as a 'black box', that is as an agent whose behaviour is unaffected by internal organization or the relations among the human assets that compose it.

The fact that issues like internal organization and the endogenous forces of growth are excluded from the analysis means that market structure remains the only framework for explaining the boundaries of the firm (Coase, 1937), in the context of this theoretical outlook. Therefore, any competitive move by a firm's management in the real world has to be understood as being shaped by – and, in turn, as itself shaping – market structure. This is precisely the approach to the phenomenon of the firm that underlies the mainstream industrial organization theory.

The literature on RJVs, which is inspired by this theoretical perspective, can perhaps be divided into two major methodological streams. One stream emphasizes the 'timing of innovation' where the winner of a 'technology race' earns the right to some exogenously or endogenously determined monopolistic return (tournament models). The analytical focus has been on determining the number of firms that enter the race, the aggregate R&D investment and its distribution across firms and time, as well as the effects of market power, technological advantage and technological uncertainty (Beath, Katsoulacos and Ulph, 1995; Reinganum, 1989). Examples of papers in this literature that investigate the relative efficiencies of competition and cooperation in R&D in speeding up innovation include two by S. Martin (1994, 1999).

The second stream has concentrated on the 'extent of innovation' (non-tournament models), usually approximated by the degree of cost reduction (Dasgupta and Stiglitz, 1980; Brander and Spencer, 1983; Spence, 1984). Firms are assumed to invest in R&D in order to decrease costs and then compete in terms of prices or outputs in product markets. A large number of static (atemporal) analyses of both cooperative and noncooperative industrial set-ups with imperfectly appropriable, cost-reducing R&D have become available since d'Aspremont and Jacquemin (1988) published their seminal paper following this stream of thought.[3] These papers investigate the relative efficiencies of competition and cooperation in R&D in raising final output production and enhancing social welfare.

In a nutshell, the major strengths of tournament models are the explicit role of time and uncertainty and their ability to handle both product and process innovations. An important weakness is that, by nature, these models relate more to discrete technical advances and may not be able to accommodate sufficiently technological competition in cases where technologies are continuously upgraded but are not radically different from their predecessors. Technological knowledge accumulates over time and there is usually more than one winner in the race in the sense that at least part of the outcome of R&D is dispersed among or somehow benefits the different players. Relatively few of the available tournament models incorporate knowledge spillovers.[4]

The strengths and weaknesses of the non-tournament models are almost the reverse. They link better to the case of continuously upgraded technologies. A large number of these models incorporate knowledge spillovers. Unfortunately, the bulk of the non-tournament literature has been confined to static (even though multistage) models of strategic interaction and 'naive' dynamic games (supergames). While multiple-stage models constitute a useful first approximation, they cannot substitute for an explicitly dynamic framework. Supergames, where a one-stage game is repeated either eternally or for a fixed number of times while nothing carries from one period to the next, have also been proved less than entirely satisfactory. The relative scarcity of formal dynamic analysis of cooperative R&D seems to be a rather serious drawback of the non-tournament literature.[5] Another is the sparse number of such models explicitly dealing with uncertainty.

TRANSACTION COSTS ECONOMICS AND INCOMPLETE CONTRACTS

We have already hinted at the aspects of the firm that the approach we just discussed could not address. This prompted attempts to open up the 'black box' of the firm in order to be able to analyse its constituent elements. The firm was thus viewed as a multi-person organization, and its existence had to be explained on the basis of the most elementary form of interpersonal relations among asset owners: the concept of contracts. Contracts were now perceived as constituting the firm, primarily by aligning the incentives under which its resources operate jointly. Transaction-costs economics is the major strand in this 'contractarian' perspective on the firm.[6]

The notion of transaction costs has been greatly refined in recent years by Oliver Williamson (1975, 1985), who attempts to operationalize it by making specific the assumptions about human behaviour – 'opportunism' and 'bounded rationality' – and the attributes of transactions – mainly 'asset specificity'[7] – that together may give rise to transaction costs. According to transaction cost economics, therefore, entrepreneurs will try different ways to organize a transaction, including displacing the market by an administrative hierarchy. The most economically efficient organizational design will ultimately prevail, assuming a market with no external interference. The boundary between the market and the firm will be determined by the relative costs of carrying out a transaction under each organizational structure. Where an administrative organization is expected to produce the highest return, arm's-length markets will be displaced; and vice versa.

Transaction costs increase steeply when contracts are incomplete, that is, when they do not specify fully the actions of each party in every contingency. A frequent cause of incomplete contracts is small number bargaining, usually a result of high asset specificity (Hart and Holmström, 1987; Williamson, 1975). A form of assets that has frequently made it very hard, or even impossible, to write complete contracts is the intangible assets belonging to a firm. The most formidable intangible asset is technological knowledge. Such knowledge can be explicit, in the form of a patent or design, or implicit (tacit) in the form of know-how shared among the firm's employees. An already voluminous literature makes a strong argument that arm's-length markets fail in the case of this particular intangible asset. The reasons are:

- Externalities (spillovers). Three types of spillovers have been considered by economists: pecuniary (market) spillovers, knowledge spillovers and network spillovers (Jaffe, 1996). Pecuniary spillovers affect embodied technology and occur because R&D-intensive inputs and outputs are not priced at their fully hedonic (quality-adjusted) value; that is, the producer of a new or improved product or process is not able to set a price that fully captures the incremental benefits flowing to the buyers. Knowledge spillovers reflect the transfer of S&T knowledge (not necessarily embodied in a product or service) from one agent to another without adequate compensation. Knowledge spillovers are either horizontal or vertical. Horizontal spillovers describe knowledge flows between competitors. Vertical knowledge spillovers describe knowledge flows between firms in different industries. Network spillovers are present when the successful implementation and economic value of a new technology is strongly dependent on other complementary technologies. Generally speaking, network spillovers are present if by undertaking an R&D project a firm creates a positive externality to others interested in complementary projects by raising their expected commercial payoff. All three kinds of spillovers are supposed to lead to market failure by adversely affecting the incentives of individual firms to invest in R&D.

- Opportunism and uncertainty. There is a difference in incentives between the buyer and the seller of S&T knowledge. The buyer needs to have extensive information concerning all practical aspects of a technology. When property rights are not well enforced, however, the seller would hesitate to present the product for full inspection before the transaction is complete since that would eliminate much of its value. Market and technological uncertainty further amplifies the problem of opportunism (Arrow, 1962). Research of broader scope with an uncertain outcome may also create a relative disincentive for the individual firm, particularly the nondiversified firm, due to its inability to exploit the expected economies of scope (Link and Tassey, 1987; Nelson, 1959).

On these grounds, the explanation of RJVs provided by transaction costs theory is quite straightforward. JVs are hybrid forms of economic organization that aim at economising on transaction costs (Menard, 1996a; 1996b; Williamson, 1996). RJVs fall into this hybrid organizational category. In the area of R&D, specifically, these costs may be very high due to spillovers, hence incomplete contracts and the possibility of opportunistic behaviour that they entail. Therefore, RJVs must be viewed as efficient governance structures for, in the case of generic research, they allow the parties to delimit the participation in the joint research effort, and thus their risks. In the case of more focused research, on the other hand, their limited time horizon allows the parties to go-it-alone at contract completion.

It has been argued, however, that transaction cost economics is limited in that its attempt to unlock the black box of the firm is based on the standard tools of neoclassical economics. The analysis is generally static and assumes that overall efficiency will sooner or later prevail. Foss (1998) summarizes the limits of this approach:

1. An implicit assumption that alternatives are given, thus depicting agents as having to choose among a clearly defined set of contractual alternatives.
2. A suppression of process, that is, a view that the optimal solution to the contract-design problem continues to be optimal throughout contract execution.
3. A set of strong knowledge assumptions, thus leaving no room to theory to conceptualize the discovery by agents of what was hitherto unimagined. In a nutshell, transaction-costs economics treats the contracting agent as a 'contract-taker' – rather than a 'price-taker', as in orthodox neoclassical price theory – rather than a learning and creative actor.

STRATEGIC MANAGEMENT APPROACHES TO INTER-FIRM COOPERATION

The formation of technical alliances in a modern business environment – where cooperation coexists with competition – is considered in this literature as a vehicle of strategic change and of shaping competition. In this context, the co-ordination and sharing of value chain with other partners, the joint creation of new value, the accumulation and reconfiguration of resources, the development of new resources, the building of new capabilities and core competencies and the organizational learning are crucial issues in the formation and operation of technical alliances as well as in the assessment of their outcomes and in the analysis of their impact.

The fact that we refer here to the strategic management literature should not be taken to mean that we are dealing with an undifferentiated paradigm. In fact, as the survey of the views on RJVs will make evident, we can think of it as consisting of a number of distinct approaches, which share, however, some distinctive common themes and concepts. In what follows, we classify these approaches into three groups, according to the specific themes and concepts that each one of them chooses to emphasise.

Shaping the Competitive Environment

There is, first of all, a group of approaches that view RJVs as efforts by firms to shape the competitive framework within which they will operate. Thus, the Competitive Force Approach (Porter, 1980; 1985; 1990; Harrigan, 1988; Hagedoorn, 1993) focuses on the consideration of inter-firm collaboration, as a means of shaping competition and improving a firm's comparative competitive position, by sharing value chains with other partners in a way that broadens the effective scope of its chain. The Strategic Behaviour Approach, on the other hand, focuses on the strategic action that a firm takes in order to influence its market environment, that is, to reduce competition by actual or potential rivals. This approach has been used to study strategic decision-making for inter-firm technological cooperation (Porter and Fuller, 1986; Hamel, Doz and Prahalad, 1989). Finally, the Strategic Network Approach is based on the network model developed by Håkansson and Johanson (1984). Networks allow the exploitation of economies of scale and scope, can lower transaction costs or raise transaction benefits – especially in cases where a high level of trust among partners is being established – and give the opportunity for the joint creation of new value through technological development.

Emphasizing Resources and Capabilities

A second group of approaches stems from Edith Penrose's (1959) seminal work. According to this approach, firm resources are valuable, rare, non-substitutable and cannot be easily imitated. Thus, firms within an industry or a strategic group may be heterogeneous with respect to the strategic resources they control. In this context, in order to fully exploit the existing stock of heterogeneous and immobile resources and to develop sustained competitive advantages, a firm may need access to external complementary resources (Richardson, 1972).

The major conceptual innovation of this 'resource-based' approach to the firm is the differentiation between the firm's resources and the services that are obtainable from them.[8] Three important implications follow from this differentiation. The first is that what a resource 'can do'[9] is something for the management of the firm to discover and promote, that is, it is subject to the exercise of entrepreneurship. Second, the mode in which the firm's resources cooperate prompts them to acquire even further capabilities, that is, to learn. Third, the capabilities they acquire depend to a large extent on their joint operation. Implied in this is that the 'knowledge' created and acquired by these resources is a sort of social knowledge, in the sense that it is shared by the human assets of the firm.

Evidently, this perspective introduces a dynamic element in the theory of the firm, as it views its growth as an incessant process of creating, developing and realigning the capabilities of its resources. Historical time is important in this context, in the sense that as firms interact with their environment, they create conditions that are genuinely irreversible. The irreversibility of time highlights the problem of uncertainty, as the condition in which any strategic decision has to be made. It is not merely the uncertainty of market configuration that is relevant here, for the interaction among the firm's resources tends to produce routines (Nelson and Winter, 1982) that are largely tacit, so that management has only a limited capacity to control them (Witt, 1998; Ioannides, 1999a; 1999b). Therefore, the growth of the firm is a path-dependent process, in the sense that the firm's history affects critically the cognitive frameworks of the members, and thus the direction and the rate at which new knowledge is obtained, and becomes effective in their joint effort. The relevance of this analytical framework for the analysis of the process of innovation is, of course, obvious.

Capabilities can be developed within the firm but can also be obtained through the market and, thus, the boundaries between these two types of institutions are not impregnable but have rather the character of a continuum of alternatives. However, the capabilities that are obtained through arm's-length market exchanges cannot be moulded according to the management's strategic aims, neither can the knowledge they obtain in the production process be unambiguously thought of as belonging to the firm. On the other hand, internal capabilities are more susceptible to reconfiguration by the management and thus more subject to strategic realignment.

David Teece (1987) has developed a very similar framework, usually referred to as the Dynamic Capabilities Approach. This is a further elaboration of the resource-based view of sustained competitive advantage through collaboration. Its novel contribution is that it views capabilities not as static attributes but, rather, as the ability of the firm to adapt to, and gain competitive advantage in, a rapidly changing environment. Furthermore, Prahalad and Hamel have introduced the term 'core competencies' to refer to the central strategic capabilities of a firm. These refer to the 'collective learning in the organization especially how to coordinate diverse production skills and to integrate multiple streams of technologies' (1990). In particular, Hamel (1991) promotes a skills-based view of the firm by considering it as a portfolio of core competencies and encompassing disciplines. Furthermore, he introduces the notion of inter-firm competition as opposed to inter-product competition. Inter-firm competition is based on knowledge acquisition and skills building. Therefore, inter-firm collaboration – alliances and joint ventures – can be seen as a mode of skill acquisition and skill building. In sum, strategic alliances – and in particular strategic technical alliances – may be, as Glaister (1996) puts it, a very effective organizational mode for the firm to gain access to resources and upgrade capabilities.

In the context of this second group of theories, therefore, the decision to form an alliance represents a strategic decision aiming at developing the resource base of a firm. In this context, three types of strategic alliance can be identified (Glaister, 1996): a) strategic alliances to gain critical mass in resources, b) strategic alliances to acquire capabilities through learning, and c) strategic alliances to generate new proprietary capabilities through the convergence of idiosyncratic capabilities from partner firms.

Emphasizing Knowledge and Uncertainty

A third group of approaches to RJVs is based on a special emphasis on knowledge and uncertainty. A first such approach considers strategic technical alliances as a consequence of the globalization of knowledge (Badaracco, 1991). As world-wide industry is facing increasing pressures (such as increasing breadth, tempo and scale of technology, decreasing product life and design time, increasing complexity of product requirements, for collaboration on technology and product development) it is widely recognized that going-it-alone is not a feasible strategy. Thus, firms in most major industries have reacted to these pressures by pursuing both formal and informal cooperative relationships. Generally, speaking, 'firms create more alliances in response to the powerful, knowledge-driven forces reshaping their economic environment' (Badaracco, 1991).

A second approach considers technical collaboration as a driving force for learning and knowledge creation. From a learning organization's perspective, there are three kinds of knowledge at the heart of every core competence: public knowledge, industry-specific knowledge and firm-specific knowledge.[10] Thus, a part of recent literature is dedicated essentially to the learning effects of cooperation (Kogut, 1988; Ciborra, 1991; Teece et al., 1994). In line with the distinction between different types of knowledge, cooperation can be an effective mechanism for transferring tacit and firm-specific knowledge (Pavitt, 1988) through the establishment of close linkages between organizations.

Granstrand et al. (1990) suggest that firms confront some difficulties in integrating competencies and knowledge that come from areas they are not familiar with. Cooperative agreements can stimulate and facilitate dealing with new technologies and technological change as firms can use cooperation for learning that enables them to enter new technological areas (Dodgson, 1991) and deal with technological and market uncertainty (Ciborra, 1991). Cooperative agreements open the range of technological options to firms as they accumulate knowledge that might be converted into new technological and organizational innovations. Two dimensions can thus be assigned to the cooperation: a driving force for learning and creating new knowledge and new competencies, and a mechanism for implementation of new knowledge and diffusion at the organizational and inter-organizational level (Llerena, 1997).

A third approach stems from the importance of uncertainty, and considers R&D collaboration as a tool to create 'options' in radically new technologies. Conventional methods for appraising *ex ante* strategic long-term investments in R&D make some implicit, but very strong, assumptions. They assume either that the investment is reversible – it can be reversed costlessly should technological and market conditions prove to be worse than anticipated – or that an irreversible investment is a now-or-never proposition – invest now or do not invest at all. However, R&D investments fall into neither of these categories. On the one hand, they are irreversible: there are significant costs associated with terminating a project prematurely. On the other, R&D investments can be delayed (in contrast to being abandoned altogether).

One can do better by taking into consideration the value of 'investment options', that is, by explicitly recognizing the 'choice to invest' aspect of multistage R&D projects. The firm is a decision-making organization constantly choosing the best among a set of potential investments for its resources (Pindyck, 1991); thus there is considerable similarity between 'real investment options' and financial options.[11] A firm might join an RJV in its effort to open up a technological frontier. In particular, it might think of the RJV as a reasonably priced call-option to the technology in question. Under the assumption that a firm would prefer to have full control of the activity, everything else being constant, it would join the RJV only if the specific technology option was otherwise unattainable. The cost of participating to the RJV is then the price of the option. At the end of some predetermined time period, the firm will re-evaluate its investment in the RJV and the prospects of the technology being sought after, assisted by the new scientific/technological information produced by the RJV as well as new information coming in from the market. At that point, either the technology is abandoned or the firm 'kills its option' by taking the second step and investing more heavily in the technology.

The fact that there is a limit to the downside risk, to which an RJV participant (option holder) is exposed, makes the value of RJV membership increase with uncertainty. This feature is of fundamental importance to understanding the explosion of inter-firm strategic technical alliances around the world since the early 1980s. It also provides a basic justification for RJV formation in the early (fluid) stages of an industry's development. The higher the technological and market uncertainty (volatility) is, the more attractive cooperation becomes for companies that are not willing to 'bet the farm'.

IMPLICATIONS FOR THE DESIGN OF EMPIRICAL RESEARCH

Our overview of theoretical approaches to cooperative R&D in the previous three sections shows that, so far, a unified framework to explain and analyse RJVs and other technical alliances has proved elusive. Most existing appraisals of strategic partnering have tended to follow one of the various theoretical perspectives discussed. Mounting empirical evidence of the modal complexity of such alliances has, however, led a number of analysts more recently to stress the limitations of 'uni-directional' analysis. Osborn and Hagedoorn (1997) argue that taking a singular view may hide more about strategic technical alliances than it reveals. They encourage researchers to abandon such singular, clear-cut descriptions of alliances and alliance networks in favour of a more sophisticated, multidimensional vision. Similar views can be found in works by Parkhe (1993) and Horton and Richey (1997).

On the other hand, our current ability to build a unified approach is to be doubted. While the answers to the research questions have varied, being sensitive to both the conceptual foundation of the analysis and the modelling technique, this may not be totally unexpected given the focus on oligopolistic industries which differ in terms of market organization, strategic interaction, and the nature of technological advance. Such differences extensively affect the objectives of inter-firm collaborative agreements. Hence, critics of model unification argue that it is improbable that a one-fits-all theoretical model will be built any time soon.

The above considerations imply that all three perspectives have important ideas to contribute towards the empirical investigation of the phenomenon of RJVs. On the other hand, while it would be epistemologically unsound to attempt to evaluate their validity on the basis of any empirical evidence, empirical research may shed light on their domain of application and thus, indirectly, inform further theoretical investigations.

Let us begin by reviewing the sets of questions that may be investigated empirically on the basis of the three approaches. The mainstream industrial organization literature points towards a set of questions that have mainly to do with the market structure or, more generally, with the 'environment' within which a firm operates. Obviously, the insights of this approach are mostly relevant in the case that the objective of an R&D activity is close to market, in which case the firm can be assumed to be able to assess the way in which the outcome of research will affect its competitive position. As a consequence, we would expect that the closer to development a research project is perceived to be by the firms themselves, the more they would tend to cooperate with universities and other research institutes rather than other firms; the more they would aim at increasing their market share; and the more concerned they would be about losing vital technological information to their research partners. On the other hand, in the case of precompetitive research we would expect cooperation to emerge in case the research project is foreseen to affect the future structure of the market decisively or in case it aims at setting common technological standards.

Transaction-cost economics points towards a different set of questions. The important issues here are the costs that arise from alternative ways of organizing the research, which themselves arise from the types of spillovers that are associated with the specific research as well as from the uncertainty of the final result and thus the possibility of opportunistic behaviour by the partners of the research consortium. As a consequence, we would expect to find a stronger tendency towards partnering in fluid technologies, or in areas where the research results can give rise only to poorly specifiable intellectual property rights. By contrast, we would expect the tendency towards partnering to be less strong when the costs arising from cooperation are anticipated to be high or when the appropriation of the research results by partners is difficult to regulate *ex ante*.

Each of the approaches that together compose the literature of strategic management place emphasis on different aspects of the phenomenon of RJVs. However, the common thread among all of them is the emphasis on knowledge, uncertainty, the irreversibility of time and, thus, on the uniqueness of the firm's competencies. In that perspective, therefore, the identity of the firm matters, as it encapsulates the set of the firm's attributes that are relevant on all these counts. At the same time, the firm's identity affects the dynamics of its development, which, in turn, the firm strives to shape through its strategy. Obviously, this perspective points to a very different set of questions compared with the other two that we discussed above. Here, the firm's decision to join an RJV must be investigated on the basis of its striving to establish access to resources – and the respective capabilities – which it does not initially possess, and to establish strategic investment options for its future development. Above all, the important issue that must be investigated in the context of the strategic management perspective is the learning processes through which the firm strives to obtain new knowledge.

NOTES

1. In this we follow the taxonomy proposed by Caloghirou, Ioannides and Vonortas (2003).
2. It is important to note that in this framework the entrepreneur is considered as both owner and manager of the firm, thus ensuring that the organization behaves as a unitary actor in input and output markets.
3. They include, for example, Spence (1984), Katz (1986), De Bondt and Veugelers (1991),

De Bondt, Slaets and Cassiman (1992), Kamien, Muller and Zang (1992), Suzumura (1992), De Bondt (1997), De Bondt and Wu (1994), Simpson and Vonortas (1994), and Vonortas (1994).

4.   An exception is the model by Katsoulacos and Ulph (1994).
5.   An exception is the model by Joshi and Vonortas (1997).
6.   The seminal contribution was Coase's paper on 'the Nature of the Firm' (1937).
7.   According to Williamson (1985, pp. 52–56), the more specific to a transaction an asset is, the costlier it becomes both for the seller as well as for the purchaser of its services to negotiate contracts attempting to safeguard him/herself against a unilateral termination of the relation by the other party.
8.   The ideas that inform this view arguably go back to Alfred Marshall (1920) and Frank Knight (1921). See Hodgson (1998).
9.   Hence the notions of 'capabilities' or 'competencies' that became fashionable later.
10. Also the classical distinction between 'tacit knowledge', 'the informal knowledge that is generated while coping with everyday problems and passed on in cafeterias', and codified knowledge, 'official rules recorded in company manuals and transmitted in compulsory training sessions', should be taken into consideration.
11. An early reference is Myers (1977). Analogies between 'real options' and financial options have been discussed in the context of strategic resource allocation in the private sector (Bowman and Hurry, 1993). Analogies with R&D in the private sector have been proposed by Dixit and Pindyck (1995), Mitchell and Hamilton (1988), and Newton and Pearson (1994). Faulkner (1996) presents a good summary of the literature.

REFERENCES

Arrow, K. J. (1962), 'Economic welfare and the allocation of resources for invention', in R. R. Nelson (ed.), *The Rate and Direction of Inventive Activity: Economic and Social Factors*, Princeton, NJ: Princeton University Press for the NBER.

Badaracco, J. L. (1991), *The Knowledge Link: How Firms Compete through Strategic Alliances*, Boston, MA: Harvard Business School Press.

Beath, J., Y. Katsoulacos and D. Ulph (1995), 'Game-theoretic approaches to the modelling of technological change', in P. Stoneman (ed.), *Handbook of the Economics of Innovation and Technological Change*, Oxford: Blackwell, pp. 132–81.

Bowman, E. H. and D. Hurry (1993), 'Strategy through the option lens: an integrated view of resource investments and the incremental choice process', *Academy of Management Review*, **18**(4), 760–82.

Brander, J. and B. Spencer (1983), 'Strategic commitment with R&D: the symmetric case', *Bell Journal of Economics*, 14, 225–35.

Caloghirou, Y., S. Ioannides and N. Vonortas (2003), 'Research joint ventures: a critical survey of the theoretical and empirical literature', *Journal of Economic Surveys*, **17**(4), 541–70.

Ciborra, C. (1991), 'Alliances as learning experiences: cooperation, competition and change in high-tech industries', in L. Mytelka (ed.), *Strategic Partnerships and the World Economy*, London: Pinter Publishers.

Coase, R. H. (1937), 'The Nature of the Firm', *Economica*, **4**, 386–405.

Coase, R. H. (1972), 'Industrial organization: a proposal for research', in R. H. Coase (1988), *The Firm, the Market and the Law*, Chicago: University of Chicago Press.

Dasgupta, P. and J. Stiglitz (1980), 'Industrial structure and the nature of innovative activity', *Economic Journal*, **90**, 266–93.

D'Aspremont, C. and A. Jacquemin (1988), 'Cooperative and noncooperative R&D in duopoly with spillovers', *The American Economic Review*, **78**, 1133–37.

De Bondt, R. (1997), 'Spillovers and innovative activities', *International Journal of Industrial Organization*, **15**(1), 1–28.

De Bondt, R. and R. Veugelers (1991), 'Strategic investment with spillovers', *European Journal of Political Economy*, **7**(3), 345–66.

De Bondt, R. and C. Wu (1994), 'Research joint venture cartels and welfare', mimeo, Economics Department, Katholieke Universiteit Leuven.

De Bondt, R., P. Slaets and B. Cassiman (1992), 'The degree of spillovers and the number of rivals for maximum effective R&D', *International Journal of Industrial Organization*, **10**(1), 35–54.

Dixit, A. K. and R. S. Pindyck (1995), 'The options approach to capital investment', *Harvard Business Review*, **73**(3), 105–15.

Dodgson, M. (1991), 'Technological learning, technology strategy and competitive pressures', *British Journal of Management*, **2**(2), 133–49.

Faulkner, T. W. (1996), 'Options pricing theory and strategic thinking: literature review and discussion', mimeo, Eastman Kodak Company, May.

Foss, N. J. (1998), 'Austrian insights and the theory of the firm', *Advances in Austrian Economics*, **4**, 175–98.

Glaister, K. W. (1996), 'Theoretical perspectives on strategic alliance formation', in P. E. Earl (ed.), *Management, Marketing and the Competitive Process*, Cheltenham, UK and Brookfield, USA: Edward Elgar.

Granstrand, O., C. Oskarsson, N. Sjoberg and S. Sjolander (1990), 'Business strategies for development: acquisition of new technologies', working paper, Chalmers University of Technology.

Hagedoorn, J. (1993), 'Understanding the rationale of strategic technology partnering: inter-organizational modes of cooperation and sectoral differences', *Strategic Management Journal*, **14**, 371–85.

Hagedoorn, J. and J. Schakenraad (1992), 'Leading companies and networks of strategic alliances in information technologies', *Research Policy*, **21**, 163–90.

Håkansson, H. and J. Johanson (1984), 'A model of industrial networks', working paper, Department of Business Administration, University of Uppsala.

Hamel, G. (1991), 'Competition for competence and inter-partner learning within international strategic alliances', *Strategic Management Journal*, **12**, 83–103.

Hamel, G., Y. L. Doz and C. K. Prahalad (1989), 'Collaborate with your competitors – and win', *Harvard Business Review*, Jan.–Feb., 133–39.

Harrigan, K. R. (1988), 'Joint ventures and competitive strategy', *Strategic Management Journal*, **9**(2), 141–58.

Hart, O. and B. Holmström (1987), 'The theory of contracts', in T. F. Bewley (ed.), *Advances in Economic Theory: Fifth World Congress*, Cambridge: Cambridge University Press.

Hodgson, G. M. (1998), 'Competence and contract in the theory of the firm', *Journal of Economic Behavior and Organization*, **35**, 179–201.

Horton, V. and B. Richey (1997), 'On developing a contingency model of technology alliance formation', in P. W. Beamish and J. P. Killing (eds), *Cooperative Strategies: North American Perspectives*, San Francisco, CA: The New Lexington Press.

Ioannides, S. (1999a), 'Towards an Austrian perspective on the firm', *Review of Austrian Economics*, **11**(1), 77–97.

Ioannides, S. (1999b), 'The market, the firm, and entrepreneurial leadership: Some Hayekian insights', *Revue d' Economie Politique*, **109**(6), 872–83.

Jaffe, A. (1996), 'Economic analysis of research spillovers: implications for the Advanced Technology Program', discussion paper, Advanced Technology Program, Gaithersburg, MD: National Institute of Standards and Technology.

Joshi, S. and N. S. Vonortas (1997), 'Dynamic cooperation in R&D with research externalities', in J. Poyago-Theotoky (ed.), *R&D Cooperation: Theory and Policy*, Macmillan.

Kamien, M. I., E. Muller and I. Zang (1992), 'Research joint ventures and R&D cartels', *American Economic Review*, **82**(5), 1293–306.

Katsoulacos, Y. and D. Ulph (1994), 'Information revelation, R&D cooperation and technology policy', research paper prepared for the Science and Technology Policies Towards Research Joint Ventures Project, SOE1–CT97–1075, Targeted Socio-Economic Research Programme, European Commission, DG XII.

Katz, M. L. (1986), 'An analysis of cooperative research and development', *Rand Journal of Economics*, **17**(4), 527–43.

Knight, F. H. (1921), *Risk, Uncertainty and Profit*, New York: Houghton Mifflin.

Kogut, B. (1988), 'Joint ventures: theoretical and empirical perspectives', *Strategic Management Journal*, **9**, 319–32.

Link, A. N. and G. Tassey (1987), *Strategies for Technology-Based Competition: Meeting the New Global Challenge*, Lexington, MA: Lexington Books.

Llerena, P. (1997), 'Cooperations cognitives et modeles mentaux collectifs: outils de creation et de diffusion des connaissances', in B. Guilhon, P. Huard, M. Orillard, J-B Zimmermann (eds), (1997) *Economie de la Connaissance et Organisations. Entreprises, territoires, reseaux*, Paris: L'Harmattan, pp. 356–82.

Marshall, A. (1920), *Principles of Economics*, 8th edn, London: Macmillan.

Martin, S. (1994), 'Private and social incentives to form R&D joint ventures', *Review of Industrial Organization*, **9**, 157–71.

Martin, S. (1999), 'Spillovers, appropriability, and R&D', working paper, Centre for Industrial Economics, Institute of Economics, University of Copenhagen.

Menard, C. (1996a), 'Of clusters, hybrids, and other strange forms', *Journal of Institutional and Theoretical Economics*, **152**, 154–83.

Menard, C. (1996b), 'Why organizations matter: a journey away from the fairy tale', *Atlantic Economic Journal*, **24**(4), 281–300.

Mitchell, G. R. and W. F. Hamilton (1988), 'Managing R&D as a strategic option', *Research-Technology Management*, **31**(3), 15–24.

Myers, S. C. (1977), 'Determinants of corporate borrowing', *Journal of Financial Economics*, **5**, 147–76.

Nelson, R. R. (1959), 'The simple economics of basic scientific research', *Journal of Political Economy*, **67**, 297–306.

Nelson, R. R. and S. G. Winter (1982), *An Evolutionary Theory of Economics Change*, Cambridge, MA: Harvard University Press.

Newton, D. P. and A. W. Pearson (1994), 'Application of option pricing theory to R&D', *R&D Management*, **24**(1), 83–9.

Osborn, R. N. and J. Hagedoorn (1997), 'The institutionalization and evolutionary dynamics of interorganizational alliances and networks', *Academy of Management Journal*, **40**(2), 261–78.

Parkhe, A. (1993), 'Messy research, methodological predispositions, and theory development in international joint ventures', *Academy of Management Review*, **18**(2), 227–68.

Pavitt, K. (1988), 'International patterns of technological accumulation', in N. Hood and J.-E. Vahlne (eds), *Strategies in Global Competition*, London: Croom Helm.

Penrose, E. T. (1959), *The Theory of the Growth of the Firm*, Oxford: Oxford University Press.

Pindyck, R. S. (1991), 'Irreversibility, uncertainty, and investment', *Journal of Economic Literature*, **29**, 1110–48.

Porter, M. E. (1980), *Competitive Strategy*, New York: The Free Press.

Porter, M. E. (1985), *Competitive Advantage: Creating and Sustaining Superior Performance*, New York: The Free Press.

Porter, M. E. (1990), *The Competitive Advantage of Nations*, New York: The Free Press.

Porter, M. E and M. B. Fuller (1986), 'Coalitions and global strategy', in M. E. Porter (ed.), *Competition in Global Industries*, Boston, MA: Harvard Business School Press.

Prahalad, C. K. and G. Hamel (1990), 'The core competence of the corporation', *Harvard Business Review*, May–June, 79–91.

Reinganum, J. F. (1989), 'The timing of innovation: research, development, and diffusion', in R. L. Schmalensee and R. D. Willig (eds), *Handbook of Industrial Organization*, Amsterdam: North-Holland.

Richardson, G. B. (1972), 'The organisation of industry', *Economic Journal*, **82**, 883–96.

Simpson, R. D. and N. S. Vonortas (1994), 'Cournot equilibrium with imperfectly appropriable R&D', *The Journal of Industrial Economics*, **XLII**(1), 79–92.

Spence, M. (1984), 'Cost reduction, competition, and industry performance', *Econometrica*, **52**(1), 101–21.

Suzumura, K. (1992), 'Cooperative and noncooperative R&D in an oligopoly with spillovers', *American Economic Review*, **82**(5), 1307–20.

Teece, D. J. (1982), 'Towards an economic theory of the multiproduct firm', *Journal of Economic Behavior and Organization*, **3**, 39–63.

Teece, D. J. (1987), 'Capturing value from technological innovation: integration, strategic partnering and licensing decisions', in B. R. Guile and H. Brooks (eds), *Technology and Global Industry: Companies and Nations in the World Economy*, Washington, DC: National Academy Press.

Teece, D. J. (1992), 'Competition, cooperation and innovation: organizational arrangements for regimes of rapid technological progress', *Journal of Economic Behavior and Organization*, **18**, 1–25.

Teece, D. J., R. Rumelt, G. Dosi and S. G. Winter (1994), 'Understanding corporate coherence: theory and evidence', *Journal of Economic Behavior and Organization*, **23**, 1–30.

Vonortas, N. S. (1994), 'Inter-firm cooperation with imperfectly appropriable research', *International Journal of Industrial Organization*, **12**(3), 413–35.

Williamson, O. E. (1975), *Markets and Hierarchies: Analysis and Anti-trust Implications*, New York: Free Press.

Williamson, O. E. (1985), *The Economic Institutions of Capitalism*, New York: Free Press.

Williamson, O. E. (1996), *The Mechanisms of Governance*, Oxford: Oxford University Press.

Witt, U. (1998), 'Imagination and leadership: the neglected dimension of an evolutionary theory of the firm', *Journal of Economic Behavior and Organization*, **35**, 161–77.

3. Subsidized research joint ventures in Europe

Yannis Caloghirou, Stavros Ioannides, Aggelos Tsakanikas and Nicholas S. Vonortas

This chapter focuses on a special form of collaborative R&D: subsidized Research Joint Ventures that have been established through project-based ventures in the European area. Research Joint Ventures (RJVs) can be defined as 'cooperative agreements engaging companies, Universities and government agencies and laboratories in various combinations to pool resources in pursuit of a shared R&D objective' (Council of Competitiveness 1996).[1] The RJVs examined here are contractual agreements among independent entities, with at least one member of the consortium being a firm. Other member entities may include firms, universities, Research Institutes and other organizations. Our analysis draws information from a new extensive database – the STEP TO RJVs Databank.

The chapter attempts to map the trends of shared funded Research Joint Ventures that have been established through EU Framework Programmes (EU-FWPs), the Union's major policy initiative for the promotion of collaborative R&D, over a period of 16 years. An overview of their characteristics is presented both at the level of the research consortium and at the level of individual participants. The overview also contrasts these ventures with those formed under the EUREKA programme. The latter are nationally funded agreements for cooperative R&D, to which a European Committee awards the EUREKA label. The descriptive analysis of this chapter provides some evidence on the following questions:

- What are the major characteristics of these RJVs? Examination of their time trend, duration, size (in terms of participants), technological areas, type of cooperation and firms' distribution.
- What are the participants' characteristics? Type of participating entities, countries' participation, frequency of memberships and activeness.
- What are the financial and sectoral characteristics of the firms participating in these RJVs?

- What are the main differences between FWP and EUREKA RJVs?
- Has repeated and presumably successive cooperation led to the creation of certain types of inter-firm networks?

The chapter is structured as follows. The next section briefly describes the reasons behind the formation of the Framework Programmes and the EUREKA initiative in Europe. We then proceed to present the data used in this chapter, to delineate collaborative research trends in Europe at both the RJV and the RJV participant levels and, finally, to introduce a more synthetic way of looking at the organizational aspects of the programmes in question through the emergence of sectoral networks across Europe.

R&D COLLABORATION IN EUROPE

The Community's (subsequently Union) involvement in R&D cooperation can be traced as far back as the Treaty of Rome, through the establishment of the Joint Research Centre (JRC) and through research funding to organizations in member countries (Caloghirou and Vonortas, 2000). However, it was in the early 1980s, when concerns began to be raised that European firms were falling behind their American and Japanese counterparts in terms of innovation and market share in global markets and especially in the IT industry, that the current profile of EU research policy began to emerge. These concerns led to the launching of a major information technology and telecommunications programme, in 1984 (ESPRIT). The model was originally taken from Japan where it was perceived to have been successful (Peterson and Sharp, 1998) and in the very beginning the participating firms were major competitors (Peterson, 1991). The European Strategic Programme of Research in Information Technologies 1 (ESPRIT 1) served subsequently as a model for the creation of a more general 'umbrella type' programme, which was referred to as the First Framework Programme on R&D. The framework was gradually widened and included various other programmes of cooperative R&D in many technological areas. The rolling Framework Programmes are renewed every four years, transforming cooperation in R&D among firms, universities and research institutes into a fundamental feature of European S&T systems.

Since 1984, five Framework Programmes have been completed (1984 to 1987, 1987 to 1991, 1990 to 1994, 1994 to 1998 and 1998 to 2002) and the sixth is currently under way (2002 to 2006), promoting extensive scientific and technological cooperation among organizations from all member countries of the European Union. A central objective of the FWPs has been to pull together the diverse and complementary technical capabilities of companies, universities and research laboratories from different European countries in pursuit of common technological goals (European Commission, 1997; Peterson and Sharp, 1998). To achieve this goal the Community 'shall encourage undertakings, including small and medium sized undertakings, research centres and universities in their technological development activities' (article 139f, Single European Act). By bringing together researchers from all over Europe and by making it possible to benefit from a larger pool of resources than those available within any single nation, the FWPs have contributed significantly in establishing an even larger number of networks stretching beyond formal collaboration: the development of trust through successful collaborations, guide future cooperation beyond FWPs, to other informal types of collaborations as well (Peterson and Sharp, 1998).

Community funds allocated to R&D have become an important source for the financing of R&D investment in the EU.[2] In the first five FWPs, the Research and Technological Development (RTD) policy of the Community is implemented through shared-cost contractual research, concerted actions, and the Community's own research. Table 3.1 sums up the total budget allocated in the five FWPs. Shared-cost contractual research refers to transnational collaborative research consortia that mainly carry out the major form of Community intervention in RTD. These consortia are made up of business firms, research institutes and universities and engage mainly in precompetitive research. The Community supports these efforts, covering up to 50 per cent of the joint research cost for the firms, whereas universities and other research institutes may opt to receive 100 per cent of the marginal or additional costs of the projects.

Table 3.1   Budget Allocation

Framework Programmes	1984–87	1987–91	1990–94	1994–98	1998–2002
Total budget (m ECU)	3750	5396	6600	12300	14960

Apart from the FWPs, European organizations have often participated in RJVs which, while endorsed by the European Union, are not directly supported by it. The EUREKA initiative was launched in 1985 by 17 countries and the European Commission and has been one vehicle for such collaboration. EUREKA is a network for industrial R&D through which industry and research institutes from various European countries and the European Commission develop and exploit technologies to strengthen European competitiveness by promoting 'market driven' collaborative RTD.[3] A project meets EUREKA criteria if it:

- is a hi-tech, market-oriented R&D project
- involves partners from at least two EUREKA members
- aims to develop a cutting edge, civilian product, process or service
- is funded by the partners themselves, who receive public financing from their national governments (EUREKA Secretariat 1993).

THE DATA

The term 'entity' describes any organization at the most aggregate national level. For business participants this is the company level. Universities, research centres and government agents are also considered to be entities. An entity may have many 'memberships' depending on the times it has been engaged in RJVs.

The EU RJV Database

One of the core databases included in the STEP TO RJVs Databank is the EU RJV database, which focuses on the transnational partnerships that were created through one of the most crucial mechanisms of promoting cooperation in Europe: The European Framework Programmes (EU-FWPs). The version of the database used in this chapter covers RJVs that started as early as 1983 all the way to those started in 1998. Thus, an extensive period of 16 years, throughout the first four Framework Programmes is represented. The basic source for the construction was CORDIS, the official EU source, which disseminates information about European RTD and related matters.

However, a selection of programmes was necessary, since the aim was to include programmes that involved industrial research. Thus, programmes whose main focus was not the creation of new technological knowledge (like forecasting, evaluations etc.) were excluded, since it would be rather difficult to properly interpret the final results.

Up to 64 programmes satisfied the above criterion and were, thus, included in the database. All the big and well-known programmes in some of the major technological areas, in which the EU promotes collaborative research, like information technologies and industrial materials, are included in the database. But some other less known programmes have also been included, since cooperation has been promoted through these research initiatives as well. Exactly ten programmes from the first FWP, 24 programmes from the second, 18 programmes from the third and 12 programmes from the fourth were ultimately chosen for inclusion in the current version of the EU RJV database.

Another criterion that was used for the construction of the database was implemented at the project level. More precisely, only those RJVs involving at least one firm in the consortium were selected, while those involving cooperation only between universities or research centres were excluded. The same applies for RJVs for which it was impossible (due to the poor quality of information) to identify whether an organization of the consortium was actually a firm or not.

The total number of RJVs in the selected programmes is 17 596. However, after the implementation of the criteria described earlier, the final number of usable RJVs reached 9335. A total number of 20 499 different organizations from 51 countries participated at least once in these 9335 RJVs, whereas all memberships recorded reached 65 476.

The EUREKA RJV Database

The EUREKA RJV database includes all RJVs that have been chosen and promoted under the EUREKA label during the period 1985 to 1996. Its structure is similar to the EU database, while the basic source of information was the EUREKA web site. Selecting only those RJVs with at least a firm in the consortium resulted in an inclusion of 1031 RJVs. In these RJVs, 6233 memberships by 4261 entities from 36 countries are recorded.

DESCRIPTIVE STATISTICS

Research Joint Venture Formation Patterns

The EU RJV database

Figure 3.1 presents the time of the RJVs by starting date. The initiation of ESPRIT 1 with nine RJVs in 1983 signals the commencement of the Framework Programmes followed by 54 RJVs in the next year. A limited number of RJVs from programmes like RADWASTOM 3C, DECOM 2C, ENNONUC 3C, AGRIRES 3C and BAP started in 1985 but the bulk of these efforts began in 1986. Generally, an increasing trend can be identified, despite some ups and downs, since the beginning of a programme usually gathers the majority of the collaborative efforts. In fact, the peaks observed in Figure 3.1 are related to the commencement of each programme. This trend for the shared-funded RJVs is clearly on the same line with the increasing trend obtained from the examination of either the strategic technological alliances (Hagedoorn, 1995) or the US research joint ventures (Vonortas, 1997). Therefore, the proliferation of cooperative agreements, especially during the last decade, is more than evident. Almost half of the

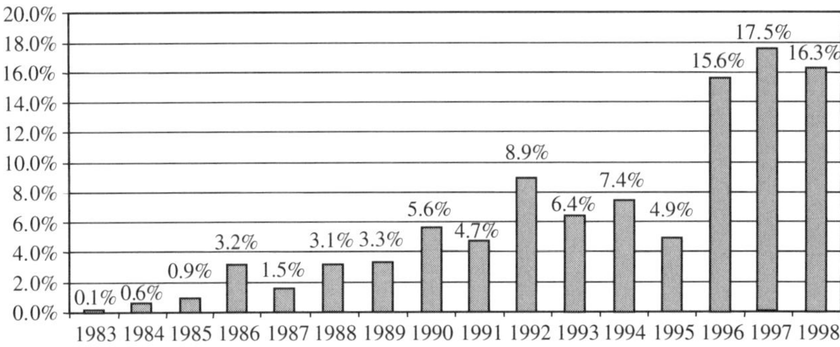

*Figure 3.1   Allocation of the EU RJVs based on their starting date
(number of observations, 8959)*

RJVs included in our database started in the period from 1996 to 1998, as many projects in many big programmes, especially BRITE/EURAM 3 and ESPRIT 4, have been initiated at that time.

The technological areas that seem to attract the greatest part of collaborative efforts in the last 16 years are mainly five: information processing/information systems, with 3118 RJVs (12.85 per cent), materials, with 2726 RJVs (11.23 per cent), industrial manufacture, with 2664 RJVs (10.98 per cent), aerospace technology, with 2417 RJVs (9.96 per cent) and electronics/microelectronics, with 2309 (9.51 per cent). They all cover more than half of all RJVs recorded and are all related with either BRITE-EURAM or ESPRIT. These programmes are the most famous and biggest in terms not only of participation, but also of EU funding. Therefore they dominate our database, concentrating the most significant part of the RJVs included throughout the time period examined.

Other technical areas with significant activity are telecommunications (1051 RJVs, 4.33 per cent) and renewable sources of energy (1040 RJVs, 4.29 per cent), whereas, on the other hand, there are some technical areas like biotechnology that present rather poor activity (below 3 per cent). This can be explained partly by the fact that usually RJVs in this specific area involved mostly universities and research centres rather than firms. Therefore, on the basis of our selection criteria, they were excluded from our database. But it is also clear that programmes related to this area (like BRIDGE or BAP) have not been at the top priority of EU policy, at least up to 1998. Table 3.2 sums up the picture.

The majority of the examined RJVs can be characterized as medium-term in terms of duration. About 37 per cent of them are in the 31 to 36 months time period and another 32 per cent last between 19 and 30 months.

Table 3.2   Allocation of RJVs in technical areas based on their starting date

Technical area	Sum	%
Information processing, information systems	3118	12.9
Materials technology	2726	11.2
Industrial manufacture	2664	11.0
Aerospace technology	2417	10.0
Electronics, microelectronics	2309	9.5
Telecommunications	1051	4.3
Renewable sources of energy	1040	4.3
Fossil fuels	904	3.7
Agriculture	734	3.0
Environmental protection	688	2.8
Other energy topics	611	2.5
Resources of the sea, fisheries	607	2.5
Biotechnology	578	2.4
Safety	532	2.2
Measurement methods	476	1.9
Standards	472	1.9
Reference materials	459	1.9
Food	458	1.9
Energy saving	429	1.8
Education, training	427	1.8
Transport	399	1.6
Other areas	1168	4.8
Total	24267	100.0

Note: The sum of the included RJVs appears to be 24267. That is because EU Programmes refer to two or even three technical areas. Double or triple counting ensues.

Generally the average RJV lasts 31 months. A significant 17 per cent could reasonably be considered longer term, since they exceed three years, while only 8.5 per cent can be characterized as very short term (below 1 year). However, this information should be interpreted carefully, since there is a bias problem related to the time limits that the EU imposes on each programme. It is unlikely that the EU would easily fund RJVs that last significantly long, thus potential participants do not apply for such projects.

Nearly half of the examined RJVs (44 per cent) had below five participants and in general the vast majority of RJVs (86 per cent) have had ten or fewer participants (Figure 3.2). Just 5 per cent could be characterized as large consortia (over 16 partners), while the average RJV consists of seven

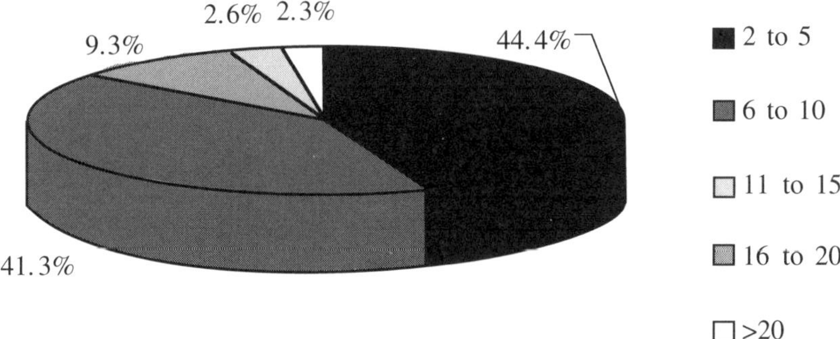

*Figure 3.2   Distribution of EU RJVs in terms of their total participants
(number of observations, 9335)*

members. Looking at the same information through time, it could be argued that the trend has been towards the formation of six to ten members' consortia. Although the proportion of small-sized RJVs is still significant, the trend is clearly for larger (middle-sized) RJVs. This could arguably be attributed to the fact that an RJV with 'more' partners is more likely to achieve EU funding than a 'poor' – in terms of members – RJV. On the other hand, it could also be an indication of a more generic research focus, although we cannot stretch this finding too far, since field research or case study work is necessary on this issue.

Figure 3.3 shows the distribution of the RJVs based on their type of collaboration. The latter refers to the type of the agents that compose the consortium. Collaboration between firms only is in the fourth place with a total of 1295 RJVs. The most frequent type of collaboration is between firms, universities and research centres (37 per cent). Industry-university links seem to have played an important role in the relationships developed through the Framework Programmes, since more than 60 per cent of the population (5218 RJVs) involve at least one university as a partner. In fact, it is not only that Universities have been very active in RJVs, but also their relative involvement has increased over time (Caloghirou, Tsakanikas and Vonortas, 2001). Furthermore, blending the two aforementioned RJV characteristics, their type and size, indicate that the vast majority of collaborations solely between firms (79 per cent), consist of two to five members, indicating a tendency for small and flexible consortia whenever firms cooperate. RJVs combining firms, universities and research centres dominate all other RJV-size groups.

Another interesting question concerns the possible relationship between technical areas and RJV size or RJV type. The objective is to identify

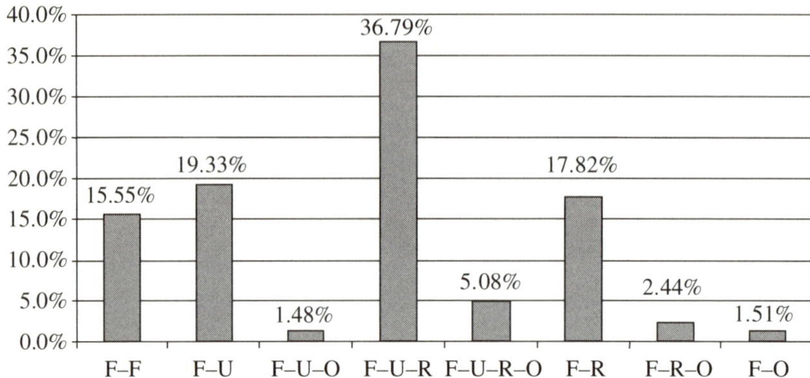

Note: F: Firm, U: University, R: Research Centre, O: Other (government agents, hospitals, libraries, etc.)

Figure 3.3   Distribution of EU RJVs in terms of their type of collaboration (number of observations, 8326)

whether certain areas seem to be concentrated in only some of the RJV-size groups or RJV-type groups. However, the analysis showed that RJVs in the five most dominant technical areas (described earlier) simply dominate every group examined. More distinguishable patterns were identified in areas with rather limited number of RJVs. Hence, RJVs in agriculture tend to be dominated by the presence of a non-private sector institution as a partner. RJVs in resources of the sea and fisheries rank high in the firm-university-research-centre and firm-university-research centre-other categories, indicating highly diversified RJVs. RJVs in the Safety area rank high in the firm-research centre-other and firm-other category, mostly indicating the importance of government bodies as participants.

The number of firms that are involved in each RJV could also provide an additional indication of whether firms actually tend to cooperate with other firms, or they prefer also other non-private agents. Table 3.3 shows that a slight majority (24 per cent) of the RJVs involves 2 firms, just outnumbering RJVs with the involvement of 1 firm (23 per cent). In another way of interpreting it, a significant 77 per cent of the RJVs involve at least two firms, or alternatively, almost one quarter of the RJVs involves cooperation between more than five firms. Examining also the data through time shows that there is a decreasing tendency in the one-firm RJVs: firms tend to cooperate with at least another firm.

Table 3.3 Distribution of firms in RJVs

Number of firms	Number of RJVs	% of RJVs
1	2100	23.1
2	2175	23.9
3	1509	16.6
4	1122	12.3
5 to 6	1255	13.8
7 to 9	620	6.8
more than 10	305	3.4
Total	9086	100.0

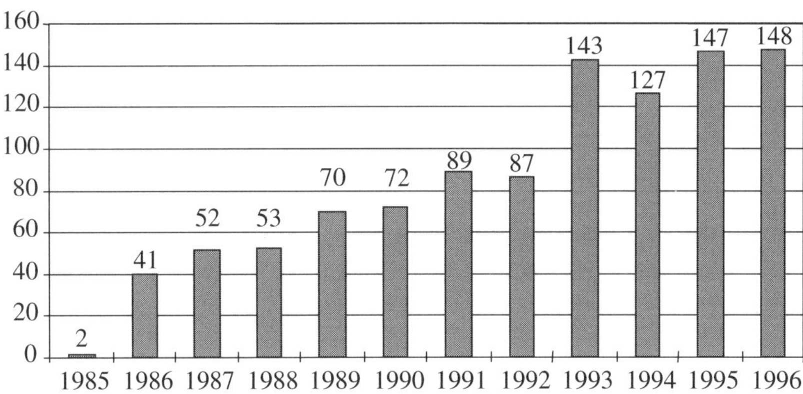

Figure 3.4 Allocation of the EUREKA RJVs based on their starting date (number of observations, 1031)

The EUREKA RJV database

Figure 3.4 presents an allocation of the EUREKA RJVs based on their reported starting date. A good part of the surge during the last four years can be explained by the fact that several countries from Eastern Europe joined EUREKA at that time.

The majority of EUREKA RJVs have been in the environment area, followed by medical and biotechnology, information technology, and robotics/production automation. In more recent years, there was a slight decrease of registered RJVs in the environmental and medical areas.

The picture changes dramatically, however, if the 'importance' of a technological area is determined on the basis of the budget allocations (Table

Table 3.4   Allocation of funding in different technological areas

Technological area	Budget (m ECU)
Information Technology	8078.14
Communications	1935.4
Transport	1487.26
Robotics/Production automation	1115.19
Medical and Biotechnology	908.83
Environment	888.87
Energy Technology	550.92
New materials	421.34
Lasers	382.31

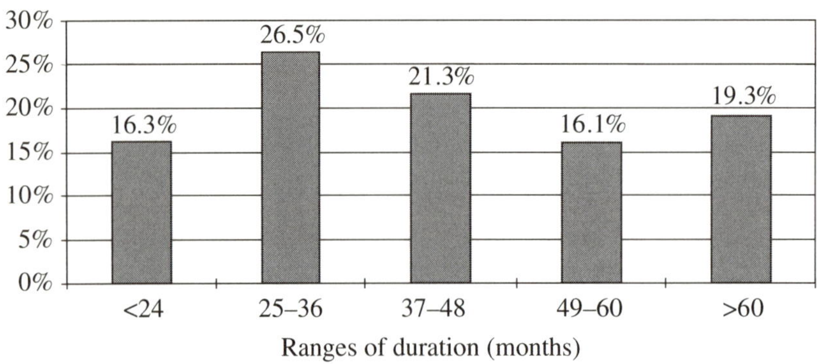

*Figure 3.5   Distribution of the EUREKA RJVs in terms of their duration
(number of observations, 1031)*

3.4). On this basis, information technology tops the list with a very significant distance from the rest. The distance is largely the result of the irregu-
larly high budgets of two major RJVs in this area, the 3.8 billion ECU
budget of the Joint European Submicron Silicon Initiative (JESSI) and the
2 billion ECU budget of the MEDEA RJV, which followed JESSI.

Figure 3.5 classifies RJVs according to their duration. The bias problem
mentioned before (in the FWPs) is absent here since this issue is decided
among partners and is not imposed to some extent from the funding body.
Therefore, a more balanced picture is obtained. Even though, as in the case
of FWPs, the medium-term ranges are more prominent, a relatively higher
percentage of RJVs are longer-term. Interestingly, 12 RJVs have reported
duration period over 10 years!

Furthermore, if RJVs' technological areas are combined with their time duration then interesting patterns emerge: environmental and medical RJVs dominate the over-60 months period, although most of the medical RJVs are in the 37- to 48-month range. The majority of RJVs from lasers have also lasted over 60 months.

Figure 3.6 allocates EUREKA RJVs on the basis of the number of participants. The majority of RJVs have had four or fewer members, thus indicating that those RJVs tend to be smaller. Moreover, Medical and Biotechnology RJVs dominate the two to four member category. The seven to ten size category features many RJVs in the environment and information technology areas. RJVs in robotics/production automation, environment, and information technology have significant percentage in the higher member categories.

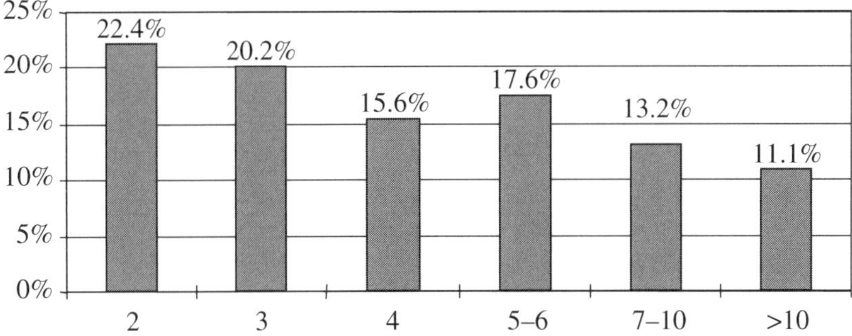

Figure 3.6　Distribution of EUREKA RJVs in terms of their total participants (number of observations, 1031)

Regarding RJV type of collaboration, the largest group of RJVs (41 per cent) involves cooperation between firms only, which seems to agree with the objective of the EUREKA initiative to pursue market oriented R&D (Figure 3.7). It comes as no surprise to see that most of the firm-firm collaborations are related to RJVs with just two partners.

Participants in Research Joint Ventures

The EU RJV database

The utilized version of the database contains 65476 memberships, corresponding to 20499 entities. Table 3.5 summarizes overall participation by entities based in various countries distinguishing also between coordinators of the RJV and partners.

While entities from a wide variety of countries have participated in the examined RJVs, it is obviously organizations from EU member states that

                    Theory and practice

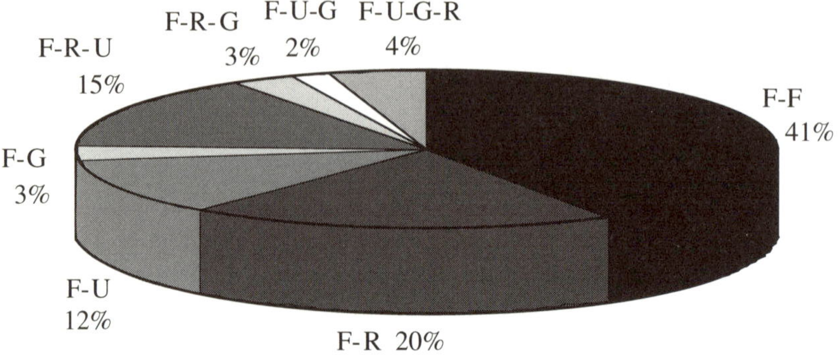

Note: F: Firm, U: University, R: Research Centre, G: Government agent

*Figure 3.7   Distribution of RJVs in terms of their type of collaboration
(number of observations, 1031)*

have, by and large, dominated participation in these RJVs. Germany ranked first both in terms of total number of participating entities and overall memberships. At the second place, we have the same number of entities from UK and France, but UK organizations are slightly outnumbered by French organizations in terms of memberships in the examined RJVs. However, UK organizations seem to have served as coordinators in larger numbers of RJVs, outnumbering the other two countries.

The unique performance of these three countries does indeed differ from all other countries in terms of participating in EU FWPs. This is easily explained taking into consideration their size and population, and also the fact that they are the most R&D intensive countries. The accumulated industry-specific competencies make firms from these countries best candidates for leading collaborative research efforts. The research activities that take place inside their region can hardly be compared to any other European country and surely represent the driving force of what we call European industry.

More than 68 per cent of all entities in the EU RJV database have participated in only one RJV (Table 3.6). A full 91 per cent have participated in less than five RJVs. A few organizations, however, seem to have spread their participation over large numbers of RJVs. Characteristically, 97 organizations have participated in 51 to 100 RJVs while 55 organizations participated in more than 100 RJVs. Not surprisingly, due to their structure and high number of skilled personnel, the majority of the 152 organizations with more than 51 memberships are universities (46 per cent), while only 28 per cent of those are firms.

Table 3.5   Participation in EU RJVs

Country	Entities	% of entities	Memberships	% of memberships	Partner	Coordinators	% of Coordinators
Germany	3501	17.08	11000	16.80	9451	1549	16.59
France	2958	14.43	10489	16.02	8753	1736	18.60
UK	2958	14.43	10408	15.90	8540	1868	20.01
Italy	2092	10.21	6789	10.37	5837	952	10.20
Spain	1609	7.85	4484	6.85	3942	542	5.81
Netherlands	1406	6.86	4628	7.07	3869	759	8.13
Belgium	998	4.87	3218	4.91	2696	522	5.59
Sweden	726	3.54	2086	3.19	1925	161	1.72
Greece	721	3.52	2679	4.09	2394	285	3.05
Denmark	663	3.23	2183	3.33	1838	345	3.70
Portugal	609	2.97	1818	2.78	1677	141	1.51
Austria	417	2.03	864	1.32	771	93	1.00
Finland	406	1.98	1178	1.80	1079	99	1.06
Ireland	392	1.91	1361	2.08	1204	157	1.68
Switzerland	296	1.44	879	1.34	869	10	0.11
Norway	296	1.44	792	1.21	727	65	0.70
Luxembourg	67	0.33	104	0.16	87	17	0.18
Other countries*	384	1.87	516	0.76	482	34	0.36
Total	20499	100.00	65476	100.00	56141	9335	100.00

Note: * Entities from 34 countries from all continents have at least once participated in these RJVs.

Table 3.6   Membership frequency

Memberships	Number of entities	% of entities
1	13980	68.2
2	2726	13.3
3	1096	5.3
4	601	2.9
5	346	1.7
6 to 10	830	4.0
11 to 20	476	2.3
21 to 50	292	1.4
51 to 100	97	0.5
>100	55	0.3
Total	20499	100.0

Because of the fact that we selected RJVs with at least one firm in the consortium, a full 74 per cent of the participating organizations are firms. Research centres represent 13 per cent, leaving universities with just 6.5 per cent. As a consequence, firms are responsible for the coordination of the majority of RJVs (61 per cent), leaving research centres at the second place with almost 21 per cent, while universities coordinate just 16 per cent of the RJVs (Figure 3.8). Interestingly, however, the percentage of firms serving as coordinators is smaller than the percentage of participations, while the increase in the percentage of universities as coordinators reveals their substantially active role in the formation and coordination of RJVs. Of course this result could be attributed to the fact that firms want to avoid the time-consuming process of writing reports and be engaged in all the administrative costs associated with compliance with EU-funded projects. That is why they probably prefer to leave these tasks to other non-firm members of the consortium.

The top 54 of the most active organizations in terms of memberships are listed in Table 3.7. These are the organizations that registered more than 100 memberships. CNRS (a public research institute) from France is the most active organization with 534 participations in our database during the examined period. The Catholic University of Leuven and the National Technical University of Athens are at the second and fourth position, which is remarkably high, taking into consideration the size and the general research activity of countries like Belgium or Greece.

Concentrating on the most active firms, Table 3.8 lists all firms with more than 50 memberships in the specific period. Large, well-known companies, with respectable research activity in their countries, are generally at the top positions.

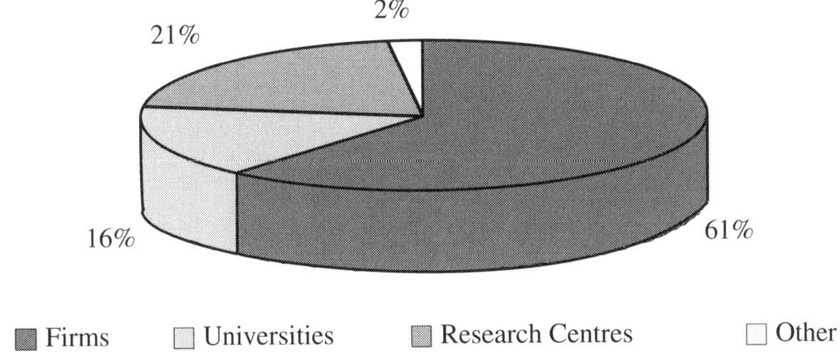

Figure 3.8   Prime contractor's type in the EU RJVs (number of observations, 8698)

The total number of firms per country is presented in Figure 3.9. Germany dominates with 2,290 firms that have participated in one RJV at least. The UK and France follow, while high relative rankings are observed for Belgian, Greek and Danish firms.

Table 3.9 gives a snapshot of the 'concentration' of memberships of each country: it shows the membership percentage of a country accounted for by the 8 most active organizations based in that country. One observes very large differences in terms of 'membership concentration' among a few entities. The highest degree of concentration is observed in Israel (51 per cent), although the country's participation is limited, in Ireland (43 per cent) and Finland (42 per cent) while the lowest is in the UK (10 per cent). Membership concentration seems to reflect the size of a country and the absolute number of R&D active organizations from that country. The relationship is, however, not linear.

Finally, a look at the sectoral distribution of the identified firms reveals some interesting trends (Table 3.10). More than half of the firms identified belong to five sectors, accounting for more than half of the memberships too: business services are at the top place, followed by electrical/electronic engineering, mechanical engineering, wholesale distribution and chemicals. The striking feature is the heavy presence of non-manufacturing firms, contrasting with the typical image of service sectors as non-R&D intensive. Similar findings have been reported in the United States where Vonortas (1997) has suggested the influence of two factors. The first emphasizes the role of RJV in facilitating supplier-customer linkages. Firms with high capital investment probably use new technologies extensively, but have little incentive in creating these technologies on their own. They participate (customers) in these RJVs as a means of influencing the research performed therein so that the outcome would better fit their needs. Suppliers of capital

Table 3.7   Most active organizations

Memberships	Organization name	Organization type	Country
534	Centre National de la Recherche Scientifique (CNRS)	Res. Centre	France
383	Katholieke Universiteit Leuven	University	Belgium
380	Siemens AG Public communication networks	Firm	Germany
297	National Technical University of Athens	University	Greece
293	CNR – Consiglio Nazionale Delle Ricerche	Res. Centre	Italy
290	Consejo superior de Investigaciones Cientificas	Res. Centre	Spain
272	Nederlandse Organisatie voor Toegepast Natuurwetenschappelijk Onderzoek	Res. Centre	Netherlands
269	University of London, The Imperial College of Science, Technology and Medicine	University	UK
266	Fraunhofer gesellschaft zur forderung der angewandten forschung e.v. zentralverwaltung (FhG)	Res. Centre	Germany
261	Technical Research Centre of Finland	Res. Centre	Finland
241	CEA Commissariat a l'energie atomique	Res. Centre	France
232	Institut National de la Recherche Agronomique	Res. Centre	France
219	Reinish-Westfalische technische hochschule Aachen	University	Germany
205	University of Stuttgart	University	Germany
202	Thomson – CSF	Firm	France
199	The University of Dublin, Trinity College	University	Ireland
197	Aerospatiale societe nationale industrielle	Firm	France
197	Nederlandse Philips bedrijven B.V.	Firm	Netherlands
190	Daimler-Benz AG (DORNIER)	Firm	Germany
185	Technical University Delft	University	Netherlands
181	Universidad politecnica de Madrid	University	Spain
178	Technical University of Denmark	University	Denmark
172	Centro ricerche FIAT S.C.P.A. (CRF)	Firm	Italy
170	Instituto superior tecnico (IST)	University	Portugal
159	Inter university microelectronics centre	Res. Centre	Belgium

157	Deutsche forschungsanstalt fur luft und raumfahrt E.V.	Res. Centre	Germany
157	Rijksuniversiteit Gent	University	Belgium
156	Bull S.A.	Firm	France
155	Universite libre de Bruxelles	University	Belgium
145	Armines-Association pour la Recherche et le Developpement de Methodes et Processus Industriels	University	France
144	Instituto de engenharia de sistemas e Computadores	Firm	Portugal
139	Riso national laboratory	Res. Centre	Denmark
134	ENEA (Ente per le nuove tecnologie, l'energia e l'ambiente)	Res. Centre	Italy
130	Universidad politecnica de Catalunia	University	Spain
129	Aristotelian university of Thessaloniki	University	Greece
128	Netherlands Energy Research Foundation	Res. Centre	Netherlands
126	Centre national d'etudes de telecommunications (CNET)	Res. Centre	France
123	University of Leeds, ITS	University	UK
117	Office national d'etudes et de recherches aerospatiales	Res. Centre	France
116	Centro Studi e laboratori telecomicazioni (CSELT)	Res. Centre	Italy
115	Atomic Energy Authority – AEA technology plc.	Res. Centre	UK
115	University of Lund	University	Sweden
114	British Telecom plc.	Firm	UK
114	Technical University of Berlin	University	Germany
113	Ins. Nat. de Rech. en Informatique et Automatique (INRIA)	Res. Centre	France
110	Robert Bosch GmbH	Firm	Germany
110	University College of London	University	UK
108	University of Southampton	University	UK
107	Ecole Polytechnique Federale de Lausanne	University	Switzerland
105	Universite de Liege	University	Belgium
104	NMRC, University College Cork	University	Ireland
102	GIE PSA Peugeot Citroen	Firm	France
102	Forth Research Centre of Crete	Res. Centre	Greece
101	University of Patras	University	Greece

Table 3.8   Most active firms

Memberships	Firm's name	Country
380	Siemens AG Public communication networks	Germany
202	Thomson – CSF	France
197	Aerospatiale societe nationale industrielle	France
197	Nederlandse Philips bedrijven B.V.	Netherlands
190	Daimler-Benz AG (Dornier)	Germany
172	Centro ricerche Fiat S.C.P.A. (CRF)	Italy
156	Bull S.A.	France
144	Instituto de engenharia de sistemas e Computadores	Portugal
114	British Telecommunication plc.	UK
110	Robert Bosch GmbH,	Germany
102	GIE PSA Peugeot Citroen	France
99	ENEL SpA – societa per azioni – centro ricerca di automatica	Italy
98	Alenia – Un'Azienda Finmeccanica SpA	Italy
88	Alcatel SEL AG (Standard Elektrik Lorenz)	Germany
87	Intracom S.A.	Greece
86	Rolls Royce plc.	UK
84	BMW Bayerische Motoren Werke AG	Germany
84	Siemens-Nixdorf Informations systems AG	Germany
78	Electricite de France	France
73	Bertin & Cie SA	France
72	SGS-Thomson microelectronics SRL	Italy
71	Alcatel bell manufacturing company	Belgium
69	Construcciones aeronauticas SA	Spain
68	Alcatel Alsthom Recherche Subcontractor of Alcatel Cable	France
68	SGS Thomson microelectronics SA	France
67	Volkswagen AG	Germany
67	BRGM – Bureau de Recherches Geologiques et Miniere	France
66	Rover group Ltd (plc.)	UK
64	Royal PTT Nederland N.V., PTT research	Netherlands
64	Dassault Electronique S.A.	France
61	International Computers Ltd (ICL)	UK
61	Telefonica de Espana S A	Spain
60	Imperial Chemical Industries plc. (ICI)	UK
58	Dassault aviation	France
55	British Aerospace	UK
55	British Aerospace (Operations) Ltd	UK
55	GEC Marconi Materials Technology Ltd	UK
54	Centro de estudio telecomunicacoes (Portugal Telecom)	Portugal
52	British Gas Exploration and Production plc.	UK
52	Dornier Luftfahrt GmbH	Germany
51	Daimler-Benz Aerospace Airbus GmbH (AG)	Germany

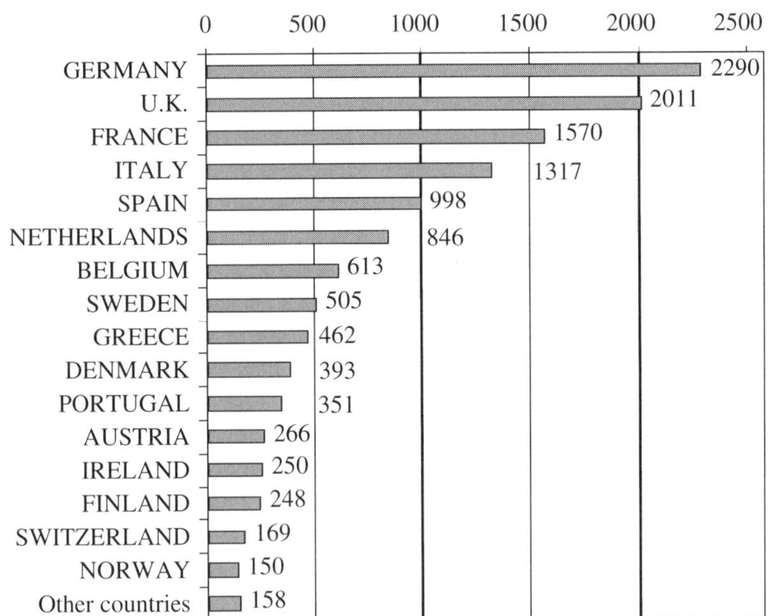

Figure 3.9   Number of firms per country in the EU RJVs

Table 3.9   Membership 'concentration' (eight most active entities)

Country	% of memberships by top 8 entities	Country	% of memberships by top 8 entities
Austria	28.7	Italy	16.2
Belgium	35.3	Luxembourg	36.5
Denmark	28.7	Netherlands	23.5
Finland	41.8	Norway	27.5
France	17.5	Portugal	34.1
Germany	14.9	Spain	20.1
Greece	35.1	Sweden	24.2
Ireland	42.6	Switzerland	38.5
Israel	51.1	UK	9.9

equipment may use these RJVs as vehicles for getting important customers on board early on in the R&D process. The second argument simply refers to the reasons behind RJVs formation: RJVs provide incentives to firms to undertake research that they would not have undertaken otherwise. So, these RJVs do exactly what they were supposed to do: add to the research efforts of their members.

Table 3.10   Sectoral distribution of the identi ed firms (2-digit)

Number of firms	%	Description	Memberships	%
402	15.4	Business services	2058	16.9
299	11.4	Electrical and electronic engineering	2067	17.0
274	10.5	Mechanical engineering	819	6.7
185	7.1	Wholesale distribution (excluding dealing in scrap and waste materials)	560	4.6
166	6.3	Chemical industry	765	6.3
94	3.6	Manufacture of metals not elsewhere specified	185	1.5
84	3.2	Instrument engineering	247	2.0
80	3.1	Food and tobacco manufacturing industries	149	1.2
75	2.9	Manufacture of non-metallic mineral products	161	1.3
68	2.6	Metal manufacturing	223	1.8
66	2.5	Manufacture and other transport equipment	911	7.5
66	2.5	Textile industry	137	1.1
64	2.4	General construction and demolition work	207	1.7
63	2.4	Manufacture of paper, paper products, printing and publishing	98	0.8
57	2.2	Production and distribution of electricity, gas and other forms of energy	434	3.6
57	2.2	Manufacture of motor vehicles and parts thereof	704	5.8
54	2.1	Manufacture of office machinery and data processing equipment	504	4.1
42	1.6	Processing of rubber and plastics	73	0.6
40	1.5	Timber and wooden furniture industries	64	0.5
38	1.5	Postal services and telecommunications	426	3.5
38	1.5	Research and development	499	4.1
304	11.6	Other areas	889	7.3
2616	100.0	TOTALS	12180	100.0

The EUREKA RJV database

Table 3.11 shows the overall participation in EUREKA RJVs by country. French agents have been dominant with most memberships and coordinators. Germany and the UK are at the second and third position respectively in terms of participations. Dutch organizations have also been very active coordinators of RJVs. Regarding the frequency of memberships (Table 3.12), results show an even more concentrated picture than in EU RJVs: the vast majority of entities have participated only in one RJV (80 per cent); an additional 12 per cent have participated in two RJVs, while only 23 entities reported participation in more than ten RJVs.

Figure 3.10 shows a similar percentage of small and medium enterprises (SMEs) and large firms in the examined EUREKA RJVs, raising the total share of firms to 76 per cent of all participating entities. The remaining are mainly research institutes (12 per cent), universities (8 per cent), and government organizations. Firms also dominate as RJV coordinators. Interestingly, SMEs outnumber large firms as coordinators in the examined EUREKA RJVs (43 per cent versus 39 per cent of cases).

Table 3.13 lists the most active organizations in EUREKA RJVs (more than ten memberships each). Universities and research institutes occupy the first six places. The first SME firm is at the 32nd position with nine memberships (not shown).

The total number of firms per country is presented in Table 3.14 (top 15 countries). The picture is proportional to the overall participations count. A significant variation between the relative shares of EUREKA RJV participation by large firms and SMEs across countries is rather evident.

Membership 'concentration' by country is shown in Table 3.15. The first column on the left of the table presents the share of memberships accounted for by the ten most active firms based in a country. Considerable variation is observed here too. While concentration is relatively low for the countries at the top, it is very high for others like Greece where the ten most active agents accounted for more than half of the overall participations from that country. The two columns on the right of the table show the number of the entities per country that are required for reaching a minimum of one fifth of the country's total memberships. UK features the most distributed membership. Greece and Ireland the most concentrated.

Comparing Framework Programmes and EUREKA RJVs

EUREKA was purposively designed in the mid-1980s to complement the Framework Programmes for RTD rather than to substitute for them. Both the Framework Programmes and EUREKA focused on international co-operative RTD among European organizations; the former were, however,

Table 3.11   Participation in EUREKA RJVs

Total entities	% of total entities	Country	Number of participations	% of total participations	Partner	Coordinator	% of coordinators
653	15.33	France	1022	16.40	829	193	18.87
604	14.18	Germany	924	14.82	852	72	7.04
448	10.51	UK	624	10.01	542	82	8.02
366	8.59	Netherlands	501	8.04	354	147	14.37
279	6.55	Italy	431	6.91	387	44	4.30
261	6.13	Switzerland	420	6.74	352	68	6.65
307	7.20	Spain	401	6.43	303	98	9.58
206	4.83	Sweden	273	4.38	234	39	3.81
176	4.13	Norway	263	4.22	210	53	5.18
160	3.75	Finland	258	4.14	209	49	4.79
154	3.61	Austria	219	3.51	163	56	5.47
128	3.00	Denmark	192	3.08	147	45	4.40
141	3.31	Belgium	187	3.00	162	25	2.44
80	1.88	Portugal	122	1.96	106	16	1.56
38	0.89	Greece	58	0.93	55	3	0.29
17	0.40	Ireland	19	0.30	17	2	0.20
10	0.23	Luxembourg	10	0.16	6	4	0.39
233	5.46	Other countries	309	4.96	282	27	2.65
4261	100.00		6233	100.00	5210	1023	100.00

Table 3.12   Membership frequency

Number of memberships	Entities	%
1	3384	79.42
2	507	11.90
3	165	3.87
4 to 6	145	3.40
7 to 10	37	0.87
>11	23	0.54
Total	4261	100.00

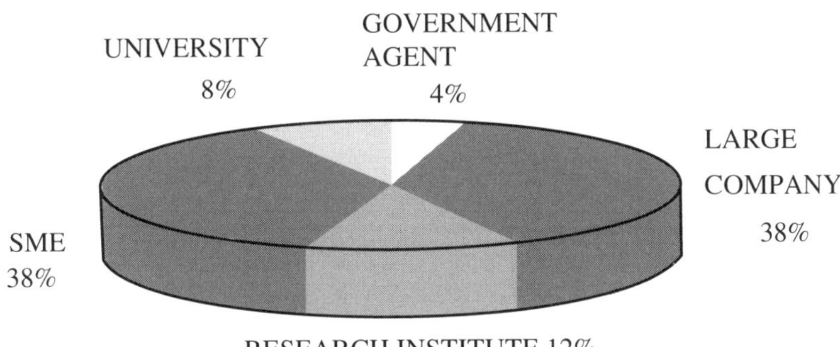

Figure 3.10   Type of participating entities in the EUREKA RJVs (number of observations, 4137)

supposed to support research projects of a different nature than the projects of the latter. Since, then, of course, both programmes have changed significantly. The basic differences can be summarised as follows:

- The first five EU FWPs were set up through a largely 'top-down' procedure, following extensive consultation between the Commission and the various stakeholders, including industry. The EU periodically announced 'focused' competitions in specific technological areas. In contrast, EUREKA has left the technological area of concentration of the proposed projects totally to the partners.
- Projects funded through the Framework Programmes were intended to involve more precompetitive (generic) research. EUREKA projects have involved more development research directly aiming at marketable products and services.

Table 3.13   Most active organizations in the examined EUREKA RJVs

Organization name	Organization type	Country	Total memberships
Frauhhofer-Institut	Res. Institute	Germany	43
Ecole Polytenique Federale De Lausanne	University	Switzerland	32
SINTEF-SI	Res. Institute	Norway	24
Technical Research Centre of Finland (VTT)	Res. Institute	Finland	22
Technische Hochschule Zuerich	University	Switzerland	19
Technical University of Wien	University	Austria	17
Aerospatiale S.N.I. S.A.	Large Firm	France	17
PSA – Peugeot Citroen	Large Firm	France	16
Center CIM de Suisse Occidentale	Res. Institute	Switzerland	15
Bull S.A.	Large Firm	France	14
Katholieke Universiteit Leuven	University	Belgium	12
Helsinki University of Technology	University	Finland	12
SAGEM Soc. D'Applications Generales D'Electricite Et De Mecanique	Large Firm	France	12
Instituto De Soldatura e Qualidade Investigacao e Desenvovlimento	Res. Institute	Portugal	12
Royal Institute of Technology	Res. Institute	Sweden	12
The Welding Institute	Res. Institute	UK	12
Universidad Politechnica De Madrid	University	Spain	11
CNRS	Res. Institute	France	11
Robert Bosch GmbH	Large Firm	Germany	11
ENEA – Ente Per Le Nuove Tecnologie, L'energie, L'Ambiente	Res. Institute	Italy	11
Universiteit Twente	University	Netherlands	11
DSM N.V.	Large Firm	Netherlands	11
Swedish Institute of Production Engineering Research	Res. Institute	Sweden	11

Table 3.14   Number of firms per country

Country	Number of large firms	Number of SMEs	Total number of firms
France	237	263	500
Germany	264	190	454
UK	184	148	332
Netherlands	140	156	296
Spain	113	112	225
Switzerland	72	128	200
Italy	135	57	192
Sweden	82	83	165
Finland	76	65	141
Norway	63	70	133
Austria	51	63	114
Belgium	56	57	113
Denmark	45	50	95
Portugal	21	19	40
Greece	15	10	25

Table 3.15   Membership concentration by country

Country	Responsible for percentage of memberships of the ten most active entities	Entities	Percentage of memberships
Germany	12.77	25	20.35
France	11.45	25	20.45
UK	10.26	28	20.19
Netherlands	13.17	20	20.36
Italy	15.55	15	20.65
Switzerland	25.95	6	21.19
Spain	12.97	21	20.45
Sweden	19.78	11	20.51
Norway	26.24	5	20.15
Finland	26.74	5	20.93
Austria	25.57	7	21.00
Denmark	26.04	8	21.88
Belgium	24.60	8	21.39
Portugal	35.25	4	22.13
Greece	51.72	2	22.41
Ireland	63.16	2	21.05

- The Framework Programmes involve subsidization (up to 50 per cent of the total research cost) by a central source (Commission). Approval by EUREKA only means a label that improves chances for (decentralized) national funding; partners can only seek public financing from their governments.
- The results of the Framework Programme research projects are the property of both the EU and the partners, whereas the results of EUREKA projects are the sole property of the partners.
- The European Commission oversees Framework Programme projects. In contrast, EUREKA projects are only supervised by the partners themselves according to the initial agreement.

These differences in the design and governance of the two policy frameworks for collaborative R&D in Europe have resulted in different sets of RJVs. The descriptive statistics in the previous sections point at the following important differences:

- *Technological areas*   EU RJVs have tended to concentrate relatively more on ICTs, whereas EUREKA RJVs have been more evenly distributed across several technical areas.
- *Duration*   Most of the examined EU RJVs (almost 70 per cent) are medium-term and only 16 per cent involve long-term efforts (more than 37 months). On the contrary the percentage of EUREKA RJVs that last beyond 37 months reaches 57 per cent. In fact, almost 20 per cent of these RJVs last over 60 months.
- *Size*   While in EU RJVs some 45 per cent are small sized (two to five partners) with another 41 per cent at the six to ten partner area, in EUREKA RJVs the small sized are significantly larger as they cover 69 per cent of the population. In fact the majority of EUREKA RJVs involve cooperation between two or three partners (42.6 per cent).
- *Type*   EU RJVs involve significant cooperation between firms, universities and research institutes; inter-firm cooperation is much more prevalent in EUREKA RJVs.
- *Coordinator*   Firms tend to be the coordinators in the majority of both EU and EUREKA RJVs. Other organizations such as universities and research institutes also tend to act as coordinators in a significant number of EU RJVs (39 per cent of the total number of RJVs formed). In EUREKA RJVs the relevant percentage is just 18 per cent.
- *Firm characteristics*   Large firms tend to participate more often, especially in the EU RJVs. On the other hand there are a large

number of SME firms that have a rather limited participation (1 to 3 times). Participation in EUREKA RJVs seems to have been more balanced between firms of different sizes.

- *Sector*   In both types of RJVs firms active in the electrical and electronic engineering and business services sectors appear to be more frequent participants than firms in other sectors. Firms active in the chemical sector tend to have higher participation in EUREKA RJVs. Firms active in telecommunications appear to participate relatively more in EU RJVs compared with EUREKA RJVs.

THE EMERGENCE OF EUROPEAN RESEARCH NETWORKS

A basic objective of the European FWPs has been to assist the formation of networks in order to transform the European economic knowledge base into economic growth. Networking is considered to provide both flexibility and a suitable environment for interactive learning. The EU RJV database provides a useful basis for network analysis due to the repeated participation of a significant number of firms and other organizations in these RJVs. This section briefly illustrates a few networks identified through a preliminary analysis of a subset of 3874 RJVs initiated during the period 1992 to 1996. The analysis was confined to companies. In this dataset, companies have made up to 32 'contacts' (participated in the same RJVs). Three main networks in the European industry can thus be observed:[4]

- *Auto-Industry Network*   Large and well-known firms from the sector of automobile industry are members of this network. Fiat, BMW, Volkswagen, Renault (Fr), Peugeot-Citroen, Volvo and Rover are some of the main members of this network. They have contacted each other through the European FWPs from 9 to 29 times during the examined five-year time period (Figure 3.11).
- *Aerospace-Industry Network*   Members of this network are firms from the aerospace industry like Construcciones, Aerospatiale, Alenia, Dassault, Dornier and others. They have contacted each other from 7 to 32 times (Figure 3.12).
- *Electronics/Telecommunications-Industry Network*   Almost all major players in the European ICT industry can be found in this network, including the major companies from each country. Thomson, Siemens, Alcatel, Bull, British Telecom, Telenor, Telefonica and others participate in this network (Figure 3.13).

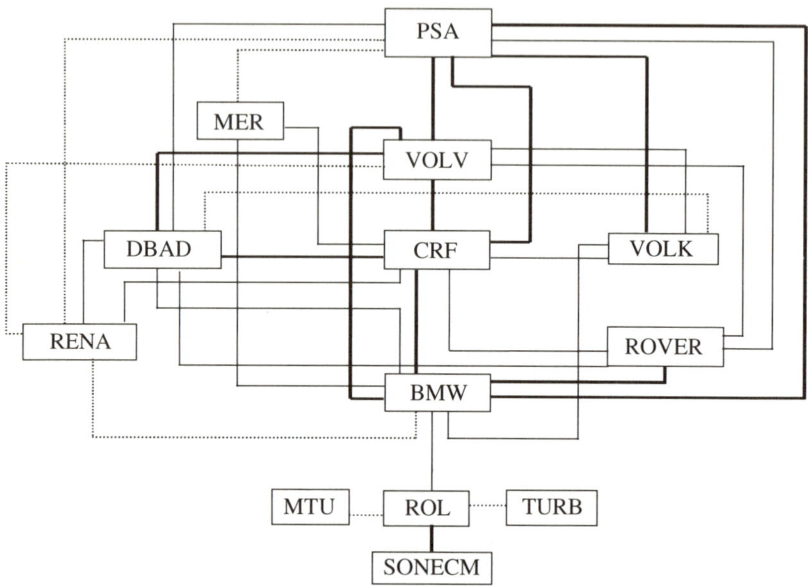

Figure 3.11   Auto-industry network

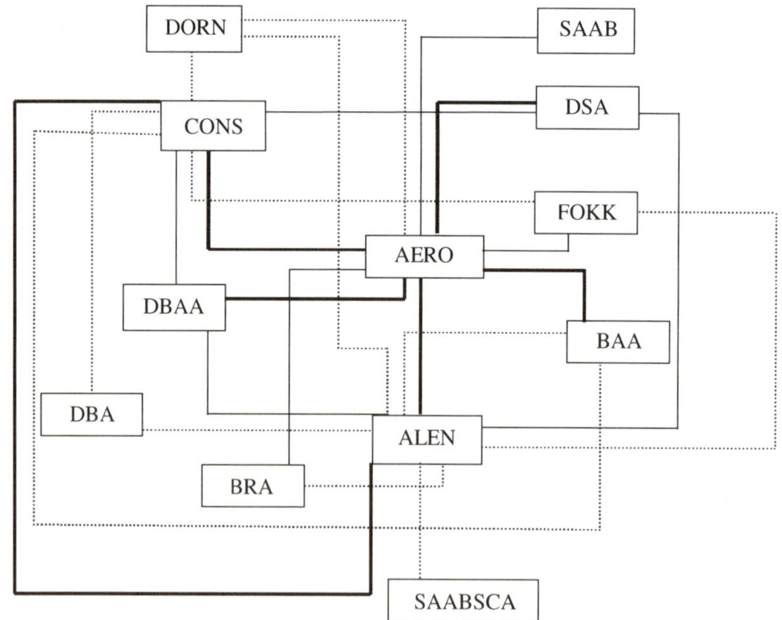

Figure 3.12   Aerospace-industry network

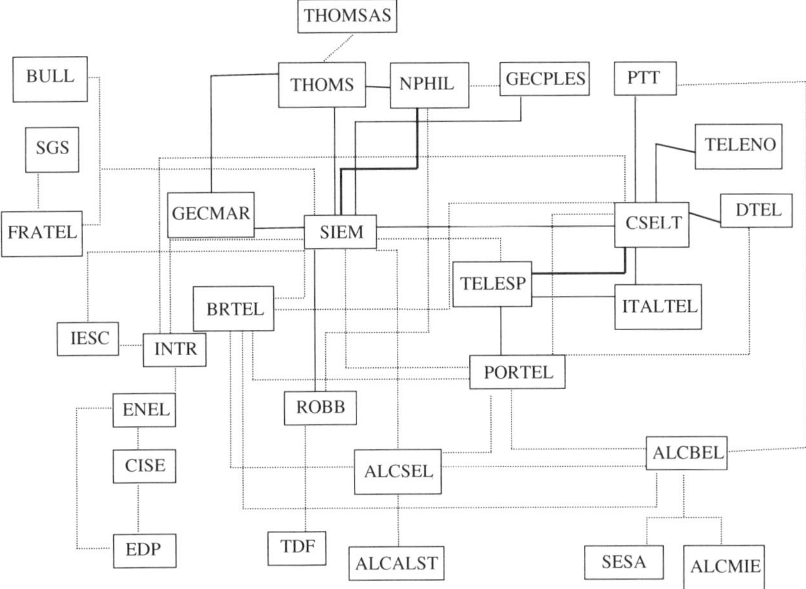

Figure 3.13   Electronics/telecommunications-industry network

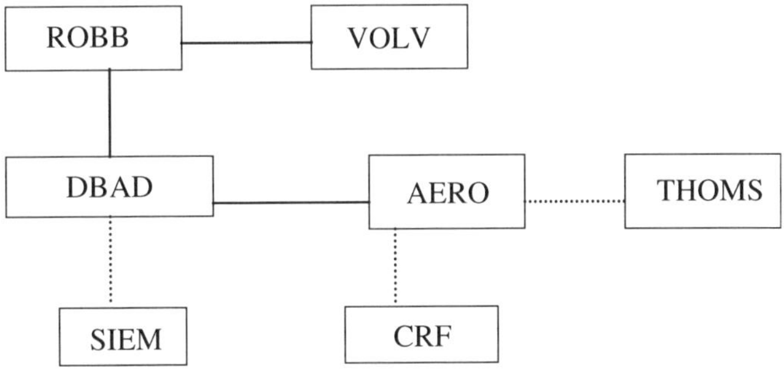

Figure 3.14   Interconnected networks

The three networks are also interconnected (Figure 3.14). The first network is connected with the second through ten links between Fiat and Aerospatiale, while the second network is connected with the third through seven links between Aerospatiale and Thomson. Finally, the first and third networks are connected through Daimler Benz and Siemens. Therefore FWPs seem to operate as a catalyst for supporting collaborative R&D networks.

NOTES

1. A taxonomy of the Research Joint Ventures is presented in Hagedoorn, Link and Vonortas, 2000.
2. In addition to the FWPs, R&D funds are allocated to member states through structural programmes. FWPs, have, however, become the most visible vehicle of Community R&D.
3. At the end of 1998, the EUREKA member countries were: Austria, Belgium, Czech Republic, Denmark, Finland, France, Germany, Greece, Hungary, Iceland, Ireland, Italy, Luxembourg, Netherlands, Norway, Poland, Portugal, Romania, Slovenia, Spain, Sweden, Switzerland, Turkey, United Kingdom and Russia. Furthermore, the European Commission is also a member of the EUREKA initiative.
4. For this illustration, we have worked with organizations contacting each other seven times or more. Linkages established through seven to ten projects are represented by the dotted line, while a simple line represents 11–15 projects. Finally the bold line means that the related firms have 'contacted' each other more than 15 times.

REFERENCES

Caloghirou, Y. and N. S. Vonortas (2000), *Science and Technology Policy Towards Research Joint Ventures*, final report of the STEP-TO-RJV's Project SOE1-CT97-1075, Targeted Socio-Economic Research Programme, European Commission, DG Research, March.

Caloghirou, Y., A. Tsakanikas and N. S. Vonortas (2001), 'University–industry cooperation in the context of the European Framework Programmes', *The Journal of Technology Transfer*, **26**(1/2), 153–61.

Council on Competitiveness (1996), *Endless Frontier, Limited Resources: U.S. R&D Policy for Competitiveness*, Washington, DC: Council on Competitiveness.

EUREKA Secretariat (1993), *Evaluation of EUREKA Industrial and Economics Effects*.

European Commission (1997), *Second European Report on S&T Indicators: 1997*, Directorate-General XII, Luxembourg: Office of the Official Publications of the European Communities.

Hagedoorn, J. (1995), 'Strategic technology partnering during the 1980s: trends, networks and corporate patterns in non-core technologies', *Research Policy*, **24** (2), 207–31.

Hagedoorn, J., A. N. Link and N. S. Vonortas (2000), 'Research partnerships', *Research Policy*, **29**(4–5), 567–86.

Peterson, J. (1991), 'Technology policy in Europe: explaining the Framework Programme and Eureka in theory and practice', *Journal of Common Market Studies*, **29**(3), 269–90.

Peterson, J. and M. Sharp (1998), *Technology Policy in the European Union*, New York: St. Martin's Press.

Vonortas, N. (1997), 'Research joint ventures in the US', *Research Policy*, **26**(4–5), 577–95.

4. RJV formation by European firms: strategic considerations

Aggelos Tsakanikas and Yannis Caloghirou

A first look at the issue of publicly funded R&D collaboration in Europe has been presented in the previous chapter, drawing on information from the EU RJV and EUREKA RJV databases. While this information is useful in determining the overall characteristics of RJVs and of participating organizations, thus illustrating the context of these ventures, it cannot assist in studying the motives of RJV participants for joining collaborative R&D ventures. The linkage of these participations with the internal activities of the firm, their special characteristics in terms of strategy, and their business environment are rather absent from such an approach. In order to study the latter in depth, it is necessary to complement the information from the databases with qualitative data at firm level, obtained through field research. This could represent a more subjective approach as the analysis is grounded on the respondents' thoughts and beliefs regarding RJVs. Therefore, field research was necessary in order to obtain the supplementary information required, which would help us evaluate effectiveness of policy towards RJVs. As Sakakibara (2001) has already pointed out, there is a surprisingly small body of empirical evidence on cooperative R&D, with comprehensive empirical research being almost non-existing. Hence, this survey provides a unique opportunity for an extensive cross-sectional and more systematic analysis on funded R&D collaborations.

The survey questionnaire was designed by taking into consideration that the decision of a firm to participate in an RJV depends both on its strategies and all its internal activities, but it is also influenced by the business environment in which it operates. Therefore, a number of questions related to these endogenous and exogenous variables were included in the survey instrument. Further information that was obtained included:

1. information on the motives and the benefits of firms of/from collaborative R&D, taking also into consideration the problems that may affect this process

2. information concerning the type of new knowledge being created, learned and transferred between RJV partners
3. information on the importance of external funding, along with the RJVs' linkage with the business activities of the participating firms
4. information on the appropriation of the results and their further exploitation.

QUESTIONNAIRE STRUCTURE

A two-pronged approach, related to the questionnaire structure, was adopted. A 'long version' of the survey used a ten-page questionnaire, containing three sections:

- general information on the company, including type, size, various financial data for the most recent six years, and strategic orientation;
- information on the specific RJV, including type of research, relation to core activities of the firm, intellectual property rights treatment, objectives and expected benefits from the specific RJV, and problems experienced in carrying out the activity; and,
- information on the particular business unit that participated in the RJV in question, including business environment affecting the decision to collaborate, technology strategy, objectives for inter-firm collaboration, and problems frequently encountered while collaborating.

The 'short version' of the survey used a six-page structured questionnaire. It abbreviated the general information section and omitted the section on the business unit, but kept the section on the RJV unchanged.

The target of the field research was set to 30 (completed) long and 70 short questionnaires from each of the seven countries participating in the survey (France, Greece, Ireland, Italy, Spain, Sweden and the United Kingdom).[1] The questionnaire was distributed to companies previously identified to have participated in RJVs either in the context of EU Framework Programmes (EU-FWPs) or in the context of EUREKA. In addition, some partners enhanced their samples with companies that had participated in nationally funded programmes. This resulted in a survey sample representing a mixture of EU-funded, EUREKA, and nationally funded projects.

Considering earlier experience with low response rates in the countries in question, it was considered prudent to allow some leeway to individual partners in selecting the final sample to be surveyed with a request for increased emphasis on RJVs funded by the EU-FWPs. The respondent would be the R&D manager of the firm or the scientist in charge of the activity related to the specific RJV. The survey was conducted in all seven EU member countries during the period from February 1999 to July 1999.

DATA AND METHODOLOGY

Table 4.1 shows the response rates in each country, in terms of firms contacted and RJVs examined, both for the long and the short version of the questionnaire.[2]

Table 4.1   Survey results

Country	Long version		Short version		Total number of firms	Total number of RJVs
	Firms	RJVs	Firms	RJVs		
France	29	30	56	57	58*	63*
Greece	88	135	–	–	88	135
Ireland	19	22	25	31	41**	48**
Italy	30	34	40	58	70	92
Spain	43	43	35	70	74**	112**
Sweden	30	30	70	74	100	104
UK	73	82	–	–	73	82
Totals	312	376	226	290	504	636

Notes:
* Most of the firms and the RJVs of the long version are included in the short as well.
**There is a small overlapping in the firms and RJVs in the two types of questionnaire

A large pool of 504 European firms and 636 RJVs was created, providing a unique dataset originating from seven EU countries for an extensive and reliable analysis. Such a dataset is, at least to our knowledge, one of the richest, multinational and cross-sectional samples that have been published. However, the analysis was limited only to the EU-FWPs funded RJVs, thus excluding those data stemming exclusively either from EUREKA or national programmes. The main reasons justifying this decision had to do mainly with the obtained results. Regarding EUREKA RJVs, it turned out that not all countries were able to present a satisfactory sample due to the sometimes low overall country participation. The same holds for the national RJVs, as only two countries (Spain, Greece) represented 88 per cent of the relevant sample. In addition, because of the fact that we needed a weighting variable for the countries included in the analysis, including these data would create problems in the construction of that variable. Therefore the dataset that is used in the subsequent analysis refers only to firms that have participated at least once in an EU-FWP funded RJV.

Based on the above criteria, the available dataset has the following characteristics: regarding general information at the corporate level of the firm, the total usable questionnaires can reach 391 firms. The part of the questionnaire that referred to the cooperative R&D activity and the related business unit was circulated exclusively through the long-type survey and resulted in a sample of 270 firms. Finally, the part referred to the cooperative R&D activity and the related business unit, which could be obtained three times at the most from the same firm, produced a sample of 467 RJVs. These numbers, and despite the fact that we excluded the EUREKA and national sourced questionnaires, still support our argument about a representative and unique – to our knowledge – survey sample, covering satisfactorily the issue of funded research partnerships in the European area.

The aim of this chapter is to present the main findings of this survey examining firms and their participation in EU funded RJVs. Therefore, the unit of analysis is the European firm that has decided to conduct cooperative R&D through this policy instrument. But in order to make any inferences about that firm and interpret the results properly, we had to make sure that our assessments clearly represent the average European firm, taking into consideration each country's relative part in that picture. Therefore, a weighting variable was used throughout the analysis, which would eliminate any possible problems or the fact that some countries like Greece, UK or Sweden were over-represented in the sample in comparison to, for example, France.

In order to create this weighting variable, the total population of firms that have participated in EU-FWPs has been retrieved from the EU RJV database, along with the total number of the RJVs that they have formed. These numbers were used for creating weights for all the relevant questions based on the usable observations.[3] Table 4.2 sums up the country results both with and without the weights in order to illustrate the differences.

As it is shown, in terms of firms' responses, Greek firms represent the majority of the sample (30 per cent), which clearly creates problems in our effort to assess the average European firm. However, in the weighted sample this is reduced to the more appropriate level of 6.5 per cent, while French and UK participations in RJVs represent more than half of the weighted sample.

Table 4.2   Mapping of the dataset

Country	Number of firms	Unweighted %	Weighted %	Number of RJVs	Unweighted %	Weighted %
Italy	*30*	11.1	18.5	*74*	15.8	19.7
France	*23*	8.5	22.1	*41*	8.8	26.7
Sweden	*19*	7.0	7.1	*57*	12.2	5.8
Spain	*33*	12.2	14.0	*58*	12.4	11.5
Greece	*81*	30.0	6.5	*119*	25.5	6.8
Ireland	*18*	6.7	3.5	*46*	9.9	3.4
UK	*66*	24.4	28.3	*72*	15.4	26.1
Total	*270*	100.0	100.0	*467*	100.0	100.0

PROFILE OF SURVEYED FIRMS

This section reports the general characteristics of the surveyed firms (profile), in order to further understand the corporate and financial identity of the RJV participants.

The firms of our sample are 94 per cent private with only 6 per cent being state owned. In most of the cases the latter are big companies operating in 'network industries' (electricity and water supply, national air transport carriers and so on), which were state owned (at least 51 per cent) at the time of the survey. Despite the huge percentage of private activity, only 4.4 per cent are family owned/run firms, while only 30 per cent are publicly traded in local or international stock exchange markets.[4] Almost 30 per cent are members of a national group, whereas a slightly smaller 23 per cent are subsidiaries of a multinational group.[5] More than half of the sample (53 per cent) report that their main business activity is in a maturity stage with a further 35 per cent being at a fast growth phase. Only two per cent are in a decline and ten per cent lie at an early stage. This result could be explained by the fact that when a firm's primary activity is at an early stage then the firm does not have a scope for long-term investments in R&D (even through public funding), as its priority is to gain a better position in the developing market area (with higher market share, and so on). Nor would a declining activity be popular for R&D, as these firms are not in a position to dispose resources to such activities. Hence, the high percentages in the other two stages seem rather logical, since firms could seek further ways to acquire sustained competitive advantage or new ways to upgrade their resources and capabilities through cooperative R&D.

Regarding the financial status of the participants, more than one third of the sample are small sized firms (less than 50 employees), with the total per-centage of SMEs (less than 250 employees) reaching 53 per cent.[6] However, there is a significant 31 per cent that employ more than 1000 employees, referring to the big European firms that have participated in the EU-FWPs. We should always have in mind that EU technology policy shifted its atten-tion to SMEs, especially in the fourth FWP, in an effort to help those firms that actually shape European competitiveness and technical change (Pavitt, 1998). These firms are supported partly because they are seen as the most dynamic sector of the economy with job-creating potential and partly because they are more clearly constrained by inadequate access to resources and capabilities (Georghiou, 2001). This explains their increased participa-tion in these RJVs and contradicts data from privately funded alliances like the strategic technological alliances of CATI database (MERIT), where a strong causality between size and the propensity to engage in such alliances is identified (Narula, 1998).[7]

Almost one third of the sample reported sales of up to €5 million per year with profits of up to €1 million, although one quarter of the sample are loss making. Furthermore, regarding R&D expenditures, more than 60 per cent of the sample spends less than €1 million, while for 57 per cent the R&D intensity lies below one per cent. In addition, the ratio of R&D per-sonnel (employees fully involved in R&D) to total employees lies below one per cent for nearly half the sample. It should be noted, however, that only 40 per cent of the original sample has reported some data for R&D expen-ditures. This suggests that the remaining respondents do not spend any amount of money for R&D, possibly making the specific cooperative activ-ity their only one in that field. Despite that, the sample could be character-ized as knowledge intensive, since almost half of it reports more than 25 per cent share as scientific personnel (scientists and engineers).

Table 4.3 sums up the picture showing the identity of the average European firm that participates in EU funded RJVs. Median values are preferred (due to data outliers) for interpretation compared to the average ones, although both are presented. Therefore, the firm in question is an SME with sales of €30 million and earnings of €320000. Despite the low R&D expenditures (one per cent of its sales), almost one quarter of its per-sonnel are scientists and engineers, while five per cent of its employees are exclusively involved in R&D activities.

In terms of sectoral profiles, Table 4.4 presents the more populated sectors that appear in our sample. Business activities referring mostly to consulting services dominate the sample (23 per cent), while another 15 per cent refers to computer and related activities. The first manufacturing sector is that of chemicals and chemical products with the rather low 6 per cent.[8] At the second part of the table we present a more complete picture

Table 4.3   Financial and corporate identity of surveyed firms

	Median	Average
Total sales	€30 million	€774 million
Profits	€0.32 million	€40 million
R&D expenditure	€0.46 million	€4.8 million
Number of employees	219	4228
% share of scientists and engineers	23%	36%
R&D employees/total employees	5%	19%
R&D expenditures/sales	1.0%	7.7%

Table 4.4   Sectoral profile of surveyed firms

Sector description	Sector code (NACE 1)	%
Most populated sectors		
Other business activities	74	22.53
Computer and related activities	72	15.02
Research and Development	73	7.99
Manufacture of chemicals and chemical products	24	5.94
Manufacturer of machinery and equipment	29	4.90
Manufacture of other transport equipment	35	4.46
Manufacture of electrical machinery and apparatus	31	4.29
All sectors aggregated		
Business Services		45.9
Manufacturing		43.3
Construction		2.3
Primary sector (mining, forestry etc)		0.4
Network Industries (telecommunication, electricity supply etc.)		3.1
Other Services (retail, miscellaneous products, insurances etc.)		5.0

with all sectors aggregated to six basic areas. Business services (mostly consulting services) and manufacturing are almost equally represented in the sample, indicating that firms from both large areas of economic activity have been attracted by the technological areas that receive the EU funding and form RJVs. However, the percentage of services is still quite large and might be striking at a first glance. One possible explanation could be taking into consideration the fact that most of these services are knowledge intensive (that is IT services). It is perhaps time to drop the old dichotomy between manufacturing as the R&D intensive sector and business services as the non-R&D intensive. A textile firm might be R&D intensive if it has incorporated new technologies in its productive processes or even at an organizational level, while another firm from the same sector might be non-R&D intensive, if it is technologically lagging. The same can hold also for a firm from the service sector. That is why a distinction between knowledge and non-knowledge intensive firms might be more appropriate.[9]

CHARACTERISTICS OF REPORTED RJVs

This section summarizes some characteristics of the 467 RJVs specified by the surveyed firms in their responses. Respondents were asked to character-ize the type of the research undertaken through the specific project. The vast majority of them involved applied research (78 per cent), whereas development takes a 34 per cent.[10] Only 14 per cent of the reported RJVs dealt with basic research. Chen (1997) suggests that the notion of precom-petitive research fails to take account of the fact that the process of inno-vation may quite well be an iterative one and may not follow the classic linear model of basic-applied-development-commercial exploitation route. It is unlikely that firms involved in R&D partnerships will confine them-selves merely to upstream precompetitive research even if public pro-grammes appear to support only such activities. Firms may opt for collaboration driven by a need for external help to complete vital R&D pro-jects. It is therefore implausible that the firms will limit themselves to pre-competitive research. Finally, it has also been suggested that basic research might be related to more sensitive technological knowledge of a firm and it is therefore preferably performed in-house (Harrigan, 1985).

Regarding the connection of the specific collaborative activity with other R&D activities of the firms, only 21 per cent of the reported RJVs are con-nected with own-funded research, while another 21 per cent were part of a previous EU project. However, about half of the examined RJVs are neither extensions nor continuations of previous projects. Most of the RJVs that were part of a previous European project involve Swedish and Greek firms, whereas continuation of own-funded activity happens mostly in UK and Ireland. A linkage between national and EU-FWPs is evident mostly in Sweden, since firms located in that country are mainly respon-sible for a low seven per cent of RJVs that were continuations of previous nationally funded RJVs.

One way to test whether the participation of a firm in a collaborative venture is well connected with a cohesive technology strategy and does not represent a random action, is to examine whether the specific cooperative

R&D was undertaken in the core activity area of the firm. The vast majority of the RJVs examined (70 per cent) were undertaken in core activity areas, indicating a close relation between cooperative R&D and the firms' main activities (Table 4.5[11]). Therefore, it seems that the research undertaken through cooperation refers to technologies that are central to the

Table 4.5   Areas of the cooperative activity

In core activity	70.3%
In secondary activity	23.1%
In totally new activities	26.8%

day-to-day activities of firms, rather than secondary or peripheral ones. It is the kind of work that is on the 'wish list' of the firm, referring to the basic technologies that it uses and that it would like to conduct, but because of shortage of resources, it cannot (Quintas & Guy, 1995). Funded RJVs seem to provide the option to the firm to get in touch with complementary actors and conduct that important type of research. This further indicates that EU subsidy seems to fulfil one of its major objectives: funding R&D that is widely connected with the central activities of firms and is of primary importance for them. Nevertheless, the 50 per cent of RJVs referring to secondary or new activities of the firms, show that collaborative R&D offers also the opportunity to pursue a wider spread of technologies and access a broader range of expertise than would otherwise be possible (ibid).[12]

The protection and exploitation of the R&D output is also an important issue regarding EU funded RJVs (Table 4.6). Our survey indicates that no patenting activity was undertaken following the completion of the project (72 per cent). This may be a result of the fact that all R&D results are supposed to belong to the funding body (EU), while there is also the requirement of a result-sharing agreement among cooperating parties. Hence, there are many difficulties in patenting the exact results of the R&D. On the other hand, for only 11 per cent of the results there were no plans for any exploitation in the market place. Almost one quarter were to be exploited through joint marketing agreements and 13 per cent through division of markets, whereas for 45 per cent, some other form of exploitation, apart from the proposed ones, was followed. This result reinforces our aforementioned argument regarding the actual limitations of precompetitive research and its applied (or not) character. Firms participating in publicly funded programmes may very well extend their joint efforts to downstream near-market activities, possibly as a result of the fact that the process of innovation tends to be an iterative phenomenon (Chen, 1997). Furthermore, Luukkonen (2002) argues that firms often carry out parallel

Table 4.6   Protection and exploitation of the results

Property rights	%	Exploitation of the results	%
Individual patenting	17.7	Joint marketing agreements	23.5
Joint patenting	6.5	Division of markets	12.9
Both	3.5	Joint product	7.8
No patents	72.3	Other	45.1
		No exploitation	10.7
Total	100.0	Total	100.0

Table 4.7   Importance of public funding

Not undertaken this research at all	59.4
Undertaken the same research project with same partners	6.7
Undertaken the same research project with different partners	11.2
Undertaken the same research project alone	22.7
Total	100.0

commercial projects and these can very well draw on a precompetitive EU funded project.

The outcome of these RJVs in terms of future actions was also surveyed. In the vast majority of the cases (92 per cent) the specific RJVs led to the initiation of new research activity either exclusively by the firm, in collaboration with others, or both. This seems to indicate that at least one of the objectives of the EU policy, the initiation of further cooperation even without the intervention of the Union, is achieved. From this result we can assume that previous experience has been successful, either in terms of the actual content of the R&D output (new opportunities to exploit), or generally in terms of relationships. Therefore, the vast majority of firms seem to be in a position to grasp the opportunity of this participation and further enhance their research activities.

Regarding the organizational way that the actual research undertaken was internally divided among partners, in an overwhelming 92 per cent of RJVs research was shared among existing laboratories of partners. In addition, learning was mainly promoted through project meetings and informal communication among partners.

Another important dimension of EU funding is the issue of additionality (Luukkonen, 2000). This means that the subsidy should function as a catalyst for the conduct of R&D that otherwise would not be conducted. This concept rests originally on the neo-classical market failure rationale, which assumes that left to themselves firms will under-invest in R&D because of their inability to appropriate all the benefits arising from it. Results show (Table 4.7) that this is accomplished to a great extent, since 60 per cent of RJVs would not be conducted in the absence of the subsidy. In addition, a significant 23 per cent shows that firms would have undertaken the specific research activity alone. Additionality R&D turns out to be very important especially for the cohesion of peripheral countries, as chi-square test reveals. Ireland, Spain and Greece have given the lowest responses regarding the conduct of the specific R&D in any case, since 79 per cent, 73 per cent and 70 per cent of the cases respectively would not have been undertaken without public funding. On the other hand, it is Italian firms that would have undertaken the same research alone, more than all other countries (36 per cent, well above the average of 23 per cent). Finally, among those that would have undertaken the research activity without the external funding, almost 70 per cent would have carried it out in a smaller scale.

STRATEGY, BUSINESS ENVIRONMENT

Corporate Strategy

Corporate strategy is the overall plan of any highly or lowly diversified company. It refers to a more general view of the firm running across all its units, dealing with its overall vision and thus distinguishing it from the business level and competitive strategy. The latter deals with the way to develop sustainable competitive advantage in a discrete and identifiable market, being therefore a more focused type of strategy. A recent definition by Collis & Montgomerry talks about 'the way a company creates value through the configuration and coordination of its multitasked activities' (1998). This definition, as pointed out, places emphasis on value creation as the ultimate purpose of corporate strategy, focuses on the multimarket scope of the corporation (product, geographical areas and so on) and takes into consideration the way the firm manages its overall activities (coordination). Both types of strategy were examined in the context of this survey.

Results show that the examined firms follow mostly a strategy of increasing market share in existing products/services, in existing markets or increasing sales through the development of new products/services. The above strategies are adopted by more than 70 per cent of the sample, since they have ranked at four or five in a five-degree Likert scale, while the mean value of their answers reaches almost four. This indicates that those firms, on the one hand, pursue new ways for customer attraction for their existing portfolio of products, while, on the other, they try to innovate through the development of new products. By contrast, diversification in totally new (unrelated) products and services is adopted by only 18 per cent of the sample, since it is generally a more difficult type of strategy: it requires special characteristics from the firm at the organizational but also at the financial level.

We performed factor analysis on the list of 11 statements that were used for capturing the variable of corporate strategy. The purpose of the analysis is to examine the underlying patterns or relationships among those statements and determine whether or not the information can be condensed or summarized in a smaller set of factors with a meaningful interpretation. Results are summarized in Table 4.8.

Table 4.8   Corporate strategy

Dimensions (items)	Factors	Mean (std)
Increase market share in existing products (services) in existing markets. Introduction of existing products (services) in new geographical areas. Increase sales through development of new products/services.	Innovative penetration	3.7 (0.9)
Vertical/horizontal integration, mergers – acquisitions	External growth	2.4 (1.0)
Diversification in related or in totally new (unrelated) products (services)	Diversification	2.6 (1.1)
Outsourcing and joining strategic alliances	Extroversion	2.9 (1.0)
Grow internally	Internal growth	3.2 (1.3)

Note: Explained variance 67.8.

The first dimension (factor) of strategy captures those activities that were also estimated as the most important. It can be named as 'innovative penetration', as it refers to the efforts of the firm to increase its sales and market share through the development of new (innovation), or the launching of, existing products/services in the same or new geographical markets (penetration). 'Internal growth' is the second most important factor, although it comprises only one item. Outsourcing and joining strategic alliances both relate to a highly 'extrovert' behaviour of the firm, representing an effort of the firm to seek for possible help in achieving its goals, outside its boundaries. 'Diversification' (in related or unrelated products) and 'external growth' are the last two factors in terms of importance. The surveyed firms do not seem to adopt strategies that include mergers or acquisitions to a great extent, either for vertical or horizontal integration. Therefore, it could be argued that generally firms involved in this type of cooperative R&D do not follow such aggressive strategies, but focus rather on innovation and new products/services for increasing their market share.

Analysis of variance (ANOVA) has shown that there are significant differences among countries in all factors except the last one ('internal growth'). More specifically, Italian and French firms differ from all other firms in terms of 'innovative penetration', as the former adopt that specific type of strategy to the greatest extent, while the latter have given the lowest responses. Italian firms hold also the highest responses regarding 'external growth', being similar only to Greek and Irish firms. This indicates a rather surprising picture of firms from peripheral economies adopting aggressive strategies, which could be explained only by the fact that mergers and acquisitions are somehow milder in that case, since they refer to smaller scale actions of this type. UK firms are the less diversified, differing significantly from all other countries, while Italian firms seem to be those with the highest degree of diversification. Finally, regarding 'extroversion' it is Spanish firms that have given the lowest values, differing significantly from almost all other countries.

Competitive Strategy

Analysis for competitive strategy shows that firms try to achieve competitive advantage through differentiation in a specific market segment in terms of product characteristics. Of the sample, 67 per cent responded with a four or five in that item indicating an effort by firms to improve their portfolio of products in a more attractive and appealing manner. The second most popular strategy is achieving cost advantage by focusing also on a specific market segment (48 per cent of the sample). Cost is highly related with the processes, which nevertheless receives a major input from the R&D efforts of the firm. On the other hand, the least popular strategy is trying to achieve competitive advantage through differentiation in mass markets in terms of marketing practices (14 per cent). Therefore these firms do not believe that they can obtain sustainable competitive advantage from changing some 'superficial' (like promotion and advertising) dimensions of their strategy. Instead they follow more essential types of competitive strategy focusing on processes and product characteristics.

Factor analysis reveals the presence of two distinct factors that characterize the firms' competitive strategies (Table 4.9). The distinction refers to the size of market area, as firms seem to focus either on the mass market,

or on market segment. However, mean values show that the second factor
is the most popular, indicating that the firms that participate in RJVs are
active in more segmented markets and focus on specific target groups. Their
main effort is to achieve differentiation in terms of product characteristics,
explaining, therefore, their need of cooperative R&D as a means for providing new innovative and differentiated products.

Table 4.9   Competitive strategy

Dimensions (items)	Factors	Mean (std)
Cost advantage and differentiation in terms of	Mass market	2.4 (1.2)
products' characteristics or marketing practices in:	Market segment	3.2 (1.1)

Note: Explained variance 67.4.

ANOVA has also shown a country effect on the business strategy
adopted by firms. More precisely, it is Swedish firms that follow to a greater
extent the market segment strategy, differing significantly from all other
countries. An interesting point would also be the fact that Greek and Irish
firms differ significantly, despite the fact that they are both peripheral and
cohesion countries, with the first having the lowest mean for this type of
strategy. In fact, Greek firms are the only ones that have reported the mass
market strategy higher than the market segment, indicating that they still
do not perceive their markets as fragmented as others. However, Irish firms
are the leaders in the market segment strategy, being significantly different
from almost all countries (except Spain and Greece).

Business Environment

The respondents' business environment seems to be characterized by
intense competition at the technology level (71 per cent of the sample with
four or five), thus affecting product-features characteristics (71 per cent) as
well. Price-based competition and, surprisingly, customers' loyalty are both
estimated important by 55 per cent of the sample, indicating that although
the environment pressures firms for technologically advanced products and
services, customers seem to stick to their preferences.

Four dimensions describe the business environment (Table 4.10). A first
factor refers to the degree of regulation (regulative) either in terms of financial system, competition, trade, labour market or IPR. Second, the environment could be market determined, if competition is intense in terms of
prices and marketing practices, or the degree of customers' loyalty and the
level of profit margins are high. The third factor extracted captures the

intensity of competition at the technological level, while the last factor explores the difficulty of the environment in terms of prediction of the future demand and competitors' movements (easily predicted). Mean factor responses show that the firm's environment is primarily a technologically intensive one, affecting the product-market characteristics. Taking into consideration the increasing pace of technological development that has taken place in the last decades, it is not surprising to find that it is rather difficult to predict changes in demand or in competitors' moves, in such an environment. On the other hand, the general regulation rules do not seem to play any significant role or to affect their actions.

Table 4.10   Business environment

Dimensions (items)	Factors	Mean (std)
Degree of regulation in financial system, competition, trade, labour market, IPR	Regulative	2.5 (1.0)
Price based and marketing competition, profit margin, customers' loyalty	Market determined	3.2 (0.9)
Technological and product-features competition	Technological	3.8 (0.9)
Future demand and competitor's movements	Easily predicted	2.8 (1.0)

Note: Explained variance 61.7.

Country differences are present in all factors. Swedish firms seem to operate in the most deregulated environment, whereas French, Italian and Greek estimations are above the overall average. In addition, Sweden takes the lead in terms of market-based competition, differing significantly from France and Italy. Technological competition is very intense in France and Italy, contrasting with the lowest ranking of Greek firms. On the other hand, the environment of Swedish firms seems to be the more easily predicted, being significantly different from all other countries, whereas the most difficult is the UK one.

Technology Development Activities

Activities that firms undertake in relation to their technological development can be considered as a proxy for their technology strategy. The firms surveyed are mainly introducing new or improving existing products along with undertaking cooperative R&D, while they also try to introduce new processes. More than 60 per cent of the sample undertake these activities

on a continuous basis, while only 14 per cent of the sample are less active
in that area, following activities like acquiring externally developed technology. This clearly indicates that the firms examined are the more technologically sensitive ones, preferring to use effective methods of handling the
necessary technology for their processes.

Table 4.11   Activities related to technology development

Dimensions (items)	Factors	Mean (std)
Introduction of new or improving/ modifying existing processes	Process development	3.4 (1.1)
Imitation of existing technology, cooperation in R&D, transforming/ improving/adapting externally acquired technology	Effective activities	2.9 (0.8)
Extramural R&D or acquiring externally developed technology (licence, patents and so on)	Inert activities	2.3 (0.9)
Introduction of new or improving/ modifying existing products	Product development	3.7 (1.0)

Note: Explained variance 68.8.

Four factors describe these activities (Table 4.11). Two of the factors
relate to technological activities that have to do with process and product
development, either through introduction of new or improvement/modifi-
cation of the existing processes or products. The remaining technological
activities are also divided into two factors, namely effective and inert activities. The first includes those activities that express a more dynamic view of
the firm, as it refers to efforts to develop the necessary technology through
various internal or external ways. Cooperation in R&D and imitation,
transformation and adaptation of externally developed technology are
closely related with R&D and show a technological and research intensive
firm. On the other hand, the inert factor includes rather easy ('light') ways
of acquiring technology, as this process is left totally outside the firm's
boundaries. Extramural R&D and licensing technology or using patents
from third parties, are the composites of this factor.

Results show that the product and process development activities are
ranked by far at the first two places, while the least adopted methods are
the inert ones. This reinforces our argument that the firms under examination are the more technologically oriented, laying special emphasis on their
technology strategy. In terms of country differences, French firms seem to

follow process development more than all other countries, outweighing the product factor. On the other hand and quite surprisingly, Swedish firms are those that use effective activities to a lesser extent, contrasting the Spanish ones that are the leaders in that area. Spanish firms, however, also take the lead in the inert activities, indicating a rather mixed picture for these firms. Greece is the country where the product development factor is underestimated, indicating a greater emphasis on processes rather than products.

Processes of Acquiring and/or Creating New Knowledge

Apart from activities that are related to their technological status, firms also adopt processes in order to acquire or create new knowledge. The firms in question conduct, mostly, internal development and applied research, as 75 and 71 per cent of the sample have ranked with four or five the specific activities. On the other hand – and despite the precompetitive nature of the EU funded RJVs, which would orientate towards basic research – conducting that type of research is the least important process of creating new knowledge, as only 33 per cent of the sample undertake it.

Table 4.12   Processes of acquiring and/or creating new knowledge

Dimensions (items)	Factors	Mean (std)
Organizing/exploiting scientific and technical information (documentation, databases), education and training, long-term forecasting and product planning, existence of procedures exploiting individual initiatives and ideas within the firm.	Internal procedures	3.3 (0.8)
Conducting applied research and development internally, design engineering	Applied R&D	3.8 (1.0)
Conducting basic research internally and patenting	Basic research	2.6 (1.2)
Developing formal/informal relationships with users/suppliers	Relationships	3.7 (1.0)

Note: Explained variance 64.9.

Factor analysis results are presented in Table 4.12. The factor that joins applied R&D and design engineering internally is the most important factor based on firms' responses. However, almost equal importance is given to the development of formal or informal relationships with users and suppliers, indicating extrovert behaviour by the firms. Internal procedures of creating new knowledge are also highly estimated, whereas conducting basic research appears to play a rather small part in that process.

Regarding country effects, Spanish firms adopt internal procedures to a lesser extent, differing significantly from all other countries except the UK, which are also below the average value. Italian firms mostly conduct applied R&D, whereas French and UK firms seem to be the 'leaders' in conducting basic research. Finally, it is Irish firms that create new knowledge mostly through the development of relationships with their users and suppliers.

Cooperation with Other Organizations

Universities and research centres are the best candidates for collaboration with firms, as 57 per cent and 44 per cent of the sample prefers them respectively. Factor analysis (Table 4.13) reveals that universities and research centres are also joined together. This result reinforces the contention that bridging the two cultures is very important in today's rapidly changing environment, since benefits can be obtained from both sides (that is, sufficient infrastructure and ability to solve problems, transfer of skilled human capital and so on). Furthermore, these results contradict claims that EU-FWPs have fostered few firm-university or firm-research institute relationships (Peterson & Sharp, 1998; Luukkonen, 2001). On the other hand, only 16 per cent and 18 per cent of the surveyed firms seem to cooperate with competitors (in the same or different geographical area), whereas cooperation with suppliers or users is much more important. This highlights the fact that collaboration among competitors is difficult, as previous research has also shown (Teichert, 1997; Luukkonen, 2002).[13]

Table 4.13   Cooperation with other organizations

Dimensions (items)	Factors	Mean (std)
Competitor firm (same or different geographic market)	Competitors	2.1 (1.1)
Public research institutions and universities	Academia – research	3.2 (1.2)
Other firms and organizations	Other organizations	2.4 (1.1)
Supplier and client firm	User/producers	2.7 (1.1)

Note: Explained variance 74.

Objectives of Cooperative R&D

Firms' motives to enter cooperative agreements have long been the subject of analysis in economic and business literature (Glaister and Buckley, 1996). Chapter 2 has presented an extensive review of that literature indicating a variety of possible motives for entering R&D cooperation. Our survey tried to combine most of the approaches that have been previously introduced.

Results show that firms' participation in RJVs is guided by the objectives of accessing complementary resources and skills (70 per cent of the sample), technological learning (64 per cent) and R&D cost sharing (64 per cent), reinforcing therefore a more resource-based view of the firm. RJVs can be considered as organizational vehicles for gaining access to resources that are difficult to transfer otherwise and do not have a market for trade. On the other hand, traditional motives of industrial-organization literature, like avoiding the unintended loss of information to competitors or creating (at a better price) new investment options, drive the participation of only ten and 26 per cent of the sample respectively. Moving the analysis to a more aggregate level, the presence of four factors that describe all the proposed objectives is evident (Table 4.14).

The first factor – with the lowest, however, mean value – gathers those objectives related to market development, since speed to market and

Table 4.14 Objectives of cooperative R&D

Dimensions (items)	Factors	Mean (std)
Improve speed to market, jointly create and promote technical standards, promote user/ producer interactions, control future market developments or create new investment options	Market development	2.9 (0.8)
R&D cost/risk sharing, reducing uncertainty, obtain funding	Cost of R&D	3.4 (0.9)
Access to complementary resources and skills, achieving critical mass in R&D and research synergies leading to cost saving or improvements in R&D productivity	Resources and capabilities	3.4 (1.0)
Technological learning while keeping up with major technological developments	Technology	3.6 (1.0)

Note: Explained variance 67.4. Avoiding loss of information to competitors was excluded from the analysis in order to reach an acceptable factor solution. It is the least preferred objective anyway.

controlling future market development are joined together, along with creating new investment options. Promoting user and producer interactions and creation of technical standards are included in this factor too and can be related to market development, as they both affect a firm's performance in that area. This result is in accordance with other nationally funded pre-competitive programmes like the Alvey Programme in UK, where such incentives were considered important by only five per cent of the participants (Quintas & Guy, 1995). Hence, the examined RJVs are probably not the best way for achieving such goals, while other organizational forms of cooperation, like strategic alliances, could function better as effective vehicles for such purposes. Glaister & Buckley (1996), examining such international alliances of UK firms, found that gaining presence in new markets and achieving easier and faster entry into markets are the main strategic motivations for the formation of these alliances.

Cost and risk sharing, along with the additional funding obtained, is a crucial dimension in a firm's objectives from funded R&D cooperation, comprising the second most important factor (cost of R&D). Equally important though, are the more resource-based-view motives (resource & capability factor), including accessing those complementary recourses and skills that are necessary for achieving research synergies and possibly a critical mass in R&D. However, as Sakakibara (1997) points out, cost-based motives are a one-time gain for the firm, while the skill-based motives remain and accumulate through time. In any case, the most important factor, which seems to drive the participation of those firms in the examined RJVs, is technology. It refers to the effort of the firm to keep up with major technological developments in the European area and learn about the relevant technologies that the RJV deals with.[14]

Country differences are also evident in all factors except the last one, which thus supports the general view that technological motives are the major driving force for these RJVs for all firms examined, irrelevant of their country of origin. Spanish firms seem to be the ones that have an eye on the market to a greater extent, since they have estimated this factor higher, differing significantly from all other countries (except France). Irish firms have the lowest responses regarding R&D cost, followed by the Greek ones. Taking into consideration the limited R&D activity that takes place in these small and peripheral economies of the EU, this result indicates that firms located in these countries do not pay attention to this factor when they enter into such cooperation. They lack the complementary resources and the knowledge to conduct R&D, since in most of the cases these cooperative ventures represent their only R&D activity. That is why reducing the relative cost is of rather secondary importance, as they do not have that wide a research agenda, which would probably force them to think about the cost as well.

The effect of firm's size on these objectives is also tested through an ANOVA.[15] Results show that there is a significant effect mostly in market development objectives and to a lesser extent in resources and capabilities objectives, while the remaining two factors are unaffected by size. More specifically, the very large firms (more than 1000 employees) seem to be those with the more market-driven incentives like improving speed to market, controlling future market developments or creating new investment options. Differing significantly from all other firms, these ones seem to enter in RJVs with a clear market-oriented perspective, being probably those that owing to their size and market power can achieve such goals despite the precompetitive nature of the RJVs. Very large firms are also those with high responses in the resources' factor, but they only differ significantly from those with over 251 and up to 1000 employees, being similar to all other firms.

The relationship between the aforementioned objectives and the areas of activity of firms is an issue that requires further investigation. Mothe & Quelin (1999) have argued that when a project is central to a firm's strategy then there is a need for more tangible results and a quicker commercialization of the R&D outcome. By contrast, when the project is less central to the firm's strategy, its expectation is essentially an increase in knowledge: firms take advantage of an occasion to see at a low cost what is happening in related activities. Although we do not have such a straightforward proxy for this 'centrality' notion, we can use in our case the areas of activity that are related to the specific R&D (see Table 4.5). A product-moment correlation matrix is presented in Table 4.15.

Table 4.15   Firm areas of activity and objectives from cooperative R&D

	Market development	Cost of R&D	Resources & capabilities	Technology
Core activity	−0.10**	0.02	−0.03	0.11**
Secondary activity	0.08*	−0.11**	−0.09**	−0.08*
New activity	−0.02	0.10**	0.07*	0.02

Note: Weighted results, **, * denote significance at the 1% and 5% level.

A positive correlation between the core activity of the firm and technological objectives from cooperation, and a negative correlation with market development objectives are identified. This indicates an emphasis of the firm on keeping up with major technological developments in the area closely related to its primary activity, hence contradicting Mothe & Quelin's results. Firms do not expect commercial returns related to their basic products and services from their participation in these funded RJVs. Instead, they seek those technological developments that will probably help them improve their processes in order to be able next to deliver new products and services. The commercialization seems to be connected with the secondary activity of the firm: when the RJV refers to that activity then the firm will probably set market development objectives, while a negative correlation with all other objectives is identified. This could represent an effort of the firm to use the RJV for further enhancing the less privileged areas of its activity, by checking out possible alternative ways of increasing its market share. The RJV is an option for examining the 'capacity' of a secondary activity to become perhaps a core activity of the firm, sufficiently supporting its function. Finally, when the RJV refers to a new activity of the firm, then the investment option is evident, since reducing the cost of such a choice and detecting the proper resources and capabilities that are necessary for its development seem to drive firms' participation.

Benefits from Cooperative R&D

Respondents have been asked to estimate the degree to which specific benefits from their cooperation were achieved. Results show that acquisition and creation of new knowledge is by far the major benefit obtained from cooperative R&D as 77 per cent of the sample consider it important or very important. Continuation and acceleration of existing research is in second place (59 per cent of the sample), while equally important is the development of new products and improvement of a unit's technological and organizational capabilities (54 per cent). On the other hand, benefits related to actual changes in the market place, such as increasing profitability or market share, were considered important by only 25 per cent and 30 per cent of the sample respectively. Although these benefits are definitely the last ones, which would possibly be realized by the firms, the percentages are rather high considering the precompetitive nature of R&D collaboration. This is an indication that a significant number of the firms under examination are able to find the way to exploit the R&D output to applicable and commercial results, translating this output in profitability and increased market share.

Factor analysis extracted three factors of possible benefits from cooperative R&D (Table 4.16). The product development impact on the benefits and the process development impact are equally important, but with a rather low mean value (2.9). The first includes benefits related to the development and improvement of products and the subsequent effect on profitability and market share, while the latter refers to the development or improvement of processes (new or existing). However, the most important impact of RJVs is on what we could call the knowledge base of the firm.

Improvement of a unit's technological and organizational capabilities, exploitation of complementary resources, new knowledge and acceleration of research are the components of this factor.[16]

Table 4.16   Benefits from cooperative R&D

Dimensions (items)	Factors	Mean (std)
Development/improvement of new or existing products, increased profitability and market share	Product development	2.9 (1.0)
Continuation/acceleration of existing research	Knowledge base	3.4 (0.9)
Exploitation of complementary resources and acquisition/creation of new knowledge, improvement of unit's technological and organizational capabilities		
Development/improvement of new or existing processes	Process development	2.9 (1.3)

Note: Explained variance 63.1.

ANOVA for country effect shows few significant differences. Swedish firms seem to benefit both at the product and process development area more than all other countries. Despite the precompetitive nature of the RJVs, these firms are in a position to exploit their participation in the market place. However, they also focus on the improvement of their processes, which are the prerequisite for new, technologically advanced products. Finally, Italian firms seem to focus more on the knowledge-base: their response on this factor is significantly higher than for all other countries.

Regarding the effect of firms' size on benefits, results show a slight effect in the product development and a greater effect in the process development benefits, whereas the knowledge-based benefits are similar to all firms, irrelevant of their size.[17] More precisely, very large firms (more than 1000 employees) are in a better position to commercially exploit their participation in these precompetitive RJVs, by developing new or improving existing products and services and having some positive gains in terms of profitability and market share, even in the long term. However, they only have such an advantage compared to the very small ones (less than ten employees), since all other firms present similar behaviour. Very large firms differ, however, significantly from the main bulk of firms, the SMEs (10 to 250 employees), in terms of process development benefits. Hence, it seems that these firms use the RJVs as a means for upgrading their technological status, at a better price, participating actively in the conduct of R&D and making sure that the final applications fit their needs best.

The correlation between the firm's areas of activity and its benefits from cooperative R&D is shown in Table 4.17. The results are rather in accordance with the relationships that were identified when examining firms' objectives from cooperative R&D. Core activity is positively connected with benefits at the process level and negatively with product development. This supports the argument about an effort by firms to use those 'core RJVs' for upgrading their basic technologies and improving their technological status in order to deliver new products and services. Commercial results are obtained only in respect of the secondary activities of firms. These areas seem to be positively influenced by the RJVs in a manner that could reach the stage of being converted to core activities. Finally, no relationship between new activities and benefits from R&D was identified.

Table 4.17   Company areas of activity and benefits from cooperative R&D

	Product development	Knowledge base	Process development
Core activity	−0.18**	−0.04	0.08*
Secondary activity	0.16**	0.07*	−0.10**
New activity	−0.00	−0.01	−0.06

Note: Weighted results, **, * denote significance at the 1% and 5% level.

Problems Arising from Cooperation

Cooperation is a rather difficult process, as it requires special effort and capabilities from the participants in order to be successful. Cooperation in R&D is even more difficult to handle as it usually involves the tacit form of technological knowledge, which suffers from great uncertainty, especially if it lies at the precompetitive level. Therefore, the degree to which the benefits examined before can be obtained from an RJV, is highly affected by the extent to which specific problems that could arise in cooperation do actually occur.

Results show that problems are not as important as might be expected. Of the sample, 46 per cent notice that different strategic interests among partners and coordination problems within the collaboration are the major sources of conflict, which usually affect the RJV and determine its success. On the other hand, losing vital technological information to partners was considered important by only nine per cent of the sample, indicating that possible leakage of information and involuntary knowledge spillovers are not important sources of tension in precompetitive R&D.[18]

Table 4.18   Problems with cooperation

Dimensions (items)	Factors	Mean (std)
Problems of appropriability of the results among partners or problems related to the broader institutional set-up (IPR, regulatory framework and so on). Loss of vital technological information to partners	Institutional set-up	2.2 (0.9)
Additional cost and time of the cooperation or inability to find suitable partners	Cost & time	2.7 (0.9)
Coordination problems within the RJV and different strategic interests among partners	Conflict potential	3.2 (1.0)

Note: Explained variance 65.6.

Three dimensions of possible problems are retrieved from firms' responses (Table 4.18). The most important one refers to so-called conflict potential, capturing the two major sources of problems, which might deter any greater efforts for the success of the cooperation. The 'correct' composition of the consortium is always considered an important success factor of joint R&D projects. Another crucial dimension is the additional cost and time needed either for managing the cooperation or even trying to find the suitable partners. Finally, the institutional set-up is the least important factor, since problems related to the appropriability of the results among partners in the broader institutional set-up, or losing vital information are not considered as important disincentives for participating in RJVs. In terms of country differences, only British firms – followed sometimes by Irish firms – seem to face some problems of the above nature, being those European firms that have ranked all three factors higher than other countries.

OBJECTIVES AND BENEFITS FROM COOPERATIVE R&D: THE EFFECT OF STRATEGY, BUSINESS ENVIRONMENT AND PROBLEMS

This section examines the relationship between internal characteristics of firms (strategies and drivers of participation, processes of knowledge acquisition and creation) and external factors (environment), on the one hand, and the objectives that drive their participation in an RJV and the anticipated benefits, on the other. Our data do not allow for an examination of the actual decision-making process of a firm when it chooses whether or not to enter a cooperative agreement, since we would need a sample of non-cooperating firms to be used as a control group. Instead, with the specific sample it is possible to analyse the type of strategies, processes and the dimensions of the environment that are related with the previously identified factors of objectives and benefits from cooperation.

The strategy that a firm adopts both at the corporate and at the business level will affect the type of incentives that guide its participation. The *ex ante* decision of a firm to participate in an RJV might suggest an effort to fill some gaps in its corporate or competitive strategy or represents at least an effort towards a more effective implementation and realization of that strategy. R&D partnerships can be driven by both strategic and tactical orientations and, thus, viewing them merely as strategic alliances offers only a very limited scope of the situation (Chen, 1997). Therefore, both the corporate and the business level strategy might be connected with the decision to enter an RJV. In addition, in the subsequent analysis the technological development dimensions are used as proxies for the technology strategy of the firm. All activities that were used in the questionnaire clearly represent actions that a firm undertakes in the direction of implementing its technology strategy. In fact, a firm's decision to participate in an RJV is highly related to this type of strategy; that is why we expect better overall results with this strategy as an independent variable.

Furthermore, the processes that a firm uses to acquire and/or create new knowledge can be used as proxies for the capabilities of the firm. They may also affect the objectives set by a firm when entering an RJV, but to a greater extent they affect the type of benefits that it can obtain. Finally, the business environment in which a firm operates might also have driven its decision to conduct cooperative R&D. Summing up, the first equation that we test refers to the objectives from cooperative R&D and can be illustrated as:[19]

$$OBJ = f \{STRAT, CAPAB, ENVIR\}$$

Regarding benefits from cooperative R&D, it is clear that the adopted strategy (corporate, competitive and technology), but also the capabilities of the firm will affect the extent to which specific benefits can be obtained from an RJV. However, we do not use the dimensions of business environment as independent variables, as we think that they do not affect the type of benefits that a firm can gain from the RJV. It is an external factor that can hardly affect the internal climate and the delicate balance of relationships that is established inside the consortium (Tsakanikas, 2002). The extent that certain benefits can be obtained rests mostly on the network relations among partners and the internal characteristics and processes of the firm. In that context, problems that can emerge in cooperation may significantly affect the process of obtaining benefits and determine whether a collaboration will be successful for all (win-win situation) or a failure. The second equation that we test is hence:

$$BEN = f\{STRAT, CAPAB, PROBL\}$$

For both equations a weighted OLS regression was used. The first equation actually consists of four separate sub-equations referring to each of the dimensions that were retrieved from the factor analysis (see Table 4.14), while the second equation consists of three sub-equations (see Table 4.16). Furthermore, each one was run three times, changing each time the level of strategy (STRAT): corporate, competitive and technology. It should also be added that three more variables have been used in the equations that were run: size of the firm, level of scientific personnel and R&D intensity, measured by R&D employees and total employees. However, due to data unavailability the sample is reduced to more than half its size, whereas certain countries (like the UK) are almost totally excluded. Therefore, the inclusion was done only for illustrative purposes in order to comment on any significant results regarding these variables.

Tables 4.19 and 4.20 present the results, when technology strategy is used as an independent variable for strategy, since this is the aspect of strategy more closely related with the participation in an RJV, providing also better overall results (better fit). However, the factors of corporate and competitive strategy, which become significant when they are used as predictors of strategy, along with their sign and level of significance are also presented.[20]

Results show that firms that adopt market-based objectives from co-operative R&D are those that introduce new products and services on a continuous basis or improve and modify the existing ones (product development activities). The fact that their business environment is highly regulated may justify their effort to overcome these difficulties through joint R&D, when introducing new products. In terms of capabilities, conduct of basic research affects positively the adoption of these objectives, whichever strategy is used as an independent variable. Both types of competitive strategies are positively significant, while firms that adopt the corporate strategy of external or internal growth – both of which can be considered as aggressive strategies – are those that want to improve speed to market, control future market development or create new investment options, through the

RJV. It should also be noted that the R&D intensity affects negatively such objectives, indicating that market-oriented incentives drive the participation of the less R&D intensive firms.

Firms that enter an RJV for R&D cost/risk sharing are those that adopt effective technological activities such as imitation of existing technology and transformation/improvement/adaptation of externally acquired technology. This is an indication that the R&D cooperation provides an alternative route for conduct of R&D, at certainly a better price for them. On the other hand, the specific firms do not follow inert activities (such as licensing technology or aiming at the development of new products), since both these factors have a negative effect on such objectives. Their business environment is characterized by intense competition at the technology level, a relationship that is re-established when both corporate and competitive strategies are considered.

In terms of capabilities, developing formal or informal relationships is positively related to such objectives, since reducing uncertainty is included in that factor. On the other hand, firms that follow internal procedures for the creation of new knowledge, or conduct applied research to a greater extent, do not pay special attention to the reduction of R&D cost. This could be a signal of a situation where firms with concrete R&D efforts and a specific R&D agenda would not use the RJV option for that type of research, preferring to conduct it internally at any cost. The same negative effect holds for the corporate strategy of innovative penetration: firms that want to increase their market share in existing or geographically new markets or develop new products and services do not enter RJVs driven by cost-based motives. Furthermore, the scientific personnel and the R&D intensity of the firm are also positively connected with such objectives, indicating that the participation of the more knowledge-intensive firms is significantly guided by the incentive of R&D cost sharing.

Motives related to a resource-based view of the firm are positively connected with effective and process-oriented technological activities and negatively with product development activities. These firms are seeking to find in RJVs those complementary resources that will help them improve their technological status, upgrade their processes and leverage their overall portfolio of resources and capabilities. It is not therefore surprising that all factors of capabilities are positively connected with these objectives, with the exception of the conduct of basic research, which turns to be out insignificant. The competition that these firms face is intense at the technological level, but surprisingly the business environment is easily predictable. Furthermore, in terms of other strategies, only two factors of the corporate strategy turn out significant. Firms that adopt the strategy described as innovative penetration do not enter in RJVs driven by such objectives,

Table 4.19   Objectives of R&D cooperation

Variables	Market development Coefficients	Cost of R&D Coefficients	Resources & capabilities Coefficients	Technology Coefficients
Constant	0.90** (0.35)	2.47*** (0.41)	0.05 (0.39)	1.82*** (0.41)
Corporate Strategy				
Innovative penetration		(−)**	(−)**	
External growth	(+)***			
Diversification				
Extroversion			(+)**	(+)*
Internal growth	(+)**			
Competitive Strategy				
Mass market	(+)***			(+)*
Market segment	(+)***			(+)***
Technology				
Process development	0.02 (0.05)	0.07 (0.06)	0.10* (0.05)	−0.03 (0.06)
Effective activities	−0.00 (0.07)	0.34*** (0.08)	0.29*** (0.08)	0.36*** (0.08)
Inert activities	0.08 (0.06)	−0.13* (0.07)	−0.00 (0.07)	−0.03 (0.07)
Product development	0.15** (0.06)	−0.17** (0.07)	−0.14** (0.07)	0.14* (0.07)
Environment				
Regulative	0.10* (0.06)	−0.09 (0.07)	−0.02 (0.06)	−0.15** (0.06)
Market determined	0.05 (0.07)	0.03 (0.08)	−0.07 (0.07)	−0.01 (0.08)
Technological	−0.01 (0.06)	0.24*** (0.08)	0.15** (0.07)	0.14* (0.07)
Easy predicted	0.00 (0.05)	0.05 (0.06)	0.11** (0.06)	0.16*** (0.06)

Table 4.19   (continued)

Variables	Market development Coefficients	Cost of R&D Coefficients	Resources & capabilities Coefficients	Technology Coefficients
Capabilities				
Internal procedures	0.09 (0.07)	−0.14* (0.08)	0.18** (0.08)	0.08 (0.08)
Applied R&D	−0.01 (0.05)	−0.14** (0.06)	0.21*** (0.06)	0.03 (0.06)
Basic research	0.10* (0.05)	0.10 (0.06)	0.05 (0.06)	0.11* (0.06)
Relationships	0.08 (0.05)	0.11** (0.06)	0.13** (0.06)	0.06 (0.06)
Adjusted R^2	0.858	0.868	0.872	0.870
Log likelihood	−266.52	−301.20	−289.12	−298.38
F statistic	110.34***	119.98***	124.45***	122.78***

Notes: Observations = 219, ***, **, * denote significance at the 1%, 5% and 10% level respectively. Standard errors in parentheses.

which is rather surprising, as an opposite sign would be expected. On the other hand, the fact that extrovert firms (following outsourcing or joining strategic alliances) adopt such objectives reinforces their effort to find the proper allies for conducting R&D and implement their vision. In addition, both the level of scientific personnel and R&D intensity, when included in the equations, turn out positively significant, indicating that despite the knowledge-intensive character of these firms, they still seek through collaborative R&D those complementary resources and new capabilities that will leverage their own portfolio of resources.

The major objective of firms in joining RJVs, technological learning, is related to effective technological activities and significant product development orientation. On the other hand, a highly regulative business environment is a disincentive for such objectives, while competition at the technological level prompts to that direction, although demand and competitors' moves are easily predicted. In terms of capabilities, conducting basic research is a sort of prerequisite for keeping up with major technological developments. Both competitive strategies of mass market or market segment positively affect these objectives, while only the dimension of extroversion in the firms' corporate strategies turns out to be significant. Finally, neither the scientific personnel and R&D intensity, nor the size of the firm affects the adoption of such objectives, indicating probably the importance of these objectives for all firms irrespective of their special characteristics.

Regarding benefits from R&D collaboration, results show that firms that manage to obtain benefits at the product development area are those that follow a technology strategy oriented to that direction, while, on the other hand, a strategy oriented towards processes is negatively related to such benefits. In terms of capabilities, internal procedures of acquiring new knowledge support the development of new products, along with the development of formal and informal relationships, which are certainly important for an improvement of market position. The corporate strategy of innovative penetration is related positively to product development, while firms that adopt a strategy of internal growth do not seem to obtain such benefits. In terms of competitive strategy, a positive correlation with massmarket competitive strategy is established. Finally, R&D intensity turns out negatively significant, indicating that the more R&D intensive a firm is, the less it tries to accomplish benefits at the level of product development.

As previous analysis has shown, the major benefits obtained by the majority of firms lie at their knowledge-base. Effective technological activities, internal procedures of acquiring new knowledge and conduct of applied R&D are those dimensions of technology strategy and capabilities that are positively related with upgrading the knowledge base of firms. This reinforces the notion of absorptive capacity of Cohen & Levinthal (1990), as it turns out that a firm must be technologically active in order to be able to realize benefits that will upgrade its portfolio of resources and capabilities. This topic is extensively addressed in Kastelli (forthcoming). Empirical work on the same sample has shown that firms gain from being involved in R&D cooperation mainly when possessing the capabilities to assimilate and exploit the knowledge outside their boundaries in order to transform it into new products, processes or services (Kastelli, Caloghirou and Ioannides, forthcoming). Innovative penetration and external growth are those dimensions of corporate strategy that are positively related with the knowledge base, along with the mass-market competitive strategy. In addition, both the level of scientific personnel and R&D intensity are significant when included in the equation, amplifying the aforementioned argument. However, size is also shown to be significant but negatively related with such benefits, indicating that smaller firms are in a better position to exploit at that level their participation in RJVs.

Finally, benefits related to the improvement of firms' processes are connected with all dimensions of technology strategy. A positive relationship is established between effective and process oriented technological activities, whereas firms following inert activities or adopting product-oriented activities are not in a position to obtain benefits at that level. A firm that aims at diversification is probably the one that manages to improve its processes to a greater extent, although the competitive advantage is pursued in mass markets and not in market segments. Problems of additional cost and time appear for the first time to be positively correlated with benefits from R&D. The specific relationship indicates that the improvement of processes might be the most difficult issue to achieve from R&D collaboration and the one that could be a source of tensions in the cooperation.

CONCLUSIONS

This chapter presented the results of a survey that was undertaken in seven countries regarding the formation of RJVs, in the context of the EU-FWPs. By summing up the main conclusions, we found out that the average European firm that participates in these RJVs is a private SME, either from the manufacturing or the business services sector, with sales of €30 million. Its main activity is mostly in a maturity stage and despite the fact that it spends only one per cent of its sales for R&D, it could be characterized as knowledge-intensive, as almost one quarter of its personnel are scientists and engineers. The RJVs that it forms deal with applied research, despite their so-called precompetitive nature, and represent mainly a new research

Table 4.20   Benefits from R&D cooperation

Variables	Product development Coefficients	Knowledge base Coefficients	Process development Coefficients
Constant	0.57 (0.44)	1.04*** (0.37)	0.46 (0.53)
Corporate Strategy			
Innovative penetration	(+)***	(+)*	
External growth		(+)**	
Diversification			(+)*
Extroversion			
Internal growth	(−)***		
Competitive Strategy			
Mass market	(+)*	(+)***	(+)**
Market segment			(−)***
Technology Strategy			
Process development	−0.13** (0.06)	0.03 (0.07)	0.54*** (0.07)
Effective activities	0.11 (0.08)	0.27*** (0.06)	0.24** (0.09)
Inert activities	0.00 (0.07)	−0.05 (0.06)	−0.21** (0.09)
Product development	0.20*** (0.06)	−0.04 (0.07)	−0.19** (0.08)
Capabilities			
Internal procedures	0.20** (0.08)	0.21*** (0.06)	0.14 (0.09)
Applied R&D	0.08 (0.07)	0.21*** (0.05)	0.14 (0.08)
Basic research	−0.02 (0.06)	0.02 (0.05)	−0.06 (0.07)
Relationships	0.24*** (0.06)	0.03 (0.05)	0.07 (0.07)
Problems			
Institutional set-up	−0.09 (0.07)	0.01 (0.06)	−0.08 (0.08)
Cost & time	0.05 (0.06)	0.02 (0.05)	0.19** (0.08)
Conflict potential	0.00 (0.06)	−0.01 (0.05)	−0.11 (0.07)
Adjusted R^2	0.792	0.885	0.736
Log likelihood	−322.25	−292.61	−376.44
F statistic	81.74***	165.32***	60.21***

Notes: Observations = 234, ***, **, * denote significance at the 1%, 5% and 10% level respectively. Standard errors in parentheses.

activity for them, related to the primary activity of the firms and their core technologies. Although no significant patent activity was identified, there are plans for the commercial exploitation of the R&D results, in the vast majority of cases. Almost all RJVs led to the initiation of new research activity either exclusively by the firms, or in collaboration with others, fulfilling one of the major EU technology policy aspirations. Additionality is also accomplished to a great extent, especially for cohesion countries.

European firms participate in RJVs aiming mostly at technological learning and keeping up with major technological developments. Accessing complementary resources and capabilities and reducing the R&D cost are equally important motives. Although market development is not a major priority, a significant part of the participants find the way to commercially exploit the R&D results. Most of the benefits that can be obtained from RJVs are related to the knowledge base of firms, while possible problems that can arise in cooperation do not act as disincentives for such activity, since they are rather unimportant. These firms constantly seek innovation; that is why their corporate strategy primarily involves new products and services and aims at penetration in new areas, focusing principally on market segments. Their strategies are conditioned by the technologically intensive business environment in which they operate, while competition is also intense in terms of prices. As a consequence of this, changes in the future demand and competitors' moves are rather difficult to predict.

These firms could be very well considered as technology and research oriented, since they follow effective technological activities aiming at the improvement of their processes and product development. New knowledge is created through the conduct of applied R&D internally, giving, however, special emphasis on the formal or informal relationships with users and suppliers. Internal organizational procedures to acquire or create knowledge are also evident, while conducting basic research is firms' least adopted activity. Finally, cooperation with universities and research centres is the most common type of R&D collaboration.

NOTES

1. Greece and UK ran only the long version of the questionnaire, while maintaining the same overall target of 100 responses.
2. The overall response rates by country were: Ireland 45 per cent, Spain 9 per cent, Italy 23 per cent, Greece 58 per cent, Sweden 33 per cent, France 7 per cent and UK 9 per cent.
3. Weights have been computed as follows: each country's total number of firms (first and third part of the questionnaire) or RJVs (second part) are divided with the usable observations. The resulting numbers are then rescaled to the smallest one (Greece in all cases) giving the final value of the weighting variable. An example illustrates the procedure: Exactly 30 firms and 74 RJVs from Italy are available, whereas the total 'Italian' popu-

lation is 1317 and 2602 respectively. This gives us in return the values of 43.9 and 35.2, which are then rescaled based on the lowest variables of Greece (5.7 and 7.5). Therefore whilst the weight for Greece is 1 (both firms and RJVs), for Italy the weight is 7.7 and 4.7 respectively.

4. In the UK, the publicly traded outweigh the non-publicly traded.

5. More than half of those from national groups belong to Italy (40 per cent) and Sweden (13 per cent), where they generally dominate their country sample. Most of the subsidiaries are located in Sweden and the UK.

6. All financial data collected refer to the period of 1995 to 1997, using a three-year average.

7. Bayona, Garcia-Marco and Huerta (2001) review the empirical literature.

8. Mothe & Quelin (1999) have also found that EU funded programmes have attracted fewer industrial companies and more research oriented entities.

9. Vonortas (1997) proposes two more explanatory reasons, since he finds similar results in US-based RJVs: the first emphasizes the special role of RJVs as facilitators of supplier-customer linkages. Firms with high capital but low R&D investments are probably using new technologies embodied in the goods they purchase, but have little incentive to create those technologies on their own. Participating in RJVs might help influence the outcome of the research so that the final products fit their specific needs better. Suppliers of capital equipment might use the RJVs as a vehicle for getting important customers on board early in the R&D process. The second explanation touches upon the main reason for the formation of an RJV: to undertake R&D that would have not been possible without it.

10. Percentages do not sum up to 100 per cent, since respondents were allowed to provide as many answers as applied. Swedish, UK and Irish firms are responsible for most of the 'basic RJVs', while, on the other hand, applied research is less common for Italian and Spanish firms.

11. Percentages do not sum up to 100 per cent, for the same reason as above.

12. Chi-square tests indicate a significant relation between country and the areas of activity. Sweden, France and Italy dominate the responses regarding the core activity, whereas Spanish firms are the lowest contributors. The latter firms are those that undertook research activity in totally new areas, along with Italian firms. Irish RJVs have the highest percentage among those that referred to secondary activity.

13. In terms of country differences results show that, especially in Ireland, cooperation among competitors is the least preferred, being similar only with the situation in Greece and the UK (all three below the overall mean value). Irish firms in general have given low values to all possible types of organizations to cooperate with. Spanish firms are low in university-research centre cooperation, whereas Italian and French firms register higher user/producer cooperation.

14. Brockhoff and Teichert's (1995) factor analysis on German firms and their objectives from R&D cooperation provides similar results: a technology factor is also identified, whereas a people-related factor (relevant to our resources and capabilities one) and an economic factor (merging the market and cost dimensions of our analysis) are extracted. However, they notice that comparison among studies with various lists of objectives is difficult, as they do not all address the same level of measurement: success refers to the fulfilment of each partner's objectives individually, or to the RJV per se?

15. A five-scaled stratifying variable was constructed, dividing the sample into five categories: less than 10 employees, 11–50, 51–250, 251–1000 and more than 1000 employees.

16. Similar benefits from cooperation were reported for Swiss firms (Reger et al., 1998).

17. We used the same stratifying variable as in the analysis of objectives (see note 15).

18. If, on the other hand, the RJVs examined referred to a more near-market collaboration (that is, product development), then this could be a major risk of such cooperation as Littler, Leverick and Wilson (1998) have shown.

19. For each variable, the factors extracted from the factor analysis are used in the analysis.

20. In all regressions the f-statistic is always significant at a p-level$<$1 per cent. Adjusted R^2 values are above 0.7 in all cases, indicating a satisfactory overall fit of the models.

REFERENCES

Bayona, C., T. Garcia-Marco and E. Huerta (2001), 'Firms' motivations for cooperative R&D: an empirical analysis of Spanish firms', *Research Policy*, **30**(8), 1289–307.

Brockhoff, K. and T. Teichert (1995), 'Cooperative R&D and partners' measures of success', *International Journal of Technology Management*, **10**(1).

Chen, S-H. (1997), 'Decision making in research and development collaboration', *Research Policy*, **26**(1), 121–35.

Cohen, W. and D. Levinthal (1990), 'Absorptive capacity: a new perspective on learning and innovation', *Administrative Science Quarterly*, **35**, 128–52.

Collis, D. J. and C. A. Montgomery (1998), *Corporate Strategy, A Resource Based Approach*, Boston, MA: McGraw-Hill International Editions.

Georghiou, L. (2001), 'Evolving frameworks for European collaboration in research and technology', *Research Policy*, **30**(6), 891–903

Glaister, K. W. and P. J. Buckley (1996), 'Strategic motives for international alliance formation', *Journal of Management Studies*, **33**(3), 301–32.

Harrigan, K. R (1985), *Strategies for Joint Ventures*, Lexington, MA: Lexington Books.

Kastelli, I. (forthcoming), 'Cooperative R&D as a means for knowledge creation', PhD thesis, Laboratory of Industrial and Energy Economics, National Technical University of Athens.

Kastelli, I., Y. Caloghirou and S. Ioannides (forthcoming), 'Cooperative R&D as a means for knowledge creation. Experience from European funded partnerships', *International Journal of Technology Management*.

Littler, D., F. Leverick and D. Wilson (1998), 'Collaboration in new technology based product markets', *International Journal of Technology Management*, **15**(1–2), 139–59.

Luukkonen, T. (2000), 'Additionality of EU Framework programmes', *Research Policy*, **29**(6), 711–24.

Luukkonen, T. (2001), 'Networking impacts of the EU Framework Programmes', in *Innovative Networks: Cooperation in National Innovation Systems*, Paris: OECD, pp. 193–208.

Luukkonen, T. (2002), 'Technology and market orientation in company participation in the EU Framework Programme', *Research Policy*, **31**(3), 437–55.

Mothe, C. and B. Quelin (1999), 'Creating new resources through European R&D partnerships', *Technology Analysis & Strategic Management*, **11**(1), 31–43.

Narula, R. (1998), *Strategic Technology Alliances by European Firms Since 1980: Questioning Integration*, Maastricht: MERIT.

Pavitt, K. (1998), 'The inevitable limits of EU R&D funding', *Research Policy*, **27**(6), 559–68.

Peterson, J. and M. Sharp (1998), *Technology Policy in the European Union*, Houndmills and London: Macmillan Press.

Reger, G., S. Buhrer, A. Balthasar and C. Battig (1998), 'Switzerland's participation in the European RTD Framework Programmes: a win-win game?', *Technovation*, **18**(6/7), 425–38.

Quintas, P. and K. Guy (1995), 'Collaborative, pre-competitive R&D and the firm', *Research Policy*, **24**(3), 325–48.

Sakakibara, M. (1997), 'Heterogeneity of firm capabilities and cooperative research and development: an empirical examination of motives', *Strategic Management*

Journal, Summer special issue 18, 143–64.

Sakakibara, M. (2001), 'Cooperative research and development: who participates and in which industries do projects take place', *Research Policy*, **30**(7), 993–1018.

Teichert, T. A. (1997), 'Success potential of international R&D co-operations', *International Journal of Technology Management*, **14**(6/7/8), 804–21.

Tsakanikas, A. (2002), 'Corporate strategy and research joint ventures', PhD thesis, Laboratory of Industrial and Energy Economics, National Technical University of Athens.

5. R&D cooperation: a case study analysis on subsidized European projects

Ioanna Kastelli and Yannis Caloghirou

The empirical analysis based on the STEP TO RJVs databank and the company survey was complemented by a series of case studies of specific cooperative R&D ventures, which were funded either in the context of EU Framework Programmes or in the context of national initiatives supporting collaboration.

In this chapter we present the findings from 21 case studies carried out in seven European countries, namely France, Greece, Ireland, Italy, Spain, Sweden and the UK, during the period May to December 1999. The value of these studies derives from the qualitative nature of information that is provided on the factors that influence the formation and evolution/development of R&D cooperation.

The unit of analysis was the R&D cooperative project. Only completed projects were appraised, each covered by two interviews: one with the co-ordinating partner and one with one of the other participant organizations. The cases to be studied were chosen so as to ensure a diverse portfolio of projects in terms of number of participants, technological areas, involvement of public actors, type of relationship among the partners (vertical and competitive), involvement of SMEs. The interviews followed a common list of basic topics that were covered during a face-to-face semi-structured discussion. These topics related to questions that are broadly discussed at a theoretical level and that have also been addressed in previous empirical work:

- Initiation of the idea for the RJV
- Relationship among partners
- Context of RJV formation
- Objectives of the participants
- Benefits from R&D collaboration
- Limitations and problems in the collaboration

- Exploitation of the R&D results
- Information-sharing among the partners
- Importance of external funding (subsidies)

The presentation that follows does not aim to make generalizations of statistical nature but analytical ones (Yin, 1989). In accordance to this distinction, the case studies are not sampling units but try to shed light upon the following questions:

1. What are the factors that enable or constrain the formation and evolution of R&D cooperation?
2. What are the effects of cooperative R&D in a knowledge-based perspective?
3. What was the role of public funding?

In a nutshell, the general gist of our case studies is that firms do indeed derive benefits from cooperating in R&D under certain circumstances, and that public subsidies to cooperative R&D do improve the R&D capacity of firms. Provided, of course that participants possess a specific strategic orientation and a potential in terms of knowledge-base and skills in order to exploit any knowledge and information flows. Especially in the case of new technologies, the closer interrelation and collaboration between European organizations fostered by European Framework Programmes proved to be of strategic value in the build up of many future activities.

In the following sections we develop the three topics above, as highlighted by the analysis on the specific subsidized projects.

FACTORS THAT ENABLE OR CONSTRAIN THE FORMATION AND EVOLUTION OF R&D COOPERATION

The study of research collaborations in Europe that have been funded either from European Framework Programmes or from National Programmes revealed the importance of some specific factors that have been also pointed out in theoretical discussions as enabling or constraining the diffusion or creation of knowledge and the rise of innovative activity of European firms. In the following section we elaborate these factors, which are also summarized in Table 5.1.

The Role of Individuals and of Personal Ties

In the Schumpeterian analysis the role of individuals was related to innovative activity through the vision of the entrepreneur, as the lone and brilliant inventor that sets in motion the process of 'creative destruction' (Schumpeter, 1934). However, industrial development in the US seemed to bring about a significant change in the organization of R&D – recognized as well by Schumpeter in his later work (Schumpeter, 1942), with huge research investments in specialized R&D laboratories of large firms. This new reality turned theoretical discussion towards routinized innovation (Pyka, 2002). The way in which inventions were perceived as emerging changed from being the result of individual ingenuity to being produced by purposive, large-scale investment in research and development (Kingston, 2001). Thus, most schools of economic thought of the past century neglected the role of the economic subject and adopted a 'scientific' line in studying economic and innovative processes (going from Taylor to Simon) (Nonaka and Takeushi, 1995). In recent years, however, a more 'humanistic' line of analysis has been developed initially from the human relations theory. Since the mid-80s, three strands of literature, consisting of the 'knowledge society' views, organizational learning theories and the resource-based approaches, have begun to put emphasis on human interaction, interactive processes within and between organizations and behavioural aspects of strategy (ibid).

Keeping in line with these approaches, the role of individual social actors, and their relations and behaviour, become again important. In this context, the process of innovation is considered to involve interaction at different levels: individuals, groups of individuals, organizations. Individuals' behaviour is embedded in their social context and inter-personal relationships become an important element of the whole innovative process in many ways. First, interaction of different actors expands knowledge in terms of quality and quantity through a spiral process of conversion betwen tacit and explicit knowledge, which tends to expand in scale and accelerate as more actors get involved in and around an organization (Nonaka, 1994; Nonaka, Toyama and Nagata, 2000). Second, concrete personal relations and structures of such relations can generate trust and discourage opportunistic behaviour (Hu and Korneliussen, 1997). In economic relationships there are elements such as mutual trust, exchange of a social and cultural kind, and common understanding, that play an important role and are emphasized as influential factors in the mechanisms of governance (Williamson, 1985; Perrow, 1986). The same goes for reciprocity based on the common understanding that every party in a relationship has both rights and obligations (Hu and Korneliussen, 1997). Finally, repeated interaction of specific individuals or organizations through collaborative R&D may establish a common understanding and a common system of values that constitutes an important lubricant in personal relations and facilitates further collaboration with the same people or organizations.

Cooperation constitutes an organizational context that promotes interaction among a multiplicity of social and economic actors. Therefore, one of the interesting questions that our case study analysis on specific cooperative R&D projects had to pursue was the specific role of individuals in undertaking R&D activities and the role of personal relationships in establishing channels of information flows and confidence among firms and other cooperating institutions. To this end, we collected information on the factors that played an important role in the origination and implementation of the research activity, on the relationships established among the partners (whether characterized by consensus or conflicts) and the type and channels of information and knowledge-sharing among them.

Our case studies revealed the emergence of a new type of actor, whom we can describe as a 'research entrepreneur'. In many cases this actor's role was critical at the initiation phase and/or the implementation phase of the project. The research entrepreneur gathers both abilities, as distinguished by Kirzner (1979), of entrepreneurial alertness and knowledge expertise. The entrepreneurial process can be divided into the phase of origination of the idea, the planning and the business establishment phase. This type of entrepreneurship played an important role in the initiation phase of the collaboration, both by giving birth to the idea and by helping in the formation of the consortium, through the exploitation of personal relationships and this actor's reputation from previous collaborations. In many cases trust and reciprocity were incrementally built through personal relationships between, for example, a doctoral student and his/her supervisor or through established channels of communication and collaboration between the scientific community and the industrial sector. The research entrepreneur also played an important role during the implementation phase, when he/she contributed to the coordination of the project and with his/her scientific expertise. Especially in the case of the coordinator, managerial and scientific abilities of the person in charge appeared to be more critical.

In some cases the role of the individual was important in taking the initiative of organizing the research activity, as there was no such activity in the company undertaken in a systematic way. These were the cases of small firms, where the entrepreneur or director was directly involved in undertaking the R&D cooperative venture. He/she was the person that inspired the whole project in the sense that they had the overall responsibility and involvement in the implementation of the R&D activity.

More specific was the contribution of people from universities or research centres that also acted with an entrepreneurial spirit. In these cases the European projects in the context of Framework Programmes gave the opportunity to academic people to undertake activities, which were more targeted. This is in line with a vision that universities should turn their interest also to entrepreneurial activities. In Europe, research funding programmes adopted a 'top down' approach in response to the innovation gap between the US and Europe and promoted the introduction of academic entrepreneurship (Soete, 1999). University-industry linkages are represented among others by established channels of informal communication among individuals that facilitate diffusion of information and knowledge and further collaboration in new areas.

Individuals appeared to contribute positively through their personal ties. First, personal ties relate to trust, which seems to be one important issue in the context of partnerships that may result in building sustainable channels of knowledge and information flows. Second, previous relationships may facilitate the initiation phase of a new project, as many partners are already known from previous collaboration, and the development phase through the establishment of a common understanding of the project's objectives. On the other hand, differences in culture and scope among partners, in many cases resulted in discouraging the continuation of the R&D cooperation.

From our case studies it appeared that trust is a major issue for collaboration. The dominant way of information-sharing among the partners was by exchanges during meetings. In many cases participation in a project created ties at a personal level that have been exploited in further informal contacts. When trust and understanding were established between two actors then informal channels of communication developed, sustaining an interactive way of operating. Experience from previous collaborations made easier the initiation of new partnerships. A dynamic process gave birth to new collaboration. The confidence that has been established due to previous collaborative experience and the high degree of understanding helped also to organize new projects better.

However, whether personal ties and initiatives still play such a positive role when there is no clear strategic orientation prevailing from the organization's side must be questioned. From the case studies of this project it is obvious that no individual efforts and experiences are adequate for exploiting systematically external sources of knowledge-flows unless these efforts are inscribed in a broader context of business strategy or vision of the overall organizational dynamic. Unless this is so, the role of individuals cannot result to sustainable situations. It should also be pointed out that the organizational context, that is the way the R&D projects are implemented, as well as the more general context in which the cooperation takes place (institutional set-up, evolution of technologies and techniques) influence and structure the way individuals behave and relationships are formed.

The Type of Interaction

Another major issue that has been pointed out in the theoretical discussions was the type of interaction and its influence on the evolution of the cooperative venture. The type of interaction refers either to the type of relationships among the partners, or to the characteristics of partners, or to the type of activities these partners are involved in and the type of competencies they possess. Partners may be competitors or related through a vertical relationship (user-producer). The cooperation may however be complementary in the sense that the partners produce complementary products or use and know complementary technologies or have complementary roles (like in the case of university-industry relationships). Finally, cooperation may take place between large and small firms, public and private organizations and so on.

The interaction approach, mainly introduced by Håkansson (1987), underlines the importance of user-producer relations in technological evolution. According to this approach, by combining experience new ideas can emerge. New knowledge in terms of new products, processes or services often emerges at the interface between different knowledge areas. In exchange situations different kinds of knowledge come together (are combined or confronted) to create innovative situations. Technical solutions developed for other situations by one of the actors can be useful to the partners. A special case is when the exchange takes place between the buyer and the seller. It means that the needs of the buyer are confronted with the possible technical solutions known by the seller. This provides an opportunity to revise and redefine both the needs and the solutions and in this way find new possibilities.

The interaction between producers and users is very important in ensuring commercialization of the R&D output. In the case of EU funded R&D cooperation, commercialization of the R&D results was not the policy goal, as almost all programmes promoting R&D cooperation were targeting precompetitive research. However, the participants did not neglect this aspect. It appeared in many cases that the absence of a manufacturer deprived the consortium of the possibility to design a prototype according to production specifications. The presence of a manufacturer that would use the R&D results for production ensured to some extent the commercialization of the R&D effort mainly through i) the strategic interest of the specific partner for commercial exploitation of the R&D outcome, ii) the distribution channels that the specific partner already possessed and iii) the linkage of the R&D content to the production process by setting production specifications to the R&D outcome. In the same line the presence of a user contributed to drive the research closer to the market and to market needs. By contrast, the absence of a buyer or user of the research outcome deprived the consortium of an expertise in market appraisal and led to a loss of the commercial focus.

When the R&D consortium involved more than one user of the research outcome, these users happened to be rivals. In these particular cases specific agreements have been signed in order to avoid any conflict of interests and thus facilitate their contribution in the project.

Complementarity was pointed as a positive element in the case of university-industry relationships, where the formation of a critical mass of R&D, for projects that are considered too difficult to be undertaken by one organization, gave the opportunity especially to small organizations to undertake R&D activities that would not be undertaken otherwise. Small firms that could not afford investment on research infrastructure or R&D expenditure on their own, chose to subcontract or collaborate with universities or research centres that have the people, the experience and the academic interest for specific research activities. For commercial companies, the collaboration with academic partners meant gaining access to research activity at the forefront of a given area. This type of interaction provided an organizational structure where resources were complemented to obtain a better solution than in the case of implementing research alone. Although the academic sector is sometimes characterized as ineffective when assessed with commercial criteria, it was observed that firms took advantage of the more basic research taking place in universities and research laboratories and of sharing experience and expertise with the academic sector.

The type of interaction also relates to the behaviour of partners within the cooperative venture. It is expected that among rivals opportunistic practices will take place and thus there will be less information and knowledge-sharing. By contrast, complementary roles allow the establishment of trust, as there is less room for a racing type of behaviour between the partners (Khanna, Gulati and Nohria, 1998). However, the converse argument has been put forth by Alchian and Demsetz (1972), who argue that cooperation may occur in similar fields because each of the partners would know better the other's work characteristics and tendencies to shirk, and thus opportunistic practices could be avoided.

Empirical evidence from our case-studies research shows that firms collaborated mostly when they came from complementary businesses. Competitors are easily brought together when the project is in a totally new area of activity or new technological field, for which there is high uncertainty regarding the final results and the possibilities for commercialization. Collaborative ventures also involved competitors in cases where there was need for establishment of technical standards that could not be established without the consensus of the main actors in the field. Such cases proved to be beneficial for the firms but at the same time against competition. European Framework Programmes allowed such restrictive practices in order to promote European competitiveness (European partners and competitors cooperate in order to face the US threat).

Competitors collaborated at a precompetitive level, whereas when the object of the project was closer to the market either they did not collaborate or if they did, they did not share crucial information. The lack of trust was more apparent when the partners were competing in the same geographical market and this could provoke conflicts within the cooperative scheme.

Firms and universities shared knowledge and experience more easily than firms with firms. There were some cases where academics shared laboratories with firms.

It was also observed in the cases studied that large firms behaved differently from SMEs when cooperating. They exploited complementary skills and knowledge and used R&D cooperation as a mechanism to cope with uncertainty (in fields where the technological output is unclear and the results from the research are not close to market exploitation). The projects did not seem to be the first priority in their R&D activities. It seems they mostly entered these projects aiming at imposing their own standards and thus influencing the context in which they operate.

Small firms seem more vulnerable within cooperative agreements because of weaker negotiation power and weaker position in terms of protecting their research outcome. Additionally, the cost of patenting was reported to be a strong disincentive for bringing the research outcome closer to the market. A small firm may face serious problems in financing the protection of its intellectual property but without protecting the first phase of research in a specific field it is very risky to proceed with the following stages of implementation and development.

The Context of the Cooperation

Economic and management literatures emphasize that cooperative agreements signify a flexible way to face increasing uncertainty and complexity due to rapid technological change and technology interdisciplinarity. Situational factors (factors relating to the context of cooperation) comprise market organization, technological complexity in the field within which research falls and uncertainty of the research outcomes. More precisely, increased competitive pressure and increased complexity and interdisciplinarity of scientific and research activities have in turn increased uncertainty regarding the research developments and costs and risks of performing R&D (Brockhoff and Teichert, 1995; Glaister and Buckley, 1996; Sachwald, 1998). Firms choose to cooperate in R&D in order to share costs and risks with other organizations and to combine and complement their knowledge and competencies in order to cope with complex tasks of the research activity (Kogut, 1988; Combs and Ketchen, 1999). These context-specific characteristics have been related not only to the decision to cooperate but also to the performance of cooperative agreements (Brockhoff, 1991; Brockhoff and Teichert, 1995).

In our case studies we observed that many organizations were incited to cooperate because of a need to align with new regulations or technical standards. Especially when these regulations refer to the international level there is more motivation for international collaborations, which appear as a way to respond to institutional changes (for example environmental regulations or technical standards in specific technologies).

The context of cooperation relates also to technology evolution and change and to the combination of technologies required for the development of complex systems. Rapid technological change in many fields creates uncertainty and burdens firms with higher R&D cost, as the lifecycle of many products tends to shorten. Many R&D collaborations were formed under this pressure. Additionally, the cooperation among organizations operating in different sectors (such as telecommunication services and semiconductors) with different strategies and corporate cultures, ensured the interaction of various assets, skills and experiences, which were not easily integrated in a single corporation.

Subsidized collaborations have occasionally been created as a response to international competition, that is, a European response to US offensiveness. In such cases, collaboration has been viewed as the most efficient way to offer more competitive prices or to capture market share.

However, institutional changes or features of competition may influence the partners' expectations from the project and may modify their interest in, as well as the performance of, the whole project. Competition between different types of technologies may also change the rules of the game for the actors undertaking an R&D project and influence the commercial performance of the research effort (for example, the case of the terrestrial flight telephone service – TFTS project – which has been displaced by the huge growth of the GSM availability and use). In some cases changes in the legal framework or the venue of new solutions for the problem on which the consortium was working had very negative effects on the performance of the project.

Table 5.1   Evolution of R&D cooperation: enabling factors and constraints

	Enabling factors	Constraints
Role of individuals and personal ties	1. Research entrepreneurship a) initiation phase: birth of idea, formation of the consortium b) implementation phase: coordination of the research activity, scientific expertise 2. Building trust and reciprocity 3. Learning to cooperate (previous experience)	1. Opportunistic behaviour in exploitation of R&D results 2. Differences in culture and attitude among partners
Type of interaction	1. Complementarity a) trust (at the initiation and development phase) b) facilitating commercialization (presence of a manufacturer or a user) c) critical mass of R&D 2. Similarity a) reducing uncertainty b) shaping markets 3. Size a) ensuring negotiation power b) financing intellectual property protection	1. Rivalry a) opportunistic behaviour b) conflict of interests 2. Differences in strategies 3. Lack of buyer and of expertise in market appraisal
Context specific factors	Motivation 1. Institutional changes 2. Regulatory requirements 3. International competition 4. Rapid technological change	Uncertainty 1. Institutional changes 2. Changes in competition

EFFECTS OF COOPERATIVE R&D

Economic and management literatures emphasize the potential benefits of cooperation between different kinds of organizations. Both the strand that focuses on minimizing cost and risk of research and technological development, as well as the strand that views cooperation as a means by which organizations learn or interact to create new knowledge and develop new products or processes, underline the positive effects that may occur from cooperating (Kogut, 1988; Combs and Ketchen, 1999).

We investigated this issue in our interviews with the participants in R&D collaborations. In most cases examined, it was difficult to determine the outcome of the collaborative R&D in terms of introduction of a final product or production process. Various explanations may account for that, including the focus of most of the subsidized programmes on precompetitive R&D, the early stage of the research effort, the time lag between research and product introduction or the failure of the collaboration.

It is, however, interesting to assess the effects of the cooperation in comparison with the objectives of the partners and the extent to which these objectives were fulfilled. We can distinguish two main groups of participants in R&D cooperation with regard to their intentions and expected benefits from collaborating:

- Organizations collaborating in areas of high uncertainty, where the research outcome was not close to market but could open new market opportunities in the future, after further development by each partner. In this group we found actors that had their own technological and organizational capabilities, were already recognized in their fields of activity and had a clear strategy regarding their business plan.

- Organizations collaborating to learn or to create the necessary technological and organizational capabilities that will enable them to improve their competitiveness. In this second group we found small-sized firms with few resources for R&D that participate in subsidized cooperation in the expectation of creating a critical mass of R&D or learning from their more experienced partners. In this group are also participants that consider cooperation a very constructive process from which they acquire experience in research in specific fields.

Generally speaking, there are differences between firms in terms of objectives to collaborate in R&D. Perhaps not unexpectedly, large firms behave differently from SMEs. As it was pointed out earlier, large firms seemed to participate in RJVs primarily to access complementary skills and knowledge and cope with technological and market uncertainty. The examined RJVs do not seem to be the first priority in their R&D activities. Many enter these projects aiming at imposing their own standards and thus influencing the context in which they operate. On the other hand, there are small firms that seem to depend more on funding for doing R&D. Public programmes subsidizing collaborative R&D play the role of indirect support for them.

Reportedly, a major benefit from participating in the cooperative ventures examined has been the acquisition of new knowledge in fields in which firms were either not willing or able to invest their own resources or they did not possess the necessary capabilities and resources to do R&D. Thus, cooperation often offered firms the possibility to access complementary assets, to open new market opportunities and develop an R&D infrastructure for which the necessary investment was prohibitive or the market which they addressed was too small. For small firms cooperation was a way to get access to more sophisticated resources that they did not possess due to extensive R&D investment needed to develop them.

For the academic sector, conducting research with firms was beneficial because of opportunities for conducting research in more applied areas and of making their research effort more visible (through publications and applications in industry).

The effects from the participation in R&D cooperation should, of course, be measured against what would have happened in the absence of cooperative R&D. Although evidence was pointing to the important benefits that would not be obtained without cooperation, the fact that these cooperative agreements are subsidized does not make it possible to obtain a counterfactual with reasonable confidence levels.

THE ROLE OF SUBSIDIES

Policy interventions to support technological development (at the European and national levels) are based upon three basic ideas/justifying arguments:

1. the need to promote knowledge flows and interaction, which in turn will enable catching-up processes,
2. the need to overcome underinvestment in R&D by firms due to appropriation problems or uncertainty,
3. the need to overcome the reluctance of firms to be involved in R&D cooperation – which is considered an important mechanism of knowledge flows – due to appropriation problems.

With regard to policy measures supporting R&D collaboration, especially EU Framework Programmes, there is a condition (the additionality criterion) of avoiding the substitution of corporate investment in R&D by public money and the undertaking of trivial R&D (Luukkonen, 2000). It is thus important to evaluate the importance of public subsidies in relation with the strategic value of the R&D from the viewpoint of the firm. We distinguish cases in which:

1. strategically important R&D would not have been carried out without
    government funding,
2. strategically important R&D would have been done in any case,
3. unimportant R&D, from the firm's viewpoint, would not have been
    realized without public support,
4. 'marginal' nonessential R&D would have been carried out anyway
    (ibid).

In our research we tried to evaluate the role of subsidies taking into
account whether the R&D would not have been carried out at all without
public subsidy and the extent to which public funding influenced the characteristics of the R&D. The importance of subsidies has been underlined
in all cases. There were differences, nevertheless, in the reasons that made
external funding important. There were cases where funding was decisive
for supporting the specific R&D activity that would not have been undertaken without financial support. There were also cases where projects
aimed at strengthening European competitiveness. Public underwriting has
created a mechanism for bringing together important economic agents that
needed an institutional framework for doing business together. Financial
support as such was, in these cases, of secondary importance.

The institutional framework also played a monitoring and coordinating
role. Once there were clear and specific guidelines for the management of
the consortium or for appropriation issues conflicts of interest tended to be
avoided, negotiated or adjudicated.

Commercial agreements were signed in some cases among some of the
partners for exploitation after the end of the project. However, according
to the funding programme's rules, all partners should have access to the
research output for their own use.

The R&D collaborative projects that have been studied revealed a specific role that could be attributed to the supporting policy initiatives: that
of creating a context fostering research entrepreneurship in the sense that
these initiatives gave the opportunity to qualified, highly skilled persons to
take initiatives and combine their ideas and competences with those of
other partners in order to undertake or implement new research activities.
Programmes supporting R&D cooperation had an impact on three essential factors (see Table 5.2) that are considered to turn individuals into entrepreneurs (Jenssen and Havnes, 2002):

1. Financial capital: they increased financial resources directed to R&D
    and cooperative schemes and supported the development of physical
    infrastructure
2. Human capital: they increased the number of researchers, they gave

motivation especially to academics to undertake initiatives that were closer to market needs, they provided a context in which the person who has an idea can organize specialized knowledge and they developed experience of participants through repeated participation
3. Social capital: they created conditions for trust in relationships, reduced information search cost, created norms and rules of behaviour and established informal ties.

Table 5.2   Support to research entrepreneurship

Financial and physical capital	Human capital	Social capital
Financial resources	Experience through repeated participation	Formal ties
Development of physical infrastructure	New researchers hired	Informal ties
	Motivational support and organizational context	Trust

In that respect, support to R&D collaboration, as it has been manifested in the seven European countries studied in the context of the STEP TO RJVs project, is expected to have more long-term effects because it establishes a common understanding for further collaboration, it improves social capital and creates communities of interaction that are conducive to knowledge diffusion and creation.

Of course, there is always the danger (long-term negative effect) that firms will depend on support from the public sector and entrepreneurs will avoid taking risks without public support.

CONCLUDING REMARKS

The case study analysis illustrates and provides some evidence to theoretical arguments and explanations concerning cooperative R&D. The main points that should be retained for further research and discussion are summarized in what follows.

From the case study analysis it appeared that cooperation may create its own dynamics through two different processes: by establishing relationships based on trust that can facilitate or even trigger further collaboration, and by offering the possibility to participants to achieve a critical mass of R&D resources in terms of financial means, physical infrastructure or human capital and improve their capabilities. It was also pointed out that there is a specific role played by individuals in initiating and implementing research activities that should not be neglected.

The above factors keep their importance and validity when embedded in a strategically clear orientation of the participant organization. Any fragmentary initiative has few chances to raise long-term benefits in terms of learning and development of capabilities.

Another interesting point, which was revealed by the case studies, was the extent of, and the way that, the type of interaction influences the evolution of cooperation. Complementarity seems to have a positive influence on the evolution of the project as it involves less conflict and enables the establishment of trust in partners' relationships. The context in which cooperation took place proved to be important in many cases both in terms of the institutional environment and technological change. Its importance was related to the objectives of firms when undertaking R&D cooperation.

Finally, regarding the role of subsidies, it was shown that public initiatives supporting R&D cooperation succeed in developing human resources and supporting research entrepreneurship, and at the same time promote important R&D activities that would not have been undertaken otherwise. However, what is not clear from the cases analysed is the creation of an independent interest for undertaking research activities and a dynamic process of transformation of R&D efforts into upgrading firms' competitiveness.

ACKNOWLEDGEMENT

The analysis of this chapter is based on 21 case studies of R&D collaborative projects. Seven research teams involved in the STEP TO RJVs project, which delivered one report per country, have carried out the interviews.

The teams and the projects on which the previous analysis is based are the following:

France: K. Barker and O. Dartois.
'Software Evolution and Reuse', 'Multimedia Creation Platform and Web Contract' and 'Multimedia Applications to Science and Technology'
Greece: Y. Caloghirou and I. Kastelli
'Development and Economic Assessment of Environmental Fuels', 'ATM Switch for Integrated Communication, Computation and Monitoring' and 'Sensor Aided Intelligent Wheelchair Navigation System'

Ireland: K. Barker, J. Evans and C. McKinlay
'Federated Healthcare Records Server', 'Verification and Launch of Integrated Digital Advanced Television in Europe' and 'Effect of processing meat on marker residues of veterinary medicinal products'
Italy: K. Barker, H. Cameron, C. McKinlay, V. Recchia and S. Torrisi
'Digital Video Broadcasting Integrated Receiver Decoder', 'ERP-Fashion – Information System for Shoe-Factories' and 'Reduction of Manufacturing Time by Using Light CFL Models Until Serial Production'
Spain: P. Kujal and E. Revilla
'Development of a hybrid garbage collection vehicle', 'Multimedia Broker' and 'Automation of the granules production in the manufacture of animal stuff'
Sweden: D. Ioannidis and E. Wikstrand
'Metropolitan Optical Network', 'Diode-Pumped Laser' and 'Safety, Availability and Maintenance Improvements and Cost Reductions in the Shipping Community'
United Kingdom: K. Barker, H. Cameron, D. Cox, O. Dartois and C. McKinlay
'Large Scale Demonstrators for Global, Open Distributed Library Services', 'Terrestrial Flight Telephone Service' and 'Flex Bioluminescence-Based Assay Eco-toxicity Test For Water Quality'

REFERENCES

Alchian, A. and H. Demsetz (1972), 'Production, information costs and economic organization', *American Economic Review*, **62**, 777–95.
Brockhoff, K. (1991), 'R&D cooperation between firms: a classification by structural variables', *International Journal of Technology Management*, **6**, 361–73.
Brockhoff, K. and T. Teichert (1995), 'Cooperative R&D and partners' measures of success', *International Journal of Technology Management*, **10**(1), 111–23.
Combs, J. and D. Ketchen Jr. (1999), 'Explaining interfirm cooperation and performance: toward a reconciliation of predictions from the resource-based view and organizational economics', *Strategic Management Journal*, **20**, 867–88.
Glaister, K. W. and P. J. Buckley (1996), 'Strategic motives for international alliance formation', *Journal of Management Studies*, **33**(3), 301–32.
Håkansson, H. (1987), *Industrial Technological Development. A Network Approach*, London: Croom Helm.
Hu, Y. and T. Korneliussen (1997), 'The effects of personal ties and reciprocity on the performance of small firms in horizontal strategic alliances', *Scandinavian Journal of Management*, **13**(2), 159–73.
Jenssen, J. I. and P. A. Havnes (2002), 'Public intervention in the entrepreneurial process. A study based on three Norwegian cases', *International Journal of Entrepreneurial Behaviour and Research*, **8**(3), 173–87.

Khanna, T., R. Gulati and N. Nohria (1998), 'The dynamics of learning alliances: competition, cooperation and relative scope', *Strategic Management Journal*, **19**, 193–210.

Kingston, W. (2001), 'Innovation needs patents reform', *Research Policy*, **30**(3), 403–23.

Kirzner, I. M. (1979), *Perception, Opportunity and Profit. Studies in the Theory of Entrepreneurship*, Chicago and London: The University of Chicago Press.

Kogut, B. (1988), 'Joint ventures: theoretical and empirical perspectives', *Strategic Management Journal*, **9**, 319–32.

Luukkonen, T. (2000), 'Additionality of EU Framework Programmes', *Research Policy* **29**(6), 711–24.

Nonaka, I. (1994), 'A dynamic theory of organisational knowledge creation', *Organisation Science*, **5**, 14–37.

Nonaka, I. and H. Takeushi (1995), *The Knowledge-Creating Company*, New York: Oxford University Press.

Nonaka, I., R. Toyama and A. Nagata (2000), 'A firm as a knowledge-creating entity: a new perspective on the theory of the firm', *Industrial and Corporate Change*, **9**(1), 1–20.

Perrow, C. (1986), *Complex Organizations. A Critical Essay*, 3rd edn, Glenway, IL: Scott-Foresman.

Pyka, A. (2002), 'Innovation networks in economics: from the incentive-based to the knowledge-based approaches', *European Journal of Innovation Management*, **5**(3), 152–63.

Sachwald, F. (1998), 'Cooperative agreements and the theory of the firm: focusing on barriers to change', *Journal of Economic Behavior and Organisation*, **35**(2), 203–25.

Schumpeter, J. (1934), *The Theory of Economic Development*, Harvard Economic Studies Series, Harvard University, Cambridge, MA.

Schumpeter, J. A. (1942), *Capitalism, Socialism and Democracy*, London: Unwin.

Soete, L. (1999), 'The challenges and the potential of the knowledge based economy in a globalised world', background paper of the Portuguese presidency of the European Union, Maastricht: MERIT.

Williamson, O. (1985), *The Economic Institutions of Capitalism*, New York: The Free Press.

Yin, R. (1989), *Case Study Research. Design and Methods*, 2nd edn, London: Sage.

6. Determinants of RJV formation – RJV returns

Yannis Caloghirou and Nicholas S. Vonortas

As mentioned in Chapter 1, a key methodological component of the research project underlying the results reported in this book was extensive empirical analysis utilizing the various forms of data created specifically for this purpose (STEP-TO-RJVs Databank). This step included statistical analysis of RJVs and RJV participants' characteristics, objectives and strategies, and econometric analysis of the determinants and impacts of RJVs.[1]

This chapter summarizes the results of econometric work on three important issues:

- The determinants of RJV formation;
- RJV performance;
- The impact of RJVs on industries and on regional economies.

DETERMINANTS OF RJV FORMATION

The econometric analysis of the incentives to form an RJV developed at two levels:

1. The first level addressed the question of why firms enter into an RJV.
2. The second level addressed the interaction between partners: why two or more firms decide to enter an RJV together.

The paper by Hernan, Marin, and Siotis (1999) addressed the first question. Their review of the theoretical economics literature showed that the mechanisms underlying RJV participation are complex. More specifically, strategic interactions in the product market affect the decision to participate in RJVs both directly and indirectly (for example, when RJVs are simply used as a vehicle to enhance the feasibility of product market collusion). Second, RJVs involve internalization of technological spillovers,

R&D cost sharing and the gathering of information that may be of strategic importance. Third, the degree of asymmetry between participating firms influences the participation decisions. Empirical research was found to have been hampered by two constraints: lack of micro data and the unobservability of a number of key parameters in theoretical models such as the degree of knowledge spillovers and the differences in absorptive capacity across firms.

Data from the EU RJV and the EUREKA RJV databases were used in an attempt to bridge the gap between theoretical and empirical analyses. They estimated two logit regressions, focusing on the probability that a firm will join an RJV on the basis of characteristics of the firm itself and of its primary sector. The first regression attempts to identify the characteristics of firms that form RJVs out of the entire universe of firms (with available data). The results allow the authors to restrict the second estimation to a subset of firms that are known to be keen on RJV formation.

The variables included in the regressions are as follows:

- R&D intensity at the industry level, hypothesizing that cost reductions due to RJVs should be higher in R&D-intensive industries.
- 'Spillover lag', a proxy of the speed at which innovations unwillingly diffuse within an industry.
- The Herfindal index of concentration for each industry, expecting the internalization of spillovers via RJV formation to be greater the smaller the number of rivals in an industry.
- Firm size, as a measure of asymmetry across firms. It is also hypothesized that size is related to absorptive capacity.
- Control variables, such as the country of the firm and the number of times it has participated in RJVs in the past.

The resulting expression is estimated twice for result robustness. The first was obtained by using the entire sample of firms. The second was limited to the firms whose characteristics make them likely to join an RJV. The final sample of RJV-active firms used in the estimations included 1042 firms that had participated in RJVs during the period 1986 to 1996.

The paper finds that:

- The examined RJVs are formed in R&D intensive industries.
- Knowledge spillovers are an important determinant of RJV formation, but their impact only emerges in R&D-intensive industries.
- Concentration has a positive effect on RJV formation, possibly because it facilitates spillover internalization and reduces the intensity of competition in the marketplace.

- Firm size is very significant, suggesting that RJV formation is primarily a large firm phenomenon.[2]
- Past experience in research cooperation greatly enhances the probability of forming a cooperative venture. This indicates that some firms, at least, appear satisfied on average with RJVs. It also implies the existence of fixed costs and strong learning effects associated with an RJV.
- Little bias associated with the country of origin of the firm was detected. When such bias is detected, it works against firms originating in large and rich countries.

The paper by Navaretti et al. (1999) addressed the second question. The paper examined which firms from a heterogeneous pool are more likely to join together and form an RJV. This has been a question of rising importance among both business and policy experts. Rather than considering both firms that entered RJVs and others that did not, the analysis considered only the former. The basic idea is to test the probability that two firms join the same joint venture against a set of variables related both to the interaction between the partners and to the RJV.

The typical incentives to collaborate in mainstream economic theory – cost-sharing, spillover internalization, complementarities and market power – provided the conceptual background of the paper. The theoretical part of Navaretti et al. (1999) introduced two significant features: (a) the opportunity that firms can also exchange information without entering an RJV (which it is hypothesized they will do if they produce complementary products) and (b) endogenous information sharing. The theoretical model shows that:

1. RJVs are more likely to form where there are significant gains to be had from research co-ordination.
2. Undertaking the R&D collectively or separately and exchanging information are strict alternatives. The gains from avoiding needless duplication arise when research paths are substitutes and are realized when the RJV operates a single lab. However, the gains from exploiting complementarities through careful research design arise when research paths are complementary, and require the RJV to keep both labs open.
3. Another potential gain from RJV formation comes from increased information sharing. However, this gain only arises when there is no information sharing in the non-cooperative equilibrium, and this will only be true when firms produce substitute products. Hence *ceteris paribus* RJVs are more likely to form when firms produce substitute rather than complementary products.
4. The effect of initial asymmetries on RJV formation is ambiguous.

The empirical analysis used information from the EU RJV and the EUREKA RJV databases. In particular, the analysis focused on pairs of firms that entered EUREKA RJVs during the 1995–1996 period and Framework Programme RJVs during the 1996–1997 period. In all, there were 148 couples for EUREKA and 1219 couples for the Framework Programmes. The counterfactual consisted of all potential couples, which did not form between firms that have participated in these RJVs (thus firms showing a positive propensity to form RJVs). Cross-section probit analysis is utilized where the probability P_{ij} that firms i and j join the same RJV is a function of:

- the number of employees of the two firms;
- the sales of the firms;
- differences between the average return on total assets of the two firms;
- a product substitutability dummy variable;
- the GNP of the countries of origin of the firms; and
- the input-output relationship of the main industries of the firms.

Following the theoretical model, the authors test for the role of product substitutability and complementarity, asymmetries and subsidies. The empirical analysis found that the probability of forming a couple is found to be larger when firms are in the same industry and when their products are complementary. This result is robust and significant for both the EUREKA and the Framework Programme RJV samples. Gains from cooperation derive from sharing information and exploiting synergies under complementary research paths. But this case is more likely to arise if firms' products are also used as inputs, hence when substitutability and complementarity arise jointly. In the Framework Programme sample, it is found that the probability of forming an RJV is larger if firms produce substitute products using complementary inputs and follow complementary research paths.

This result does not hold equally well in the EUREKA sample. Here complementarity appears to be less important than substitutability, particularly if compared with the Framework Programme sample. RJVs are in this case less likely to be formed when firms are both in the same industry and follow complementary research paths.

The introduction of asymmetries into the picture sheds more light on this matter. It is found that, for firms producing substitute products, the probability of forming a couple is higher, the lower the asymmetries between them. According to the authors, this is precisely what one would expect for firms in substitute industries with complementary research paths.

Results on asymmetry indicators are muddled for the EUREKA RJV sample. In contrast, for Framework Programme RJVs, the larger the asymmetries, the more likely RJVs are to be formed. It is conjectured that this result is probably driven by policy design: a key objective of Framework Programmes is to favour research cooperation between small and large firms.

Finally, the paper examines the role of the countries of origin of the two partners. It confirms that EUREKA couples are more likely to take place between firms both based in northern countries, but the relationship is not significant for Framework Programmes, again showing a policy bias in favour of firms based in Southern European countries. As the geographic location (north and south) reflects mildly the level of development, the authors also control for relative GNP. For both samples, couples are more likely to be formed, the more similar the GNP of the countries of origin.

Summing up, the empirical results are consistent with theoretical predictions, but there are quite noticeable differences between the Framework Programme and the EUREKA samples. Framework RJV firms are more likely to be asymmetric and in complementary industries than EUREKA firms.

PERFORMANCE

As shown in Chapter 2, a blossoming theoretical economics and business literature has offered a long list of useful concepts regarding the objectives and expected benefits of private sector firms for collaborating in R&D. Firms have been urged to join research partnerships in order to share R&D costs, pool risk, reduce R&D duplication, access complementary resources and skills, internalize R&D spillovers, exploit research synergies, diversify, create new investment options and so forth. Unfortunately, the empirical literature has struggled with thorny issues regarding both methodology and measurement of the outcome of collaboration (Geringer and Hebert, 1989; Glaister and Buckley, 1992). An example is the long-standing debate on whether financial or other objective measures of performance – such as partnership survival, duration and stability – should be preferred over subjective measures of performance. Another example is the debate over whether the appraisal of the performance of equity partnerships should (or could) be similar to the appraisal of the performance of non-equity partnerships. Yet a third example of disagreement is the debate on whose view on performance counts, given that different partners may have different objectives in the same partnership.

Much of the problem resides in the controversy concerning the measurement of organizational performance in general (Cameron, 1986; Eccles, 1991). As Glaister and Buckley (1998a) summarise it, one problem here has been the choice of the appropriate yardstick, another has been the extent to which the surrounding environment affects the performance of an organization, and a third problem has been the differentiation between the indicators of performance and the determinants of performance.

Such difficulties get compounded in the case of hybrid organizational forms where, not surprisingly, there is no consensus concerning either the definition or the measurement of performance (Geringer and Hebert, 1989; 1991; Glaister and Buckley, 1998a). The following have been important stumbling blocks. First, there is no clear definition of partnership success. There is disagreement on whether objective (for example, financial) or subjective measures of success are more appropriate in appraising success. Objective measures are more widely available. Financial measures of performance such as profitability and growth as well as other objective measures such as partnership survival, duration, and stability have been used on several occasions (for example, Franko, 1971; Gomes-Casseres, 1987; Harrigan, 1986; Kogut, 1988b; Killing, 1983; Lecraw, 1983; Stopford and Wells, 1972). However, objective measures may not adequately reflect the extent to which a partnership achieved its short and long term objectives, which are often diverse (Anderson, 1990; Contractor and Lorange, 1988; Killing 1983). For example, rather than profit generation, a partnership may be set up to improve the strategic positioning of the partners (Glaister and Buckley, 1996) or to enhance one partner's access to the intangible assets of the other partner. Other subjective measures, including qualitative ones, must also be appraised for determining performance. Subjective measures are considered to be closer connected to partner objectives. Moreover, the available evidence concerning the correlation between objective and subjective measures of partnership performance is mixed (Geringer and Hebert, 1991; Geringer 1998; Glaister and Buckley, 1998a; 1998b).

Second, even when subjective measures can be constructed, there is difficulty in assigning values to individual measures of success for the partnership as a whole. Various partners usually have different expectations from the same partnership, thus making several authors argue against generalizing from one partner's evaluation (Beamish, 1984; Beamish and Banks, 1987; Schaan, 1983). 'Triangulation' of partner evaluations has thus been suggested (Geringer, 1998).

Third, the availability of information concerning the explanatory variables, most of which are subjective, is fairly scattered (collected by occasional surveys) and discontinuous. Fourth, the literature providing the foundations for the various hypotheses is diverse, not necessarily sharing the same views concerning basic conceptual building blocks – such as, for example, deciding what is the ultimate goal of a firm. This naturally complicates the interpretation of empirical results. For example, alliance volatility and short duration can be an indicator of either failure or success depending on what the theoretical assumptions are concerning the operation of the parent firm.

It should be evident from the above that the appraisal of the performance of non-equity research partnerships – like those we are dealing with in this project – is not a straightforward exercise. The main problems include the following (Tucci, 1996). First, there is no central organization as a stand-alone company, rendering most venture-level financial indicators meaningless. Second, a good number of research partnerships are designed to last for a limited time period, making the objective performance measures of survival, duration, and stability irrelevant. Third, partners often have different objectives regarding the venture, making venture-level subjective measures useless and cross-partner comparisons of firm level measures difficult to assess.

One can concentrate instead on the appraisal of the returns of the partnership to individual members. Partnership success is, then, defined to be the degree to which partner objectives are met or surpassed (Brockhoff and Teichert, 1995). The achievement of firm-level strategic goals can be used as a measure of performance of partnerships (Yan and Gray, 1994; Tucci, 1996). This convention was adopted in this project.

Given the disagreement on whether objective (for example, financial) or subjective measures of success are more appropriate in appraising success, and our fortunate position of having access to data allowing the construction of both, it was decided that we should follow both approaches. The data from the EU RJV and EUREKA RJV databases were used to create 'objective' measures of success from the point of view of the participating firms (Benfratello and Sembenelli, 1999). The data from the RJV survey database were used to create 'subjective' measures of success, again from the point of view of the participating firms (Caloghirou, Hondroyannis and Vonortas, 2003). The results from these two approaches are not directly comparable, however, as the samples of RJVs and firms they are based on overlap only partly.

IMPACT OF COLLABORATION ON RJV PARTICIPANTS

An 'Objective' Measures Approach

The paper by Benfratello and Sembenelli (1999) tests whether participation in EU-sponsored RJVs has a positive impact on participating firms' performance. This is compared with the impact of EUREKA RJVs on firm performance. The authors extract 1339 manufacturing firms that participated in Framework RJVs initiated during 1992 to 1996. They also extract 750 manufacturing firms that were members of RJVs selected by EUREKA during 1985 to 1996. For all these firms, financial data for the period 1992 to 1996 were obtained from the Amadeus database. Their final sample used in the estimations comprises 411 manufacturing firms, out of which 253 had joined at least one Framework Programme RJV, 101 had entered at least one EUREKA RJV, and 57 at least one RJV in both programmes. A control sample of 3621 firms was also created from Amadeus according to the following criteria: i) similar cross-tabulation of firms by country and industry, ii) firms not involved in the RJVs covered in the two data sets; iii) firms with complete balance sheet data.

The empirical analysis focuses on three performance measures: labour productivity, total factor productivity and price-cost margin. The first two variables measure productivity. The former is only a partial measure but it is less likely to suffer from measurement errors. The latter is more satisfactory, in principle, since it takes into account both production factors (labour and capital). On the other hand, the capital stock is difficult to measure, also because some of the relevant data, including investment flows, are not available in Amadeus and consequently have to be estimated. Finally, price-cost margin can be considered, admittedly rather crudely, a proxy for firm's market power.

Labour productivity has been constructed as the ratio of the value added at constant prices to the average number of employees. The price-cost margin variable is simply computed as the ratio of value added net of labour costs to sales. Finally, total factor productivity (TFP) is computed as the ratio of deflated value added to a weighted average of two input factors: labour and capital.

Descriptive statistics provide a preliminary, yet indicative, picture. Focusing on mean values, RJV participating firms show higher TFP, labour productivity and price-cost margin values than control sample firms. The ranking is confirmed for all variables but TFP if the median is used. Interestingly, firms in EUREKA RJVs are characterized by higher labour and total factor productivity but by lower price-cost margins than firms in Framework Programme RJVs.

While suggestive, such descriptive statistics are inadequate as a statistical basis for testing for the impact of RJVs participation on firm performance. First, it is at best naïve to assume that participation in an RJV has an instantaneous impact on performance, also bearing in mind that the average length of observed projects is three years and above. Second, if the impact of RJV participation is additive, also the number of RJVs a firm participates in is likely to matter. Third, as already mentioned, the control sample is constructed in order to mimic the industry/country distribution of our sample of 411 firms. However, given a possibly different industry/country composition of the EUREKA and the Framework Programme samples of firms, comparisons do not take fully into account industry and/or country specific differences.

To circumvent the first problem, Benfratello and Sembenelli split the sample period (1992–96) covered by their data into two sub-periods, labelled as 'pre' (1992–94) and 'post' (1995–96) respectively. The idea here is to focus only on firms participating in RJVs in the 'pre' period and to test whether this participation has had an impact on performance in the 'post' period. On average, this implies allowing a two-year period between the RJV's start and the performance evaluation time. Data limitations precluded taking a longer time interval. In the 1992–1994 period, 242 firms (out of 411) have entered at least one RJV. Of those, 55 firms entered at least one RJV sponsored under the EUREKA framework, 199 one RJV financed under the Framework Programmes, and 12 at least one RJV in both programmes. About two thirds of the 242 firms have entered only one RJV during the examined time period. This figure is much higher if we restrict our analysis to EUREKA RJVs (78.2 per cent), whereas it is slightly lower for RJVs under the Framework Programmes (65.8 per cent).

The main result of this analysis is that firms participating in EUREKA have experienced a significant improvement in their 'adjusted' performance measures between the 'pre' and the 'post' period. Furthermore, for two of the variables (labour productivity and price-cost margins) participating firms also show a lower than average performance in the pre-period but a higher than average performance in the post-period. On the contrary, firms participating in Framework Programme RJVs do not show any clear pattern.

Both parametric and non-parametric tests do not suggest any impact of Framework RJVs on firm performance. On the contrary, firms participating in EUREKA RJVs show a general increase in the values of the three performance variables. Also, for the labour productivity and price-cost margin variables, this increase is (rather comfortingly) significant in both the parametric and the non-parametric approach.

Benfratello and Sembenelli (1999) argue that, on the one hand, these empirical findings are seemingly broadly consistent with the common wisdom on EUREKA and Framework Programme general objectives. EUREKA RJVs are commonly perceived to be relatively more 'market' oriented. From this perspective, it is not unreasonable to assume that EUREKA RJVs are more likely to have a direct, or at least faster, impact on firm performance. A more radical explanation in the same vein is that

Framework Programmes do not aim at all at improving firm level performance but have more general and indirect objectives such us promoting cooperation between firms, universities and research centres or stimulating the development of European networks.

A different, and perhaps competing, explanation is grounded on the institutional differences occurring between the two programmes. EU officials, who also directly finance accepted projects in exchange for the monopoly on property rights, define the broad objectives of Framework Programme RJVs. On the contrary, within the EUREKA framework, participating firms define RJVs' objectives and projects are much more based on decentralized funding. Framework Programme institutional characteristics might then induce an adverse selection process, where firms carry out less profitable, long term and very risky projects only if they can have access to public money through FPST funding. This in turn might explain these results.

A 'Subjective' Measures Approach

The paper by Caloghirou, Hondroyannis and Vonortas (2003) also investigates the performance of RJVs from the point of view of individual industrial partners, this time using subjective information from the Survey-RJV database. Successful partnerships are defined to be those that meet or surpass partner objectives. The extent to which partner objectives are met (or surpassed) is hypothesized to depend on a long list of characteristics of the partnership, characteristics of the firm, and characteristics of the business unit directly involved in the partnership under question.

Rather than appraising the 'success' of the partnership as a whole – an elusive concept as discussed above – the paper focused on the performance of research partnerships as perceived by individual partners. The paper presents evidence on:

1. partnership 'success' in meeting/surpassing partner objectives, and
2. factors affecting important objectives of R&D collaboration.

More specifically, the paper investigates two sets of hypotheses. The first set of hypotheses examines the impact of a number of behavioural and situational characteristics of the partnership and of the partner on the success of the partnership in meeting (and surpassing) the set of objectives of the responding partner as a whole. The second set of hypotheses examines the relationship between each of several objectives of the responding firm and each of these behavioural and situational characteristics of the partnership and of the partners.

This paper brings to bear the rich set of survey information in the STEP TO RJVs Databank to empirically investigate the performance of a large set of RJVs. This dataset documents the replies of business executives of 568 firms participating in 636 research partnerships to an extensive questionnaire focusing on business strategy, objectives and expected benefits from collaborative R&D. Respondents included the specific business units that participated in the partnerships spread out in seven EU member countries. The sample consists entirely of non-equity RJVs.

Perceived partnership success is shown to depend significantly (a) on the closeness of the cooperative research to the in-house R&D effort of the firm, (b) on the extent to which the firm makes a concerted effort to learn from the partnership and its partners, and (c) on the absence of problems of knowledge appropriation between partners. The chances of partnership success decrease as a result of venturing far away from familiar technological territory. In contrast, chances of success increase with efforts to absorb both background knowledge (pre-existing, carried by partners) and foreground knowledge (created in the partnership) and with effective intellectual property protection mechanisms.

Moreover, the empirical analysis successfully explains two central company objectives for engaging in research partnerships, both relating to R&D collaboration as a mechanism to mitigate risk and uncertainty associated with new technologies. One of these objectives is to collaborate in order to share risks and decrease market and technological uncertainty. The other is to collaborate in order to create new investment 'options' and place bets on future technologies more safely. Firms are shown to pursue these objectives in both vertical and horizontal partnerships when the research is far apart from their in-house R&D and when the expected outcome is not easily appropriable.

IMPACT OF COLLABORATION ON INDUSTRIES AND ON REGIONAL ECONOMIES

Empirical analysis in this project also considered the effects of international cooperative R&D on short-term productivity gains among European manufacturing firms and the role of spillovers in technological diffusion. More specifically, the paper by Bussoli (1999) assesses whether a short-term technological convergence process has been taking place among manufacturing firms in the seven EU member countries represented in the consortium. It uses a dataset of 4171 firms with detailed information about balance sheets, which allows measurement of technological change at the level of the firm by calculating TFP and examination of technological convergence for the whole sample of firms and within the sub-sample of firms that participate in the examined RJVs.

The empirical analysis proceeds in three steps. First, the paper assesses the presence of countrywide and sectoral technological convergence among all firms in the sample. Second, after short-term convergence is established, the paper studies the role of the characteristics of international RJVs in this process. It concentrates on a sub-sample of firms participating in RJVs to better understand the process of convergence and technological diffusion within the group of firms that join RJVs. Finally, the paper investigates the extent to which the presence of RJVs in the different manufacturing sectors affects the technological gap between a given firm and the best performing firm in the sector. Thus, the final step of the analysis is to construct the productivity gap (dispersion, distance), which is comparable across sectors, and to explain the distance measure in terms of firm and RJV characteristics. The idea here is that, if new technological knowledge developed in RJVs is transmitted to firms outside RJVs, then the productivity of firms should be relatively higher in sectors with larger presence of RJVs.

The dataset supporting the conclusions of this paper was drawn from the EU RJV and the EUREKA RJV databases. It consists of a group of 434 firms that participated in RJVs and had complete financial information for the 1992–1996 time period. For 40 of them there are data on R&D investment for the whole period. The dataset also includes a counterfactual 3700 firms that did not join the examined RJVs. The counterfactual sample was randomly drawn from the Amadeus database, which was the most representative of European firms at the country and sectoral level. The selected 21 sectors are at the three-digit level (NACE 91) and represent manufacturing.

The analysis across countries and across different manufacturing sectors in Europe supports the hypothesis that RJVs favour technological convergence at the country level (this effect is not statistically significant for Germany and the UK) and at the sectoral level for 14 of the examined 21 sectors, excepting clothing, ferrous products except machinery, office machinery and computer, radio, TV and telecommunication, medical equipment, measuring instruments and watches, and furniture and other manufacturing.

Regarding the second question – do international RJVs increase technological convergence among firms that participate in them? The analysis concentrated on firms from six countries (Belgium, France, Germany, Italy, the Netherlands and the UK) and 18 sectors (tobacco, wood products, furniture and other manufacturing industries were excluded). The results support the hypothesis of convergence among all countries except Germany and the UK. The convergence effect is found to be stronger the higher the degree of asymmetry among firms joining the same RJVs.[3]

The third question concerned whether the level of firm TFP is affected by international R&D cooperation. Here, the paper appraises the determinants of a dispersion term measuring the gap between a given firm and the sector's best-performing firm. The results show that such cooperation has a positive impact on the technological productivity distance. Larger firms are found to have a greater distance from the best-performing firm in their sector: they are less likely to achieve higher levels of technological productivity.

On the whole, the paper finds:

1. substantial evidence of short term convergence across firms in Europe;
2. the overall convergence process is positively influenced by the presence of international R&D cooperation;
3. symmetric RJVs increase productivity to a greater extent than RJVs between asymmetric firms.

NOTES

1. This work was carried out by various partners of the STEP-TO-RJVs consortium. See references in the following sections.
2. This argument needs to be qualified with the fact that only firms of certain size and kind (for example, publicly traded) are usually represented in publicly available databases like Amadeus used here to draw financial data.
3. Firm asymmetries are defined in terms of efficiency as measured by profit margins or return on total assets.

REFERENCES

Anderson, E. (1990), 'Two firms, one frontier: on assessing joint venture performance', *Sloan Management Review*, **31**(2), 19–30.

Beamish, P. W. and J. C. Banks (1987), 'Equity joint ventures and the theory of the multinational enterprise', *Journal of International Business Studies*, **18**(1), 1–16.

Benfratello, L. and A. Sembenelli (1999), 'Research joint ventures and firm level performance', working paper prepared for the STEP TO RJVs project, Fondazione Eni Enrico Mattei.

Brockhoff, K. and T. Teichert (1995), 'Cooperative R&D and partners; measures of success', *International Journal of Technology Management*, **10**(1), 111–23.

Bussoli, P. (1999), 'An empirical analysis of technological convergence process and RJVs in Europe at the firm level', working paper prepared for the STEP TO RJVs project, Fondazione Eni Enrico Mattei.

Caloghirou, Y., G. Hondroyannis and N. Vonortas (2003), 'The performance of research partnerships', *Managerial and Decision Economics*, **24**(1), 85–99.

Cameron, K. S. (1986), 'Effectiveness as paradox: consensus and conflict in conceptions of organizational effectiveness', *Management Science*, **32**(5), 539–53.

Contractor, F. J. and P. Lorange (1988), *Cooperative Strategies in International Business*, Lexington, MA: Lexington Books.

Eccles, R. G. (1991), 'The performance measurement manifesto', *Harvard Business Review*, Jan.-Feb., 131–37.

Franko, L. G. (1971), *Joint Venture Survival in Multinational Corporations*, New York: Praeger.

Geringer, J. (1998), 'Assessing replication and extension. A commentary on Glaister and Buckley: measures on performance in UK international alliances', *Organization Studies*, **19**(1), 119–38.

Geringer, J. and L. Hebert (1989), 'Control and performance of international joint ventures', *Journal of International Business Studies*, **20**(2), 235–54.

Geringer, J. and L. Hebert (1991), 'Measuring performance of international joint ventures', *Journal of International Business Studies*, **21**, 249–63.

Glaister, K. W. and P. J. Buckley (1996), 'Strategic motives for international alliance formation', *Journal of Management Studies*, **33**(3), 301–32.

Glaister, K. W. and P. J. Buckley (1998a), 'Measures of performance in UK international alliances', *Organization Studies*, **19**(1), 89–118.

Glaister, K. W. and P. J. Buckley (1998b), 'Replication with extension: response to Geringer', *Organization Studies*, **19**(1), 139–54.

Gomes-Casseres, B. (1987), 'Joint venture instability: is it a problem?', *Columbia Journal of World Business*, **22**(2), 97–107.

Harrigan, K. R. (1986), *Managing for Joint Venture Success*, Lexington, MA: Lexington Books.

Hernan, R., P. Marin and G. Siotis (1999), 'An empirical evaluation of the determinants of Research Joint Venture formation', working paper for the STEP TO RJVs project, Universidad Carlos III de Madrid.

Killing, P. J. (1983), *Strategies for Joint Venture Success*, New York: Praeger.

Kogut, B. (1988), 'A study of the life cycle of joint ventures', in F. J. Contractor and P. Lorange (eds), *Cooperative Strategies in International Business*, Lexington, MA: Lexington Books.

Lecraw, D. J. (1983), 'Performance of transnational corporations in less developed countries', *Journal of International Business Studies*, **14**(1), 15–33.

Navaretti, G. B., P. Bussoli, G. von Graevenitz and D. Ulph (1999), 'Information sharing, research co-ordination and membership of Research Joint Ventures', working paper for the STEP TO RJVs project, Fondazione Eni Enrico Mattei.

Schaan, J. L. (1983), 'Parent control and joint venture success: the case of Mexico', unpublished doctoral dissertation, University of Western Ontario.

Stopford, J. M. and L. T. Wells (1972), *Managing the Multinational Enterprise*, New York: Basic Books.

Tucci, C. L. (1996), 'Firm heterogeneity and performance of international strategic technology alliances', paper presented at the Strategic Management Society Annual Meeting in Mexico City, October.

Yan, A. and B. Gray (1994), 'Bargaining power, management control, and performance in United States-China joint ventures: a comparative case study', *Academy of Management Journal*, **37**(6), 1478–517.

7.   RJVs in Europe: trends, performance, impacts

Yannis Caloghirou and Nicholas S. Vonortas

The economic and business literature on cooperative R&D has proliferated since the early 1980s in parallel to the rapidly unfolding phenomenon of strategic technology partnerships. Until recently, this literature was subject to a serious handicap: the lack of systematic and extensive evidence to validate its theoretical underpinnings. This is not to say that evidence on motives for, and outcomes of, collaboration has been missing altogether. It can be strongly argued, however, that available evidence has been fragmented because of the lack of extensive data-collection on the subject by statistical agencies. Empirical analysis has depended on either multiple case studies on a small number of well-known RJVs, on one hand, and on (often limited) databases created by academic researchers and private sector companies, on the other. Some well known examples of widely utilized academic databases of this sort include CATI, covering technical strategic alliances announced globally since the late 1970s, and the NCRA-RJV and CORE databases, covering RJVs registered with the US Department of Justice since 1985.[1] Unfortunately, such data have not necessarily been compiled for the same purpose, overlap only partially in terms of coverage, and use different primary sources of information. Even so, research has hitherto reached important conclusions and has provided useful insights into business strategy and technology policy.

A major, if not the most important, contribution of the research project underlying the material presented until now in this book has been the creation of a new source of information on cooperative R&D, focusing exclusively on Europe. This is the STEP TO RJVs databank,[2] made up of four separate databases. First, the EU RJV database contains information on all RJVs with at least one business participant that were funded through the European Union's Framework Programmes for RTD since 1984. It also contains financial and industrial classification information for a large number of identified business participants. Second, the EUREKA RJV database contains similar information on all RJVs selected by the EUREKA programme since 1985 and on their business participants. Third, four national databases contain information on RJVs funded by the governments of four EU member states: Greece, Spain, Sweden and the United Kingdom. Finally, the RJV Survey database contains detailed information from an extensive survey of European firms participating in RJVs. The latter is really one of the most extensive databases of its kind containing detailed information on the characteristics, strategies, and incentives and benefits from cooperative R&D for several hundreds of business respondents.

The link across all the databases in the STEP TO RJVs databank is the private sector: covered partnerships include at least one member organization from the private sector. They have all been constructed under the objective of allowing the study of the incentives for, and impacts of, cooperation on the private sector. The distinguishing feature of the STEP TO RJVs databank as a whole is that it focuses solely on government supported RJVs, with the partial exception of the RJV Survey database that also includes non-subsidized RJVs. In addition, the databank combines diverse kinds of information – subjective (quantitative) and objective (qualitative and quantitative) – on diverse kinds of RJVs (in terms of sources of funding). It thus allows the most direct undertaking of analyses matching the objectives for, and impacts of, policies supporting cooperation in the creation and dissemination of new technological knowledge.

This first part of this book reported the main results of a multi-faceted analytical approach that used the different databases in the STEP TO RJVs databank and a large number of RJV case studies to address several issues in the following broad topical areas:

1. Trends in RJV formation in Europe.
2. Determinants of RJV formation.
3. RJV performance and impact on participating firms.
4. Impact on European industries and regions.

The outcomes of a fifth area of interest – policies supporting RJVs – is the subject matter of the second part of this book.

TRENDS IN RJV FORMATION

The study showed in considerable detail the formation of RJVs funded through the first four Framework Programmes on RTD during 1984 to 1998.

- Starting with ESPRIT in 1983, RJV numbers increased considerably into the 1990s. Formation seems to follow a cycle that peaks about two years into a Framework Programme, no doubt as a result of available funding.

- Information processing and information systems, and electronics and microelectronics have taken more than a quarter of all RJVs. Other important areas have been materials, industrial manufacture, aerospace, telecommunications, and renewable energy sources.
- More than three-quarters of the RJVs extended up to three years, with half of that around the three-year range.
- Various organizations participate. The largest single category of RJVs has firms, universities and research institutes as members. The next three largest involve firms collaborating again with non-private sector organizations in various combinations.
- RJV size, duration, and combination of members indicates concentration on pre-competitive research.
- Firms are by far the most frequent coordinators of the examined RJVs.

The EUREKA data was compiled in order to have a point of reference. EUREKA and the Framework Programmes are, of course, very different. The EU Framework Programmes have largely reflected a top-down procedure, following extensive consultation with stakeholders that has been implemented through 'focused' competitions in specific technological areas. This contrasts EUREKA practice. On the other hand, unlike the Framework Programmes, EUREKA has concentrated on applied research aiming at the development of marketable products and processes. In addition, whereas Framework Programmes involve subsidization, approval by EUREKA only means a label that improves chances for national funding of individual partners. Finally, whereas the Commission oversees Framework Programme projects whose results are the property of both the Commission and the partners, nobody else but the partners oversee EUREKA projects or own their results.

The different design and governance of the two policy frameworks for collaborative R&D have resulted in different sets of RJVs. Important differences include:

- *Technological areas*: Framework Programme RJVs have tended to concentrate relatively more on ICTs, whereas EUREKA RJVs have been more evenly distributed across several technical areas.
- *Duration*: Most of the examined EU-funded RJVs (66 per cent) are medium-term. A larger percentage of EUREKA RJVs are longer term. However, it is worth noting that this 'average' and 'cumulative' picture hides an emerging trend: the gradual decrease in the duration

of EUREKA RJVs. On average, EU and EUREKA RJVs initiated
since the mid-1990s tend to last about the same time.

- *Size*: Most EU RJVs are middle sized (six to ten partners), whereas
  the majority of EUREKA RJVs have been small-sized (two to three
  partners).
- *Type*: EU RJVs involve significant cooperation between firms, universities and research institutes; inter-firm cooperation is much more
  prevalent in EUREKA RJVs.
- *Coordinator*: Firms tend to be the coordinators in the majority of
  both EU and EUREKA RJVs. Other organizations such as universities and research institutes also tend to act as coordinators in a significant number of EU RJVs (38 per cent of the total number of
  RJVs formed); not so in EUREKA RJVs.
- *Business firm characteristics*: Large firms tend to participate more
  often, especially in the EU RJVs. On the other hand there is a large
  number of small and medium enterprises that have a rather limited
  participation (one to three times). Participation in EUREKA RJVs
  seems to have been more balanced between firms of different sizes.
- *Sectoral representation*: In both types of RJVs, firms active in the
  electrical and electronic engineering and business services sectors
  appear to be more frequent participants than firms in other sectors.
  Firms active in the chemical sector tend to have higher participation
  in EUREKA RJVs. Firms active in telecommunications appear to
  participate relatively more in EU RJVs compared to EUREKA RJVs.

DETERMINANTS OF RJV FORMATION

The first question here was why firms enter RJVs. The analysis addressed
important questions in the theoretical economic literature. The main findings of the econometric studies based on the EU RJV and EUREKA RJV
databases include the following:

- Knowledge spillovers are an important determinant of RJV formation, but their impact only emerges in R&D-intensive industries.
- Industry concentration is positively related to the rate of RJV formation. One reason may be that concentration may facilitate the internalization of spillovers. It also reduces the intensity of
  competition in the marketplace.
- Firm size is a very significant determinant of participation in RJVs.
  This finding may be qualified by the fact that only firms of certain
  size and kind (for example, publicly traded) are usually represented

in publicly available databases like Amadeus, used here to draw financial data.

- Past experience in research cooperation greatly enhances the probability of forming new cooperative ventures. This may indicate several things. First, it may indicate that firms appear satisfied on average with RJVs, as they show a clear willingness to repeat the experience. Second, it may indicate that there are fixed costs and strong learning effects associated with an RJV.

The second question was what determines the exact pairs of firms that collaborate. In other words, why the observed couples of firms and not others? The main findings included the following:

- The probability of forming a couple is larger when firms are in the same industry and when their products are complementary.
- For firms producing substitute products the probability of forming a couple is higher, the lower the asymmetries between them.
- In the Framework Programme, the larger the asymmetries between firms, the more likely RJVs are to be formed. This result should, however, be taken with caution as it may simply reflect the design of these Programmes.
- EUREKA couples are more likely to form between firms both based in Northern European countries. This relationship is not significant for Framework Programmes, showing a policy bias (cohesion) in favour of firms based in Southern European countries.

Tabulations of subjective information from the RJV Survey database revealed the importance of the following objectives of firms to join specific RJVs (listed by order of importance):

- Establishment of new relationships.
- Access to complementary resources and skills.
- Technological learning.
- Keeping up with major technological developments.

Concerning the objectives of firms to generally collaborate in R&D, they were reported as follows (in order of importance):

- Access to complementary resources and skills.
- Keeping up with major technological developments.
- Technological learning.
- R&D cost sharing.

The RJV Survey aggregated the competitive strategy of surveyed firms into two broad categories, focusing on either existing large markets (mass markets) or smaller market segments (niches). Both kinds of strategies correlated with the same four objectives of companies for engaging in co-operative R&D:

- Create new investment options.
- Control future market developments.
- Keep up with major technological developments.
- Improve speed to market.

The mass market-oriented strategy was highly correlated with creating new investment options (apparently reflecting the use of RJVs as a mechanism for differentiation in new markets) and with controlling future market developments (probably reflecting the size of the respondents, their invested interests in existing large markets, and their fear of losing control as a result of new technologies). Such firms may be using RJVs for casting their nets wide: be present when something exciting happens. In contrast, the market segment-oriented strategy was highly correlated with improving speed to market, and least correlated with keeping up with major technological developments. Such firms would seem to have identified the technologies they are interested in and to be using RJVs in order to access the necessary complementary resources to bring their products to market quicker.

An important question to policy decision-makers is the difference that public funding makes in forming the RJV. Almost two thirds of the responding firms (total 456) said that they would not have undertaken the specific research (cooperatively or otherwise) without government funding. The other third would have gone forward even without such funding. Importantly, for between two thirds and three quarters of the respondents, this information related to cooperative research that falls within their core business activity.

RJV case studies also offered particularly valuable insights into the question of RJV formation. More specifically:

- Previous relationships among partners (personal or institutional) played a critical role in several of the examined cases.
- The importance of the role of a 'research entrepreneur' cannot be overestimated. Such people often are responsible for the original idea for the specific R&D and its implementation through the RJV.
- Successful collaboration depends on trust. Initiating a partnership is always easier by experience from previous collaborations. Trust building is an important dynamic process.

- Firms in complementary business collaborate frequently. An important reason tends to be the complexity of the product under development that requires complementary capabilities. Cooperation among firms operating in different, but related, sectors (such as telecommunications services and semiconductors), with different strategies and corporate cultures, allows the necessary interchange of assets, skills, and experiences.
- Competitors will collaborate either when there is no major market challenge or to establish technical standards. Otherwise, competitors will limit their collaboration to precompetitive research.
- Firms and universities share knowledge and experiences more easily than firms with firms.
- The institutional set-up and regulations (environmental, technical standards, and so on) often provide the motive for new collaborations.
- Government-subsidized RJVs are often set up in response to international competition.
- Many RJVs are formed under the pressure of high uncertainty and rising R&D expenditures due to rapid technological change.
- Another way to slice the observed objectives to collaborate in R&D is between large, established firms and small, less resource-rich firms. The former tend to collaborate in areas of high uncertainty, where the research outcome is not close to the market but may open new market opportunities in the future, after further development by each partner. The latter firms collaborate to learn or to create the necessary technological and organizational capabilities that will enable the firm to compete internationally and to leverage their own limited R&D resources.
- Small firms that cannot afford extensive R&D investment occasionally choose to subcontract or to collaborate with universities or research centres that have the people and infrastructure for specific research activities.

PERFORMANCE

The available literature has identified a number of problems in analysing the performance of alliances. The most important involve:

- differences in the definitions of RJV success among individual member organizations;
- lack of appropriate empirical measures of performance;

- disagreements over the relative appropriateness of objective versus subjective measures of performance; and,
- the fact that some of the most important indicators can only be expressed through subjective evaluations.

By design, this research project allowed access to data suitable for the construction of both objective (such as financial) and subjective (survey) measures of RJV success. It could thus support a two-pronged econometric and statistical approach to the question of performance. The data from the EU RJV and EUREKA RJV databases were used to support an objective-measure approach while the data from the RJV survey database were used to support a subjective-measure approach. Even though the results from these two approaches are not directly comparable, due to partly different RJV and firm samples, they are both informative and relatively rare for combining both methodological venues.

The 'objective measures' analytical approach focused on the impact of participation in either Framework Programme or EUREKA RJVs on firm performance.

- Descriptive statistics indicate higher productivity (on average) for RJV participating firms than for non-participants. Firms in EUREKA RJVs were shown as relatively more productive than firms in Framework Programme RJVs.
- Econometric analysis was able to establish a positive impact of EUREKA RJVs on the examined firms but no clear trend for Framework Programme RJVs.

The downside is that these results depend on relatively small samples and with short time lags between the initiation of the research and the measurement of performance. This may be important given the general orientation of Framework Programme RJVs for more precompetitive R&D that is expected to affect performance in longer time period than the development research, which is the primary focus of EUREKA RJVs.

The 'subjective measures' analytical approach (using RJV Survey data) was able to handle more complicated issues, related to strategy. Straightforward tabulations of the responses revealed the following as the most important expected benefits from specific RJVs they had participated in (listed by order of importance):

- acquisition/creation of new knowledge;
- development of new products;
- improving the technological and organizational capabilities of the participating unit.

Successful partnerships were considered to be those that met or surpassed the objectives of partner firms. Important findings of the econometric analysis here include:

- The success of the examined RJVs in meeting or surpassing the overall objectives of individual industry partners was found to increase:
  1. the more related the cooperative research is to the existing activities of the firm;
  2. the lesser the problems of knowledge appropriation between the partners;
  3. the higher the effort of the specific business unit involved in the RJV to learn from it through various channels.
- The incentive of a firm to join an RJV in order to share risks and decrease market and technological uncertainty:
  1. is positively correlated with cooperation with supplier and buyer firms, and cooperation with competitors;
  2. is negatively correlated with cooperation with universities and public research institutes and with the degree of appropriability of the cooperative R&D.
- The motivation of a firm to join an RJV in order to create new investment options:
  1. is positively correlated with cooperation with competitor firms;
  2. is negatively correlated with cooperation with universities and public research institutes and with the degree of appropriability of the cooperative R&D.

A persistent question in the literature relates to the apparent asymmetric benefit of various partners in an RJV. In other words, what accounts for the apparently disproportionate benefits of some partners over others from the same RJV? Each of a long list of learning mechanisms (for creating and acquiring new knowledge) was correlated to three broad categories of benefits from RJVs: direct product development and profitability benefit, process development benefit, and benefit on the firm's knowledge base. The results were of interest:

- The strongest relationships were found with respect to the knowledge base benefit, which was correlated with all learning mechanisms, including:
  1. Undertaking basic research internally;
  2. Undertaking applied research internally;
  3. Undertaking development research internally;

4. Undertaking design engineering internally;
5. Developing formal relationships with users and/or suppliers;
6. Developing informal relationships with users and/or suppliers;
7. Observing and imitating processes of other firms;
8. Learning from patents;
9. Learning from codified scientific and technical information (databases and so on);
10. Using employee training and education;
11. Engaging in long-term forecasting and product planning;
12. Institutionalizing procedures for exploiting ideas and initiatives from individual employees.

- Undertaking of internal (independent) development R&D proved the best facilitator of benefits to the knowledge base of the firm.
- Product development benefit also correlated positively with all learning mechanisms (except number 12 above), particularly so with developing formal and informal relationships with users and/or suppliers, and undertaking development research internally.
- Process development benefit was positively correlated with imitation of other firms, and undertaking internal applied and development research.
- Undertaking independent, similar R&D to that of the RJV was found strongly correlated with the ability of firms to maximize their benefits from the RJVs they participate in. Such R&D especially helps them to acquire and create new knowledge, improve their technological and organizational capabilities, increase market share and exploit complementary resources.
- Mass-market oriented strategy is correlated with process development benefits from RJVs. Market segment (niche) oriented strategy is correlated with product development benefits from RJVs.

Such results confirm earlier findings in the literature that independent research effort in the firm enhances considerably its ability to benefit from RJVs and, more broadly, from knowledge in the public domain. They also strongly indicate more general benefits from RJVs (knowledge base) than those tied to specific products and production processes.

RJV case studies also offered valuable insights into the question of RJV performance. More specifically, it was found with respect to benefits:

- In most examined cases, it was difficult to determine the outcome of the collaborative R&D in terms of introduction of a final product or production process. While various explanations exist, outright failure to reach the RJV's objectives should not be excluded from the list of possible reasons for this disappointing finding.

- A major reported benefit from participating in the examined RJVs has been the acquisition of new knowledge, in fields in which either responding firms were not willing or able to invest their own resources or they did not possess the necessary capabilities to tackle on their own.
- Cooperation often provided the possibility to access the complementary assets of partners, including technological knowledge, human capital, financing and so forth.
- RJV participation also opened new market opportunities for firms and gave opportunities to the academic sector to make their research efforts more visible.

Reported problems in the RJV can be grouped into two main categories:

- *Problems due to the funding programmes.* In many cases the participants of subsidized RJVs reported problems resulting from the rigidity of the programmes, more specifically relating to budget allocation changes and partner changes. Especially for the latter, it was pointed out that although the responsibility of the prime contractor is clearly defined, the flexibility of dealing with problems with the partners is low. Moreover, reporting requirements, budget changes, and bureaucratic rigidities were mentioned as impediments.
- *Problems related to the cooperative scheme.* The opportunities for commercialization of the R&D results are one main concern of RJV participants from the private sector. Lack of appropriate consideration concerning how to bring the results of R&D to market was a frequently reported problem.

Not surprisingly, the importance of government subsidies has been pointed out in all examined cases. There were differences, nevertheless, in the reasons that made subsidies important:

1. Cases where funding was decisive for supporting the specific R&D activity.
2. Cases where projects aimed at strengthening European competitiveness. Public underwriting has created a mechanism for bringing together important economic agents that needed an institutional framework for doing business together. Public funds as such were of secondary importance.

Some interviewees commented on the potential value of spreading funding over more projects in future Framework Programmes. This would reportedly result in participation incentives resting more on higher visibility and networking than access to funds. Some of the subsidized projects could arguably proceed without funding beyond administration expenditures.

IMPACT ON INDUSTRIES AND REGIONAL ECONOMIES

Has collaborative R&D supported by the Framework Programmes on RTD and EUREKA contributed to the convergence of firms based in different regions of the European Union? Has such R&D contributed in narrowing the technological gap between participating firms? Has it contributed to narrowing the technological gap between firms in manufacturing?

Based on a sample of RJVs drawn from the STEP TO RJVs databank, econometric analysis has found substantial evidence of short term convergence across firms in Europe, and positive effect of international R&D cooperation on the overall convergence process. More specifically, regarding the first question, the analysis across countries and across different manufacturing sectors in Europe supports the hypothesis that RJVs favour technological convergence both at the country level (this effect is not statistically significant for Germany and the UK) and at the sector level for 14 out of the examined 21 sectors. Regarding the second question, the results support the hypothesis of convergence among all countries except Germany and the UK. Regarding the third question, the results show that cooperative R&D has a positive impact on closing the technological productivity distance between firms in a sector. The higher the number of RJVs in which a firm participates, the smaller the deviation from the highest productivity firm in its sector.

A different approach was also used to map the networks formed in a subset of 3874 Framework Programme RJVs during 1992 to 1996. Network formation can reasonably be expected to contribute to technological and economic convergence. Considering a 'link' between two firms to exist if they cooperated at a minimum in seven RJVs during this time period, researchers were able to identify three major networks in the automobile, aerospace, and electronics and telecommunications industries. In all three cases, large, well-known corporations based in the core countries of the European Union have central positions. The three networks are also connected with each other through links between certain important members of each network.

One implication of dense networking is that the European Framework Programmes on RTD have established an important mechanism for transferring knowledge and experience across traditional sector boundaries as well as across national and regional boundaries. Another implication may be the use of the European programmes by large corporations for anticompetitive reasons (Mytelka, 1995; Van Wegberg and Van Witteloostuijn, 1995; Vonortas, 2000). The potential for collusion through publicly supported RJVs is a subject that would deserve further study – anticompetitive behaviour would, of course, run counter to the objectives of the European Commission in the Framework Programmes.

NOTES

1. CATI is maintained by John Hagedootn and his colleagues at the University of Maastricht. NCRA-RJV is maintained by Nick Vonortas at the George Washington University. CORE is maintained by Al Link at the University of North Carolina.
2. The STEP TO RJVs databank is currently maintained by Yannis Caloghirou and his colleagues at the National Technical University of Athens.

REFERENCES

Corvers, F., R. Hassink, M. Slabbers and B. Verspagen (1994), 'Monitoring technology policy in Europe: with an application to the consequences of the rise of South-East Asian countries', report, Maastricht Economic Research Institute on Innovation and Technology (MERIT), University of Maastricht.

Ergas, H. (1987), 'Does technology policy matter?', in B. R. Guile and H. Brooks (eds), *Technology and Global Industry: Companies and Nations in the World Economy*, Washington, DC: National Academy Press.

European Commission (1994), *The European Report on Science and Technology Indicators: 1994*, Directorate-General XIII, Luxembourg: Office for Official Publications of the European Communities.

European Commission (1997), *Second European Report on Science and Technology Indicators: 1997*, Directorate-General XII, Luxembourg: Office for Official Publications of the European Communities.

Kemp, R., I. Demandt and B. Dankbaar (1996), 'Monitoring technology policy in Europe: the role of public research institutes', report, Maastricht Economic Research Institute on Innovation and Technology (MERIT), University of Maastricht.

Mytelka, L. K. (1995), 'Dancing with wolves: global oligopolies and strategic partnerships', in J. Hagedoorn (ed.), *Technical Change and the World Economy*, Aldershot, UK and Brookfield, VT: Edward Elgar.

Nelson, R. R. (ed.) (1993), *National Innovation Systems: A Comparative Analysis*, New York: Oxford University Press.

Organisation for Economic Co-operation and Development (1998), *Science Technology, and Industry Outlook 1998*, Paris: OECD.

Organisation for Economic Co-operation and Development (2000), *Science, Technology, and Industry Outlook 2000*, Paris: OECD.
Van Wegberg, M. and A. Van Witteloostuijn (1995), 'Multicontact collusion in product markets and joint R&D ventures: the case of the information technology industry in an integrating Europe', in J. Hagedoorn (ed.), *Technical Change and the World Economy*, Aldershot, UK and Brookfield, VT: Edward Elgar.
Vonortas, N. S. (2000), 'Multimarket contact and inter-firm cooperation in R&D', *Journal of Evolutionary Economics*, **10**(1–2), 243–71.
Wolters, A. and M. Hendriks (1997), 'Monitoring science and technology policy III', report, Maastricht Economic Research Institute on Innovation and Technology (MERIT), University of Maastricht.

PART II

Policy

Introduction to Part II

Science and technology (S&T) is one area with relatively little to show in terms of harmonization and cohesion between the policies of European Union (EU) member countries. There is ample evidence that European national innovation systems (NIS) remain rather dissimilar due to historical, cultural and other factors related to the development stage and consequent needs and capabilities.[1] The work underlying this part of the book demonstrates the same phenomenon in one specific area of S&T policy: cooperation in R&D.

Diversity is increasingly viewed as a strength of the European Innovation System. Still, the more recent concept of a European Research Area presupposes a certain degree of cohesiveness and basic goal harmonization across member states. One way the Commission has tried to address the discrepancies – in terms of R&D funding levels, areas of focus, and specific policy tools – has been through formal Community programmes to support R&D since the early 1980s. Framework Programmes on RTD (FWPs) were first established in 1984. They have been successive four-year programmes supporting R&D in somewhat broadly defined, and yet selective, technological areas. Cooperative R&D has been the most frequent organizational mode of the RTD undertaking supported by the Framework Programmes. Cooperation involves business firms, universities, and government institutes based in more than one member country in any combination.[2]

The two-year research project on intra-European R&D collaboration whose results supported the discussion in Part I of this book also appraised the underlying policy climate affecting the formation and conduct of cooperative R&D in Europe. Consortium partners prepared policy position papers for their respective countries as well as for the European Union as a whole, for Japan and for the United States. Japan was included because it has been a pioneer in the past few decades in cooperative industrial research. The United States was included because it has introduced significant policy changes since the early 1980s, first creating the legal infrastructure for cooperative R&D and then putting in place various programmes to support cooperative RTD.

Policy position papers summarized the S&T policies related to cooperative RTD during the past couple of decades. In addition, the papers investigated competition policies and the intellectual property rights (IPR) policies that directly affect both the incentives of economic agents to participate in, and the returns from, cooperative RTD.

The papers indicated extensive differences between the policies of individual EU member states. Policy decision-makers across industrialized countries have typically actively promoted cooperative R&D during the past couple of decades but have tried to do so through largely different approaches. Policies have ranged from the almost complete indifference to the issue of R&D cooperation until recently (Ireland), to refocusing attention (UK), to lukewarm policies in anticipation (Greece, Italy), to well established, specialized network systems (Sweden), to highly determined programmes to assist cooperative industrial R&D (France, Spain). The level and type of support has varied widely as have the specific programmes, their technological focus, and the numbers and kinds of economic agents that have participated. Amidst this variability, the European Commission's policies have played a boosting and cohesive role. The visibility (and funding) of European programmes has increased to the extent that member state governments perceive them as complements to their own S&T policies.

As expected, the policies of Japan and the US have also been quite different from those in Europe. In Japan, the emphasis on cooperative RTD continues. Government-sponsored RJVs, however, seem to have made the transition in the 1980s from mechanisms for assisting whole sectors to catch up with world best practice to mechanisms for creating a broader technological superstructure to assist a large group of high technology sectors.

The US has followed a rational approach to increasing attention to cooperative R&D. During the 1980s, it changed its institutional structure and relevant legal system. During the first half of the 1990s, it tried to put in place specific programmes to actively promote cooperative R&D. Political developments and the decreasing pressure from the 'competitiveness camp', due to particularly favourable economic conditions for the American industry in the second half of the previous decade, lessened the attention of policy makers to research partnering. Cooperative R&D is still considered a potent S&T policy mechanism, however, surely to surface again as soon as the currently relentless pace of economic growth slows down. Policy experts are currently focusing their attention on the value of RJVs in assisting industry to decrease the high levels of uncertainty associated with opening up new emerging product markets.

The EU approach seems to have been the reverse of the US approach, but equally rational.[3] Faced with a wide collection of nationally-based S&T policies, the Commission tried first to put in place its own supra-national programmes for cooperative R&D before harmonizing policies across its member states. Harmonization efforts and 'cohesion' efforts have continued, of course, but the process has naturally been a slow one due to path dependencies and vastly different S&T capabilities among the European core and the periphery. The Commission apparently hoped that a series of well-established and funded Framework Programmes for R&D would increase the chances of success for these efforts. And, in fact, support for the sixth Framework Programme was drummed up under the argument that, having succeeded to bring the European players together with the first five FWPs, Europe now needs greater coordination between policies at different levels of governance (EU, national, regional) and R&D efforts that meet a critical minimum mass necessary to sustain and enhance the international competitiveness of European industry. The first five FWPs may well have accomplished their core mission. What came out clearly in the consortium's work is that EU policies have become a force well reckoned by individual agents and by member state governments. National and regional governments have increasingly shaped their policies at the image of those of the European Commission.

The rest of this part of the book consists of seven chapters. The first six deal with the policies of individual countries and one region. Chapters 8 to 13 appraise the policies of the European Union, the United Kingdom, France, Italy, Spain and of the United States of America respectively. Consortium partners have contributed the chapters on the United Kingdom, Italy, and Spain. Another expert has contributed the chapter on France. The coordinating partner is responsible for the chapter on the United States. Chapter 14 closes this Part by tracing the common policy threads across countries.

NOTES

1. See, for example, Corvers et al. (1994), European Commission (1994, 1997), Ergas (1987), Kemp et al. (1996), Nelson (1993), and OECD (1998, 2000) and Wolters and Hendriks (1997).
2. In addition to FWPs, cooperative RTD is also being supported through the structural programmes. Structural funds usually supplement member-state funds and are distributed by member-state agencies within their national territory.
3. See also Vonortas (2000) for a comparison between the EU and US S&T policies in general, and collaborative R&D policies in particular.

REFERENCE

Vonortas, N. S. (2000), 'Technology policy in the United States and the European Union: shifting orientation towards technology users', *Science and Public Policy*, **27**(2), 97–108.

8. European Union science and technology policy, RJV collaboration and competition policy

Katharine Barker and Hugh Cameron

This chapter outlines two major themes concerning the evolution and current status of research joint ventures (RJVs) in the European Union in four sections.[1] Section 1 outlines the basis of competition policy set out in the EC Treaties. These apply to all member states of the European Union, and determine the extent to which RJVs are permitted without contravening competition rules. The European Commission is responsible for administering competition policy in the European Union. The Directorate General for Competition covers competition policy and regulation, including antitrust, mergers, market liberalization, state aid to industry and international aspects of competition policy. It will be seen that competition policy in Europe is different in tone and emphasis to that of the USA, and the resulting evolution of RJVs in the EU is therefore distinctive to this region. But the European Commission also has a significant role in funding research and technology development (RTD) throughout the EU, much of which involves forms of RJVs. Section 2 outlines the development of this activity which has had a major impact on the growth of RJVs in Europe. Section 3 discusses the structure of projects and the associated intellectual property requirements and exploitation issues. The final section draws together some conclusions about the interplay between the two areas of policy and the development of RJVs in the EU.

SECTION 1: EUROPEAN UNION COMPETITION LAW AND RJVs

1.1 Background

Economists and industrialists have for more than a century debated the merits and drawbacks of competitive and monopolistic market structures and their resulting welfare losses and transfers in the economy as a whole. In general there has been a presumption against monopoly for both theoretical and practical reasons. Competition is thought to be a main driver of economic progress as firms attempt to gain advantages over their competitors in production and sale of goods and services. Anticompetitive markets structures and practices have been legislated against for many years, for example in the USA, from the Sherman Antitrust Act (1890) against the railway trusts of the nineteenth century to the recent actions against Microsoft's alleged monopoly power in the software market.

However, economists have always been divided, for changing reasons, about the merits or otherwise of monopolies. With the focus on the economic importance of technological change resulting from research and development, support for Schumpeterian or evolutionary analyses, in place of orthodox neo-classical views, has become more prominent. Competition as a process rather than as a state leads to rather different conclusions: the incentive effects of pursuit of monopoly profits may have an important part to play in rapidly developing economies, sometimes outweighing static efficiency arguments for competition.

In the European Union, the two, sometimes conflicting, trends have been at the heart of policy making. RTD has become one of the most significant areas of mutual cooperation within the Union, intended as a means of improving the competitiveness of EU industry in comparison with the United States and with the Far Eastern economies. EU rules concerning competition and regulation of mergers are administered by the European Commission. Yet it is also clearly seen that cooperation in RTD, by means of joint projects, may be in conflict with the regulations concerning overall competition policy within the Union. It has been necessary, therefore, to provide specific exemptions to agreements concerning research, and also exemptions for joint ventures, which are necessary if such work is to proceed.

This section considers aspects of the competition law of the European Union relevant to RJVs and technological collaboration.

1.2 European Competition Law

The Treaty of Rome, which established the European Community, gave competition law a constitutional character. It required the institution of a system to ensure that competition is not distorted, and gave the Commission competence to implement and enforce the competition laws and to levy heavy fines on infringers. Competition is dealt with more specifically under Articles 81 and 82:[2]

- Article 81 deals with agreements which may affect trade between member states by restricting or distorting competition within the (now) European Union.
- Article 82 prohibits abuse of a dominant position by one or more undertakings.
- Article 87 (the 'State Aids' provision) is also relevant. This prohibits the grant of aid by any state that distorts or threatens to distort competition insofar as such aid may affect trade between member states.

Article 81(1) prohibits anticompetitive practices in very broad terms: all undertakings, decisions by associations of undertakings and concerted practices which may affect trade between member states and which have as their object or effect the prevention, restriction or distortion of competition within the Union. These include price-fixing agreements, production limitations or market-sharing agreements. Companies making agreements must notify the Commission of the details of these, and a decision on their legality is issued, though sometimes with a considerable delay. The European Commission can levy heavy fines on participants in agreements found to be anticompetitive. Appeals may be made to the European Court.

Clearly, agreements by companies to collaborate in RTD projects and programmes could be open to charges of anticompetitive practices. For example, projects aimed at generating industrial standards, though these may be beneficial to the companies, non-participant companies (under certain conditions) and consumers, must involve a significant number of the industrial companies which are potential adopters of the new standard, and so could be classified as anticompetitive. Limitations have therefore been produced to cope with these (and other) problems. Particular refinements have addressed the problems of small and medium-sized enterprises (SMEs). For example, the Notice of Agreements of Minor Importance exempts companies which have a relatively low turnover, a limit which is increased from time to time.

In the field of RTD, the major influence has been Article 81(3), which provides the basic grounds for exemptions from Article 81(1). Any agreements which contribute to improving production or distribution of goods or to promoting technical or economic progress, while allowing consumers a fair share of the resulting benefit, are exempt from the prohibitions. However, the agreements must not include any restrictions which are not indispensible to the objectives above, nor must they give any undertakings as to the possibility of eliminating competition in a significant part of the markets in question. Only the Commission may grant or refuse exemptions, and only after their formal notification. Exemptions may be granted to all or some of the parties to an agreement.

Article 82 prohibits the abuse by any undertaking of a dominant market position within the EU, or in a substantial part of it insofar as it may affect trade between member states. The evolution of the meaning of 'dominant position' took some time to refine, with variations being given by the Commission and by the Court. One Court version is:

> [dominant position] . . . relates to a position of economic strength enjoyed by an undertaking which enables it to prevent effective competition being maintained on the relevant market by giving it the power to behave to an appreciable extent independently of its competitors, its customers and, ultimately, of consumers. In general, a dominant position derives from a combination of several factors which, taken separately, are not necessarily determinative.

This point of law has interesting implications for RJV formation, as is explained below.

1.3 Block Exemptions

Collaborative RTD projects and programmes, whether within or independent of public policy schemes, are always aimed at improving the competitive advantage of enterprises in some way (that is, towards creating a stronger market position). Thus they have had an ambiguous status within European competition law, particularly Article 82 outlined above. Technological advance is almost universally seen to be crucial to economic competitiveness, in particular in relation to the global marketplace. The EU, as will be seen later in this chapter, has explicitly funded and promoted technological collaboration and RJVs, most significantly through the successive Framework Programmes of research in technological development. Yet commercial collaboration is viewed with some suspicion, to the point of being generally illegal. Thus, special exemptions are made for RTD agreements within EU law.

Under the block exemptions, enterprises are not required to notify the Commission of agreements. These came into being, beginning in 1962, primarily to reduce the delays which were encountered in producing Commission opinions of notified agreements. The scope of block exemptions has not always been clear, however, and several times agreements have been notified in order to clarify whether they are covered by exemptions. As this tended to negate the whole purpose of reducing Commission workflow, an 'opposition process' was instituted in 1985, which applies to agreements that fall in part outside the scope of the block exemptions. Under this procedure, notified agreements become valid after six months unless the Commission opposes exemption. Block exemptions have been put in place to allow RJVs to form, and in the areas of patent licensing and know-how,

which are crucial for exploiting the results of RJVs. These are discussed
below.

1.3.1   RJV block exemption

In recognition of the benefits of RJV collaboration, such as avoidance of
duplication, and production efficiency gains, agreements in this field have
been given a specific block exemption. RJV projects and exploitation
projects qualify for exemption under certain conditions:

- R&D must be carried out within a framework in which it is clear
  which field is addressed
- all parties must have access to the results; if the agreement provides
  only for R&D, then each party must be free to exploit the results
  independently

Additionally, where collaborating parties are not competing manufacturers of the product in question, the exemption can last for the duration
of the project plus a further five years from the date of the first marketed
product. This may be extended as long as the combined production of
the parties does not exceed 20 per cent of the total market for such
products.

If the parties are competitors, the exemption will only apply if the combined production does not exceed 20 per cent of the market. The block
exemption does not apply to joint exploitation of the products of the
research and development, unless there are competitive factors outside
the EU which could result in individual exemptions being made by the
Commission.

Some other conditions may be allowable under the agreement. For
example, collaborations may require participants to continue to exchange
information subsequent to the conclusion of the work, such as details of
exploitation problems or later improvements. Confidentiality may have to
be preserved, and royalties may be payable.

1.3.2   The patent licensing block exemption

This concerns both patent licensing agreements and agreements which
combine patent licensing and communication of 'know-how' between two
parties. It allows agreements to:

- restrict licensees' rights to license third parties in specific parts of the
  European Union
- restrict licensees' rights to exploit the licence in territories reserved for
  the licensor or other licensees

- restrict the use of the patent after the licence has terminated so long as the patent is still in force
- require the licensee to use the licenser's trade mark or distinguishing features of the licensed product

'Know-how', or confidential knowledge, is included in the regulation only as far as needed to exploit licensed patents.

Some conditions are not permitted in agreements, including:

- prohibiting the licensee from challenging the patent
- extension of the agreement beyond the term of the patent
- charging license fees (royalties) on partly patented products
- restrictions on quantities of production or on prices, or on supply restrictions

1.3.3 Know-how exemptions

In recognition of the increasing importance of know-how agreements, in 1989 the Commission produced a block exemption defining know-how as information which is secret, substantial and identified in an appropriate form. The provisions are generally similar to those concerning patents; indeed mixed patent/know-how agreements are treated under either of the block exemptions according to the predominance of the type of intellectual property addressed.

There are specific exempted provisions for licensers, as well as licensees. These include the allowance of provisions which prevent the licensee from:

- exploiting the licensed technology in territories reserved for the licensor;
- manufacturing or using the licensed item in EU territories licensed to other licensees;
- limiting production of the licensed item to the quantities required for manufacturing of own products;
- selling the licensed product only as an integral or replacement part for own products.

The time limit on these agreements is rather less than that for patent agreements; ten years (from the date of signature of the first licence agreement) as compared with 20 years (from the date of the first marketed product) for patents agreements. The market limitation arrangements are limited to five years duration.

1.4   Joint Ventures

Joint ventures may be of several different types: companies, partnerships and also enterprises set up to manage appropriate parts of separate enterprises for a specific purpose. Systems of cross-licensing are also included in the definition of a joint venture. They are recognized as having a value in legitimate operations, for example in RTD where individual companies may not command sufficient resources, or to minimize risk, or to share production facilities.[3] Such joint ventures may be covered by the block exemptions outlined above, as they may have the effect of increasing competition. However, they may have the effect of imposing barriers to entry to potential new market entrants, by fixing prices or by excessive market concentration.

If ventures are not covered by the block exemptions, they may still be eligible for Article 81(1) exemption if they offer substantial economic benefits and do not reduce competition in the market. Such exemptions are treated on a case-by-case basis, but the general guidelines require that the necessity of the joint venture be shown, for example that the necessary investment is beyond the capacity of individual participants, and that the provisions do not go beyond what is necessary in, for example, geographical restrictions or duration.

1.5   State Aid

The European Treaty regulates state aid provided by its member states in Article 87. The regulation of state aid is an important part of EU competition law, seeking to ensure a level playing field for European businesses, which could obviously be distorted by public subsidy and favourable treatment by one or more states. However, state aid may be crucial for developing the Union, for example in assisting poorer regions to modernize, and in pursuing the objective of making the EU the most competitive economy in the world by 2010.[4] State aid may be justified where it corrects market failures or where it produces externalities such as improved employment or benefits to the environment. It has been a prominent source of conflict between the member states and the European Commission over a very broad range of industrial support policies.

In general, state aid is not allowed under EU competition law, but a variety of mandatory and discretionary exceptions have been developed. For example the rules do not apply to aid to SMEs and aid to certain industrial sectors such as the motor vehicle industry.

Public subsidy of industrial R&D has been a major element of the science and technology policies of many member states for a considerable time. The justification has been the social and economic externalities arising from R&D. Thus R&D has been considered as an area where state aid may produce beneficial externalities which offset distortions to competition and this has been explicitly recognized in the Commission's framework for research and development (European Commission, 1996). This is still in force until the end of 2005, despite having been considered for amendment in 2001.

Large companies in the EU have expressed dissatisfaction with the existing framework.[5] The US does not control or monitor the level of public support for private R&D as does the EU's Competition Directorate (and has a higher proportion of business expenditure on R&D financed by government than does the EU). The WTO rules have expired and new ones are not yet in place.[6] Thus, EU rules on state aid for R&D constrain public R&D funding for EU firms (SMEs are not included) compared with their global competitors (EICTA, 2000).

The 1996 Community Framework for state aid for R&D distinguishes between fundamental research, industrial research, precompetitive development and prototyping, product development and manufacturing. R&D subsidy is not allowed beyond initial prototyping, pilot projects or initial demonstrators. This rule is based on the widely discredited sequential (or linear) model of innovation, a view which supports strict limitations on public subsidy to private R&D and innovation. The Community Framework for state aid even appears inconsistent with the block exemption for RJVs (see section 1.3.1) which defines R&D more broadly. It is certainly at odds with the many EU funded RJVs which include user interaction and validation of technological systems, and with any notion of public financial support for the development of a European innovation policy (see section 2.2).

1.6 Conclusion

It can be seen from this account that European competition laws and their effects upon RJVs are complex and the application of the rules is not always clear. However, in general European policy is more favourable towards industrial technological collaboration, formal joint ventures, and joint exploitation of results than is the case in the USA. More emphasis is placed on the promotion of innovation and dynamic competition, rather than policies which are suspicious of any form of collusion between firms.

The RJV block exemption in particular clears the way for national and trans-European RJVs. Thus, competition law clearly allows collaborative programmes and independent RJVs. The EU's own Framework Programmes for RJVs (see next section), and the EUREKA[7] initiative (a large European

RJV programme independent of the EU) could therefore exist, but within the state aid rules, which are fairly stringent.

SECTION 2: EUROPEAN UNION PROMOTION OF RJVSs

2.1 Introduction

The European Union has had the promotion and subsidy of RJVs, involving partners from different member states, as a major element in its research and technology policy from its beginnings. The objectives of this have been variously the promotion of European cooperation, the competitiveness of European industry and the well-being of its citizens. The EU has developed, as the main strategic research policy instrument, successive 'Framework Programmes' within which RJVs and other research policy mechanisms are organized.[8] This section will provide a brief account of the evolution of EU policy for cooperative industrial research, review the successive Framework Programmes and comment upon the impacts of EU-funded RJVs.

Much attention has been given to providing economic explanations for the growth of industrial collaboration in scientific and technological research. There has been an additional motivation for international collaboration in Europe. The founding of the European Community, subsequently Union, produced the circumstances in which: S&T was accepted to be within the competence of the Commission, and EU policies were in general limited to transnational (or transstate) activities, due in part to the subsidiarity principle which prevents EU intervention in purely national-level issues. Thus, support for collaborative research in trans-European RJVs seemed to be particularly appropriate for Commission interventions. It is only since 1982 that there has been a formal legal basis for EU science and technology actions across all fields, yet in that time there has been a steady growth of funding and of the perceived significance of RJVs for industry and EU competitiveness, as well as advancing the subsidiary aim of increasing European cohesion (raising the scientific and technical capabilities of the less developed EU member states and regions).

Before introducing the factors which have affected the development of EU research and technological development (RTD) policy, it is salutary to note a few statistics. The EU entire budget represents only 2.4 per cent of member states' total public expenditure, and 1.1 per cent of Union GDP. Though it has steadily grown, the EU RTD budget is 3.9 per cent of the EU's total budget (2002). Figure 8.1 shows that only about 5 per cent of European R&D (non-military) spending by governments is under the control of the Commission. Less than 16 per cent of all European R&D involves cross-border cooperation (Stajano, 1999). The small scale of funding relative to national, industrial, and defence spending on R&D, not to mention US and Japanese public and private spending, has several implications. EU-funded RJVs represent a minority activity in the big picture of EU R&D, but nevertheless, as will be shown below, have been expected to meet ambitious goals of competitiveness, cohesion and social well-being.

2.2 Evolving Rationales

The evolution of EU policy in this area has not been simple or straightforward. It has certainly not been born out of purely technical or economic judgements, but has involved institutional and political negotiations and trade-offs which have often been inconsistent and in conflict. Caracostas and Muldur (2001) analyse the development of EU research and innovation policy in terms of a co-evolution with European integration and the general evolution of the EU from a primarily economic construction to a political one. For example, the RTD policy of the Union has been viewed at times as a means of competition against the USA and Japan, as an instrument of industrial and trade policy, and as a method of helping to achieve rapid development of disadvantaged European regions. At the same time as it was seen as a means of achieving rapid and fundamental

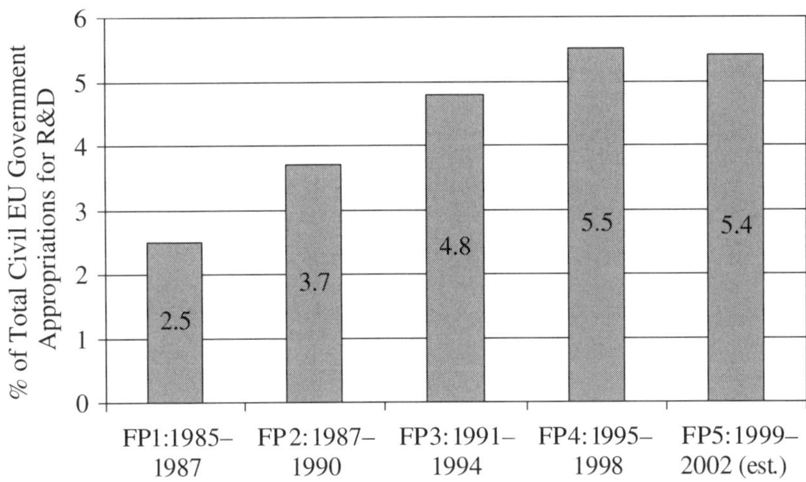

Source: European Commission Directorate General for Research, *Science, Technology and Innovation Key Figures 2002.*

Figure 8.1   European Commission R&D appropriations 1985–2002

structural economic change, other parts of the Union were simultaneously devoting overwhelmingly greater resources to achieve the opposite objective: in particular, restricting structural change in the agricultural sector.

Politically, RTD policy seemed to offer the Union a new means of restarting the integrationist movement which had almost stopped by the end of the 1970s. In addition, it was seen as a means of escaping from the identification of Community policies with support for declining industries (iron and steel, coal mining, agriculture and so on) and towards the dynamic new industries of the future (electronics and information technologies, telecommunications, biotechnology, new materials and so on). Moreover, the failure of collaboration, under the Euratom Treaty, to produce a European civil nuclear industry to compare with that of the USA, gave impetus to finding more successful modes of collaboration (Williams, 1973). The rationale for European technology policy was couched in terms of global economic competition, with Europe being the poorest performing member of the 'Triad' compared with the USA and Japan, and later with the emerging Asian economies (Guzzetti, 1996). This rationale has persisted despite the addition of other objectives.

RTD policies of EU member states concentrated during the 1970s on identifying and supporting their national champions in vital technology industries, in particular in the face of the Japanese economic threat. Failures of these national policies (in particular the poor performance of national electronics 'champions' in the UK, France, Italy and Germany) encouraged Europe-wide policy initiatives to counter the economic threat.

An important, and convenient, conclusion at that time was that Japan's success was identified with the mechanism of collaborative research and development used by major Japanese companies to produce generic ('enabling') technologies in 'precompetitive' programmes,[9] with government assistance. Later it became clear that these Japanese programmes were not all successful, nor were the companies necessarily keen on enforced collaboration with commercial rivals. However, European national, and later Community[10] programmes were instituted, aiming to achieve competitive scales of operation, beginning with the European Strategic Programme of Research in Information Technologies (ESPRIT), which was modelled on the Japanese VLSI programme. The large companies which were consulted about this policy were enthusiastic to receive the financial support for their R&D, though not perhaps for the associated opening up of their protected markets. ESPRIT and subsequent programmes thus adopted a collaborative, precompetitive and multinational format, which was accepted to be within the competence of the Commission: the EC had to fund industrial research through collaborative mechanisms (Peterson and Sharp, 1998). Thus, RJVs became a key component of European RTD policy.

The formal expression (in the early 1980s) of the policy rationale for Community action in the field of support for industrial RJVs was contained within the 'Reisenhuber criteria' (named after the then German research minister). These initially set out the following criteria:

- 'research conducted on so vast a scale that single Member States either could not provide the necessary financial means and personnel, or could only do so with difficulty';
- 'research which would obviously benefit financially from being carried out jointly after taking account of the additional costs inherent in all actions involving international cooperation';
- 'research which, owing to the complementary nature of work carried out at national level in a given sector, would achieve significant results in the whole of the Community for problems to which solutions call for research conducted on a vast scale, particularly in a geographic sense';
- 'research which contributes to the cohesion of the common market, and which promotes the unification of European science and technology, as well as research which leads where necessary to the establishment of uniform laws and standards' (Guzzetti, 1995, p. 84).

In 1987, promotion of cohesion among member states and regions was added to the list. These criteria attempt to define the boundaries between national and Community level policy for the promotion of RJVs.

A new generation of perceived European problems and associated solutions emerged in the 1990s. After a decade of programmes designed to generate new technologies, it was found that many of these were under-exploited by European industry, so diffusion became a new aim. Also, the 'European paradox' was identified, for example in the 1995 Green Paper on Innovation:

> . . . Compared with the scientific performance of its principal competitors, that of the EU is excellent, but over the past fifteen years its technological and commercial performance in high-technology sectors such as electronics and information technologies has deteriorated. The presence of sectors in which the scientific and technological results are comparable, if not superior, to those of our principal partners, but where the industrial and commercial performance is lower or declining, indicates the strategic importance of transforming the scientific and technological potential into viable innovations. (European Commission, 1995)

And, from the Second European Report on S&T Indicators:

> There is a growing perception that Europe's science and technology system is in a paradoxical situation. Although Europe's educational and scientific research

base is acknowledged to be of high quality, it seems to be failing to convert this advantage into strong technological and economic performance. (European Commission, 1997a, p.175)

So, after more than a decade of 'technology-push' policies, it became accepted at the EU level and in many other countries that a more sophisticated understanding of the innovation system was required as a basis for policy (Sanz-Menendez and Borras, 2001). This was easily agreed for a number of reasons. It still implied that collaboration was the best means of improving economic performance, though the emphasis would be on interactions between all contributors to the innovation process (research performers, commercial producers, users and so on), rather than between similar companies in efforts to achieve scale efficiencies.

The EU was also consistently failing to achieve high levels of employment creation, again compared with Japan and particularly the USA. The 1993 White Paper on 'Growth, Competitiveness and Employment' (known as the Delors Report after the then President of the Commission), identified:

> The depth of the present crisis is largely due to insufficient progress in adapting the structures of the Community's economy to the changing technological, social and international environment . . . Only through the structural adaptation of industry can the twin requirements of higher productivity and more jobs be achieved. (see Peterson and Sharp, 1998, p. 12)

This introduces another of the factors influencing the objectives and structure of EU collaboration. One of the features perceived to contribute to the USA's success in innovation and job creation has been the health of new SMEs in new industries: Silicon Valley has had a particularly strong influence on European policy makers. This fitted well with the collaborative imperative for the Commission. Collaboration between SMEs, and between SMEs and other actors in the innovation system, would at the same time achieve scale economies, reduce 'duplication' of research efforts, and promote diffusion of technologies and their exploitation. RTD policy has therefore also become a tool of structural adjustment in the European economy. Particular attention is now placed on the need to devote resources to SMEs in all areas of its RTD programmes, including promoting SME involvement in RJVs.

This proliferation of the rationales and goals for EU research and technology policy (with RJVs as the main mechanism) was given further impetus in the late 1990s. A major change was the recognition of the need for economic and social acceptance of the technologies and other results which have come from funded research. The Panel assessing the achievements of Framework Programmes in 1997 concluded that:

The Fifth Framework Programme needs . . . to be based on the twin pillars of scientific excellence and social and economic relevance, and can only be made relevant if it is the result of a strategic approach . . . However, scientific excellence and relevance have to be accompanied by European added value, which . . . must be the essential criterion for selecting programmes and projects in future Framework Programmes. (European Commission, 1997c)

The Commission's document setting out the broad lines of the fifth Framework Programme claimed:

[research] . . . is not an end in itself but a means of meeting common objectives . . . Hitherto research has been based largely on technical achievement. The aim now is to make research more efficient and increasingly directed towards meeting basic social and economic needs by bringing about the changes which each individual citizen desires.

Thus, RJVs were now expected to bring about social and economic changes for the benefit of Europeans, as well as restructuring industry and creating economic competitiveness.

Another stage in EU RTD policy has been reached with the design of the sixth Framework Programme, commencing in 2003. The European problems of research fragmentation, under-investment in R&D and a lack of coordination of S&T were emphasized by the new Commissioner for Research, Philippe Busquin. The underpinning idea for RTD has become the European Research Area (ERA) (European Commission, 2000). This encompasses aspirations for a highly integrated European research capacity, coordinated S&T policies of member states and integration of the accession countries.[11] Heads of state endorsed the ERA at the Lisbon summit in March 2000. The image used by policy makers is one of a single market for research, fostering excellence, competitiveness and innovation through collaboration at all levels, with the ERA to make a significant contribution to the goal of the EU becoming the most competitive and dynamic knowledge-based economy in the world by 2010. At a subsequent summit (Barcelona) in March 2002, heads of state discussed the issue of relative under-investment in research in Europe compared with the US and Japan (European Commission, 2002a). So the sixth Framework Programme also takes on this problem, at least at a political level.

In summary, RJVs (as part of the EU Framework Programmes), have been seen almost as a 'cure-all' to address the various problems and political agendas of the European Union, in particular:

- low rates of R&D spending compared with the USA and Japan and other emerging economies;

- low rates of economic growth, and of job creation;
- poor general economic performance measured by competitiveness, innovation, market shares, trade performance and so on;
- structural adjustment: that is the need to achieve a dynamic economy, moving out of declining industries and into new high value and growth sectors;
- regional policy: to assist the disadvantaged regions of the Union and accession countries to catch up with the mainstream.

It is clear that with such a broad range of objectives, EU RTD policy is unlikely to achieve all of its goals satisfactorily.

2.3   The Framework Programmes and RJVs

This section provides a view of the evolution of RJVs within the Framework Programmes in terms of the types of RJV supported, the technical areas promoted by the EU for subsidy, and the participants making up the consortia. It is perhaps worth repeating some key points at this stage: each Framework Programme has specified and legally agreed technical areas (the 'work-programme') to which self-organizing consortia of firms, higher education establishments, public and private research organizations and users submit proposals for RJVs which are selected by peer review. Successful RJVs enter contracts with the Commission to undertake the work, receiving up to 50 per cent of the costs.[12] RJVs (called shared cost contract projects by the Commission) form one element of the Framework Programmes; the other main elements are 'concerted actions' (coordination costs only for large European networks), funding of the Commission's own research institution (the Joint Research Centre) and mobility grants for scientists. Thus, a Framework Programme does not equate to RJV support, but most of the budget is devoted to it.

There have been some changes in the organization of the Framework Programmes, mainly in an attempt to make them less a collection of numerous sub-programmes (18 within the fourth Framework Programme) and activities and more of a coherent and strategic whole. As described in section 2.2, the fifth programme was a step change from what had gone before, not only in its embracing of socio-economic goals, but in its organization into four 'thematic programmes' containing 'key actions' and three cross-cutting or 'horizontal programmes', including innovation and SME actions. One can trace the continuous evolution of the programme areas into the thematic and horizontal programmes.

The structure of the sixth Framework Programme builds on that of the fifth in having three groups of actions: research and related (organized in seven S&T areas), structuring the European Research Area and strengthening the foundation of the European Research Area. In the fifth and sixth Framework Programmes, the Commission specifically supports RJVs in two of its funding instruments: research and innovation projects and co-operative research for SMEs.[13]

2.3.1 Emergence of the Framework Programmes

The European Community's involvement with research long predates the Framework Programmes, becoming established in the 1950s with the European Coal and Steel Community and EURATOM, for European collaborative research on those industries and in nuclear energy and associated health and safety. It was not until the 1970s that industrial policy became an area of activity for the Community and that RTD became linked with such policy (Guzzetti, 1996, p. 71). In January 1974 the Council adopted a resolution for an action programme in the field of S&T, and by 1977, programmes were under way. However, there was not a high profile link with industrial policy as envisaged by the Commission (Kastrinos, 1997). In 1979 Community spending on industrial technologies was 9.7 per cent of its R&D budget, half of which was devoted to the coal and steel sectors. Thus, at this stage, there was no significant policy support for RJVs, and little support for RJVs in the 'new' technological areas such as microelectronics.

The shift towards Commission involvement in the development of new technologies came with the establishment of the ESPRIT programme, orchestrated by Commissioner Davignon (responsible for both science and technology and industry). He worked closely with heads of European IT companies to discuss the technological and market threats posed by Japanese competitors. The Commissioner generated support from what were then the national champions (and highly competitive with one another) for a European collaborative R&D initiative involving large and small firms, universities and research institutes. It was focused on precompetitive research to comply with EU competition rules. After demonstrable success in attracting proposals, it became the template for future RJV support, quickly spawning programmes in materials, biotechnology, communications technologies and telematics, all based on the precompetitive model of collaboration. By the 1990s, RJVs were an established part of EU RTD policy (Guzzetti, 1996; Peterson and Sharp, 1998).

The notion of a Framework Programme also dates back to European Commission (1997c). The first Framework Programme merely gathered together the existing Commission RTD activities, and it was not until the second programme that there was an explicit legal basis in the Single European Act. The subsequent Treaty on European Union (1993) introduced an additional component of coordinating RTD policies of member states and gathered together all EU RTD into the Framework Programme. Thus, the Framework Programmes would include basic research, applied research and technology development as well as demonstrations of new technologies.

Table 8.1 summarizes the dates, legal basis and main rationales for the successive Framework Programmes.

2.3.2 Changing priorities

Table 8.2 shows the changes in the scientific and technical areas promoted by successive Framework Programmes, which can broadly be interpreted as the areas in which the EU has supported RJVs. The content of each programme is decided through negotiation between the Commission, member states and European scientists and industrialists.

A striking feature of the changing priorities are the rise in life sciences from 5 per cent of the first Framework Programme to 20 per cent of the sixth, and the decline of the share given to energy-related research from around half the budget to 13 per cent. Thus, in the first Framework Programme, the 'new' information and communication technologies (ICTs), biotechnology and new materials were not given prominence, although the actions on traditional industries were seeking to update technologies to include ICTs. Energy was still seen as a key issue for Europe. Information technology appeared seriously in the second Framework programme, where it took 42 per cent of the budget (European Commission, 1997a). The proportion of each successive Framework Programme devoted to information and communication technologies has declined, to 23 per cent of the sixth programme. (Bear in mind that the overall budget has increased substantially – see Table 8.1.)

The above account is necessarily brief. Each sub-programme (such as ESPRIT and its successors) has undergone evolution since the 1980s, not only in technical content, but in the focus and type of RJVs promoted. It is generally agreed that ESPRIT supported much more exploratory research, while the recent Information Society Technologies programmes have been more focused on targeted technology development and validation with users – in summary, a shift to nearer market RJVs.[14]

2.3.3 Participation

The Commission has estimated that more than 5000 RJVs were funded in the fourth Framework Programme, with over 20000 participations (European Commission, 1997a, p. 516). These figures will be even higher for the fifth programme, and represent the creation of numerous trans-European collaborative links between small and large firms, universities and public and private research centres.[15] In the fourth Framework Programme the average number of participants in an RJV was seven, from an average number of 4.2 different member states.

Table 8.1   The Framework Programmes: dates, legal basis and main rationale.

Instrument	Dates	Budget	Legal basis	Emphasis of rationale
First Framework Programme	1984–87	3270m ecu	European Coal and Steel Community, EURATOM, Article 235 of EEC Treaty	Strengthen S&T basis of industry, increased global competitiveness (technological catch-up with global competitors)
Second Framework Programme	1987–91	5360m ecu	Single European Act, 1987	As for first FP, plus technology transfer and mobility
Third Framework Programme	1990–94	6600m ecu	Single European Act, 1987	As for second FP
Fourth Framework Programme	1994–98	13120m ecu	Maastricht Treaty, 1993	Industrial competitiveness and employment
Fifth Framework Programme	1998–2002	14960m ecu	Amsterdam Treaty, 1997	Socio-economic objectives and European added value
Sixth Framework Programme	2002–2006	17500m euro	Amsterdam Treaty, 1997 (Nice Treaty unratified at end 2002)	European Research Area

Source: Adapted from: Caracostas and Muldur (2001).

Table 8.2   Changing priorities between EU Research Areas (% of budget)

Research Area	FP1 1984–86	FP2 1987–91	FP3 1990–94	FP4 1994–98	FP5 1998–2002	FP6 2003–06
Quality of life (life sciences, biotechnology, biomedical research)	5	7	10	13	17	20
Information society (IT, communications, telematics)	25	42	38	28	27	23
Competitive and sustainable growth (industrial and manufacturing technologies including aeronautics)	11	16	15	18	19	18
Environment (including transport)	7	6	9	9	8	6
Energy (nuclear and non-nuclear)	49	22	16	18	14	13
International co-operation	–	*2*	*2*	*4*	*3*	*2*
Innovation/dissemination and optimization of results	–	*1*	*1*	*3*	*3*	*2*
Improving human potential	*3*	*4*	*9*	*7*	*4*	*18*
Socio-economic	–	–	–	–	*1*	*2*

Note: Rows in italics are not relevant for RJVs.

The allocation of fifth Framework Programme funding between types of participants is shown in Figure 8.2. It can be seen that the three biggest recipients of funding (and also most frequent participants in EU RJVs) are higher education establishments, public research centres and firms. There has been a trend away from the early domination of the programmes by large firms to a more balanced breakdown between small and large firms.

Within the Framework Programmes, two main areas have provided by far the greatest concentration of industrial RJVs, these being industrial and material technologies (including aeronautics) and information technology and communications. Non-nuclear energy programmes, notably the

Thermie demonstration programme, also attract a high proportion of industrial participation, though the number of participations is smaller than for the above-mentioned programmes. Higher education and public research institutes have been more dominant in programmes on socio-economic research, biomedicine and biotechnology, environment and climate, and agriculture. As might be expected, the UK, Germany and France have most participations and take the most subsidy.

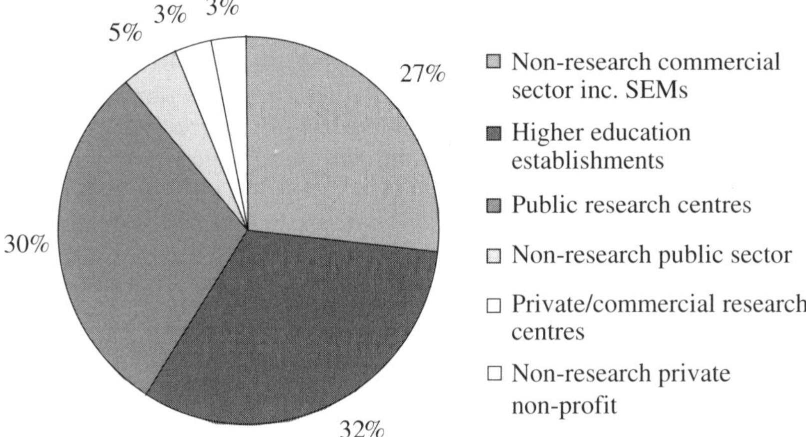

Source: European Commission Directorate General for Research *Science, Technology and Innovation Key Figures 2002.*

Figure 8.2   Fifth Framework Programme, percentage of EC contractual funding by type of participant

2.4   Impacts of EU RJVs

Following the now lengthy experience of large scale public funding of EU RJVs, it is natural to ask what impacts can be identified in return for the expenditure of such large sums of public funds. Questions of impacts and effects are of great concern to the Commission, as well as to the member states and parliaments for purposes of accountability and justifying the continuation of the policy. Indeed, the Framework Programmes and the subprogrammes within it have undoubtedly contributed to the development of R&D evaluation and impact assessment because of the support for studies and methodological development by the Commission. These questions were addressed by the STEP TO RJVs project by bringing to bear novel mixes of methodology and developing new analytical tools, as described elsewhere in this volume. For the purposes of this chapter, it is sufficient to briefly indicate the types of impacts which have been found in previous studies.

The methodological difficulties in measuring the impact of R&D are well known, and become even greater when studying the effects of RJV policies (Callon, Larédo and Mustar, 1997). There are problems of time scale of impacts, attribution of impacts to a particular piece of public funding for R&D, and difficulties in valuing 'intangible' but possibly very significant impacts such as improvements in human capital and access to networks (Georghiou and Roessner, 2000). For studies of rates of return, there are difficulties in estimating all the input costs, which can be overcome partly by systematic methods. Evaluations also need to take into account the different strategic motivations which firms have for entering RJVs in order to understand their exploitation and impacts (Hagedoorn, Link and Vonortas, 2000).

The impact of the Framework Programmes has been addressed in numerous studies (European Commission, 1997a, pp. 562–81). The Commission's systematic evaluation, first formally introduced in 1983 building upon previous practice, includes a Five Year Assessment of each programme area and of the Framework Programme as a whole, plus a raft of other studies commissioned by programme managers. The Five Year Assessments and many of the other studies are conducted by panels of eminent experts, and it may be argued are largely political validation exercises rather than in-depth evaluations of policy impacts (Georghiou, 1995).

Studies of completed projects in the BRITE-EURAM programmes (manufacturing technologies and materials) have produced high impact ratios (benefits/costs calculated in various ways). Though the methods of calculation are of necessity fairly crude, the main defence has been that numerous studies all producing positive impacts tend to reinforce each other, and convince policy makers. Against this is the general criticism of methods used, for example the use of gross benefits rather than the net measure, which would take account of activities displaced by the RTD work.

Partnership reinforcing and formation of networks have prominence as effects. The network effects of EU RJVs seem to be clearly demonstrable. Although difficult to quantify, improving collaboration between, for example, universities and firms, is likely to be of considerable long-term significance to the performance of European industry (Larédo, 1995). The creation of regional RTD activities and networks are also an important feature. More recently, impact studies have demonstrated employment effects and have gathered evidence about indirect effects of EU RJVs, taking the economic and policy environments into consideration (TAP-

ASSESS Consortium, 2000). In the area of communications and other standards, there have been some notable successes from Framework Programme RJVs.

In general, then, although it is problematic to point to simple cause and effect, there is enough evidence to point to positive impacts from the Framework Programmes for participants in RJVs (and of course some negative ones too). These are both in terms of narrowly defined competitive and economic benefits, but also less easily measurable impacts upon collaborative behaviour. EU funding usually makes up only a small part of overall commercial R&D budgets, but it is common for the effects upon commercial and technology strategies to be far greater than this would imply. While many criticisms have been made of EU RJV programmes, it would be unfair to give a negative verdict on their performance purely because EU industry has not been transformed in its performance.

2.5   Conclusion

The EU has a firmly established policy for subsidizing RJVs in specific technical areas as a core component of its RTD policy. It has mobilized many thousands of firms to enter RJVs and, despite their sometimes exaggerated political rhetoric, the Framework Programmes appear to have generated both direct and indirect socio-economic effects.

SECTION 3: STRUCTURE AND INTELLECTUAL PROPERTY RIGHTS IN EU FUNDED RJVs

Many thousands of collaborative projects have been carried out under the Framework Programmes. This section outlines the nature of these projects, and how intellectual property rights (IPR) are treated in this structure.

3.1   Structure of Collaborative Research Projects

EU RJVs involve two or more participants (from at least two member states), referred to as 'partners' or 'contractors'. Usually one of these will be responsible for coordination or project management, or this may be shared out between some of the members, but the participants are jointly and severally responsible for carrying out the work-plan. The participants may be commercial enterprises, university or independent research organizations, consultants, or other entities including subsidiaries of non-EU corporations. The conditions for geographical ownership or operations have been relaxed over the years, and now require that any participant must carry out substantial research within the EU. Associated partners may be included in the work of a project (performing sub-contractor roles), and complementary partners may have relationships with the project if they are involved in other EU RTD projects or programmes. Lastly, complementary contractors are defined to be companies controlled by, or controlling, one of the contractors, within EU territory.

Several types of legal agreement may be used in each project. As projects are part-funded by the Commission, it is necessary to conclude a contract between the Commission and each contractor in turn. The details of this, in particular the IPR conditions, will be addressed in a separate section below. For most projects the Commission's standard ('Model') contract is used,[16] with the detailed work-plan included as an annex (the 'technical annex': Annex I). In the sixth Framework Programme, the Commission requires the participants themselves to conclude a consortium (or collaboration) agreement which will contain any additional requirements for rights and duties between the members due to the particular nature of the project in question.[17] Though the Commission is not a party to this, nor does it approve it, it does provide a checklist of points to be considered for inclusion in a consortium agreement.[18] The Commission contract conditions take precedence over any internal consortium agreement conditions in the case of any conflicts. Associated contracts and complementary contracts may also be concluded between appropriate actors in each project. Figure 8.3 shows the relationships between the Commission and participants, and the legal agreements involved.

Each of these formal agreements has a legal status, and is expected to

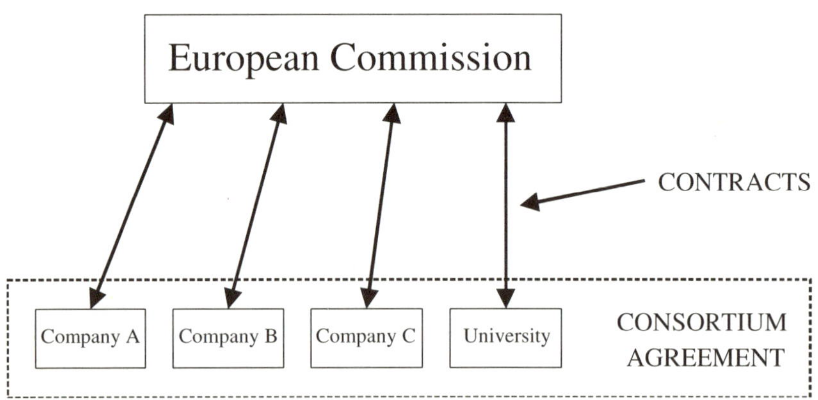

Source: Compiled by the authors.

Figure 8.3   Structure of EU RJVs

address all the issues which may be expected of collaborative RTD work. They will include rights and responsibilities, financial management and reporting, applicable legal systems and arbitration procedures, default procedures and liability, confidentiality, and, in particular, IPR conditions.

3.2 Treatment of IPRs

From the early experiences of collaborative RTD projects supported by the Commission, it was clear that major issues surrounded questions about the nature, origin and division of intellectual property rights between participants. Indeed, IPRs were a major factor in the motivations for participation, as well as the composition of project participations. In Framework Programmes prior to the sixth Framework Programme, detailed IPR conditions were specified by the Commission. In a complex set of rules, access to project results had to be ensured for all project participants, but under differing conditions, for example depending upon the nature of the intellectual property (IP), the use to be made of it, and licensing conditions. IP was also to be available to other Framework participants, or other EU companies, under differing levels of remuneration. The latest set of rules formulated for the sixth Framework Programme has been simplified, leaving considerable flexibility to adapt to the specific requirements of particular projects (European Parliament, 2001). Essentially, each project is expected to produce a consortium agreement which addresses the IPR issues.

> The rules governing the dissemination of research results should promote the protection of the intellectual property and the use and dissemination of those results. They should ensure that participants have mutual access to pre-existing know-how and to knowledge arising from research work to the extent necessary to conduct the research work or to use the resulting knowledge. At the same time, they should guarantee the protection of the participants' intellectual assets. . . . These agreements may form part of a consortium agreement. (European Parliament, 2001)

The Commission distinguishes between 'knowledge' generated during the contract that did not exist before (usually called 'foreground' knowledge; see below), and 'preexisting knowledge' ('background' knowledge) comprising IPR owned by the partners before the start of the project or created outside the project during its duration ('sideground' knowledge). Ownership of knowledge resides with the project participants generating it, but there may be some limitations on transfer of ownership.

Table 8.3 summarizes the conditions for the sixth Framework Programme.

*Table 8.3   Intellectual property rights in sixth Framework Programme
                RJVs*

	Access rights to pre-existing know-how	Access rights to knowledge
For carrying out a project	If a participant needs them for carrying out its own work under the project	
	Royalty-free unless otherwise agreed before signing the contract	Royalty-free
For use (exploitation) and/or further research	If a participant needs them for using its own knowledge	
	Non-discriminatory conditions to be agreed	Royalty-free unless agreed before signature of contract
	Possibility for participants to agree on exclusion of specific pre-existing know-how before signature of contract (or before entry of a new participant).	

Source: European Commission (2002c).

3.3   Exploitation Issues

To explain the reasons for these conditions, a brief review of the motivations of participants is useful. Commercial enterprises may at first be viewed as having only one motive (competitive advantage or even profits). But the detailed means of pursuing this objective are more complex. They may range from acquisition of IP from other participants for direct commercial products, to methods for design and production processes, software or hardware, artefacts or data acquisition.

Universities will clearly have other motivations, from pursuit of knowledge to publication of learned papers (for researcher's career progression). Much institutional and financial advantage is gained by researchers who achieve support for their research activities.

Commercial research agencies will have more commercial objectives, but will also use collaborations to make contacts in the industrial world, construct new areas of expertise for future exploitation, and keep a watching brief on competitors or emerging technologies.

A further distinction may usefully be made. Projects can be characterized (rather simplistically, but as 'category types'), as 'vertical' or as 'horizontal' according to the nature of the participants' interests. Early theories of collaboration tended to concentrate upon the latter, in which companies with similar market positions (say as consumer products manufacturers, or oil companies, and so forth) joined forces to achieve economies of scale in RTD. Empirical studies, however, have pointed out the predominance of 'vertical' projects in which participants with differing market interests (sometimes geographical as well as functional) and competences have cooperated. Direct commercial competitors rarely cohabit in RJVs, unless for the purposes of developing technological standards or in long term basic research (Georghiou et al., 1993).

Section 2.4 demonstrated that the results and impacts of EU RJVs are varied and often intangible. So the view that 'outputs' were in general those outcomes of projects that resulted in marketable or easily valued products, with easily traced provenances, must now be seen as simplistic. When the wide variety of outputs is recognized, we can also see that the nature of exploitation of these outputs will vary greatly. The commercial product is of course important, but many are used for internal company purposes, in particular for further research or development.

Some of the main motivations for supporting and participating in such work centre on the sharing of participants' existing IP, and the production and exploitation of results, or foreground (European Commission, 2002b). Yet this area has generated many of the problems in EU RJVs. A prime case of this is in the software field. Let us take a fictitious but realistic example to outline the problems (European Commission, 1997b). In a project aiming at producing process control software for a manufacturing industry, a project may involve one or more software houses, hardware providers (sensors and instrumentation), systems integration consultants, and several 'users' who provide realistic cases on which prototypes may be modelled and tested. For the purposes of the project there are sufficient common interests to produce a coherent work-plan. Each of the partners has a commercial interest in success, and the resulting product may be exploited in ways which do not involve direct competition between them. The software house will sell products and maintain and improve them, systems will be sold, users will improve efficiency, and so on. However software rights are complex; how far do collaborators have rights to access the software background intellectual property? A condition is that background is made available for the purposes of the project, and under different conditions for exploitation, but should source code be available, when this may represent the main capital asset of the software house? It seems reasonable to expect that some restriction be placed on the extent of access in this case. If the software company is an existing major supplier to the industry in question, substantial release of background IP (in order to exploit foreground) to users may entail a loss of potential revenues to the company. From the user viewpoint, will confidential data on its operating processes and efficiencies be used in production of software that is available to its direct market competitors? The web of interlocking IPRs, which are generated by collaborative projects, quickly becomes difficult to manage. In addition, it can easily be seen that the foreground from one generation of Framework projects becomes the background for a successive generation, in which different combinations of participants may be involved, each having a different and dependent set of IPs of their own.

The fears of many potential participants regarding the leakage of IP through partners has in some cases discouraged involvement in EU projects, or sometimes promoted reluctant involvement and cooperation within projects. However, despite the attention given to IPR issues, relatively few serious problems have occurred in practice. This does not imply that resources were wasted on negotiating agreements, as negotiations focused the minds of participants on the real problems of collaboration and exploitation.

3.4 Conclusion

A major conclusion of analysis of EU collaborative RTD is that IPRs should not be seen just as an unavoidable 'add-on' to promising technological projects, or even merely as an important part of successful RJVs. Rather, it is clear that detailed consideration of the intellectual property implications of collaborative work is the main determining factor in the choice of projects and participants of collaborative projects (European Commission, 1999). Companies assemble partners or choose to join projects, because they judge that the gain in IP from projects outweighs the potential loss. Thus, there is in general a preference for collaborating with non-competitors, either by function or geography (Georghiou et al., 1993; EUREKA Secretariat, 1993). RJVs are assembled from their first stages with a view to the intellectual property implications.

SECTION 4: CONCLUSIONS

This chapter has attempted to set out the two elements of EU policy relevant to RJVs: regulation of competition, and the support of RJVs in the Framework Programmes. It provides the background for the investigations of the STEP TO RJVs project, which empirically investigated the effects upon firms of RJV participation. Policy analysis in this domain is necessarily complex. European Union policies, even more so than those of single states, are products of political negotiations, battles between interest groups (for example, European industry sectors) and global positioning, which seem far removed from the practical experience of industrial research collaboration. We therefore have to look at the implementation of the policies to understand their significance to research performers in Europe.

EU competition policy remains based on a linear model of innovation, and a precompetitive model of RJV collaboration. Both are now recognized as outdated and over-simplistic. However, until economists are able to work with the concepts of knowledge creation and use in the economy and the importance of intangibles, this conceptual basis is likely to remain.

Compared to the strict regulation of competition in the USA, the EU seems more flexible in embracing technological cooperation as a principle, and in allowing control of intellectual property and its exploitation by collaborating firms. The threat of economic competition from the US and Asia combined with the fragmented nature of European industry has led not only to the relaxation of the rules but to policies encouraging the formation of RJVs. However, regulation of state aid in the EU is more stringent than in the USA and according to some parts of industry is holding back investment in R&D. Whether this might be relaxed in the face of the Barcelona objective[19] remains to be seen.

EU RJV policy has also adopted a precompetitive model of collaboration, partly influenced by the competition perspective. The fact that most RJVs do not conform to this model seems unimportant to the way that policy is formulated, particularly now that exploitation, impacts and effects are stressed by the Commission as expected outcomes of RJVs. The transnational requirement for Framework Programme RJVs is partly to fulfil the EU's mission of economic and political integration, but also to conform to the competition framework. It would have been impossible at a political level for EU RTD policy not to support European collaborative science and technology, and the industrial goals of the Framework Programme made RJVs an obvious choice for its implementation. The regulations on treatment of intellectual property in Framework Programme RJVs are certainly bound by competition law, which recognizes the importance of diffusion of knowledge but with means to protect the owners from free-riders. An adequate balance has been struck between achieving private and public benefits from the R&D undertaken.

We have seen that, despite the changes in the policy environment and high level rhetoric of the EU, the instrument of providing partial subsidy for R&D within RJVs has persisted as a main pillar of EU RTD policy. Why is this so? From the stance of the policy maker, part of the answer lies in the compatibility of RJVs with EU competition policy and integration.

RJVs are a very flexible instrument and have been suitable for implementing the changing RTD policy agenda of the EU: as tools for developing and diffusing key technologies, for addressing social and environmental problems which require inputs from users and social scientists, and more recently for promoting the scientific and technological integration of the accession countries to the Union.

From the viewpoint of participants in RJVs, another, and we believe very important, part of the answer lies in the collective experience gained by both the Commission and industry in managing RJVs over the past decade and a half. There is evidence from systematic studies and evaluations that large firms, and also a population of technology-based small firms, have learned how to use the Framework Programme for best effect: how to collaborate, how to undertake RTD in networks, how to protect proprietary knowledge while collaborating with others, how to manage partners and how to move to exploitation.[20] Thus, there is a constituency of support for their continuation in European industry and academia.

However, the subsidy of free-standing RJVs within programmes may be reaching its limits as a policy measure. With the emergence of innovation as the dominant theme for economies, policymakers realize that added value comes from setting RTD in a systemic context. RTD is now almost always used as part of a wider objective such as structuring networks and building capacity. The Commission has partly addressed this in the sixth Framework Programme through the new instruments of the 'Networks of Excellence' and larger RJVs ('Integrated Projects'), but these are concerned with integrating research capacity and less so with innovation and networks. RJVs that address larger challenges, such as innovation in public goods, require regulators and other arms of government to combine with firms from different parts of a technological and market system, including the service sector, thus encompassing an 'innovation' joint venture rather than the traditional research joint venture.

As a final note, we cannot escape the fact that the EU needs a better environment for R&D, in terms of investment, availability of capital and skilled labour, and rates of return on investment. RJVs have helped in a limited way with promoting networking and technological collaboration, but these other issues remain a very difficult challenge.

NOTES

1. This chapter provides the policy background for the empirical research conducted in the STEP TO RJVs project, the results of which are reported elsewhere in this volume.
2. From 1 May, 1999, the Treaty of Amsterdam renumbered the Articles of the EC Treaty; therefore some documentation may still refer to the original numbering. Thus the

original Article 85 became Article 81, Article 86 became Article 82, and Article 92 became Article 87 under the new scheme.

3. It is worth emphasizing that the 'Research Joint Ventures' promoted by the EU Framework Programmes, and similar collaborations promoted by national European Governments, are very rarely incorporated as joint ventures in the formal sense. Rather, they are structured by contracts between the partners, and so are constituted as agreements. However, there are numerous examples of formal joint ventures in Europe with a primary mission in RTD and they often take part in EU programmes in order to attract project funding.

4. A stated goal of the EU decided by Heads of State in Lisbon in 2000.

5. For example, the European Information and Communications Technology Industry Association (http//www.eicta.org).

6. Formerly there was a maximum allowable 75 per cent subsidy for industrial research and 50 per cent for precompetitive development.

7. This chapter has restricted its consideration of EU RJV policy to the Framework Programmes. EUREKA is important in the story of European RJV policy, but is outside the remit of the European Commission. See Georghiou, (2001).

8. There have been five successive Framework Programmes to date. The Framework instrument represents the basis for RTD funding and promotion. The content and mechanisms for the life of each programme are adopted by a co-decision between the European Parliament and Council of Ministers.

9. 'Precompetitive' denoting that after collaborating on joint research, the partners would develop and market new products alone and in competition with one another.

10. The 'European Communities' became the 'European Union' after the Maastricht Treaty of 1992.

11. In 2002, the EU agreed terms for accession of ten new member states, primarily from Eastern Europe and the Baltic.

12. Participants must be from more than one member state and may include those from the accession countries and states with agreements with the Commission.

13. http://www.cordis.lu/

14. This has been accompanied by increasingly stringent monitoring of milestones and deliverables by the Commission, and a forced focus upon exploitation of the results of RJVs in some areas of the Framework Programme.

15. Final figures for the fifth Framework Programme were to be contained in the European Commission's *Third European Report on Science and Technology Indicators*, due for publication in 2003.

16. Rules for participation in projects are given in Regulation (EC) No. 231/2002 of the European Parliament and of the Council (16 December, 2002), see http://ftp.cordis.lu/pub/documents

17. Up to and including the fifth Framework Programme, the Commission 'strongly encouraged' participants to conclude a consortium agreement.

18. ftp://ftp.cordis.lu/pub/documents

19. To raise the business expenditure on R&D to three per cent of GDP in the EU.

20. One should also add learning to deal with Commission bureaucracy to this list.

REFERENCES

Callon, Michel, Philippe Larédo and Philippe Mustar (eds) (1997), *The Strategic Management of Research and Technology – Evaluation of Programmes*, Paris: Economica International.

Caracostas, Paraskevas and Ugur Muldur (2001), 'The emergence of a New European Union research and innovation policy', in Philippe Larédo and Philippe

Mustar (eds), *Research and Innovation Policies in the New Global Economy: An International Comparative Analysis*, Cheltenham, UK and Northampton, US: Edward Elgar, pp. 157–204.

EICTA (2000), *EICTA Position on the revision of EU rules on State Aid for R&D*, Brussels: EICTA.

EUREKA Secretariat (1993), *Evaluation of EUREKA Industrial and Economic Effects*, Brussels: EUREKA Secretariat.

European Commission (1995), *Green Paper on Innovation*, 20 December.

European Commission (1996), 'Community framework for state aid for research and development', *Official Journal*, C45/06.

European Commission (1997a), 'Beyond the European paradox', Chapter 4 in *Second European Report on S&T Indicators*, Brussels: European Commission EUR17639.

European Commission (1997b), *IPR Handling in Collaborative RTD*, Brussels: European Commission (DG III), accessed at http://europa.eu.int/ comm/research/era/ipr_en .html.

European Commission (1997c), *Five Year Assessment of the European Community RTD Framework Programmes: Report of the Independent Expert Panel Chaired by Viscount E. Davignon and the Commission's Comments on the Panel's Recommendations*, Brussels: European Commission Directorate-General Science, Research and Development.

European Commission (1999), 'Strategic dimensions of intellectual property rights in the context of S&T Policy', ETAN working paper, Brussels: European Commission (DG Research).

European Commission (2000), 'Towards a European research area', communication from the Commission to the Council, the European Parliament, the Economic and Social Committee and the Committee of the Regions, COM 6.

European Commission (2002a),' More research for Europe: towards 3 per cent of GDP', COM(2002)499, 11 September.

European Commission (2002b), 'Working paper expert group report on role and strategic use of IPR (Intellectual Property Rights) in international research collaborations', Brussels: European Commission DG Research, http://europa.eu .int/comm/research/era/ipr_en.html.

European Commission (2002c), *Participation and Dissemination Rules and Contracts FP6: Specific Targeted Research Projects (STREP) Coordination Actions (CA)) Specific Support Actions (SSA)*, Brussels: European Commission (DG Science, Research and Development). http://europe.eu.int/comm/ research/conferences/2002/resources/bas-sanchez-model-ppt-6cu.pdf

European Parliament (2001), 0202(COD) PE-CONS 3647/02, accessed at http://europa.eu.int/comm/research/fp 6/pdf/rules_en.pdf.

Georghiou, Luke, Hugh Cameron, Josephine Anne Stein, Maria Nedeva, Martin James, John Yates, Marilyn Pifer and Mark Boden (1993), *The Impact of European Community Policies for Research and Technological Development upon Science and Technology in the United Kingdom*, London: HMSO.

Georghiou, Luke (1995), 'Assessing the Framework Programmes – a meta-evaluation', *Evaluation*, **1**(2), 171–188.

Georghiou, Luke (2001), 'Evolving frameworks for European collaboration in research and technology', *Research Policy*, **30**(6), 891–903.

Georghiou, Luke and David Roessner (2000), 'Evaluating technology programs: tools and methods', *Research Policy*, **29**(4–5), 657–78.

Guzzetti, Luca (1995), *A Brief History of European Union Research Policy*, Luxembourg: European Commission.
Hagedoorn, John, Albert L. Link and Nikos Vonortas (2000), 'Research partnerships', *Research Policy*, **29**(4–5), 567–86.
Kastrinos, Nikos (1997), 'The European Community Framework Programme as technology policy: towards an assessment', PhD thesis, University of Manchester.
Larédo, Philippe (1995), *The Impact in France of the European Community Programmes for RTD*, Paris: Presse de l'Ecole des Mines.
Peterson, John and Margaret Sharp (1998), *Technology Policy in the European Union*, Basingstoke: Macmillan.
Sanz-Menendez, Luis and Susana Borras (2001), 'Explaining changes and continuity in EU technology policy', Chapter 2 in Simon Dresner and Nigel Gilbert (eds), *The Dynamics of European Science and Technology Policies*, Aldershot: Ashgate.
Stajano, A. (1999), 'EU R&D programmes, technology policy and European integration', EU/US Science and Technology Policy Conference, Atlanta, GA, 9–10 April.
TAP-ASSESS Consortium (2000), 'Socio-Economic and Industrial Assessment of FPIV Telematics Applications Projects completed between 1996 and 1998', Brussels: European Commission, DG Information Society.
Williams, Roger (1973), *European Technology: The Politics of Collaboration*, London: Croom Helm.

9. United Kingdom public policies and collaboration in R&D

Katharine Barker, Luke Georghiou and Hugh Cameron[1]

INTRODUCTION

This chapter will consider the attitude of the UK government towards industrial collaboration in research and development. Of course, this cannot be isolated from public policies towards research and technological development and their role in creating economic prosperity and national security. Industrial R&D collaboration is not, however, shaped by R&D policy alone, but by the broader context of operation of industrial firms.

Below is given a brief account of the status of industrial R&D in the UK, and the main characteristics and concerns of science and technology policy in recent years. The format, though not the scale, for public support of industrial R&D collaboration has been remarkably stable over the past two decades. For this reason a historical perspective is adopted to show the development of these policies and their underpinning rationales. The 'flagship' policy to promote R&D collaboration in the 1980s was the Alvey programme for advanced information technology, which is described and reviewed. In many ways Alvey provided the model for both UK and other European schemes to support collaborative R&D. Its successors, and the shift to an emphasis upon promotion of R&D collaboration between industry and the science base, are then considered. European collaborative programmes have affected UK industrial participation in R&D collaboration and domestic policy in the area: both the Framework Programmes and EUREKA have been important. In line with the other chapters in this volume, domestic competition policy and the regime for the protection of intellectual property are considered, particularly as they have impinged upon R&D collaboration.

The chapter concludes by considering the future role of industrial R&D collaboration in the UK. The argument is made that the deliberately low profile for industrial policy in the UK has left science and technology policy in a prominent position but, within those policies, there is by international standards a low level of financial support for R&D collaboration between firms. Instead, the emphasis has shifted to support for industry–science linkages. However, broader changes in the industrial landscape may have reduced the scope for collaboration between firms.

RESEARCH FUNDING AND POLICIES IN THE UK

1. Investment in Research and Development – Business

The low level of investment by the UK in research and development has been an almost continuous theme of debate since science and technology policy first emerged in the modern sense at the beginning of the twentieth century. Business expenditure on R&D (BERD) is also relatively low and has been declining. There was a real terms increase in BERD during the 1970s and early 1980s, but a downward trend in the mid-1990s. An increase at the end of that decade to £11.3 billion lagged behind the rise in OECD as a whole. The area which fell most sharply was office machinery (which includes computer hardware). The highest expenditure by product groups was in pharmaceuticals (accounting for 22 per cent of the total in 1999), aerospace (11 per cent) and motor vehicles and parts (9 per cent). The seeming inability of the government to raise the level of investment in research and innovation by firms is again an often heard refrain in national economic policy debates.

There is concern about the lack of business R&D investment relative to international competition. The DTI-sponsored annual survey of R&D expenditure in firms, the UK R&D Scoreboard (Department of Trade and Industry, 2001a), showed that the average UK company R&D intensity is about half of the international intensity. However, the Scoreboard points out that interpretation of this figure needs to take into account two big differences between the UK and other developed economies. The UK has a substantially R&D intensive pharmaceuticals sector (which accounts for nearly 40 per cent of all UK R&D) and a large oil and gas sector (accounting for 31 per cent of the total sales of all the R&D Scoreboard companies). The first is highly R&D intensive and the second has a very low intensity – the two largely cancelling out one another in the overall average.

Of particular importance in considering the environment for research joint ventures is the high degree of internationalization of the UK's business R&D. While 23 per cent of intramural BERD came from overseas in 1999, 38 per cent of extramural R&D expenditure by UK firms was spent overseas.

2. Government Funding of Research and Development

The overall context is that the UK's gross expenditure on R&D (GERD) was £16.7 billion in 1999, equivalent to 1.83 per cent of GDP. In real terms this has fallen from 2.2 per cent in 1985 and places the UK below the OECD average and just above the EU average (Office of Science and Technology, 2001). Since 1997 there has been a slight increase, somewhat larger in civil R&D. However, knowledge-based industries provide 51 per cent of business sector value-added and grew at 4.1 per cent per annum in the period 1985–96 (both figures place the UK fourth highest among OECD countries, according to the OECD Science and Technology and Industry Outlook, 2000). Scientific performance is also strong. With one per cent of the world's population, the UK funds 4.5 per cent of the world's science, produces 8 per cent of the world's scientific papers and receives 9 per cent of citations (Rigby and Georghiou, 2002, p. 109–58).

Figure 9.1 shows the main actors involved in the funding and performance of research in the United Kingdom and Figure 9.2 shows the flow of funding between them. Key features to note are that industry is the largest performer of R&D, accounting for 66 per cent of the total, followed by universities with 20 per cent and government laboratories with 13 per cent. Industry is also the largest funder of R&D, spent mainly in its own premises but also accounting for 7.27 per cent of higher education research income. Defence remains a large sector of the economy.

Universities are funded for research through what is known as the dual support system. Higher Education Funding Councils (separate bodies for England, Scotland, Wales and Northern Ireland, with funds derived from ministries responsible for education) provide general funding, used mainly for academic salaries and research infrastructure, while Research Councils (with funds derived from the Office of Science and Technology in the Department of Trade and Industry) provide funding for projects (including salaries of contract researchers), research training and centres on a competitive peer-reviewed basis. Some of the Research Councils also operate their own institutes. The other principal funding source for research is the charitable, non-profit sector, notably the Wellcome Trust which is the largest single funder of medical research. Universities and Research Council institutes collectively form what is generally referred to as the 'Science Base'.

Other Government Departments may commission research from universities or from Research Council institutes, as well as from their own current and previous (now privatized) laboratories and from the private sector. This research is almost entirely applied and oriented to the mission of the ministry concerned.

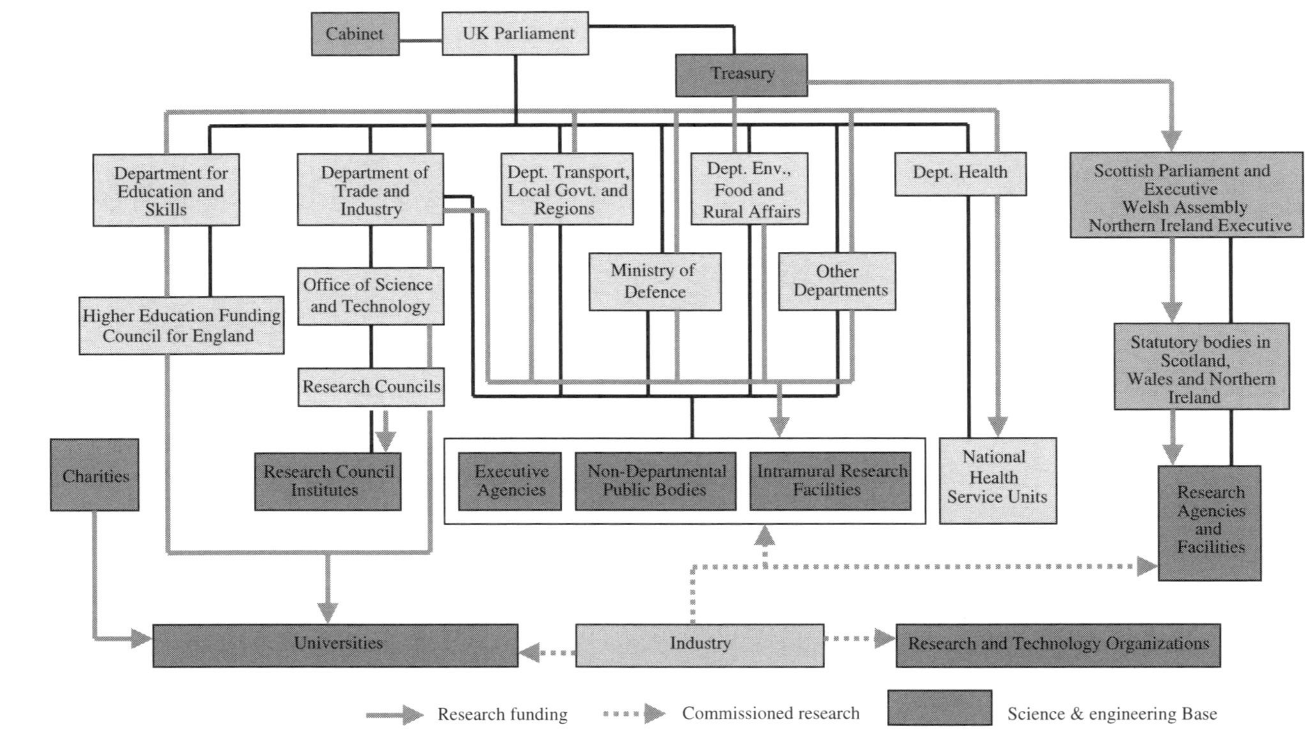

Source: Paul Cunningham, PREST.

Figure 9.1   UK funding and performance of R&D

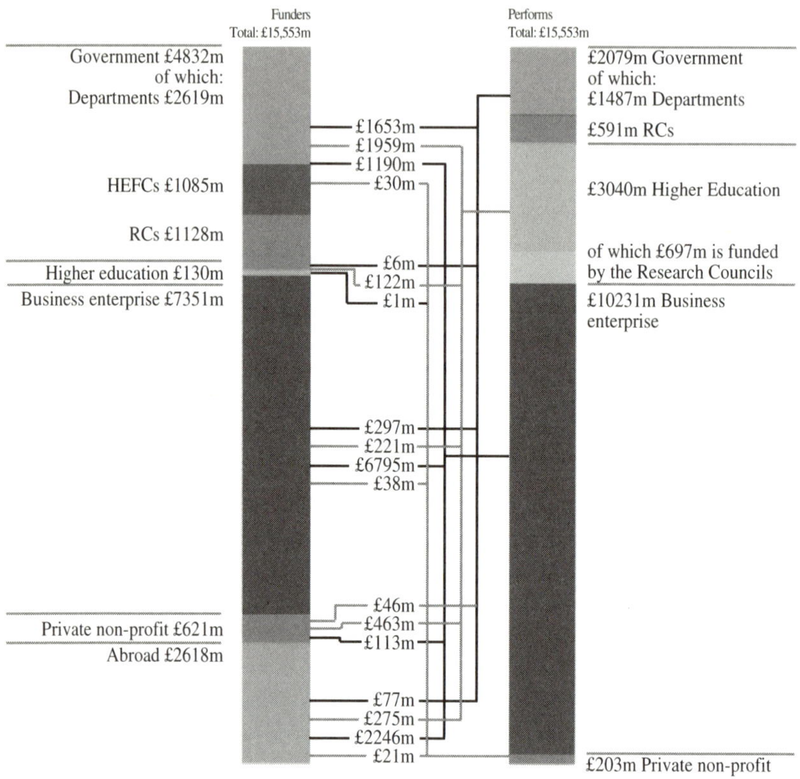

Source: SET Statistics 2000, Office of Science and Technology.

Figure 9.2   The flow of funds for UK R&D, 1998–99

THE RISE OF COLLABORATIVE R&D – THE ALVEY PROGRAMME

The first major programme to promote collaborative R&D in the UK – and in Europe – (in parallel with the beginnings of the European Commission's ESPRIT Programme) was the Alvey Programme for research in advanced information technologies, named after the chairman of the committee recommending the initiative. The programme, which began in 1983, was planned to have a five-year duration, and had a budget of £350 million, of which £100 million would come from industry and £250 million from government departments (Defence, Industry, and the academic research councils). It covered four major areas of information technology: software engineering, man-machine interface, silicon architectures (VLSI) and intelligent knowledge-based systems.

It was remarkable that a programme on this scale could have emerged during the early years of Margaret Thatcher's Conservative administration. A combination of pressure groups (including the indigenous IT sector, users of IT, academic researchers and the popular and technical press and media) managed to convince the responsible minister to support the programme, despite the prevailing government policy at that time of minimal intervention in industry.

The rationale for the programme was based upon several factors. The general background was that the UK was experiencing a period in which, for the first time, the 'information revolution', or 'micro-chip revolution' became constant themes of public debate. It was recognized, moreover, that IT was not just a single industry, but one which was necessary to all other industries. More directly, the perceived threat of far-eastern, particularly Japanese, industrial competition became an insistent part of economic policy-making. The United Kingdom's experience of devastating competition in the automobile, shipbuilding, motorcycle and consumer electronics markets led commentators to predict which industries would be next to be targeted. When the Japanese 'Fifth Generation' computer research initiative was announced, with the rather ambitious stated targets characteristic of such programmes in Japan, UK policy-makers (along with their European and US counterparts) were panicked into considering their own. The structure of the Alvey Programme was also a response to the Japanese 'threat'. It was thought that the Japanese form of cooperative R&D (archetypally in MITI's VLSI programme: see Guy and Arnold, 1986), with many industrial partner firms which subsequently commercialized separately, was particularly suitable for the IT sector. For the UK, the proposed response was that academic and defence research would have to be harnessed, together with the large and small firms composing the IT sector. The research was to be collaborative (government, industry, academia), and focused on 'enabling technologies', in a precompetitive market environment.

In support of this diversion from orthodox government policy, standard economic arguments were rehearsed concerning the 'public goods' aspects of research activities. It was recognized that performers of research were not able to appropriate the full benefits of their work, and that, therefore, there was a strong argument for government subsidy in order to redress the free-market bias against precommercial research. However, this argument was a convenient rationalization of the exceptional policy being followed. The rationale with which the government felt most comfortable was that of their main political concern: the economic success of the UK. Thus, the primary rationale for the Alvey Programme was 'to increase the competitiveness of the UK IT sector'. The means for doing this were threefold: to increase the effective size of the units performing research, whose results would then feed through into commercial markets, and to harness the undoubted strength of the research institutions of the UK in a mode calculated to generate wealth, rather than purely to win Nobel Prizes. Also, the strength of defence-related research could be transferred to the civil sector: an aim much pursued by governments of all persuasions. Academic researchers in these areas found that their chances of gaining funding outside the programme were extremely limited.

The Alvey Programme also broke new ground in an entirely different way: it was subject to the earliest, and perhaps largest ever, formal 'real-time evaluation' of an R&D policy initiative. This was carried out with the dual objective of assisting the management of the Programme, and to assist with future policy initiatives of a similar type. Indeed the evaluation fed back into the rationale for subsequent collaborative research by identifying at an early stage the key motivations of participants for collaborative R&D. Notably, it established the predominance of the desire to acquire complementary expertise, with smaller numbers of participants taking advantage of opportunities for risk and cost-sharing and the establishment of standards. The final report of the evaluation, published in 1991, summarized the various impacts which Alvey had produced (Guy et al., 1991).

The main focus of attention in the earlier part of the Alvey Programme was, naturally, the success it had in producing new research results in the area of enabling technology. In one respect the judgement was that it had been very successful in this, most of the individual projects having fulfilled their initial objectives. However, the political sponsors of the initiative had not appreciated the lags which are involved in commercializing these results, and their feeling was that the Programme had been unsuccessful in producing the quick, commercial results which they had expected. Proponents of the 'long-view', however, are even now, years after the end of the last Alvey project, seeing commercial products and industrial processes which owe their existence to work within the Programme, including major products in mainframe computing and mobile telephony. The strategy that focused on 'enabling technologies' by definition would not produce quick results, and it would have been inappropriate for public subsidy to private firms to be aimed at this. On the negative side, even in areas of technological success, the results were sometimes not exploited because of the withdrawal from appropriate markets of the firms concerned, or even the demise of firms. For example, in the VLSI area, the largest single recipient of funds was GEC, which withdrew from most of the markets addressed even before the conclusion of projects within the Programme.

The Alvey Programme did give a head start to UK firms in the experience of R&D collaboration. It began before the large-scale European R&D programmes, and UK firms therefore had been forced to address the practical problems of collaboration in R&D. These problems included managing distributed research projects, addressing the issues of intellectual property rights which have since come to dominate discussions of collaboration, as well as the other problems encountered when working with commercial competitors. UK firms took a prominent part in European programmes subsequently, and often became project managers (of course the use of English as the means of communication inside projects also had an important effect here).

The impact upon the volume, or quantity of research carried out was not possible to determine with confidence. The timescale of the Programme, its small scale in relation to overall industry R&D spend, and the external environment of economic recession, all tended to cloud the impacts. Certainly no direct estimates of the impact on 'the competitiveness of the UK IT industry' were thought convincing. The judgement of the evaluators was that, at best, the Programme slowed down the decline in competitiveness of the UK IT industry. With some notable exceptions, this seems to have been borne out in the years since.

However, it was significant that the firms involved did change their views of the commercial environment. Rather than identifying their UK counterparts as their prime source of competition, they began to see the European, or even the world, markets as their arena, and competition as global. Again, this ran alongside similar changes in other industries, so it is wrong to attribute this change to Alvey alone.

THE SECOND PHASE OF COLLABORATIVE SUPPORT: ADVANCED TECHNOLOGY PROGRAMMES

Alvey had initially been intended as a ten-year initiative (Oakley and Owen, 1989). Plans for a follow-up to the Alvey Programme began in 1986 when a committee recommended a programme of applications, involving users, as well as continuing collaborative research. After a long delay, in 1988 the Government responded in a White Paper (Department of Trade and Industry, 1988), which rejected the applications programme but accepted that 'some resources should be devoted to a national initiative complementary to ESPRIT'. This was the first sign of shift to a position where the Framework Programmes were regarded as providing sufficient support for collaborative R&D in the UK. At a national level there would be two mechanisms, Advanced Technology Programmes, which would principally cater for company-company collaboration, though also with academic involvement where appropriate, and LINK, an initiative where the focus was more on academic-industrial collaboration. In general, the White Paper emphasized priority for projects demonstrating mixed scientific and technological disciplines and distance from the market, though offering a good prospect for market exploitation. It also marked the formal end of government support for innovation in single companies (except on a small-scale for SMEs).

Support for research joint ventures also encountered a significant change in the funding rules. Industrial participants in Alvey had received matching funds from government with their academic partners receiving full additional costs in the normal model for academic support. Under the new rules (known as 'LINK rules' but also applied to the Advanced Technology Programmes (ATPs) including Alvey's successor) a 50 per cent ceiling for government subsidy was imposed upon the project as a whole, with any funds for academic partners counting towards that total. Since academics would and could not work for less than they had previously received, the effect was to substantially depress the sums available for industry. With the much smaller programmes that were becoming common, these schemes were no longer supporting strategic national projects. Larger firms could either take the more favourable terms available from EC programmes or else make a judgement that the low funding levels did not justify the bureaucracy of taking part. At least one IT company decided to take part without any subsidy precisely to avoid these constraints.

The direct successor to Alvey, the Information Engineering Advanced Technology Programme (IEATP), was addressing a much changed industrial structure in the IT sector. Larger electronics companies had consolidated through a series of mergers and acquisitions, with GEC predominant. Overall, however, the industry had become less concentrated, leading the IEATP to focus more on the needs of smaller companies than had been the case with Alvey. A second major trend had been the rise of foreign ownership, with North American companies accounting for well over 50 per cent of the computing and software sub-sector by value and the UK's leading company, ICL, acquired by Fujitsu. The total public contribution to the IEATP was £56.7 million, of which £32.1 million was for industry.

IEATP was the largest ATP by far. Other ATPs and LINK programmes were much more focused on specific technologies. However, the mechanism was not to last for long. When the seminal White Paper on Science, Engineering and Technology 'Realising Our Potential' (Office of Science and Technology, 1993) was published it was accompanied by an announcement from DTI that innovation policy was to be refocused. The new innovation policy was to place much greater focus on technology transfer and access to technology and services. The ATP mechanism was abandoned, though LINK was retained with more restricted support. The change was partly motivated by a realization that a small number of large firms were the primary beneficiaries of these schemes, while a large majority of smaller firms were not being reached by innovation policies. Hence, the UK was left without a policy instrument which has as its main focus the promotion of industry-industry R&D collaboration.

PROMOTION OF INDUSTRY-ACADEMIC RESEARCH COLLABORATION

Promotion of better academic-industry links was a preoccupation of the UK's policy for research, technology and innovation throughout the twentieth century (Georghiou, 2002), with the problem usually being defined in terms of the disparity between successful scientific performance and somewhat less spectacular performance in industrial innovation. Nonetheless, in the present period such linkages are at record levels. A survey on behalf of the Higher Education Funding Councils found that there had been large-scale growth in the scale, number and variety of linkages (Howells, Nedeva and Georghiou, 1998). For example, research funding of universities by UK industry had grown by 30 per cent in three years to a level of £188 million in 1996/97, a total of 11 per cent of all research income. This figure does not include research income from national and European collaborative programmes. Research commissioned directly by industry accounted for 59 per cent of the total, income received in the context of European collaborative schemes 27 per cent and income received in the context of national collaborative schemes 9 per cent, with the balance coming from regional collaborations. On the negative side, collaboration with industry is highly concentrated, with seven universities accounting for one third of the total, while the bottom half collectively only received eight per cent of the total.

While universities are motivated to collaborate primarily by the access to research funding, the survey found that collaboration generally only took place when the goals of both partners were being satisfied. Mutual trust and a professional business-like approach by the academic partners are seen as the keys to success. The major barriers arose from changes in corporate objectives during the lifetime of the project making the project less relevant (in some cases caused by a change of ownership and others by a change of strategy). From the academic side the main barrier was the lack of incentive structures in universities to reward successful collaborators.

Policies to promote such linkages have built cumulatively over time.

Before the 1970s, linkages were generally informal or else involved bilateral contracts. During that decade areas of university research of particular relevance to industry (for example, polymer engineering) began to be 'ring-fenced' by the Research Councils and given more active management with some industry participation (a model known as 'Directed Programmes'). Two of the most successful schemes began in that decade and are still running: Co-operative Awards in Science and Engineering (CASE) studentships target PhD projects on problems of particular interest to firms, which co-fund and co-supervise them; the Teaching Company Scheme involves graduates working for firms on specific projects under academic supervision (Senker and Senker, 1994). As described above, the 1980s were dominated by collaborative R&D programmes. Of these, the one with the most specific remit to promote academic-industry links was the LINK initiative.

1.   The LINK Initiative and Recent Policy Developments

Since 1986, LINK, a government-wide initiative, has been the Government's principal mechanism for supporting research partnerships between the industry/commercial sector and representatives of the science base/research base such as universities, research council institutes, government research establishments, hospitals or independent research organizations. Its principal aims are to aid innovation and wealth creation and promote the quality of life. LINK is mainly managed through programmes covering discrete technology or generic product areas and research is precompetitive and strategic. Each programme receives sponsorship from relevant government departments or research councils and consists of a number of collaborative research projects involving industrial and academic/science base partners. Within each two to three year project, up to 50 per cent of funding is received from the sponsoring department or research council with the industrial partner providing the balance of the funds. There are currently 72 LINK programmes of which 27 are open to new proposals.

In response to a review, the LINK programme was re-launched in 1995 with a streamlined administration and greater strategic focus. Subsequent programmes have been closely aligned with priorities emerging from the Foresight Programme (see below).

Since 1997, 441 LINK projects have been approved involving the participation of over 800 different companies. For flexibility, the LINK family also includes three LINK 'franchises' (including EPSRC's Innovative Manufacturing Initiative), and a number of 'stand alone' projects including the Foresight LINK Awards. Government expenditure on LINK projects was £41million in 2000–2001 (from DTI, other departments and the research councils). This sum was more than equalled by support from industrial participants.

In response to priorities identified by Foresight, six new LINK programmes, a stand alone project and the Foresight LINK Awards have been announced since September 2000, worth at least £154 million, of which the Government contribution is £77 million. These include the largest ever LINK programme, E-Science Grid technologies (£40 million). Additionally, two existing LINK programmes have been extended, with Government providing a further £15.5 million. The third Foresight LINK Awards competition was run in 2001 for research projects in specific Foresight priority areas outside the coverage of current LINK programmes. The seven winning projects were announced in July 2001 and are supported by £12 million funding from DTI.

In 2002 LINK was the subject of a strategic review. This aimed to consider the fundamental rationale for LINK and how it fits in the overall pattern of innovation policies. Since LINK was launched there have been many changes in the policy landscape. Of most significance has been a shift in emphasis away from support for the larger firms which perform most R&D in the UK (see above) and towards policies aimed at stimulating entrepreneurship and the formation of new science-based firms. Other initiatives such as Faraday Partnerships seek to link universities and independent research and technology organizations with small and medium-sized firms. The most recent policy initiative (as at June 2003) has been the announcement in the 2002 Budget of a tax credit for R&D expenditure applying to firms of all sizes (a previous initiative was restricted to small firms). During a long consultation period industry lobbied successfully for a credit based upon the total volume of spending rather than the incremental credit which would have been the government's preference.

There has been no visible knock-on effect on the amount of funding available for other industry support schemes to date, though a broad review of business support was undertaken by the Department of Trade and Industry. The principal issues raised during consultations have been that there are too many schemes, with many having a low value and impact, and that there is a lack of a strategic overview. A new organizational structure for the Department is based upon three strategic priorities, Innovation, Enterprise and Competitive Frameworks (Department of Trade and Industry 2001b). However, it is likely that the existence of the fiscal incentive is likely to preclude any significant expansion of direct support for collaboration.

Table 9.1   Departmental/Research Council expenditure on LINK programmes (£k)

	1995/96	1996/97	1997/98	1998/99	1999/2000	2000/01
Dept of Trade & Industry[1]	12551	13033	11691	9498	7475	7431
Engineering & Physical Sciences Research Council/SERC[2]	10565	9941	8393	14878	15532	17161
Ministry of Agriculture, Food & Fisheries	2741	4038	3062	5171	5038	6848
Biotechnology & Biological Sciences Research Council/AFRC	2206	2531	2483	2844	3932	3314
Dept of Transport	729	382	N/A	N/A	N/A	N/A
Dept of Environment, Transport & the Regions[3]	N/A	N/A	960	863	943	1254
Dept of Environment	296	429	N/A	N/A	N/A	N/A
Natural Environment Research Council	670	968	1154	1300	1028	817
Medical Research Council	632	540	911	1070	1197	1696
Dept. Health	364	724	1029	1452	1795	1511
Ministry of Defence	244	234	N/A	N/A	N/A	N/A
Scottish Office/Scottish Executive	191	144	139	154	382	447
Economic & Social Research Council	N/A	N/A	64	215	280	582
Northern Ireland Office	N/A	N/A	N/A	120	N/A	N/A
Home Office	N/A	N/A	N/A	N/A	N/A	50
Total[4]	31188	32965	29884	37566	37601	41110

Source: LINK Directorate.

Notes:
1: Includes expenditure in 1997/98 to 1999/2000 through the Environmental Best Practice Programme (joint fund with DETR).
2: Figures include IMI LINK spend from 1998/99.
3: DoT and DoE merged to form DETR in July 1997.
4: Figures may not add up due to rounding.

EUROPEAN PROGRAMMES: THE FRAMEWORK PROGRAMME AND EUREKA

1. UK Participation in the Framework Programme

UK organizations are enthusiastic participants in the EU's Framework Programme, not least because of the scarcity of national resources for collaborative R&D. This is not coincidental – it should be noted that the UK operates a system of attribution, whereby the UK contribution to the Framework Programme budget is attributed to and normally deducted from the budget of the national ministry, which is responsible for the area concerned. The intention is to make national administrators treat these programmes as part of their own budget and, in theory at least, to optimize the balance between national and EU support. There are obvious flaws in this logic since it cannot account for the situation where the two types of spend are complementary and synergistic. In 1997–98 a sum of £190.9 million was attributed to the Department of Trade and Industry (excluding the Office of Science and Technology), which, since the UK receives approximately what it contributes, provides a reasonable estimate of the sums being spent on industrial participation in EU research joint ventures, together with some other EU innovation policy measures. Though not yet clearly visible in the statistics, there is a strong suspicion that the level of industrial participation by the UK in the Framework Programme has declined substantially as a direct consequence of the decline in R&D in the ICT sectors in the UK.

2. UK Participation in the EUREKA Initiative

It should be remembered that since its launch in 1985 the UK has been a participant in the EUREKA Initiative. Since EUREKA is funded and largely administered on a national basis, this should be counted among the array of national policy instruments for the support of collaborative R&D. EUREKA has sought to differentiate itself from the Framework Programme by offering a 'bottom-up' structure, giving firms wide discretion in terms of the technological areas covered, and positioning itself closer to the market. Some EUREKA projects (for example JESSI and Prometheus) have been large strategic initiatives, effectively programmes within a programme. While still continuing, EUREKA funds within the UK have declined over the years and since the 1993 Science Engineering and Technology White Paper have largely been confined to small firms. EUREKA is unusual in providing a collaborative R&D initiative in which some industrial participants do not receive funding at all, though evaluations have shown that these R&D collaborations are less likely to achieve success. Despite a history of being one of the most popular countries in terms of the provision of partner firms, the UK's current EUREKA participation has dwindled to a small proportion of its former levels, largely as a result of lack of funding, combined with a lack of priority for assigning personnel to promote the initiative. The UK is now far behind its former peers in France and Germany and lags behind medium-sized participants such as the Netherlands and Spain. An attempt is being made to stop this decline through the allocation of a dedicated budget for EUREKA project participants for the first time (previously UK EUREKA project participants had to compete for funds from other existing government programmes). It is too early to say whether this will encourage greater participation of UK firms.

FORESIGHT AND THE NEW INNOVATION POLICIES

The centrepiece of UK innovation policy from 1993 to the end of that decade was the Foresight Programme (initially called the Technology Foresight Programme). This has pursued the objectives of stimulating partnership between industry and the science base, identifying priorities for public support for science, and promoting a foresight culture in UK industry. Panels of experts, usually industry-led, consulted widely before reporting on the future for their areas. A major programme of dissemination and support for networking followed, with many intermediary bodies taking part. The connection to collaborative R&D comes in more than one way. At a strategic level the initial enthusiasm of industry for foresight may be seen as a recognition that innovation frequently takes place in a collaborative context. With this in mind, a process which facilitates the creation of a shared vision of the future with competitors, suppliers, customers and research collaborators becomes an attractive component of strategy-making (Georghiou, 1996). More practically, the follow-up activities to foresight are oriented towards networking, including a dedicated R&D support programme to fund foresight priorities. In its first round this was known as the Foresight Challenge fund and involved £30 million of public spending, matched and exceeded by industrial funding. As with LINK, the focus is on academic-industrial partnership but most projects involve multiple firms. The scheme is now known as Foresight LINK Awards (see section 5.1 above). There is an upper size limit of £2 million on the total public sector contribution to a project.

Other DTI schemes to support technology transfer, access and management best-practice do not directly support collaborative R&D but may advise firms to seek collaborative solutions to their problems and give them assistance with improving their management capabilities. This trend has continued under the Labour government. In its first major innovation policy statement, the 1998 Competitiveness White Paper 'Our Competitive Future: Building the Knowledge Driven Economy', a whole section was entitled 'Collaborate to Compete'. However, most of the measures here concern learning, benchmarking and the promotion of industrial clusters, particularly in biotechnology. Out of DTI's innovation budget of £207 million in 1998, itself small by international standards, about 13 per cent was spent on cooperative research, principally for the industrial component of academic-industry cooperation.

COMPETITION POLICY AND RESEARCH JOINT VENTURES

1. Overview

The United Kingdom has pursued policies to maintain competition between firms and the efficient working of markets for several centuries. The basis of modern competition policy, to prevent restrictive trade practices, was established in the 1970s but has been evolving since the 1948 Monopolies and Restrictive Practices (Inquiry and Control) Act (Fishwick, 1993). The 1998 Competition Act came into force in March 2000. This new Act seeks to greatly strengthen UK competition policy and align it with that of the EU. None of the UK policies specifically deal with industrial R&D collaboration, since it is not normally concerned with the market end of business practice. However, as will be described below, consideration of research and development has not been absent in the regulation of mergers, and it may be that the new regime will be required to acknowledge the specific issues associated with collaborative research and its exploitation.

2. The Basis of UK Competition Policy

UK policy has been concerned historically with the monitoring and regulation of restrictive agreements between firms (presumed to be against the public interest) and with the control of merger behaviour. The implementation of merger policy has been through various forms of commission (first named the Monopolies and Restrictive Practices Commission, now called the Competition Commission). While attending to matters of the public interest in consideration of mergers, there has also been a long-standing tendency to encourage 'concentration and rationalization to promote greater efficiency and international competitiveness in British industry' (Pickering, 1974). This is worth bearing in mind when considering the UK's attitude to regulation of competition and collaboration.

The basic outlines of competition policy in the UK today (Young and Metcalfe, 1994) were consolidated by the introduction in the 1973 Fair Trading Act. It created a Director General of Fair Trading (DGFT) with support from an Office of Fair Trading (OFT). The DGFT was legally able to refer cases of restrictive practice to the Monopolies and Mergers Commission (MMC). Once a referral had been made, the MMC was charged with deciding, on a case-by-case basis, whether there was in fact a monopoly, and, importantly for the context of considering research and development, whether or not it operated against the public interest. For this, the Commission had to balance questions of efficiency gains against the abuse of market power. The Commission was expected to consider factors such as the maintenance of competition of supply in the UK, the balance of industrial activity and employment in the UK, the competitiveness of UK firms in foreign markets and cost reductions due to implementation of new technologies and techniques. Where the MMC found that the firm(s) were acting against the public interest, then they were legally prevented from pursuing the activities. Investigations under this Act could be very slow (as they required an assessment of the structure of demand and supply throughout the market for the reference product) and were often perceived to be ineffective.

The Competition Act of 1980 allowed the DGFT to investigate and subsequently refer to the MMC an allegation that a single firm, not necessarily possessing a 25 per cent share of any market, was carrying out a specific 'anticompetitive practice'. This set up a much simpler procedure (six months) for the investigation of conduct by one company. The 1980 Act also brought within the remit of the MMC the utilities ('public monopolies'), which were being privatized during those years (Office of Fair Trading, 1981).

3.   Research and Development and Competition Policy

Given the parameters of the law, it is hardly surprising that research joint ventures have not themselves been the subject of any MMC investigation. However, the Commission has examined claims as part of evidence in merger cases that R&D might suffer or benefit. A high profile case between two major participants in the Alvey Programme for collaborative research (see above), GEC and Plessey, was considered by the MMC in 1986 (HMSO, 1986). GEC argued that Plessey would not be able to sustain the

R&D needed for future survival, and that merger with GEC would allow a more diverse and cost-effective R&D portfolio. Plessey held the opposite view: that a merger would reduce the variety in research. Interestingly, the Ministry of Defence and Department of Industry put forward conflicting evidence, and the MMC decided that a rationalization of R&D would not make up for the potential loss of competition in research between the two existing research organizations. Three years later the MMC allowed GEC and Siemens to acquire Plessey, but only after specifying undertakings relating to access to technology and the ownership and management of R&D (HMSO, 1989).[2] Since 1980 it has been possible for the DGFT to investigate single issue cases of anti-competitive practice, but none has arisen involving R&D.

4. 'A New Dawn for Competition Policy'?[3]

The 1998 Competition Act, which came into force in March 2000, is seen as a marked change towards domestic competition policy in the UK. It replaces the previous legislation and aligns UK domestic competition law with the Treaty of Rome Articles 81 and 82 (formerly Articles 85 and 86). It prohibits both anti-competitive agreements and the abuse of a dominant position and gives greater powers of investigation and enforcement to the DGFT. Significant fines will be payable for breaches of the prohibitions. The Act is part of other measures related to competition and industry regulation (for example of the utilities), which seek to put the consumer in a stronger position.

In April 1999 the MMC was replaced by a Competition Commission[4] which will hear appeals against decisions under the prohibitions, as well as taking on the existing reporting functions of the MMC. The new Commission has tougher powers of investigation and stiff penalties for firms which breach the prohibition. Interim measures allow cartels and serious abuses of market power to be halted pending investigation. It is the government's aim to reduce anti-competitive behaviour in the UK economy, while at the same time reducing the burden for firms by being fully in line with the EU's policies.

The new Competition Act is not likely specifically to affect the formation, or operation, of UK domestic R&D collaboration, as anti-competitive behaviour is generally judged to be at the market, rather than research, end of the collaborative spectrum. However, the broadening of the competition regime and the general nature of the prohibitions mean that if R&D agreements are reported as having an anti-competitive effect then it is likely that the claim would be investigated seriously. It remains to be seen, however, how strict the new competition regime will be in practice.

IPR POLICY

Legal protection of intellectual property rights in the UK goes back more than 500 years. Patents were introduced in order to encourage the import of skills and technology from abroad, and thus gain economic benefits for the monarch, as well as reward the efforts of inventors and innovators. These were followed quickly by the concept of copyright which was a response to the introduction of the new printing technologies. The IPR system has over time gained more specialized forms, and at present can include patents, copyright (now the main instrument for software protection), trade marks, industrial or registered designs, rights in performances and plant varieties. In addition to these, the common law gives other rights, including those concerning confidential commercial information, passing-off and trade libel (Bainbridge, 1994, p. 5).

In general, these rights have been the result of the introduction of new technologies, and have shown remarkable flexibility in their application to novel and unpredicted innovations. However, there have been constant pressures to revise the legal framework, as a result of new technologies and also international harmonization. The UK is party to all the major international agreements in the field of IPRs, from the Paris Convention of 1883 and the Berne Convention of 1886, to the more recent Patent Co-operation Treaty (in force from 1978) and the Agreement on Trade-related Aspects of Intellectual Property Rights (TRIPS), (in force from 1995). As the source of much intellectual property, the UK has been in the forefront of activities aimed at regulating and enforcing IP regulations, for example in the illegal copying of popular music works, and also concerning the pharmaceuticals sector, industries which are amongst the largest exporting industries for the country.

It is increasingly well recognized that IP is the source of wealth in many areas of economic activity in the UK, with the result that more attention is being paid to their protection in many fields, in particular the music, pharmaceuticals and computer industries, but also in the academic research field which had little previous expertise in IP until twenty years ago.

A UK patent is a legal monopoly, granted for a limited duration of 20 years, allowing the owner exclusive rights to use an invention and return on the investment of time and resources which produced the invention. The main legislation is the Patents Act of 1977. Patents are applied for through the UK Patent Office (UKPO), and are awarded on the 'first-to-file' basis in common with most industrial countries (except, of course, the USA). About 70 per cent of applications come from UK residents, and half of the remainder come from Japan and the USA. The European Patent Office (EPO) opened in 1978, causing a decline in numbers of UKPO applications, which were at a level of about 60000 per annum previously, to about 25000 per annum at present.

From an innovation policy perspective, past measures in this field have focused upon improving awareness on patenting and associated issues. Recent measures have included the abolition of patent application fees (in part to enable application through the internet) and measures to simplify tax rules relating to intellectual property (Cunningham and Boden, 1999). IPR continues to be an area of policy concern, particularly the reluctance of small firms to use methods of protection other than secrecy because they lack confidence in their ability to defend their rights. This is seen as a barrier to corporate alliances with larger partners (HM Treasury and Department of Trade and Industry, 1998). A second problem area is that of academic-industrial collaboration where the academic research culture may not be conducive to the establishment of secure IPR. Disputes as to ownership are also a problem.

In national schemes for the support of collaborative R&D, participants are expected to comply with a general framework defining the rights and obligations of those involved during the project and in subsequent exploitation. Participants are also required to produce a signed collaboration agreement. In the Alvey Programme this led to major delays in the commencement of projects as a result of the inexperience of participants (particularly universities which had only just been given property rights from non-collaborative Research Council funding) and through logistical loads on companies' legal departments. In later programmes the benefits of learning and a collaborative culture were evident as the problem largely disappeared. Substantial issues which remain include access to background IP, especially in the software field (Cameron, 1997). While most managers agree on the importance of a legal framework for collaborative R&D, evaluations have shown that it is rarely if ever used in practice.

CONCLUSION

This review of policy support for collaborative R&D in the UK over the past few decades has tracked first the emergence of collaborative research as the dominant policy mechanism in the mid-1980s. At that time it was perceived as the only form of direct support to large firms which could clearly be demonstrated to address a market failure, because of the costs of learning to collaborate and the potential externalities arising in the more open conduct of collaboration. This was followed by an accelerating decline in funding support prompted by a desire to cut spending, a recognition that support was focused upon a small number of relatively profitable large firms, and the decision to leave this type of support to the EU while concentrating the restricted domestic resources upon an information and networking infrastructure. Today, a limited amount of financial support remains, largely linked to Foresight and to a lesser extent EUREKA, but the focus is upon academic-industrial collaboration, with industry-industry cooperation supported either in this context or through non-financial promotion, by means of networking advice and events.

The initial rationale for support for collaborative R&D in the UK, as applied during the planning phase of the Alvey Programme, was in many ways an ex post rationalization of a fait accompli – a government with a strong free-market ideology had nonetheless been persuaded that there was a real threat from developments in Japan and the USA which merited public investment in R&D. To avoid the charge of picking winners, the concept of precompetitive R&D was used as a shield by arguing that firms would work together only until the market phase, at which point they would compete fiercely. This interpretation was backed up by the mistaken view that this was a part of the reason for Japanese success in the MITI-organized collaborative programmes. The identified market failure was that firms would have to overcome a natural reluctance to collaborate, and also that the act of collaboration involved a threshold of overheads, which needed to be offset by subsidy.

As empirical evidence began to accumulate, which demonstrated that collaboration with direct competitors was restricted either to areas such as standards or to technologies which were applied in different national markets, a new emphasis appeared in such programmes. In their second phase they tended to run along the more natural lines of collaboration between users and producers, and promoted the involvement of the science base. However, by this stage, the desire by government to cut public expenditure left industry programmes as an easy target, particularly when it could be argued that the type of alliances which were needed were more likely to emerge at a European level than nationally, and hence that support for collaboration was principally the task of the Framework Programme.

As the systems failure rationale for technology policy began to take hold, the lack of linkages between innovation actors received renewed prominence, but this time, as emphasized throughout this chapter, the focus was on industry-science linkages. Encouragement of direct links between firms remained a goal but the instruments aimed to identify and demonstrate opportunities rather than provide direct incentives.

Finally, a number of factors may have reduced the scope for research joint ventures. It could be argued that a shift in emphasis to bio-sciences has left less room for collaborative R&D. The short distance from the lab to intellectual property in life-science based industries makes industrial collaboration much more difficult than it is in physics-based industries. Another environmental change is the growth in outsourcing of R&D (Howells, 1997), which has tripled its share of business R&D. It can be hypothesized that much of the 'precompetitive R&D' which was the subject of such collaborations is now outsourced to universities or to specialist R&D companies. The internationalization of R&D may also have overtaken the need for national collaboration. Mergers and acquisitions have substantially reduced the number of major players, and in some cases led to an international reorganization of R&D assets. Global firms with global customers will certainly be engaged in technological collaboration (Coombs and Georghiou, 2002) but this may be beyond the scale of public support. Lastly, and most controversially, there is a sense that UK governments have failed to perceive that their international competitors have consistently offered higher levels of support for collaborative R&D and continue to do so, either at national or at regional level. An attempt to level the national playing field may have left the international field biased against UK-based firms. The relative decline of industrial R&D in the UK means that the efficacy of policies in this area remains an issue of pressing national concern.

NOTES

1. The authors would like to acknowledge the contribution of Carole McKinlay in collecting information for this chapter, and of Paul Cunningham who produced Figure 9.1.
2. Of course in these cases there were issues not only of competition but national security, both GEC and Plessey being involved in defence products.
3. Derek Morris, Chairman of the new Competition Commission gave a speech on 24 November 1999 entitled 'A new dawn for competition policy in the UK'. See http://www.mmc.gov.uk/
4. http://www.competition-commission.gov.uk/

REFERENCES

Bainbridge, D. (1994), *Intellectual Property*, London: Pitman.
Cameron, Hugh (1997), 'IPR Handling in Collaborative R&D', report to the European Commission DG III, Brussels: European Commission.
Coombs, Rod and Luke Georghiou (2002), 'A new "industrial ecology"', *Science*, **296**, 19 April, 471.
Cunningham, Paul and Mark Boden (1999), 'Monitoring, updating and disseminating developments in innovation and technology diffusion in the member states', report to DGXIII, EIMS 98/181, 98/182, 98/183, Luxembourg: European Commission.
Department of Trade and Industry (1988), *The Department for Enterprise*, Cmnd 278, London: HMSO.

Department of Trade and Industry (2001a), *UK R&D Scoreboard 2001*, London: Department of Trade and Industry, available at http://www.innovation.gov.uk/ projects/rd_scoreboard/introfr.html.

Department of Trade and Industry (2001b), *Progress Report on Two Reviews*, November, London: Department of Trade and Industry.

Fishwick, F. (1993), *Making Sense of Competition Policy*, London: Kogan Page Ltd.

Georghiou, Luke (1996), 'The UK Technology Foresight Programme', *Futures*, **28**(4), 359–377.

Georghiou, Luke (2001), 'The United Kingdom national system of research, technology and innovation', in Philippe Larédo and Philippe Mustar (eds), *Research and Innovation Policies in the New Global Economy. An International Comparative Analysis*, Cheltenham, UK and Northampton, US: Edward Elgar.

Guy, Ken and Erik Arnold (1986), *Parallel Convergence*, London: Frances Pinter.

Guy, Ken, Luke Georghiou, Paul Quintas, Hugh Cameron, Mike Hobday and Tim Ray (1991), *Evaluation of the Alvey Programme for Advanced Information Technology*, London: HMSO.

HMSO (1986), 'The General Electric Company PLC and The Plessey Company PLC Monopolies and Mergers Commission case', Cmnd 9795, May, London: HMSO.

HMSO (1989), 'The General Electric Company plc, Siemens AG and The Plessey Company plc Monopolies and Mergers Commission case', Cmnd 676, April, London: HMSO.

HM Treasury and Department of Trade and Industry (1998), 'Innovating for the Future: Investing in R&D', consultation document for the 1998 budget, London: HM Treasury.

Howells, Jeremy (1997), 'Research and Technology Outsourcing', CRIC discussion paper 6, University of Manchester, England, http://les1.man.ac.uk/cric/papers .htm.

Howells, Jeremy, Maria Nedeva and Luke Georghiou (1998), *Industry-Academic Links in the UK*, Bristol: Higher Education Funding Council for England.

Oakley, B. and K. Owen (1989), *Alvey – Britain's strategic computing initiative*, Cambridge, MA:The MIT Press.

Office of Fair Trading (1981), *Monopolies and Anti-competitive Practices – A Guide to the Provisions of the Fair Trading Act 1973 & the Competition Act 1980*, London: UK Office of Fair Trading.

Office of Science and Technology (1993), *Realising Our Potential: a Strategy for Science, Engineering and Technology*, Cmnd 2250, London: HMSO.

Office of Science and Technology (2000), *SET Statistics 2000*, London: Office of Science and Technology.

Office of Science and Technology (2001), *SET statistics 2001*, London: Office of Science and Technology.

Organisation for Economic Co-operation and Development (2000), *Science, Technology and Industry Outlook 2000*, Paris: OECD.

Pickering, J. B. (1974), *Industrial Structure and Market Conduct*, Oxford: Martin Robertson.

Rigby, John and Luke Georghiou (2002), 'Industry-science relationships in the United Kingdom', in *Benchmarking Industry-Science Relationships*, Paris: OECD.

Senker, Peter and Jackie Senker (1994), 'Transferring technology and expertise from

universities to industry: Britain's Teaching Company Scheme', *New Technology, Work and Employment*, **9**(2), 81–92.
Young, David and Stan Metcalfe (1994), 'Competition policy', chapter 5 in M. Artis and N. Lee (eds), *The Economics of the European Union: Policy and Analysis*, Oxford: Oxford University Press.

10. Collaborative research and technology policy in France

Mireille Matt

The aim of this chapter is to characterize the French technology and research system with a specific focus on R&D cooperation between the different economic actors.

To provide an idea of the characteristics of the French S&T system this chapter underlines the following facts. France has developed a vast public research sector. More than 20 public research organizations and 160 universities and 'Grandes Ecoles' execute 37 per cent of the total R&D and employ 53 per cent of all researchers in the French economy. On the business side, R&D efforts are concentrated on a small number of sectors and a small number of firms, mainly large companies. In order to innovate, firms collaborate with the private sector but not very often with public research actors.

The public support of industry is rather small: in 1999, 12 per cent of research conducted by firms was funded by public funds. Of these public funds devoted to industry, 85 per cent were distributed to carry out defence and large-scale programmes. Mission-oriented policy tools are largely predominant in financial terms. Moreover a very restrictive number of firms benefit from these funds: mainly the national champions created by these policies. The organization of these programmes, in which secrecy is important and subcontracting is not, entails few externalities. The general French industrial policy, which includes technology policy, reinforces this concentration effect: creation and control of large companies, public monopolies and protected cartels. The European Union forced France to open up its protected sector (telecom, air traffic, gas and so on) to competition.

This general configuration of the system explains why France exhibits strong scientific capabilities in fields far from the market, a rather weak position in patents with a specialization in aerospace and earth transportation (the large-scale programmes effect). This statement could be interpreted by the fact that the public research sector meets with difficulties to transfer research results and to diffuse knowledge towards the private world. This partial conclusion is reinforced by inadequate connections between the two worlds. It is also reinforced by the lack of incentives for public researchers to diffuse their results and by the lack of attention given to SMEs.

Since the mid-1990s, the French innovation policy has followed new orientations reinforced in 1999 by the innovation bill. The general objective was to reduce the above-mentioned weaknesses. More precisely, one of the aims is to create connections by inducing R&D cooperation between a wide range of actors in the national arena, with a specific attention paid to SMEs. The new tools cover actions such as the funding of innovation networks, the creation of public incubator structures and seed-capital means, supporting specific disciplines, supporting the creation of new innovative firms, providing incentives in the public sector to diffuse their knowledge. These changes will probably induce an evolution of the French system, but the financial resources devoted to these new tools remain very small.

Fostering R&D cooperation between a wide range of actors is a rather new strategy in the French S&T policy. This could probably explain why the French competition law did not devote any provision to the specific case of agreements: that is, R&D cooperative agreements belong to the category of agreements which could be exempted by decree but no decree exists to this end.

THE FRENCH S&T POLICY SYSTEM

The objective of this part is to present the main characteristics of the French innovation system. France is characterized by a decline of the national R&D effort, by a vast public research sector and by a concentrated private one. Even if the importance of defence contracts and large-scale technological programmes has decreased since the eighties, they still constitute major technology policy tools in monetary terms.

1.   General Trends and Actors

A decline of the national R&D effort and a decrease in the proportion of public funding

The overall R&D structure can be synthesized through the main aggregates in terms of funding and execution published by the French Ministry of Research and Technology.[1]

The national R&D expenditure (DNRD) represents the funding of R&D by the public and the private sector. In 1999, it amounted to 196 billion FF (2.2 per cent of GDP). Since 1994, we witness a decrease of the ratio DNRD/GDP. The proportion of publicly funded research decreased

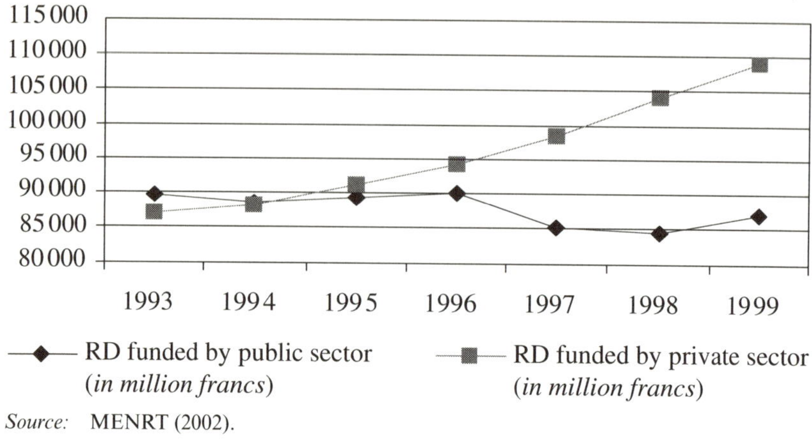

Source: MENRT (2002).

*Figure 10.1   Evolution of the R&D funded by the public and the private
           sectors*

from 70 per cent in the 1960s to 44.4 per cent in 1999. Since 1995, the part
of industry in the overall funding is larger than that of the government (see
Figure 10.1).

Domestic R&D expenditure (GERD) expresses the R&D activities
carried out on the national territory. For 1999 it amounted to 193.7 billion
FF (2.2 per cent of GDP). Business firms carry out 63.2 per cent of the
GERD. The ratio GERD/GDP^2 grew from 1.7 per cent in the 1970s to 2.45
per cent in 1993, and has decreased since 1993 (see Figure 10.2).

By spending 2.2 per cent of the GDP on domestic R&D, France
accounts for 6 per cent of the total OECD R&D expenditure, as compared
with the United States which accounts for 42 per cent, Germany 8.6 per
cent and Japan 18 per cent. This ratio places France in the fourth position
compared with 3 per cent in Japan, 2.7 per cent in the USA and 2.4 per cent
in Germany.

An important public sector

In 1999, 160 800 researchers and engineers were active in the French
economy. The public sector (military and civil) employed around 85 400 scientists, or 53 per cent of all scientists, of which 3000 were employed in the
defence sector. The private sector employs around 75 400 researchers.
France exhibits a ratio of 6.1 researchers per 1000 working persons. By
comparison this ratio amounts to 7.4 in the United States, 5.9 in Germany,
3.3 in Italy, 5.1 in the United Kingdom, 9.2 in Japan and 8.6 in Sweden
(MENRT, 2002) (see Figure 10.3).

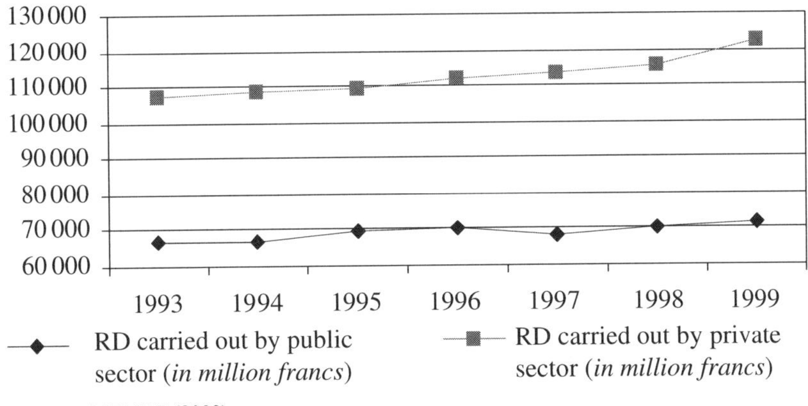

Source: MENRT (2002).

Figure 10.2 *Evolution of the R&D carried out by the public and the private sectors*

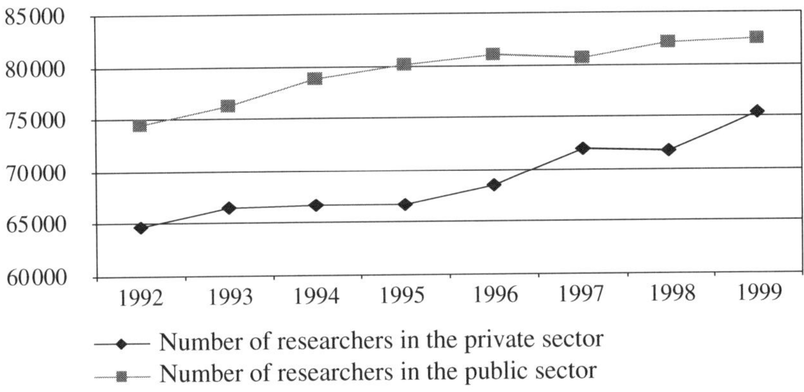

Source: MENRT (2002).

Figure 10.3 *Evolution of the number of researchers in the public and the private sectors*

The public sector (civil and military) conducted research for an amount of 71.3 billion FF (10.9 billion Euros) in 1999 (36.8 per cent of the total R&D carried out). In France we distinguish between civilian and military public sector. The civilian sector conducted 92.8 per cent of the total public research. The civilian public sector involves three different organizations: Public Research Institutions (20 different organizations), higher education

(160 universities and 'Grandes Ecoles') and non-profit associations. In 1999, the French Public Research Organizations except National Centre for Scientific Research (CNRS) executed 42.1 per cent of the R&D of the public sector. They are empowered to establish subsidiaries, to acquire shares in companies, to seek cooperation with scientific and industrial partners and to transfer technologies towards industry. Universities, 'Grandes Ecoles'[3] and CNRS executed 46.6 per cent of the public R&D, Associations 4.1 per cent and defence 7.2 per cent. The missions of universities are education, research and, since 1982, transfer of technologies towards firms. In the public sector, the researchers are all civil servants and their career prospects depend only upon their publications. This situation differs from the US, the UK and Germany, which allocate permanent positions only at a tenured level (Duby, 2000)

The existence of a large number of public research institutions may be explained historically. Since the Second World War, innovation policy has been characterized by large public programmes in telecommunications,[4] the nuclear and space sectors, civil aeronautics and so on. The innovation policy was an archetypal 'mission-oriented' policy (Ergas, 1987; Foray and Llerena, 1996). This policy induced the creation of a number of public research institutes such as Atomic Energy Commissariat (CEA), National Space Research Centre (CNES) and so on. France also created a number of other mission oriented public research organizations in domains such as health (INSERM), agricultural development (INRA), transport (INRETS) and so on. Their mission was to answer the needs of different ministries (Larédo and Mustar, 2001). In addition, France developed the CNRS, to compensate for weak fundamental research activities in the universities. In 1999, the CNRS employed 11 700 researchers and covered all scientific areas. Few European countries have a PRO equivalent to the CNRS (Germany, Spain and Italy) in terms of size and research areas covered. Originally the French research system was characterized by the separation between CNRS and the universities. Since the 1960s both entities have developed associated and joint research units, in which personnel from both institutions work together and are evaluated as a single research unit. We will see in a forthcoming section of this chapter, that the need for a better coordination of resources in the public research sector will entail the generalization of this association procedure.

A concentrated private sector ...
French industry is concentrated in terms of R&D expenditure not only by firm size but also by sectors (OCDE, 1999; 2000; 2001). Table 10.1 shows that in 1999, 2.8 per cent of firms (that is 150 firms) carrying out R&D, realised 56.4 per cent of the private R&D activity, employed 50 per cent of the

researchers and benefited from 81.5 per cent of public funds (tax credits excluded).

Five sectors are responsible for 60 per cent of the private R&D effort: radio and communication equipment, aeronautics and space industry, precision and medical instruments, pharmacy and automobile industry. Moreover, the first three mentioned sectors benefit from more than 75 per cent of public funds (aeronautics accounts for 41 per cent of public subsidies).

This concentration has been observed for a long time, but some changes have occurred (Larédo and Mustar, 2002). Since 1980, the R&D carried out by firms has grown more rapidly than the GDP and tangible investments. The number of firms conducting R&D has been multiplied by four.

. . . publicly funded through defence and large programme contracts
In 1999, firms conducted research for an amount of 122.4 billion FF. This research was financed mainly by themselves (79.5 per cent). The government provided 14.3 billion FF to the private sector (11.7 per cent of their research effort) to which 3 billion FF could be added, devoted each year to R&D tax credits. Firms benefited also from international resources (European Union, firms and other international organizations), representing 8.82 per cent of the research they carried out (see Table 10.2).

According to Tables 10.1, 10.2 and 10.3 public funding of firms exhibits the following features:

- defence research contracts and large technological programmes are still predominant (85.5 per cent of the public funds allocated to firms in 1999)
- the share of public contracts decreased from around 25 per cent in 1980 to 11.7 per cent in 1999
- SMEs employed 29 per cent of the private researchers but benefited only from 10.7 per cent of public funds.

Public resources are still concentrated on a small number of firms and technological areas. According to Duby (2000), SMEs should benefit much more from public funds. The national policy is exclusively interested in high-tech SMEs. By comparison, the German policy differentiates its programmes towards SMEs (high-tech or not, supplier or customer).

These figures clearly show that France still has an important mission-oriented technology policy. Defence and large-scale technological programmes still represent major policy tools even if their share has decreased. In 2001, the large technological programmes accounted for 35 per cent of the public civil R&D budget (MENRT, 2002) and in 1980 for 51 per cent.

Table 10.1 Degree of concentration of private R&D (MENRT, 2002)

Total number of employees in 1999	Firms		Number of researchers		R&D carried out		Public Funding	
	Number	% total	FTE*	% total	MF	% total	MF	% total
<500	4714	87.7	21868	29.0	24467	20.0	152	10.7
500–1000	328	6.1	7348	9.7	11772	9.6	64	4.5
1000–2000	181	3.4	8815	11.7	17099	14.0	48	3.4
2000–5000	96	1.8	10572	14.0	16190	13.2	366	25.7
>5000	54	1.0	26787	35.5	52841	43.2	795	55.8
Total number of firms	5373	100	75390	100	122369	100	1426	100

Note: *Full time equivalent.

Table 10.2   Origin of funds for the private sector (MENRT, 2002)

In %	1993	1994	1995	1996	1997	1998	1999
Share of public funds	17.73	16.20	14.12	13.61	11.49	10.35	11.66
Share of international funds	11.26	11.22	11.11	11.36	10.57	9.36	8.82
Share of private funds	71.01	72.58	74.77	75.04	77.95	80.29	79.52
Total R&D carried out by private sector	100	100	100	100	100	100	100

Table 10.3   Evolution of public funds allocated to the private sector (MENRT, 2002)

In %	1993	1994	1995	1996	1997	1998	1999
Defence and large technological programmes	89.56	89.61	88.88	88.14	86.84	86.52	85.52
Other civil funds (specific ministers, regions etc.)	10.44	10.39	11.12	11.86	13.16	13.48	14.48
Total public funds allocated to the private sector	100	100	100	100	100	100	100

We will see later that to compensate for the decrease of the large programmes and to support a larger number of actors, new policy tools have been implemented since the late 1990s, but with very small budgets.

2.   Towards New Objectives for the French S&T Policy

The characteristics of the above described system highlights some weaknesses that the policy makers have to overcome. To understand the new challenges of the French S&T policy, we should briefly describe the influence of the European context.

The European context

The 'European paradox' arises from the conjunction of excellent European scientific performances (30 per cent of world publications and 35 per cent of US) and the lower technological performance of Europe compared with that of the US or Japan, in terms of the respective shares in the patents granted both in the US and in Europe. The extent of this paradox differs between European countries due to the variety of national systems of innovation. This paradox is not apparent for instance in Germany or the

Netherlands; it is stronger in the UK, Sweden and Spain; while France and Italy are fairly average.

The new policy tools being adopted as national measures in France must therefore be considered in a broader European context. At the European level, initiatives have been taken to avoid obstacles to innovation. On the basis of the Green Paper on Innovation published by the Commission in 1995, an Action Plan for Innovation was elaborated in 1996, which stressed three major objectives: to strengthen the links between research and innovation; to develop a culture of innovation; and to adapt the administrative, legal, financial and fiscal environment. These policies have been implemented and have produced a general tendency to implement similar and complementary measures at the national level.

The French paradox and the need for new policy objectives
The Guillaume Report, published in 1998, showed that the weakness of the French innovation system was due to a lack of linkages between public research organizations and firms. These shortages were analysed in comparison with the perceived performance of the US, which is seen as a reference model (Mowery, 2001). The gap between the French scientific production and technological development is part of this argument.

In 1982, the share of French scientific publications in the world (OST, 2000) was close to 4.3 per cent and reached 5.2 per cent in 1997 (an increase of 21 per cent). In Europe, the French share increased from 14.8 per cent to 15.5 per cent between 1982 and 1997. This increase is particularly true for mathematics (7.1 per cent of the world publications) and sciences of the universe. France is also specialized in fundamental biology, physics and chemistry.

Between 1990 and 1997, the share of French patents decreased both in the European Patent System (from 8.5 per cent to 6.8 per cent) and in the US system (from 3.7 per cent to 3 per cent). France is more specialized in aerospace and earth transport (that is, the large programme effect) and less specialized in electronics and chemistry.

The inadequate connections between the research and the technology systems may be explained by the following reasons:

- Researchers have few incentives to move from the public system towards industry and more generally to diffuse their results.
- The number of joint laboratories between public research and industry is limited.
- The public domain is largely concentrated on research targets, far from the market, and not on technology development (there is not much research in engineering sciences).

- Cooperation in R&D between different actors was not a widely used policy tool before the 1990s.

These weaknesses may also be partially explained by the absence of property rights policy in public institutions, even if a legal framework to retain such rights exists.[5] Public institutions do not reap significant returns from the results of contractual research with industry. In general the property rights are claimed by the industrial partner and institutions do not even consider the possibility to patent themselves. This is due to a lack of competencies and organizational structure to support the development of patenting activities in public research laboratories.

To face these problems, the French government has implemented new policy tools and reforms. The objectives were to develop public research-industry interactions, to promote the diffusion of scientific results throughout industry and to encourage entrepreneurship. The remaining part of this paper will present these new measures, which are characterized by new forms of R&D cooperation.

R&D COOPERATION IN FRANCE

In this part we will focus first on how the French government regulates R&D cooperation, taking into account European rules. The absence of a decree authorizing R&D agreements confirms somehow that these kinds of tools were not commonly used by the French S&T policy to foster innovation. In a first step, we will briefly present the French competition legislation. Second, we will underline the recent policy changes, which aim to induce new forms of R&D cooperation in order to reduce the above-mentioned weaknesses.

1.   Competition Policy and R&D Cooperation

Competition versus industrial policy
Numerous OECD countries have formulated new competition legislations or have revised existing legislations (on mergers, monopolies and other restrictive agreements) for creating a more competitive economic environment and eliminating barriers to the entry of new firms.

The French competition policy is part of the industrial policy. According to Cohen and Lorenzi (2000, p. 15), in France we can distinguish between three types of industrial policies: policies concerning structure (concentration, rationalization and specialization), large projects in high tech industries (integration of technology policies, public procurement and large infrastructure networks) and policies concerning sectors in difficulties (coal, steel, textile and shipyards 'plans'). The French structure policy favoured concentration, promoted national champions and even organized cartels. For a long time the defence of consumer interest was a concept unknown by the techno-industrial French elite. The large technological programmes (often with a political-military origin) gave rise to national champions (such as Alsthom-Alcatel, Elf and Aerospatial), to large equipment programmes (railways, telephone network, nuclear and so on) and to strong exploitation companies (Electricité de France, France-Telecom, and the like).

Competition policy is now divided into an interventionist industrial policy and an allegiance to the European model of consumer protection and privatization of a number of protected sectors (water, telecommunications and airlines). A vast debate was launched during the 1990s about the notion of 'public service', which is a strong French juridical concept. In the network domain France has been introducing some competition to meet European constraints: openness of telecommunication services, airlines, and so on. The breaking up of public monopolies is continuing (for example, in air transport, telecommunications and electricity) with the elaboration of a new regulatory framework and a change in corporate behaviour.

The French control body (Conseil de la Concurrence) concerned with competition, consumption and fraudulent practices is in charge of ensuring the proper functioning of the market. Since 1987, it is this particular independent body that detects and analyses illicit agreements and abuse of dominant position distorting the way the market functions. It also examines concentration among firms and promotes the opening up of protected sectors to competition. Its legal bases for intervention are the Treaty of the European Union and the decree of 1 December, 1986, as amended in 1996.

R&D cooperation in the French and EU competition law

Concerning R&D cooperation, the French competition law transposed the block exemption system of the European Union under some conditions. In order to understand the differences between the EU and the French regulation, let us first briefly present the rules applying to R&D cooperation in the EU.

By applying Article 81.3 CE (formerly Article 85.3 of the Rome Treaty), which allows exemptions to the prohibition of agreements, the Council of Ministers authorized the Commission (by Regulation) to promulgate block exemptions (cf. Bout et al., 2001). In December 1971, Regulation 2821/71 gave the Commission the right to exempt R&D agreements from the application of Article 85.1 (now Article 81.1). In 1985, Regulation 418/85 granted a block exemption to R&D arrangements. Koelliker notices that 'the 1985 Regulation . . . allowed not only joint R&D efforts, but also "exploitation of results", which includes manufacturing and licensing, but not marketing. However, this permission is subject to a series of conditions reaching from the character of the agreement to questions related to the market share and the duration of the collaboration. Concerning the exploitation of the R&D results, the exemption is usually limited to five years and in case of horizontal agreements, the market share must not exceed 20 per cent.' (2001, p. 37)

This *a priori* definition of the economic justification conditions of agreements has long been an important difference between the French and the EU system (Brault, 1997). The French approach was more characterized by *a posteriori* controls. The block exemption system was paradoxically transposed to the French competition law. Article 10.2 of the order No. 86-1243 (drawn upon the EU regulation) states that prohibition underlined by Articles 7 and 8 (concerning agreements and dominant position) is not applicable if 'the authors of such practices can justify that these practices promote economic progress and that they reserve to users a fair share of the resulting profits . . .'. This order underlines that it is by decree that some agreements can be recognized as satisfying the exemption conditions. R&D agreements and patent licensing agreements belong to the categories of agreements, which may be exempted by decree. In France only two decrees have been published and they concern agricultural agreement exemptions. To sum up, R&D agreements may be potentially exempted, but for the moment no decree has been published.

This means that *a priori* the French State may support R&D cooperation. What about supporting R&D? Public R&D support may be considered as a case of competition distortion within the Common Market. In the EU some state aids are considered as incompatible with the Common Market, some others not. A regulation of the Council authorizes the Commission to declare that the following categories of aids are compatible with the Common Market: aids in favour of SMEs, R&D, employment, training and so on. Fundamental research is the only full exception. In case of applied R&D, development and all other cases the Commission fixes some thresholds that the state aids cannot exceed (for instance 50 per cent of the cost for industrial research). The control of state aids and the power to stop such aids are executed on behalf of Article 88 CE by the Commission. The control is executed on existing aids and on new ones: state aids must be notified by the member states and authorized by the Commission before they can be applied. This means that the French State has to consult the Commission before modifying its policy.

2.   R&D Collaboration Supported by French S&T Policy

The aim of this part is to show that new measures, devoted to ease and broaden cooperation between the different actors of the French system, have been implemented. One important part of the argument will be to underline that very small budgets have been allocated to these new measures, as compared to large technological programmes.[6] The latter will be progressively abandoned because they raise many problems (Foray, 2000): complex bureaucratic organizations, industrial competitiveness distortion (creation of national champions) and low externalities (non-disclosure rules, secrecy and little subcontracting with the rest of the industry).

Recent evolutions of the system

An innovation bill[7] was promulgated on 12 July, 1999. Its main aim is to ease the connections between science and technology, thus increasing diffusion of scientific knowledge. Its objectives are:

- to ease the creation of firms by researchers who want to value their research results;
- to favour the creation of new companies (to set up incubators inside the academic system and to provide for shareholding and creation of private subsidiaries by universities);
- to favour, within public research organizations, the creation of new organizational structures able to manage their research contracts, commercial, industrial and patenting activities.

The intention of the 1999 Innovation Law was to alter the incentive structure and organizational possibilities both for individual researchers and for public research organizations and universities in order to increase interactions with industry. As noted earlier, during the same period, the French public research system had also to deal with a relative decrease in financial resources and of large research programmes. To further its goals of improving interactions and to mitigate some of the effects of the budgetary adjustments, the French government developed a further set of policy tools:

- 'research and technological innovation networks' have been created and largely developed;
- the creation of new firms has been encouraged;
- fiscal, financial and legal actions have been taken in favour of innovative companies; and
- a limited number of research themes (life sciences, ICT, social and human sciences, energy, transport and so on) will be sustained.

Table 10.4   Priorities of the civil R&D budget

Priorities of the Civil R&D budget	2001 (in MF)	%
Public Institutions (CNRS, INRA, INSERM, INRIA etc)	26 231	45.7
CNES (National Centre for Space Studies)	8 695	15.1
CEA (Atomic Energy Commissariat)	6 102	10.6
Industrial research and aeronautic programmes	5 515	9.6
University research	2 710	4.7
FRT	1 000	1.7
FNS	885	1.5
Others	6 308	10.9
Total Civil R&D Budget	57 446	100

In the remaining part of this chapter we will show why these new instruments will foster cooperation and allow for a better diffusion of knowledge. But first, we feel it is important to highlight that a very small public budget is devoted to these activities (see Table 10.4). These small financial resources will not induce a rapid switch from a mission-oriented to a diffusion-oriented policy system.

To implement the new policy, the government created two funds: the Fund for Technological Research and the National Fund for Science. These two funds account respectively for 1.7 per cent and 1.5 per cent of the total civil R&D budget. It should be recalled that 35 per cent of the civil R&D budget is still devoted to large technological programmes. The huge financial difference between the two funds and the technological programmes does not need any further comment.

The Fund for Technological Research (FRT)
The FRT is a funding and a coordination instrument. It is the main tool used to induce the emergence of partnerships between public and private research. Its objectives are to ease technological transfers from public research organizations towards industry.

The technological innovation and research networks constitute the most important tool of the FRT (56 per cent of the FRT). They were launched in the mid-1990s in order to replace some of the large industrial programmes (especially in telecommunication and transport), which benefited only large firms. The objective of these networks is first, to induce collaboration between public actors and a large part of industrial research laboratories active in new technological fields and second, to encourage the creation of new firms. Cooperation between different organizations is a prerequisite for being selected. The Ministry of Research with other ministries, public research organizations and firms finance these networks. They are seen as complementary to the European Framework Programme and to EUREKA. The main national research networks are: the national network of research in telecommunications; the PREDIT in transport; the Micro and Nano-technologies Network; the Fuel Cell Network; the Human Genome Network and so on. The most recent ones concern software technologies, new materials and technologies for health. The Ministry of Research reports that in 2000, SMEs benefited from 51 per cent of the subsidies and large companies from 8 per cent. The situation was the reverse five years earlier. This obviously does not mean that SMEs are more subsidized than large companies in general!

In 1999, the Ministry of Research launched a competition which favoured the creation of new innovative firms with a budget of 100 MF, representing ten per cent of the FRT; 244 projects were selected. This action was continued in 2000. This new measure allowed the creation of some 500 firms in two years.

The French government has also created National Centres of Technological Research, which associate public research laboratories and industrial research departments of large companies and, in some cases, SMEs. These centres are located in specific places and work on selected areas. The idea is to concentrate human, financial and material resources in order to foster technology transfers and innovation and to increase industrial competitiveness. These centres should for instance reinforce local industrial development and support teams working in innovation and research networks. Of these centres 12 were created in 2000, but no public budget was allocated.

In order to foster the creation of new technological firms, and to value the results of public research, the government decided to implement incubators with seed-capital means in higher education and research organizations. A call for tenders was launched in 1999. These organizational structures should offer to the new firms buildings, training, management and marketing support, and so on. The seed-capital should bring financial means to the public research organizations that should help them (with complementary partnerships) to finance the creation of new firms. In May 2000, 29 incubator projects were selected. The budget devoted to this action accounts for 10 per cent of the FRT.

In Europe, since 1985 more than 1400 projects obtained the EUREKA label for a total investment of 115 billion FF. France participated in more than 480 projects representing an R&D effort of more than 32 billion FF (in 2000, the French budget of EUREKA represented 5 per cent of the FRT). The amount of subsidies has largely increased for SMEs and decreased for large companies.

The National Fund for Science

The National Fund for Science (FNS) is also a coordination and funding instrument. Its main objective is to support research efforts in priority sectors and in fundamental research able to generate wide applications. It supports mainly public organizations.

The selected programmes should be able to generate new research disciplines, teams and specialists in areas considered as very important by the government. Some programmes are more fundamental in the sense that they only involve public research teams, often with a multidisciplinary approach. Public-private collaborations are sustained as often as possible. Of the FNS, 70 per cent is devoted to life sciences and more particularly to genomic, but also to medical technology programmes and AIDS-Malaria ones. Some of these programmes induce cooperation between public research, industry and the medical sector. Other programmes (called Incentive Actions) are devoted to questions related to cognition, the organization of labour, and the town development.

The multi-annual contracting procedures

The French research system is composed of more than 20 public research organizations and 160 universities and 'Grandes Ecoles'. This diversity implies cooperation structures and mechanisms in order to coordinate human resources, equipment and competence allocation and to cover all technical and scientific domains with few redundancies. The main coordination and cooperation mechanisms are the following: the association of university researchers and PRO researchers in common laboratories, as done by CNRS, and the creation of Public or Scientific Interest Groups, allowing research organizations, universities and sometimes private research labs to pool resources.

Each public research organization signs a four-year contract with the corresponding ministry, in order to coordinate the State priorities and the research objectives and projects of the PRO. Universities also sign a four-year contract with the Ministry of Research and Technology. In many cases these contracts are tripartite (CNRS or other PRO, State and University). In terms of research, these contracts formalize the university scientific objectives, the 'valuation' of research results and the State financial contribution. Since 1982, research organizations and higher education organizations involved in research have the explicit mission to value their research results towards the economic world and industry. Each organization has to define a valuation policy adapted to its characteristics and to create an appropriate structure. The new innovation law mentioned under the recent evolutions section, should favour this activity.

Regional policy

One of the objectives of the government policy is to encourage the dissemination of technologies over a wide range of sectors and regions. In order to promote the geographical spread, local administrations have set up an increasing number of Technological Resource Centres (CRT) and Technology Transfer Centres at regional level, which fulfil directly the expressed needs of firms (largely SMEs). The CRT is a type of quality label allocated to technology transfer centres in order for SMEs to identify the most efficient centres.

Regions have also seen the emergence of Technological Diffusion Networks. Their main objective is to support the technological development of SMEs through technological diffusion, the analysis of their projects, the connection with adequate financing structures and technological competencies. These networks exist in 21 regions. They are financed by the State (via ANVAR) and by local administrations.

ANVAR (National Agency for the Valuation of Research) is a public organization in charge of two main missions: financing innovation programmes and valuing the results emerging from technical and scientific research via a technology transfer policy. The agency established 24 regional delegations allowing local contacts and a better monitoring of the different actions.

ANVAR calls on a whole range of procedures: financing and helping SMEs to develop new products, processes and services; helping the creation and the development of new technological firms with the partnership of public and private venture-capitalists; favouring technology transfer between different kinds of economic actors; recruiting R&D managers and engineers for SMEs; and making it easier for SMEs to access technological, financial and commercial partnerships.

CONCLUSION

In this chapter, we characterized the different actors who are active in the French innovation system, and the way they are connected. The French public research sector is vast and the private research sector is very concentrated in terms of size, sector and public funds. For a long time, these two sectors were badly connected. The French industrial and technology policy was oriented towards the creation of large companies and national champions, sustained by important connected PROs. France recently opened up its protected sectors (under European Union pressure). It also decided to involve a larger variety and number of actors (SMEs) in its public policies.

Large-scale programmes and defence contracts remain predominant in monetary terms, but since 1998 the French innovation policy has followed new orientations. It implemented a diversity of new cooperative tools mainly devoted to better connect public and private research areas (exploit the strengths of both kinds of actors). Some tools such as the innovation networks have to be considered as complements (and not as substitutes) to the EU Framework Programme. The European FWP plays an important role in the French research system. In the fourth FWP, French actors participated in 42 per cent of the launched projects. In 1997, French actors benefited from 3.2 billion FF of shared actions. The private sector benefited from 49 per cent of the funds (mainly large companies), academic labs (universities and CNRS) from 27.7 per cent and other public labs from 23.3 per cent. Telecommunication-electronics-informatics are the most important funded areas. This corresponds to a reinforcement of the French competencies.

Cooperation has a multivariate meaning and has to be understood as such in this paper. The cooperative tools used by the French government in order to foster innovation are diverse: cooperative research contracts or networks, creation of research groups or autonomous structures, of common research centres and laboratories, technological transfer contracts and incubators inside universities and public research organizations. The performance of cooperative policies is closely linked to the degree of commitment of agents, their incentives, their ability to communicate and to generate trust, their previous experience, the existing knowledge base and absorptive capacity. These elements have to be taken into consideration to understand the impact of cooperative policies on the economic performance of the involved actors and the economy as a whole.

NOTES

1. The annual report 'projet de loi de finance' for 2000 and 2001. See MENRT (2000, 2001).
2. OST, 2000.
3. To understand the specific role of 'Grandes Ecoles' in France see Chesnais (1993), but also Quéré (1999) and Larédo (1999).
4. cf. Llerena, Matt and Trenti (2000).
5. In February 2001, the incentives to individual researchers were increased. The inventor could get 50 per cent of the revenue of a patent (under the previous regulation this was only 25 per cent).
6. We disagree with Larédo and Mustar (2001) who claim that France is no more a Colbertist state. Some organizational changes have occurred to compensate the decrease of large technological programmes, but the monetary resources are far too small to invert the tendencies.
7. For a critical analysis of the real impact of this law upon universities see, Llerena, Matt and Schaeffer (2002).

REFERENCES

Brault, D. (1997), *Droit et politique de la concurrence*, Paris: Economica.

Bout, R., M. Bruschi and S. Poillot-Peruzzetto (2001), *Droit économique, concurrence, distribution, consommation*, Paris: Editions LAMY.

Chesnais, F. (1993), 'The French national system of innovation', in R. Nelson (ed.), *National Innovation Systems*, Oxford: Oxford University Press.

Cohen, E. and J. H. Lorenzi (2000), 'Des politiques industrielles aux politiques de compétitivité en Europe', in *Politique industrielle en Europe*, rapport CAE 26, La Documentation Française

Duby, J. J. (2000), 'La politique française d'innovation et la concurrence internationale', complément B in *Politique industrielle en Europe*, rapport CAE 26, La Documentation Française.

Ergas, H. (1987), 'The importance of technology policy', in P. Dasgupta and P. Stoneman (eds), *Economic Policy and Technological Performance*, Cambridge: Cambridge University Press.

Foray, D. (2000), 'On the French system of innovation: between institutional inertia and rapid changes', workshop innovation paradigm, the impact of economic ideas on RT policies, 4S/EASST Conference, 27–30 September, Vienna.

Foray, D. and P. Llerena (1996), 'Information structure and coordination in technology policy: a theoretical model and two case studies', *Journal of Evolutionary Economics*, **6**(2), 157–74.

Francois, J. P. and F. Favre (1998), 'L'innovation technologique progresse dans l'industrie', les 4 pages du Sessi, Ministère de l'Economie, des Finances et de l'Industrie, 89, Avril.

Guillaume, H. (1998), *Rapport de mission sur la technologie et l'innovation*, Rapport au Premier Ministre.

Koelliker, A. (2001), 'Public aid to R&D in business enterprises: the case of the US from an EU perspective', *Revue d'Economie Industrielle*, 94, 21–48.

Larédo, P. (1999), 'S&T policy in EU countries and at EU level: towards complementary roles', International Conference on Knowledge Spillovers and the Geography of Innovation – A Comparison of NSI, 1–2 July, University Jean Monnet, St-Etienne, France.

Larédo, P. and P. Mustar (2001), 'French research and innovation policy: two decades of transformation', in P. Larédo and P. Mustar (eds), *Research and Innovation Policies in the New Global Economy. An International Comparative Analysis*, Aldershot: Edward Elgar, pp. 447–96.

Larédo, P. and P. Mustar (2002), 'Innovation and research policy in France (1980–2000) or the disappearance of the Colbertist state', *Research Policy*, **31**(1), 55–72.

Llerena, P., M. Matt and V. Schaeffer (2001), 'Evolution of the French innovation policies and the impact on Universities', presented at the NPRNET workshop, May, Paris.

Llerena, P., M. Matt and S. Trenti (2000), 'Public policy procurement: the case of digital switching systems in France', in C. Edquist, L. Hommen and L. Tsipouri (eds), *Public Technology Procurement and Innovation*, Boston/Dordrecht/London: Kluwer Academic Publishers, pp. 197–216.

MENRT (2000), 'Etat de la recherche et du développement technologique', projet de loi de finance, Ministère de l'Education Nationale, de la Recherche et de la Technologie.

MENRT (2001), 'Etat de la recherche et du développement technologique', projet de loi de finance, Ministère de l'Education Nationale, de la Recherche et de la Technologie.

MENRT (2002), Bureau des études statistiques sur la recherche du Ministère de l'Education Nationale et de la Recherche, http://cisad.adc.education.fr/reperes/public/chiffres/default.htm.

Mowery, D. C. (2001), 'The United States national innovation system after the cold war', in P. Larédo and P. Mustar (eds), *Research and Innovation Policies in the New Global Economy. An International Comparative Analysis*, Aldershot: Edward Elgar, pp. 15–45.

OCDE (1999), 'France: Etudes Economiques de l'OCDE – Politiques structurelles, recherche et innovation', Paris: Organisation for Economic Co-operation and Development.

OCDE (2000), 'France: Etudes Economiques de l'OCDE', Juillet, Paris: Organisation for Economic Co-operation and Development.

OCDE (2001), Outlook 2000, France, Paris: Organisation for Economic Co-operation and Development.

OST (2000), *Indicateurs 2000, Rapport de l'Observatoire des Sciences et des Techniques, sous la direction de Rémi Barré*, Paris: Economica.

Quéré, M. (1999), 'The French innovation system: some insights into the analysis of the institutional infrastructure supporting innovation', International Conference on Knowledge Spillovers and the Geography of Innovation – A Comparison of NSI, 1–2 July, University Jean Monnet, St-Etienne, France.

11. Italian policy regarding cooperative R&D

Maria Rosa Battaggion and Patrizia Bussoli

Italy seems to lack an organic policy to promote cooperative research, in particular when Italian Science and Technology (IS&T) policies are compared to those of other European countries. This aspect becomes even more evident with regard to Research Joint Ventures (RJVs). Several weaknesses persist and prevent the Italian industry from becoming more competitive in high technological sectors: lack of advanced and original technological capabilities, a fragile technological infrastructure supporting innovation processes and unstable links between universities and industry. However, the Italian public research system is undergoing a process of reorganization. In recent years, a great effort has been made to support and promote innovative activities in general, with some efforts to encourage technological cooperation.

Public policy favouring research was mainly focused on mature technologies and scale intensive sectors (chemical industry, steel-making industry and car manufacture) until 1980. A major reform was adopted in 1982 (Law 46), which provided new instruments to implement a policy for innovation and research. The new tools were either directed to applied research, or were to create prototypes at a precompetitive stage or to promote cooperation in both basic and applied research.

In terms of policy for R&D cooperation, a coherent set of tools to support cooperation and joint ventures among firms, and between public research centres and firms, has not been set up yet. However, in the last decade Italian firms, universities and research centres have been actively involved in the programmes financed by the European Commission, as already emphasized previously in this book.

Furthermore, S&T policies are not only related to the promotion of innovative activity, especially at the cooperative level, but also to technological effects on market competition and Intellectual Property Rights (IPR). Therefore we will focus on the characteristics of Italian competition policies and IPR as well as on their links to R&D strategies. Antitrust policy is rather young in Italy, since it was implemented in 1990 and it is based on Articles 85 and 86 of the Treaty of Rome. Italian legislation on IPR has incorporated European legislation. Both competition policy and intellectual property rights are complementary means of promoting innovation, technical progress and economic growth to the benefit of the consumer and the whole economy. The key question is to establish when the exercise of an intellectual property right ceases to be legitimate and becomes anti-competitive. A specific legislation has not been established yet, but some common principles have been derived on the basis of existing cases.

In what follows, we will first present the involvement of Italian firms in R&D activity and in collaborative R&D activity. We will then examine the Italian innovative system, and in particular S&T regulatory policies and the Government's intervention to support innovative activity, both at the non-cooperative as well as at the cooperative level. Finally, we will analyse anti-trust policy and IPR.

ITALIAN R&D ACTIVITY

R&D efforts in Italy show a relative delay compared to R&D investments in the US, Japan and most countries in Europe. In fact, in 1998 Gross Expenditure on R&D (GERD) was USD 12976 million (ppp), much below the level of other European countries and the US (Table 11.1). This amount accounts for 1.03 per cent of the GDP, while in other industrialized countries the average ratio between GERD and GDP is more than 2 per cent (Table 11.2). The ratio between business expenditure for innovative activity (BERD)[1] and GDP (Table 11.3) in Italy decreased in the 1990s, as on average in the European Union, but it is lower than in other countries (0.57 per cent, around half of the European Union average).

Table 11.1　　Gross expenditure in R&D (million $, ppp)

	ITA	FRA	GER	UK	USA	JAP	EU	OECD
1993	11482	26442	36459	21258	165868	74506	121680	390649
1994	11343	26520	37310	21743	169270	75116	124522	401283
1995	11481	27595	39366	21604	183694	85256	130206	439746
1996	12100	27791	39851	22362	196995	85271	134454	466090
1997	12276	27890	41913	22618	211928	90208	139389	495431
1998	12977	28711	43175		227934			

Source:　OECD, 2001, Main Science and Technology.

Table 11.2   GERD as a percentage of GDP

	ITA	FRA	GER	UK	USA	JAP	EU	OECD
1986	1.13	2.23	2.73	2.25	2.85	2.74	1.91	2.32
1987	1.19	2.27	2.88	2.19	2.82	2.81	1.95	2.33
1988	1.22	2.28	2.86	2.14	2.78	2.84	1.95	2.31
1989	1.24	2.33	2.87	2.15	2.73	2.95	1.97	2.32
1990	1.30	2.41	2.75	2.18	2.78	3.04	1.98	2.36
1991	1.24	2.41	2.61	2.11	2.81	3.00	1.95	2.28
1992	1.20	2.42	2.48	2.13	2.74	2.95	1.92	2.24
1993	1.14	2.45	2.42	2.15	2.62	2.88	1.92	2.19
1994	1.06	2.38	2.32	2.11	2.52	2.84	1.87	2.14
1995	1.01	2.34	2.31	2.02	2.61	2.98	1.84	2.16
1996	1.02	2.32	2.30	1.95	2.66	2.83	1.83	2.18
1997	1.00	2.24	2.31	1.87	2.70	2.91	1.82	2.21
1998	1.03	2.20	2.32		2.77			

Source: OECD, 2001, Main Science and Technology.

Table 11.3   Business expenditure in R&D, as a percentage of GDP

	ITA	FRA	GER	UK	USA	JAP	EU	OECD
1986	0.66	1.31	2.00	1.55	2.06	1.82	1.25	1.60
1987	0.68	1.34	2.08	1.50	2.04	1.86	1.27	1.60
1988	0.70	1.35	2.07	1.47	1.99	1.93	1.27	1.59
1989	0.73	1.41	2.07	1.49	1.94	2.06	1.28	1.60
1990	0.76	1.46	1.98	1.51	1.98	2.15	1.29	1.63
1991	0.69	1.48	1.81	1.42	2.05	2.13	1.23	1.58
1992	0.67	1.51	1.70	1.42	1.98	2.03	1.21	1.53
1993	0.61	1.51	1.62	1.44	1.85	1.90	1.19	1.47
1994	0.56	1.47	1.54	1.38	1.78	1.87	1.16	1.43
1995	0.54	1.43	1.53	1.32	1.88	1.94	1.14	1.46
1996	0.55	1.43	1.52	1.27	1.95	2.01	1.14	1.49
1997	0.53	1.37	1.56	1.22	2.01	2.10	1.14	1.53
1998	0.56	1.37	1.57		2.08			

Source: OECD, 1997, Main Science and Technology.

In 1995 intra-muros R&D expenditure (direct investment by firms and public enterprises) was ITL 17864 billion, equal to an increase of 2.7 per cent with respect to the previous year. Provisional data show that R&D expenditure growth was 7.8 per cent and 6.8 per cent in 1996 and 1997 respectively, while its level increased to ITL 19249 billion and ITL 20556 billion respectively in the same two years. Since 1991, although levels of both private and public research have increased, their yearly growth rates have decreased. So far, Italy ranks 20th compared to other OECD countries in terms of R&D investments over GDP (Istat, 1998).

Conversely, with regard to output measures, Italy seems to be rather dynamic in patent performance. In particular, considering the number of patent applications filed at the European Patent Office (EPO) in Munich, it is clear that the Italian share continually increased from the early 1980s throughout the 1990s.[2] Despite this positive trend in patent applications by Italian firms, the quota of patents registered at EPO is lower than that of major industrialized EU countries (Table 11.4). In terms of number of patents on GDP, Italy's position is less than one third with respect to France and Germany (Archibugi, 1993).

An index showing Italian progress in terms of technological convergence towards other more advanced countries is the coverage ratio of the Technological Balance of Payment[3] (OECD, 1998). It has increased since 1992 and in 1997 it was around 79 per cent, close to the performance of Germany and France. This positive result is partially due to the increase in

Table 11.4   Patent applications for some EU countries (EPO, %)

Countries	1978–84	1985–1991	1992–1994	1995–1996
Italy	2.1	3.4	3.4	3.4
Belgium	0.9	0.8	0.8	0.8
France	10.7	8.9	8.1	8.0
UK	6.9	6.3	5.2	4.2
Germany	24.6	21.2	18.9	19.8
Netherlands	4.1	4.1	2.9	3.2
Spain	0.1	0.3	0.4	0.3
Sweden	2.1	2.5	1.4	1.5
Switzerland	5.3	4.0	3.3	3.1
Japan	14.5	20.3	20.9	20.5
United States	26.7	26.3	29.6	28.8
Rest of the World	1.9	1.9	5.1	5.7
Total	100	100	100	100

Source: CESPRI-EPO database (1998).

Table 11.5   Technological balance of payments – coverage ratio

	ITA	FRA	GER	UK	USA	JAP
1989	0.50	0.83	0.78	0.91	5.47	1.00
1990	0.58	0.76	0.91	0.76	5.31	0.91
1991	0.60	0.71	0.79	1.01	4.42	0.94
1992	0.55	0.72	0.72	1.08	4.04	0.91
1993	0.57	0.71	0.70	1.12	4.31	1.10
1994	0.58	0.73	0.80	1.17	4.56	1.25
1995	0.77	0.73	0.80	1.19	4.38	1.43
1996	0.57	0.76	0.76	1.14	4.14	1.56
1997	0.79	0.72	0.86	1.70	3.60	1.90

Source: OECD, 2001, Main Science and Technology.

net technological exports following the Lira devaluation in 1992 (Table 11.5).

Both dimensional and intensity indicators of innovative activity show that Italy is still far from the major industrialized countries in terms of resources invested in formal research and innovation output (patents), but some of them witness an improvement since the mid 1990s. Innovative activity of Italian firms is characterized by specialization patterns, geographical distribution and size of the firms.

Areas of Specialization in Terms of Patents

A deeper analysis of the trends and characteristics of the Italian pattern of specialization is provided, to shed light on the sectoral characteristics of the areas of specialization and non-specialization (Breschi and Mancusi, 1997).

The revealed technological advantage[4] (VTRS>0) in the 1995–1997 period (Table 11.6) shows that Italy specialises in traditional sectors, such as footwear, clothing, furniture, agriculture and industrial specialized machinery. A positive value for VTRS has been found for industrial auto-mation, electronic classes (domestic appliances and light) and aerospace. Specialization is stronger in those sectors, which are internationally com-petitive in exports. In term of the dynamic of specialization, the data show that the pattern of specialization has grown stronger in time. This evolution suggests that cumulative patterns of specialization and path dependence coexist in the Italian innovation system. Considering VTRS values, no spe-cialization exists for core R&D sectors, even though a convergence towards

Table 11.6　Technological classes that Italy specializes in

	1° VTR	2° VTR	3° VTR
1978–1984	Clothing/Footwear (0.64)	Artificial and Natural Fibres (0.57)	Furniture (0.49)
1985–1991	Clothing/Footwear (0.69)	Artificial and Natural Fibres (0.53)	Furniture
1992–1994	Clothing/Footwear (0.67)	Furniture (0.64)	Artificial and Natural Fibres (0.56)
1995–1997	Clothing/Footwear (0.62)	Electrical devices (0.53)	Artificial and Natural Fibres (0.48)

Source:　CESPRI on EPO database.

industrialized countries has been detected over the last decade with patent quotas moving from 1.3 (1978–84) to 1.9 (1985–91) (Malerba and Gavetti, 1996). The pattern of specialization is very unstable in high technology, while it is stable and cumulative in the traditional sector.

Geographical Pattern

Innovative processes and organizational patterns of innovation systems are interdependent, that is, systems of innovation are affected either by the specific evolution of national industrial structure or by the specific characteristics of each industrial sector. In fact each sector is characterized by specific technological imperatives that affect the pattern of specialization and the geographical distribution of innovative activity.

Patent data show that the north-west is the leading region in Italy with more than 80 per cent of patents (in electronics classes). For those classes in which Italy is specialized (traditional sectors), the north-west and the east account together for 80 per cent of total innovation. As for type of innovation, the north-western regions are characterized by product innovation, while in southern and central regions process innovation prevails. Data show that in Italy there is a geographical distribution of innovative activity. North-western regions maintain a leading position in innovative activity, while southern regions, apart from aerospace, play a marginal role. The emerging dynamic market is formed by central regions (Emilia-Romagna, Tuscany, Marche, Umbria and Veneto).

SMEs Versus Large Firms

The participation of small and medium-sized enterprises (SMEs) is a characteristic of the Italian actors of the innovation system. The presence of small firms is stronger in traditional industries (textile, clothing, footwear and so on), even if recently their presence has emerged in more dynamic sectors such as robotics and automation. These firms have been growing internationally, especially by adapting and tailoring to customer needs and to ever-changing demand (Malerba, 1993).

As shown in Table 11.7, in Italy the largest firms, defined as those with more than 500 employees, are the most innovative ones in terms of innovation activity characteristics. R&D and productive investments are the main

Table 11.7   Characteristics of innovation activity in Italy (1990–1992) per employee (% on total)

Employees	Innovative firms	Firms with R&D	Employees of innovative firms	Sales of innovative firms
20–49	25.9	11.7	27.5	2931
50–99	40.8	23.4	41.6	43.0
100–199	48.0	33.3	48.7	47.8
200–499	58.5	47.5	59.8	67.3
500–999	74.0	61.0	74.5	79.1
>999	84.3	78.5	9135	95.9
Total	33.1	18.6	61.5	70.7

Source: Archibugi et al., 1993.

sources of innovation for both SMEs and large firms, the former being the major source of innovation for large firms while the latter for small firms. Patents and licences are an innovation tool for medium-sized firms. Large firms are the most involved in R&D cooperative activity, in particular in activities in collaboration with universities and foreign firms and the National Research Centre (CNR). Small firms show a preference for co-operation with other firms (both national and foreign) instead of collaboration with other entities (Table 11.8).

In high technological sectors (Table 11.9), 120 large firms own 58.8 per cent of patents. Large firms represent 21.5 per cent of firms of which size information is available. Medium enterprises, which are 34.5 per cent of the sample, applied for 917 patents, that is, 28 per cent of the total, while 44 per cent of the sample, represented by small firms, own only a 13.2 per cent share of patents (Malerba, 1998).

Table 11.8　Cooperation among firms and other institutions (% values on total firms with R&D)

	Number of Employees					
Cooperation with:	0–49	50–199	200–499	500–999	>999	Total
Other Italian firms	18.8	20.2	22.1	35.7	48.2	30.1
Other foreign firms	18.8	15.2	20.8	35.7	69.4	33.9
Of which: EU	12.5	15.2	11.7	21.4	47.1	23.5
Outside EU	6.3	0.0	9.1	14.3	22.4	10.3
Italian universities	12.5	14.1	18.2	35.7	51.8	27.9
Foreign Universities	0.0	3.0	10.4	9.5	27.1	11.9
Of which: EU	0.0	3.0	5.2	4.8	15.3	6.9
Outside EU	0.0	0.0	5.2	4.8	11.8	5.0
Scientific and technological parks	0.0	2.0	1.3	2.4	10.6	4.1
Consortia cities research	0.0	2.0	1.3	2.4	10.6	4.1
CNR	6.3	10.1	13.0	11.9	44.7	20.1
ENEA	0.0	4.0	9.1	11.9	21.2	10.7
Other	0.0	0.0	2.6	0.0	1.2	0.9
Consortia cities research	0–49	50–199	200–499	500–999	>999	Total

Source: Confidustria, Tendenze dell'Industria Italiana, Giungno 1998.

Table 11.9　Innovative firms size in high tech sectors

Employees	Firms	% of firms	Patents	% of patents	Ratio
0–50	156	27.91	278	8.49	0.30
51–100	90	16.1	156	4.76	0.30
101–250	128	22.9	370	11.29	0.49
251–500	65	11.63	547	16.7	1.43
501–1000	47	8.41	237	7.23	0.86
>1000	73	13.06	1688	51.53	3.95
Total	559	100.00	3276	100.00	

The reason behind the fact that large firms are more innovative than SMEs may depend on two factors: first, there is a long formalized and expensive procedure[5] to apply for patents; second, SMEs carry out only a small part of formal R&D and introduce incremental innovation through channels like learning by doing, interacting processes and acquisition of new machinery.

In short, we can describe the actors of the Italian innovation system as follows: an oligopolistic core of large firms accounts for most of the Italian research activity. Besides this innovative core, there is a small set of small firms operating in the high technology sectors and a large sample of SMEs in the traditional sectors or in micro-mechanics and instrumental mechanics, specialized in customized production of final and intermediate products. Italy is characterized on the one hand by a weak and unorganized system of instruments to favour R&D, and on the other hand by firms which are behind their European competitors in terms of R&D activity.

GOVERNMENT'S ACTIONS TO PROMOTE INVESTMENTS IN R&D

1.   Promotion of R&D

Several policy tools, which may affect the innovation process at the firm level, are at the disposal of governments. These tools can be briefly summarized in three broad categories: taxation schemes, public procurement for high-tech products/services and direct financial subsidies for research activities.

The Italian government's action to encourage private R&D activity consisted primarily of financial incentives, namely facilitated credits and grants. This policy started in the reconstruction period. At that time, the impressive diffusion of R&D laboratories inside firms was considered an important element of economic growth and this process was strengthened by technological public policy. A generic subsidization of R&D expenditure was thought to be more effective than the government's intervention in specific areas of research: the government offered financial arrangements to decrease research costs, without targeting specific projects or particular technological fields. Neoclassical and also Schumpeterian analyses provide a theoretical argument to support this choice: financial incentives or tax reductions are optimal means to increase R&D expenditures up to the point where private and public returns are equal. This strategy was pursued until the early 1980s, through a wide range of instruments aimed at sustaining the production and the diffusion of technological knowledge.

The first attempt to make the government's intervention more selective is Law 46, 17 February, 1982, which provides different incentives to sustain specific sectors of national relevance. On the basis of this law, two funds, the 'Fondo Speciale per la Ricerca Applicata' (FRA) and the 'Fondo Speciale Rotativo per l'Innovazione Tecnologica' (FRT), were set up.[6] The former was created to support applied research and diffusion of its results.

The latter was meant to sustain relevant technical advances in the last stages of applied research.

This new approach allows firms, research societies, consortia and public entities to autonomously submit projects, which are subsequently selected for subsidization by the Ministry of University, Scientific and Technological Research (MURST). According to the specific technological area, selection criteria are based on the originality and the follow-up chances of the projects in the business world in the short to medium run. Therefore, Law 46 is a tool to direct R&D activity in the specific technological areas of national interest.

FRA

FRA is meant to sustain R&D projects of private firms, consortia, public entities, societies for research, private centres of research and consortia between private firms and public entities. The applications for research projects funds filed by a single entity are continuously decreasing, while the demands submitted by consortia of firms and public entities are growing.[7]

Funds for FRA are granted by the Istituto Mobiliare Italiano (IMI) upon submission of requested documents. Subsidies are ex-post, that is, they are distributed after the firm has undertaken R&D costs, in an average span of five years. The total amount of funds will be determined each year on the basis of the government's financial budget.

According to Law 46/82, updated by Law 652/92, a 20 per cent share of the total fund is devoted to SMEs, while 40 per cent is reserved for activity in the South of Italy and a 10 per cent share is devoted to international projects.

Articles 2 and 7 of Law 46/82 define the mechanism for the provision of financial resources. Projects carried out by SMEs with a cost lower than ITL 2.5 billion receive a subsidy up to 70 per cent of the global cost of the project and up to a maximum amount of ITL 1750 billion. Projects carried out by companies, consortia and research centres with a cost between ITL 2.5 and 10 billion are funded by grants and by subsidized loans, decided by a decree of the Ministry of Industry, following the advice of a technical committee. Each phase of the project, from applied research to experimentation, has to be developed in Italy. Law 346/88 regulates applied research projects whose cost is greater than ITL 10 billion. A fixed share mechanism to allocate resources for this type of project is not established under this law.

FRA represents the most relevant support to high-tech projects for Italian manufacturing. In 1990, its subsidies amounted to ITL 806.1 billion, accounting for roughly 8.2 per cent of BERD. Unfortunately, FRA was not active between 1994 and 1995 for bureaucratic reasons. On average, the resources distributed by the fund are around ITL 1000 billion per year.

Looking at the characteristics of the subsidized firms and their geographical distribution, two features emerge. First, there is an asymmetry between large and medium to small companies. The latter account for almost 50 per cent of the total funds demanded, but they receive only roughly 10 per cent of the total funding, which is dramatically lower than their reserved share of 20 per cent. Second, the percentage of funds granted by FRA to Southern Italy is lower than the reserved share of 40 per cent, although it has increased since 1990.

Despite its ambitious aims, FRA activity has been extensively conditioned by the discontinuity and insufficiency of financial funds, which depend on the budget constraint of the Italian administration. Moreover, its activity has been influenced by the European Union legislation, which implies the communication of all projects involving a minimum cost of 20 million ECU. Due to this procedure, large corporations seem to be more oriented to small size, low risk projects with a poor technological content, which require lower financial grants,[8] than to more costly projects. Thus, FRA turns out to be inadequate not only for SMEs, which receive in practice a low share of the funds, but also for large companies. In the meantime, the projects presented between 1992 and 1994 decreased in terms of dimension from ITL 3300 to 1380 billion, and in terms of number from 200 to 90, as an effect of economy slowdown, money cost and privatization on the one side, and as an effect of the access to other programmes, which may guarantee a higher probability of success for firms on the other side. Interestingly, the simplification in the application rules for SMEs and the reduction of the project evaluation time positively affected the number of applications for FRA funds. In fact, in 1995 applications increased by 50 per cent with respect to the previous year (Malaman, 1997).

FRT

FRT has been created to promote relevant technological advances in the last stages of applied research activity. The subsidized costs are related to all the precompetitive stages of research activity, from design to experimentation. FRT's activity shows that the total FRT intervention increased in the 1990s as well as the part of intervention dedicated to SMEs, with the firms in Northern and Central Italy remaining the main beneficiares.

Law 317/91 introduced further facilities for SMEs under FRT, in terms of the procedure to submit demands. On average, a share of 25 per cent of the total amount of the fund is targeted to SMEs. A higher share of SMEs is subsidized by FRT than by FRA. This trend can be explained by a peculiarity of SMEs' innovative activity. Innovative efforts are primarily focused on incremental innovation, imitative activity and technological renewal. In this respect, FRT seems to be an instrument suited to promote SMEs' innovative efforts and, consequently, to sustain R&D activity in the Italian manufacturing field. If SMEs do not conduct research activity inside R&D laboratories they are denied access to FRA funds.

The competence and the areas of intervention for the two funds are not clearly defined, creating some confusion and overlapping of action. Moreover, to increase the efficiency of both FRA and FRT it would be necessary to drastically reduce the time between the application and the decision to provide a subsidy (which is around eight months).

With regard to the diffusion of technical knowledge, Law 46/82 does not explicitly introduce any mechanism to promote technological follow-up. In particular, relative to the possible diffusion of the research results, Article 11 says that the State owns research outcomes. However, productive exploitation of the innovation and patent use by the firms members of the agreement are allowed for. More precisely, the property right can be relinquished to the members of the agreement against payment.[9]

More generally, the government has promoted the process of diffusion by facilitating investments in new machinery or renewal of production equipment. A successful example of these types of policies is represented by Law 1329/65 (Sabatini Law, 1965). The number of projects funded under this law jumped from 3953 in 1983 to 17596 in 1992, with a yearly average increase of the funds granted of around 38 per cent in the period 1983 to 1992. Initially, Law 1329/65 was introduced to subsidize specialized machinery firms, but within a few years it had changed into a relevant instrument to promote technological diffusion. In fact, SMEs innovate mainly by the acquisition of new materials, machinery and technological components. The objective of speeding up the technological development of SMEs has been pursued also by the introduction of Law 696/83, modified by Law 399/87, which allows firms to buy new high-tech machinery by means of subsidized credits. In 1988 the number of projects which benefited from the law was 2478 compared to 848 in 1987 and it oscillated around 2000 in the following years.

Technological agencies
As far as technological agencies are concerned, the Ministry of Industry announced the creation of an agency, called Agitec, for innovation and technology transfer. This agency, organized as a society, whose main partners are Mediocredito Centrale, Enea and Unioncamere, is mainly devoted to designing and implementing programmes of technological investments for SMEs and to the creation of new high-tech firms. In addition, it offers some complementary services like technological check-up, recruiting of domestic and international partners for research projects and information and documentation for accessing national or Community funds for R&D

expenditures. Following this example, some other centres of technological diffusion have been created: they are based on the collaboration among universities and firms and their activity is oriented to regional areas (ARPA, ASTER, and so on), and others are societies where ENEA cooperates with other firms in specific fields (for example Polo tecnologico).

A relevant intervention by the government to diffuse technological knowledge and know-how has been the creation of scientific parks and technological agencies, which will be analysed below in relation to measures to support cooperative R&D activity.

2.   Promotion of R&D Cooperation

The intrinsic characteristics of the Italian industrial structure as well as the public policies pursued during the last fifty years have reduced or impeded the opportunities of interactions between public and private research institutions. On the one hand, public authorities set up a series of policy tools, such as fiscal and financial incentives, which sustained long-term research, mainly basic research. On the other hand, the industrial pattern of specialization biased towards traditional products and small firms, expressed a low demand of scientific knowledge. However, a new trend in policy-making is emerging, a trend to implement policies designed to promote cooperation between research centres and industry, other than financial incentives. An example of this new trend (De Marchi et al., 1998) is the creation of an interface structure: INFN, ASI, ENEA and so on, to establish commercialization structures for research products; the creation of service and innovation centres, to locally support technology transfers and also to promote the creation of high tech firms; a patent office to provide information and assistance on patent application.

At present, the legal layout of the cooperation agreements is relevant for revenue laws. However, in Italy there are no tax credits to provide incentives for technological cooperation among firms. In fact, government action takes the form of facilitated credit instead of tax facilities.

Regarding the government's role in directly influencing technological cooperation, we should distinguish three different types of cooperation. The first is cooperation among firms, for instance short-term contracts regarding a project of research or the joint use of R&D laboratories, the commercialization of a new product, the licensing of a patent, the creation of a RJV and so forth. The second is cooperation between private and public institutions, namely cooperation between private firms and universities and public research centres. Third there are new structures for co-operation, such as technological parks, public laboratories and research centres.

The Italian government's action has mainly privileged the first two types of intervention. The main focus has been on increasing cooperation between firms, universities and public entities and on supporting private joint activity of technological research. Although a systematic and coherent line of action to promote cooperative R&D is missing, we consider a set of specific programmes, which have been quite influential in promoting joint R&D.

Progetti Finalizzati (PF)

CNR established a programme to fund specific innovative projects, Progetti Finalizzati. This programme aims at promoting research coordination between public and private laboratories and research centres, in particular between universities and companies. It is focused on the precompetitive stage of research and on high risk and delayed return projects of research. Areas of interest are energy, food, health, environment and advanced technology. The broad objectives of PF are: i) the decrease of Italy's technological dependency on foreign countries; ii) the improvement of human capital; iii) the development of Southern Italy and in general of all the less industrialized regions.

Three different categories of PF can be distinguished. The first type of PF has essentially the role of stimulating basic research and it is mainly addressed to universities and to the public system of research. In this sense these projects have promoted cooperation between public research centres inside and outside academia. The second type of PF is meant to support concrete public action. In other words, this type of PF supports the public operator's demand of knowledge in order to improve the quality of public services or to provide the necessary information and knowledge for long-term planning and intervention. Finally, the last category of PF aims at promoting technological development. These PF support fields of research where important technological follow-ups for the productive sector are expected in the short and medium term. Six fields of national interest have been promoted, namely: food, health, environment, advanced technology, energy and a last one specifically addressed to the analysis of some peculiar features of the Italian economy. Firms' participation is allowed in all three categories of PF, but in practice it is limited to the last category.

It is a common opinion that the third type of PF is the most effective in promoting innovation and that it has produced the most promising results.[10] These PF have efficiently developed high-risk projects, with promising follow-up as, for instance, in the case of electronics and telecommunications. They also offered many SMEs a chance to cooperate in high-tech projects, and they have effectively promoted cooperation between firms and universities.

Programmi Nazionali di Ricerca

The National Programmes of Research (PNR) are research programmes organized by MURST, but directly addressed to promote industrial research in the private sector. They represent the natural extension of PF and are based on knowledge, competence and information created by PF. They are addressed to firms, to carry out high-risk projects characterized by a multidisciplinary approach. Ten per cent of the total subsidies is reserved for the training of researchers.

Recent legislation comprises part of the EC norms: the Italian President's Decree D.P.R. 240/1991 introduces EC regulation 85/2137, 1985, which establishes the European Group of Economic Interest (GEIE). The GEIE is an instrument to promote cooperation between firms and between private entities and public institutions. The GEIE's goal is not of attaining its own profit, but of promoting partners' development and profitability. Therefore, it is particularly useful in the case of R&D activity jointly conducted by several partners. The GEIE is particularly valuable in the case of cooperation among SMEs. In fact, it allows the creation of a group even without capital; partners can choose to contribute to the group with cash, but also with assets or services. For this reason it is a relevant institution in Italian S&T policy.

Another effort of Italian policy makers to foster firms' cooperation is Law 95/95 Article 3. For the period 1995 to 1997 it planned the allocation of five per cent of the authorized budget in favour of CNR, ENEA, and FRA, which aimed at promoting cooperation among firms, universities and research centres.

The involvement of Italian firms in European programmes to promote R&D cooperation is substantial.[11] At present, more than ten per cent of the Italian industrial R&D effort is performed through international cooperative programmes and two thirds of these collaborations are financed by public subsidies.[12] European Community funds are the third source of R&D funding for Italian firms after FRA and FRT. Italian participation is considerable in the fields of energy, industrial technologies and information. Italian participation is characterized by the large contribution of SMEs, as opposed to the domestic case where the share of SMEs is relatively small. Conversely, technologically advanced countries such as Germany, France, Great Britain and the Netherlands show a strong presence of large firms in comparison to SMEs.

Consortia

Consortia represent a new structure to support R&D cooperation. They were established in 1980 (Law 382) to promote cooperation in educational activities, students' curricula and complex research. Law 46/82 does not foresee specific incentives for the creation of consortia or other forms of R&D cooperation. Examples of consortia are CILEA focused on electronics and the Italian institute for physics. Since 1985 other entities, such as firms and research centres, have been involved. It is relevant to point out that CNR, like universities, can be a partner in such consortia. So far CNR has taken part in 26 projects where many industrial firms were involved.

Scientific and technological parks
In 1990 the Ministries of Treasury, of University and Research, and of Extraordinary Interventions in Southern Italy signed the Agreement Programme (Programma di Intesa 7/12/1990) to promote and develop scientific and technological parks in Southern Italy, as instruments for the implementation of policies to promote and diffuse technology. The Agreement Programme was established in response to the need of developing scientific and technological skills, to allow technological transfer to small firms and to create synergies between firms and public centres, in particular in Southern Italy. Scientific and technological parks have been created as consortia or societies. This agreement was in line with European policies to promote technological regional development and with Italian policies for the development of Southern Italy. Based on this agreement, approved by the ministerial decree (D.M.) 25/03/1994 n.225,[13] thirteen technological parks have been created in Southern Italy since 1997. Cooperation among firms, universities and scientific institutions in the parks is devoted to sustaining precompetitive research, development, planning and the creation of new products, in particular in the high technological industrial sector. The aims are various and range from sustaining local growth and the creation of new innovative firms, to the creation of services for new small enterprises.[14]

Local programmes
Programmes promoted by local authorities are also worth mentioning, for example regional regulations in Lombardia: Laws 34/1982 and 34/85 (Article 6) define two specific types of intervention. The first one considers financial facilities for research agreements between SMEs and specialized centres of research (up to 40 per cent of the cost of the project and up to ITL 300 million is covered by a grant). The second one provides subsidized credits repayable in the medium term to finance product innovation by small-sized firms. The Regional Law (r.l.) 7/93 introduces capital account subsidies for process and product innovations in Lombardia. Finally, r.l. 35/97 provides grants for the participation of firms in Lombardy to applied research programmes. Another example is provided by the autonomous province of Trento, which passed a law aimed at fostering cooperation between industry and university (Malerba, 1993).

Finally, we summarize the features of Italian S&T policies. First, the role of the state in R&D activity is dominant: basic research is mainly carried out by public institutions and a large share of private R&D efforts is supported by the government through financial subsidies; in the period between 1990 and 1996, the government financed on average 12 per cent of BERD.[15] Second, S&T policies are based on broad goals and do not offer clear guidelines for technological efforts at the firm level. Moreover, the Italian government did not pursue a top-down approach with the aim of stimulating private R&D by means of public procurement and the launch of advanced projects of research related to both civilian and military needs. Equally, it has not followed a bottom-up approach, in order to stimulate R&D effort at the firm level, to speed up the diffusion of technological know-how and to strengthen the link between firms and universities/research centres. Finally, S&T policies are haunted by delays and discontinuities. Various efforts in the direction of promoting R&D cooperation have been implemented, however, further effort is needed to create an organic and unified policy framework, specifically related to RJVs.

Given that we examined Italian R&D activity and policies, focusing in particular on cooperative R&D, we follow the analysis concentrating on the question of whether cooperation in R&D may affect competition among firms. In fact, RJVs may lead to collusive behaviour not only at the R&D level but also at the product level. For this reason, we will cast a glance at the characteristics of competition and antitrust policies in Italy and at their relationship to RJVs.

ANTITRUST POLICY

Competition policy in Italy began in 1990, even though the original draft legislation dates back to the early 1950s. The essential material has been transformed into law, defining the economic behaviour to be controlled and the procedures for so doing (in particular with the institution of the Autorita' Garante delle Concorrenza e del Mercato, the Antitrust Agency).

Italian antitrust policy is regulated by Law 287/90, which is derived from European antitrust law. The implementation of the norms reflects precisely articles 85 and 86 of the Treaty of Rome. Regulation of agreements, abuse of dominant position and mergers and acquisitions are essentially the same as the EU's. In particular, in Italy, as at the EU level, exceptions for limited periods may be granted to agreements or categories of agreements restricting competition provided that they improve supply conditions and result in substantial benefits to consumers.

There is, however, a distinguishing feature at the sectoral level between

Italian and EU law. Italian antitrust law does not include any special provision for the agriculture and the transport sectors, while European law provides a special treatment for these two sectors. Italian antitrust policy has special provisions aimed at protecting the international competitiveness of Italian firms. These provisions reflect the strong presence of SMEs in the Italian economic environment. However, these exemptions can only be applied whenever anticompetitive actions of Italian firms do not affect competition in the European Union (Vanzetti and Di Cataldo, 1996).

Like the European one, Italian law considers the firm as the unit to be regulated. The concept of firm for both the European and the Italian antitrust is rather broad: it includes business activities with and without legal personality, including non-profit institutions.

The enforcement powers are vested in an independent agency, Autorità Garante, which has a total organizational independence and the freedom to spend the financial resources it receives every year from the Parliament. The independence of the Autorità Garante in terms of extent of its action is peculiar to Italy: in fact the antitrust agencies in France, Germany, the United Kingdom or even the US do not have the same degree of independence and autonomy as the Autorità Garante. The government can only influence the activity of the Autorità Garante in general terms but not in respect of individual cases. Moreover, the enforcement powers over certain sectors are vested in other institutions (Banca di Italia for credit, Garante per la Radiodiffusione e l'Editoria for broadcasting and publishing).

The industries which are most often investigated by the Autorità Garante are the chemical industry (traditionally characterized by high concentration degrees for technical/economic reasons) and the food industry for mergers and acquisition; the cement and concrete industry and the insurance business for cases of agreements; and the telecommunications industry and airport sector, for cases of abuse of dominant position (Gobbo and Ferrero, 1998).

If antitrust policy is related to RJVs, we find out that antitrust laws and RJVs are linked in two ways. On the one hand, antitrust law regulates the restriction of competition to which the type of the agreement may lead per se (Article 85 of the Treaty). On the other hand, it investigates whether patents, and more generally intellectual property rights originating from RJVs, may result in an abuse of dominant position by an individual partner or by all members collectively (Article 86 of the Treaty). This last concern will be examined below.

R&D agreements and joint ventures are not considered by European law as restrictive to competition: '. . . agreements to carry out common research projects and develop the results till the industrial application stage will not influence the competition position of the partners' (Ghidini-Hassan, 1991).

However, special agreements among partners may fall under the brunt of the antitrust legislator when they limit R&D activity, or the access to pre-existing knowledge or the use of research results by one or more partners. Specifically, the legislation is against agreements restricting partners' activities outside the joint venture (even jointly with non-member firms). Moreover, the agreement should not prevent or restrict the circulation of research results to non-member firms, unless such results are protected by patents. There are exceptions to these general rules, on a case-by-case basis, whenever restrictions are useful in order to enhance research benefits. So far, the activities of the Autorità Garante have never dealt with RJVs.

INTELLECTUAL PROPERTY RIGHTS

Intellectual property laws pursue the following goals: rewarding innovators for their creative efforts, disseminating innovations and promoting a more competitive environment through the development of new products or productive processes. On the other side, protection of this right and the exclusive use of innovation may raise concerns in terms of competition policies. However, both policies play a complementary role in providing sufficient incentives for innovation and economic growth. This is particularly true as far as pool patenting is considered, in relation to RJVs, which not only promote innovation but may also raise a concern for market concentration, as emphasized in the previous section.

In what follows, first the Italian patent regulation system is presented and second, the IPR and competition policy links are analysed.

1. Italian Patent Regulation System

The first law about property rights on invention in Italy dates back to 1939. This law, n.1127/39, has been continuously modified up to Law n.338/1979 which conforms the national regulations to European standards. Thus, the Munich agreement (5 October, 1973) and the European Patent have also been introduced into the Italian patent system. This implies that Italian innovators can choose whether to file their inventions with the European or the National patent system. The European system will grant property rights within some or all the states subscribing to the Munich agreement while the national one will do so just within national boundaries.

European legislation mostly overlaps with national norms and the effects of the European patent are the same as the national one, even though some important differences exist. As for Italy, the most relevant difference is that Italian patent can be granted without an examination, unlike the European ones. In fact, in Italy the inventor submits his/her request to the Italian Patent Office and, although the legislation provides for a formal examination of the request, the examination does not deal with technical details and it analyses neither the originality nor the patentability requirements. The time of submission is important, as in the case of conflict between inventors the Italian system works on the 'first to file' criterion. In contrast, when the inventor submits the request to the European Patent Office, there is a compulsory preventive examination before receiving the patent aimed at assessing the originality of the invention.

In what follows we will focus on the Italian patent, in particular on an aspect that is specifically relevant for RJV: the rights concerning patents in the case of a team invention. There are two kinds of rights related to the patent: the right to obtain it and the right to the economic exploitation of the results of the invention.

The right to obtain the patent
By Article 29 of Invention Law (l.i.), all the co-inventors have the right to obtain the patent. The law considers as co-inventors those members of the group that developed research activities aimed at the creation of the new invention, but not those that worked on other parts of the research projects or whose activity was not creation-oriented. As for the rules concerning team patents, the patent law refers to the standard rules on joint ownership. The problem is that such rules only regulate the sharing rules of the patent once the patent is obtained. There is no specific law defining the rights for co-inventors to file for patents. However, according to common practice, the decision to ask for a patent has to be taken by the majority of the co-inventors. When the application for the patent is submitted by just one or a minority of co-inventors, this is equivalent to the application for the patent by an individual without legal rights. In any case the absence of norms makes the situation unclear and imprecise.

The right to the economic exploitation of the results of the invention
As reported above, there is no specific legislation regarding the economic exploitation of the results of the invention. Normally the general norms on joint ownership are applied. Ownership is held equally by all co-inventors unless otherwise specified; the ownership share is transferable and each partner has a right of pre-emption on it; the patent is an indivisible object; the decision on its use and licensing should be taken by the majority of the co-inventors (Article 1105), while the decision on exclusive licensing should be taken unanimously (Article 1108, comma 3, C.C.).

Article 20 of the Invention Law establishes that these are the norms for the mentioned rights, except in case of different agreements among the parties involved. Particularly, if the parties form a society to carry out the research project, the business law will rule the above mentioned rights.

Special sectors
Italian patent law was born to protect inventions in the mechanic sector. Some special developments have characterized specific sectors. Special provisions regard in particular the patent for the chemical sector, for new vegetable varieties and for microchips.

In chemistry, some special norms have been introduced to determine what a new finding is and the requisites of novelty and originality, necessary to deliver the patent. Novelty requires particular criteria when the compound is described in chemical and physical terms. Originality, instead, is related to both the structure and the function of the compound found by the inventor.

In the case of new plant varieties the patentability requisites are modified; particularly the requirements for novelty are less strict, as well as those for originality. Homogeneity and stability are *ad hoc* for this kind of invention. Moreover there is a system of double protection for new plant varieties that allow the request for the usual patent or for the special protection. The process to obtain the patent requires an examination by the Ministry of Agriculture and Forestry.

The microchips sector is characterized by high amounts of investments and high risk of copying. Following the European Commission directive, 16 December, 1986, n.54/1987, special provisions for microchips have been introduced by Law n.70, 21 February, 1989. This law's approach is similar to the one for patent law, but the word registration is used instead of patent (Vanzetti and Di Cataldo, 1996).

2.   Patents and Monopoly

Competition policy and intellectual property laws are both founded on the intent to promote economic advance, technical progress and consumer welfare. Antitrust laws seek to prevent certain behaviours that may restrict competition to the detriment of consumer welfare. In a long run view, consumer welfare depends also on the availability of new products and on the increased quality of existing goods. Thus, both competition policy and intellectual property rights are complementary means of promoting innovation, technical progress and economic growth to the benefit of the consumer and the whole economy. For the purpose of antitrust analysis two issues should be considered: (i) intellectual property should be regarded as comparable to any other form of property; (ii) the possession of an intellectual property does not necessarily confer market power upon its owner.

The mere possession of an intellectual property right does not necessarily guarantee the possibility to exercise anti-competitive practices. IPR intrinsically have a monopolistic aspect, given that they may limit production, exchange and imports of the patented products. Market power arising from holding IPR may be used to restrict competition between technologies that are economic substitutes or to exclude new technologies from the market. Further restrictions to the economic activity and competition derive from the fact that national patents impose the implementation of the innovation within national borders and may protect from competition of imported foreign substitute products.

The privileges granted by the patent do not imply *per se* a restriction to competition or an abuse of dominant position, as referred to in Articles 85 and 86. The key question is to try to identify a borderline between the IPR legislation and competition law. A specific legislation has not been established yet, but on the basis of existing cases some common principles have been derived.[16]

A restriction of competition should be considered with respect to the global competitive structure of the market and not only in relation to the parties involved. The exploitation of the patent through contracts and agreements is acceptable by the legislator, as far as it enhances economic and technological progress: Article 85 n.3 (Tavassi, 1998). With this respect the ENI/Montedison case is an example of the application of Article 85 n.3. In this case cross-licensing of patents and know-how in the chemicals and thermoplastics industries are involved. The agreements between ENI and Montedison related to their efforts to rationalize their production in certain chemical feedstock and in thermoplastics, industries suffering from serious overcapacity in the EU. The firms agreed to reduce their cracking capacities at the feedstock level and to specialize at the thermoplastic level, with each firm ceasing the production of certain thermoplastics. Patents and know-how were cross-licensed on a non-exclusive basis in connection with the plan. The Commission exempted the agreements under Article 85 n.3, as they helped to resolve a serious problem of overcapacity more quickly and completely than would otherwise have been possible. Moreover, the fact that each firm retained cracking capacity and the right to use its own intellectual property (the patents and know-how were licensed non-exclusively), meant that each firm remained a potential competitor in the thermoplastics field it had abandoned, limiting the restraint on competition (OECD, 1989).

Consequently, there is an overlapping between the patent and the antitrust legislation and it is not always obvious which of the two should be applied. The patent law is applied as long as there is no dominant position, while the antitrust law is applied whenever the patent right will constitute dominant position and/or lead to an abuse of dominant position. Thus, the uncertainty boils down to the difficulty of defining a dominant position and the relevant market concerning such abuse (Sena, 1990, 1998).

So far the Autorità Garante has taken a stand in a couple of cases involving an intellectual property licensing agreement. In one of the two,[17] the Autorità Garante stated that competition rules apply to the exercise of intellectual property rights. In particular, the exercise of an exclusive intellectual property right may infringe competition rules if it prevents, restricts or impedes competition to a significant and unjustifiable degree on any of the markets in which the right is exercised. The Autorità Garante ruled that the contracts were to be considered prohibited agreements, on the grounds that the exclusivity clause was not necessary to enhance market efficiency (OECD, 1998). In the other case,[18] the Autorità Garante expressed its negative opinion on the patentability of some models, since patents could distort competition in the relevant market and create an economic damage for consumers (Sena, 1998, Tavassi, 1998).

Patent pooling and cross licensing is an area where competition law can and should be applied to restrict anti-competitive use of IPR among firms, which are actual or potential competitors, as in the case of RJVs. Patent pooling is normally pro-competitive if it is strictly confined to sharing complementary patents. However, companies could seek to combine substitute technologies and thereby reduce horizontal competition. This could happen in the context of settling patent litigation. Even where pooled technology clearly combines complementary rather than substitute technology, concerns are raised regarding treatment accorded to non-members and to technology improvements. Patent pools could amount to collective boycotts, which significantly reduce the competitive power of existing or future competitors. Consumers also stand to lose if the patent pools require such generous sharing of any technological improvements that the incentive to make improvements is significantly reduced. A rule of reason approach seems eminently suitable to review the effects of patent pooling.

CONCLUDING REMARKS

The Italian system of innovation shows some specific features. On the one hand, there is a clear gap between Italian expenditures in R&D and those of most industrialized countries. On the other hand, Italy shows a good level of technological dynamics carried out by SMEs especially in traditional sectors.

S&T policy to promote innovative activity covers a considerable share of R&D expenses and in the last decade some incentives for cooperative R&D have been introduced.

The Italian government's action for innovative activity has been analysed from two different points of view: research promotion and promotion of cooperative R&D. Research promotion has primarily taken the form of facilitated credits and grants to stimulate innovative activity and to speed up the diffusion of technological knowledge. With regard to the promotion of R&D cooperation, several governmental instruments have been analysed, however a specific and coherent strategy to sustain RJVs does not yet exist in Italy.

Italian Antitrust Policies and Intellectual Property Rights mainly derive from European legislation. The analysis proposed shows that there are no specific features discouraging or encouraging the creation and the performance of RJVs.

NOTES

1. BERD is a subset of GERD and comprises only business expenditure.
2. Source: EPO-CESPRI database.
3. The TBP registers the commercial transactions related to international technology transfer. The coverage ratio is the coefficient obtained by dividing receipts by payments. It shows to what extent a country covers its own requirements of technological imports by its corresponding exports.
4. VTR is computed taking into account 49 technological classes (Malerba, 1998) $VTR_{ij} = (P_{ij} / \Sigma_i P_{ij})/(\Sigma_j P_{ij}/\Sigma_i \Sigma_j P_{ij})$, where P_{ij} is the amount of R&D expenditure in country i in sector j. The normalized index used in the tables is defined as $VTRS_{ij} = VTR_{ij} - 1/VTR_{ij} + 1$, whose values range between -1 and $+1$, with a positive value showing specialization in that sector.
5. For a detailed analysis of the Italian high technological sector refer to Malerba (1998).
6. Actually FRA was created by Law 1089 in 1968, but only the following legislation n.46/1982 rigorously explained the fund's objectives and functioning procedures.
7. Source: CER-IRS, *La Trasformazione Difficile* (1993).
8. Source: Falzoni in *La Ricerca Scientifica* (1990) and CER-IRS (1993) on IMI data set.
9. For an analysis of pool patents, refer to the section 'Intellectual Property Rights'.
10. S. Ginebri in *La Ricerca Scientifica* (1990).
11. Refer to Part I of this book.
12. G. Antonel and R. Malaman in *La trasformazione difficile* – Sesto rapporto CER-IRS (1993).
13. The procedures for the creation of the parks were established by the Conversion Law (legge di Conversione) 5/11/1996 n. 573.
14. For more specific detail refer to the D.M. 25.03.1994, n.255.
15. OECD, Main Science and Technology Indicators, n.2, 1997.
16. The Ciba-Geigy/Sandoz merger case is an example of the degree to which competition policy interacts with IPR. This merger combined two of only a few entities capable of commercially developing a broad range of gene therapy products, and threatened to significantly reduce competition to innovate in that area. The merger reduced incentives for other companies to enter a field where they would, in future, have only one source of necessary IPR instead of two and only one potential buyer for resulting technology. Accordingly, the competition authority abstained from blocking the merger only after the parties agreed to certain compulsory licensing conditions (OECD, 1998). Other cases, in which the above distinction is established by the Court of Justice, are Park Davis, Sirena Emi Records, Renault and Volvo, Warner Bros, Emi Electrola and Magill.

17.	The proceeding related to two agreements concluded between Associazione Italiana Calciatori (AIC) and the Panini SpA. According to these agreements, the AIC had assigned to Panini the exclusive right to use images of the soccer players wearing their team colours, by publishing and marketing them on self-adhesive stickers, together with albums for stickers and other published items for collection.
18.	This is the case about cars' spare parts (Riv. Dir. Ind., 1994).

REFERENCES

Archibugi, D., R. Evangelista and M. Pianta (1993), 'Forze e debolezze del sistema Innovativo Italiano', *Economia e Politica Industriale*, **79**, 137–66.

Breschi, S. and M. Mancusi (1997), 'Il Modello di Specializzazione tecnologica dell'Italia: un'Analisi Basata sui Brevetti Europei', in D. Archibugi and G. Imperatori (eds), *Economia Globale e Innovazione: la sfida dell'industria italiana*, Rome: Donzelli.

CER-IRS (1993), 'La Trasformazione Difficile', sesto rapporto CER/IRS sull'industria e sulla politica industriale italiana, Bologna: Il Mulino.

CER-IRS (1997), 'Più tecnologia, più concorrenza', ottavo rapporto CER/IRS sull'industria e sulla politica industriale italiana, Bologna: Il Mulino.

CESPRI (1998), 'Analisi della performance brevettuale e della localizzazione dell'attività innovativa delle imprese italiane nei settori ad alta tecnologia', rapporto tecnico, Università Bocconi.

Confindustria (1998), Tendenze dell'Industria Italiana, Giugno.

De Marchi, M., B. M. Potì, E. Rocchi and A. M. Sarda (1998), *Il Sistema Scientifico Pubblico in Italia*, Milan: Franco Angeli.

Falzoni, A. (1990), *La Ricerca Scientifica* and CER-IRS (1993) on IMI data set.

Gavetti, G. and F. Malerba (1996), 'Il sistema innovativo italiano e l'Europa', *WP Cespri*, **85**, January.

Ghidini, G. and S. Hassan (1991), *Diritto Industriale e della Concorrenza nella CEE*, Milano: IPSOA.

Ginebri, S. (1990), 'I progetti finalizzati del CNR ed i programmi nazionali di ricerca. L'intervento pubblico di tipo progettuale nell'ambito della ricerca tecnologica italiana', in F. Malerba and F. Onida (eds), *La Ricerca Scientifica*, Rome: SIPI.

Gobbo, F. and M. Ferrero (1998), 'The Interaction between community and national competition policy: the Italian case', in S. Martin, *Competition policies in Europe*, Amsterdam: North Holland Elsevier.

Malaman, R. (1997), 'Verso una nuova politica per l'innovazione tecnologica', in *Più tecnologia, più concorrenza*, CER/IRS.

Malerba, F. (1993), 'Italy', in R. R. Nelson (ed.), *National Innovation Systems: a Comparative Study*, New York: Oxford University Press.

Malerba, F. and G. Gavetti (1996), 'Il Sistema Innovativo Italiano e l'Europa, *Economia e Politica Industriale*, **89**, 231–60.

Malerba, F., S. Breschi and G. Villa (1998), 'Analisi della Performance Brevettuale e della Localizzazione dell'Attività Innovativa delle Imprese Italiane nei settori ad Alta Tecnologia', in S. Ferrari, P. Guerrieri, F. Malerba, S. Mariotti and D. Palma (eds), *L'Italià nella competizione technologica internationale secondo rapporto*, Franco Angeli.

OECD (1997, 1998, 2001), *Main Science and Technology Indicators*, Paris: OECD.

OECD (1986), 'Technical Cooperation Agreements between Firms: Some Initial Data and Analysis', DSTI, SPR 8620, Paris: OECD.

OECD (1989, 1998), *Competition Policy and Intellectual Property Rights*, Paris: OECD.

Sena, G. (1990), *I Diritti sulle Invenzioni e i Modelli Industriali*, Milan: Giuffrè.

Sena, G. (1998), 'Proprieta' Intellettuale: Esclusiva e Monopolio', in E. A. Raffaelli (ed.), *Antitrust between EC Law and National Law*, Brussels: Giuffrè Editore-Bruylant.

Tavassi, M. (1998), 'Diritti della Proprieta' Industriale e Antitrust nell'Esperienza Comunitaria e Italiana', in E. A. Raffaelli (ed.), *Antitrust between EC Law and National Law*, Brussels: Giuffrè Editore-Bruylant.

Vanzetti, A. and V. Di Cataldo (1996), *Manuale di Diritto Industriale*, Milan: Giuffrè editore.

12. Science and technology policy in Spain: 1980–2000[1]

Pedro L. Marín and Georges Siotis

Spanish Science and Technology (S&T) policy was non-existent prior to 1977. The legislation adopted in that year was to form the embryo of the Spanish national system of innovation (NSI). The notion of NSI, popularized by Nelson and Winter (1982), describes the interaction between firms and research institutions (both private and public) that carry out research activities. The functioning of an NSI, then, refers to the mechanisms through which these entities interact to generate and/or distribute the economically valuable output of scientific research across the economic fabric. In that sense, a Spanish NSI did not exist prior to 1977, and it is only during the 1980s that a more comprehensive set of legislation was adopted with the objective of developing a coherent S&T policy.

The OECD established the distinction between NSIs that are mission-oriented and those that are diffusion-oriented. Spain clearly falls in the latter category. The stated objectives, as well quantitative results, indicate that efforts have been concentrated in fostering the adoption and diffusion of existing technology. Public policy has focused on fostering links between public research centres and private firms, the twin objective being to improve the technological base of Spanish enterprises and, at the same time, encourage public research entities to undertake economically valuable research. To that end, resources have been devoted to building the basic technology infrastructure, which would allow the Spanish NSI to take shape. Some initiatives have resulted in a certain degree of duplication, for instance between the regional and national levels, but also across national initiatives. In that sense, the Spanish NSI is still in its formative years and its shape in constant evolution. Preliminary results indicate a certain degree of success, as the number of projects involving Research Joint Ventures (RJVs) has grown substantially during the 1995–1998 period. However it has flattened since then.

Spain's entry into the EU acted as a catalyst for change with respect to S&T policy. First, decision-makers realized that a more pro-active policy, and in particular in the S&T fields, was necessary if industry was to remain 'competitive' within the Single Market. Also, the consensus was that Spanish firms had the potential for large productivity gains as there were opportunities for upgrading production techniques at low cost (in fact, that is what happened in many instances of foreign direct investment in the form of the acquisitions of existing Spanish facilities). To use the terminology christened by Abramovitz (1986), Spain presented large opportunities for catch-up. Second, the prospect of EU accession required substantial changes in the Spanish legal framework in areas that affect the functioning of Spain's NSI. In some cases, legislation did not exist or was poorly applied (for example competition law), while in others, it was inadequate or obsolete (for example intellectual property rights protection). Third, Spanish accession coincided with the development of European-wide cooperative research efforts in the form of five-yearly Framework Programmes and EUREKA. As a consequence, Spanish firms and research institutions were given the opportunity to participate and benefit from pan-European collaborative research endeavours. Fourth, EU membership has resulted in a substantial overhaul of the legislative framework applicable to S&T. In practice, current Spanish legislation is a 'direct translation' of the *acquis communautaire* in that area. Last, authorities are keen to fully integrate the Spanish S&T community into the nascent European research area.

This chapter is organized as follows. The first section broadly describes Spain's S&T efforts. We then present the institutional and legal framework which surrounds Spain's NSI. The plethora of legislation adopted during the late 1980s, the large number of new initiatives, and the adoption of the first multi-annual S&T plan, clearly indicate that these were the formative years. It emerges that public authorities have put much emphasis on fostering diffusion, and efforts were made to improve co-ordination across S&T initiatives. The next section outlines the characteristics of supporting Spain's S&T efforts. The last section presents some general observations on the functioning of Spain's NSI.

S&T POLICIES IN SPAIN: BROAD TRENDS

According to Buesa and Molero (1990) the following features characterized the Spanish situation during the 1960s and 1970s. First, growth was based on industries with low technological content, which relied on the use of foreign technology. Second, resources devoted to R&D activities were limited in comparison with other western economies. In particular, R&D expenditure represented 0.65 per cent of GDP, while in France, the UK, Germany, Japan, and the US, these were about four times greater. Third, few companies had proper R&D budgets; of these, 25 per cent were foreign subsidiaries. The latter represented 43 per cent of total R&D expenditures, public companies spent another 20 per cent, while private local companies accounted for the remainder. This situation resulted in a slow pace of adoption and diffusion of innovations.

1.   Spanish R&D Effort

As can be seen from Table 12.1, gross expenditure on R&D as a percentage of GDP increased considerably during the 1980s, and continued to do so in the 1990s, but at a slower pace. Despite these increased efforts, Spain's R&D effort is still only half the EU average, the GERD/GDP ratios (Gross Expenditure on R&D over GDP) are only above those of Greece and Portugal. Table 12.1 also shows that R&D personnel as a proportion of the labour force grew very fast during the 1980s, but despite these advances, Spain remains still well below the EU average. The percentage of GERD performed by the Spanish business sector decreased during the period 1981

Table 12.1   Main science and technology indicators: Spain and the EU

	1981	1985	1990	1995	1996	1997	1998	1999	2000
Spain (GERD/GDP)	0.41	0.53	0.81	0.81	0.83	0.82	0.90	0.89	0.91
EU (GERD/GDP)	1.69	1.87	1.96	1.81	1.81	1.80	1.81	1.85	NA
Spain (BERD/GDP)	0.18	0.29	0.47	0.39	0.40	0.40	0.47	0.46	0.48
EU (BERD/GDP)	1.05	1.20	1.27	1.13	1.13	1.14	1.15	1.20	NA
Spain (BERD/GERD)	0.44	0.55	0.58	0.48	0.48	0.49	0.52	0.52	0.53
EU (BERD/GERD)	0.62	0.64	0.65	0.62	0.62	0.63	0.64	0.65	NA
Spain: R&D personnel/1000	2.7	2.9	4.5	5.0	5.4	5.3	5.9	6.2	NA
EU: R&D personnel/1000	8.6	9.0	9.4	9.5	9.5	9.4	NA	NA	NA
Spain: Inventiveness coeff.	0.46	0.56	0.58	0.53	0.59	0.58	0.59	NA	NA
EU: Inventiveness coeff.	2.24	2.32	2.24	2.28	2.61	2.48	2.58	NA	NA

Notes:
GDP: Gross Domestic Product
GERD: Gross expenditure on R&D
BERD: Business expenditure on R&D
R&D personel/1000: R&D personnel per thousand labour force.
Inventiveness coefficient: (resident patent applications/10 000 population).

Source: OECD (2001), *Main Science and Technology Indicators.*

to 1999, standing at 52 per cent in 1999. Again, this percentage is lower than the EU average (65 per cent in 1999). This reflects the fact that higher education institutions and government research institutes play a more important role in the Spanish innovation system than they do in the rest of the EU. Scientific output, as proxied by the inventiveness coefficient (resident patent applications per 10000 population) is perhaps the weakest point in the Spanish NSI. For the last year for which data is available, Spain's inventiveness coefficient stood at 0.59 against 2.58 for the EU as a whole. This reflects the weakness of Spain's NSI in the sense that little output is produced from R&D efforts. However, it also reflects the fact that Spain's NSI is diffusion oriented and is therefore less prone to produce patentable outputs.

Business enterprise expenditure on R&D as a percentage of GDP (BERD) increased during the 1980s, and has hovered around 0.45 per cent of GDP since then. Table 12.2 indicates that the number of firms performing R&D activities, and total R&D personnel in enterprises have experienced a steady growth since 1990. However, the proportion of R&D researchers employed in firms has declined throughout the 1990s.

Table 12.2   R&D in the Spanish enterprise sector – selected indicators

	1990	1992	1994	1996	1998	2000
No. of industrial firms with R&D activities	NA	NA	4360	5531	4742	6452
Total R&D personnel (No. of FTE)*	69684	73320	80399	87264	91098	120617
(% employed in firms)	(40.9%)	(39%)	(34%)	(33.7%)	(35.7%)	(39%)
Total R&D researchers (No. of FTE)*	37676	41681	47867	51633	60269	76669
(% employed in firms)	(29.2%)	(27.8%)	(23.1%)	(21.5%)	(23%)	(27.2%)

Note: * number of full-time equivalent.

Source: Comisión Interministerial de Ciencia y Tecnología, CICYT, 'Memoria de Actividades de I+D+I Año 2000'.

Table 12.3 shows the distribution of R&D related public funds granted to private R&D in 1992. Public Administration financing is mainly directed towards small and medium size firms, towards firms without foreign capital, and towards public rather than private firms.

Table 12.3   Distribution of public funds by size and firm ownership (1992)

	R&D expenditures	R&D public financing	R&D expenditures / R&D public financing
Size (No. of employees)			
<100	16.5	23.6	1.4
100–500	23.3	30.5	1.3
>500	60.2	45.9	0.8
TOTAL	100	100	
Property			
Without foreign capital participation	43.8	67.3	1.5
With foreign capital participation	56.2	32.7	0.6
TOTAL	100	100	
Type			
Public	18.4	35.4	1.9
Private and others	81.6	64.6	0.8
TOTAL	100	100	

Source: CICYT.

2. Preliminary Remarks

As a general rule, Spanish R&D effort is weakest in technology intensive
sectors. These are sectors such as chemicals, office equipment, precision
instruments, and pharmaceuticals. The situation is comparatively better
than the average in traditional industrial sectors such as food products,
shoe and leather industries, textiles and printing industries. There are also
some sectors, of medium-to-high technological intensity, in which the
results are better than the average. These are industries such as machinery
and transport equipment.

If we undertake an international comparison of R&D efforts during the
period 1981 to 2000, two features emerge:

- The volume of resources directed to R&D activities in Spain is two
  to three times smaller than in other similar countries.
- This gap has been slightly reduced during this period.

Importantly, during the nineties the effort in R&D expenditures has become stagnant. In 1994, around 1800 companies undertook R&D activities systematically and continuously, and approximately 2600 did it occasionally with the total summing to 4360 (Table 12.2). These firms are of different sizes and sectors and are controlled by different types of capital. More than one half of them are small, usually having less than 100 employees, and a third of them can be regarded as medium size companies, as they employ between 100 and 500 workers. Many of these companies are relatively young and started operations during recessions, especially at the beginning of the eighties.

Spanish residents control 71 per cent of companies that develop R&D activities. Another 25 per cent are branches of multinational companies operating in Spain and the remaining 4 per cent belong to the public sector. However, this distribution differs when we analyse company expenditures on R&D activities, since the effort made by foreign owned and publicly owned companies is much larger than the effort made by private local companies. The relatively small average size of Spanish companies partially explains this finding.

The industries with higher R&D expenditures are electronic material, chemical products, cars and other transportation material. Companies in these industries employ about one half of the corresponding resources. A second group of industries accounts for another quarter of total R&D expenditures: office and electric machinery, education and research services to other companies.

R&D activities in companies employ on average 16.4 workers, which represents 6 per cent of the total workforce during the late 1990s. However, the distribution is extremely asymmetric as more than two thirds of these companies have research teams that employ less than ten people, and in almost three quarters of them, the percentage of workforce employed in R&D activities is below average.

There are significant differences between Spain and the European Union. For a start, there is a different distribution of researchers among public and private sectors – in Spain only 30 to 35 per cent of R&D personnel work for the private sector while in the EU, this percentage is as high as 56 per cent. In addition, both the sources of R&D financing and the volume of R&D expenditure differ. In particular, in Spain the contribution of the Public Administration is more than ten points larger than in the EU and the volume of R&D expenditure is about half that found in the EU as a whole.

These weaknesses have translated into poor results in terms of total factor productivity (TFP) growth (OECD, 2000). While the macroeconomic performance has been quite satisfactory over the last few years, growth has mainly stemmed from the accumulation of tangible factors of production (labour and capital). By contrast, TFP growth has lagged behind that of the rest of the EU.

3. Institutional Framework and the National Plans

Before the eighties, there was almost no piece of legislation related to the promotion of R&D activities. The *Asociaciones de Investigación* (Research Associations) and the *Planes Concertados* (Coordinated Plans) were receiving some subsidies from the *Comisión Asesora de Investigación Científica y Técnica* (Scientific and Technical Research Advisory Commission – CAICYT), but resources and political interest for S&T were scarce.

The first attempt to reorganize the R&D Spanish policy was made in 1977, during a profound recession and the political transition to democracy. The *Centro para el Desarrollo Tecnológico Industrial* (Industrial Technological Development Centre – CDTI) was created within the *Ministerio de Industria y Energía* (Industry and Energy Ministry – MINER). Its main task was to promote the technical capabilities of Spanish firms by different means: financing R&D projects, technically advising firms and helping in the development of technological markets. In order to achieve these goals the CDTI was financing at low or zero interest rates, and managing two types of technological projects undertaken by firms. First, *Proyectos de Desarrollo Tecnológico* (Technological Development Projects) in order either to create or to improve existing products or productive processes, which were going to be incorporated by the firm in the short run. Second, *Proyectos de Innovación Tecnológica* (Technological Innovation Projects) to incorporate new technologies in firms that wanted to improve their productive organization.

The first piece of legislation related to R&D activities approved during the eighties was the *Ley Orgánica de Reforma Universitaria, 25/08/83* (University Reform Act – LRU). It recognized the importance of research activities for the social, cultural and economic development of entrepreneurial activity. In particular, articles 11 and 45, and their subsequent developments, established the mechanisms to support and promote co-operative R&D activities which could involve both firms and universities.

The LRU, which was approved in 1983, was followed by the *Ley de Fomento y Coordinación General de la Investigación Científica y Técnica, 24/04/86* (Scientific and Technical Research Promotion and Coordination Act – LFCICT). This legislation reorganizes the institutional framework for the Spanish scientific and technological policy by defining the *Planes Nacionales de Investigación Científica y Desarrollo Tecnológico* (National Plans for Scientific Research and Technological Development) as the main instrument for the promotion, coordination and planning of R&D activities. A new institution was created to define the aim of the plan and monitor its performance, the *Comisión Interministerial de Ciencia y Tecnología* (Science and Technology Inter-ministerial Commission – CICYT, which also coordinates domestic and international R&D activities. Additionally, this law created two new institutions to coordinate national and regional R&D policies,[2] and to establish a link between the scientific community and the CICYT.[3] Figure 12.1 provides an overview of the various actors involved in S&T policy).

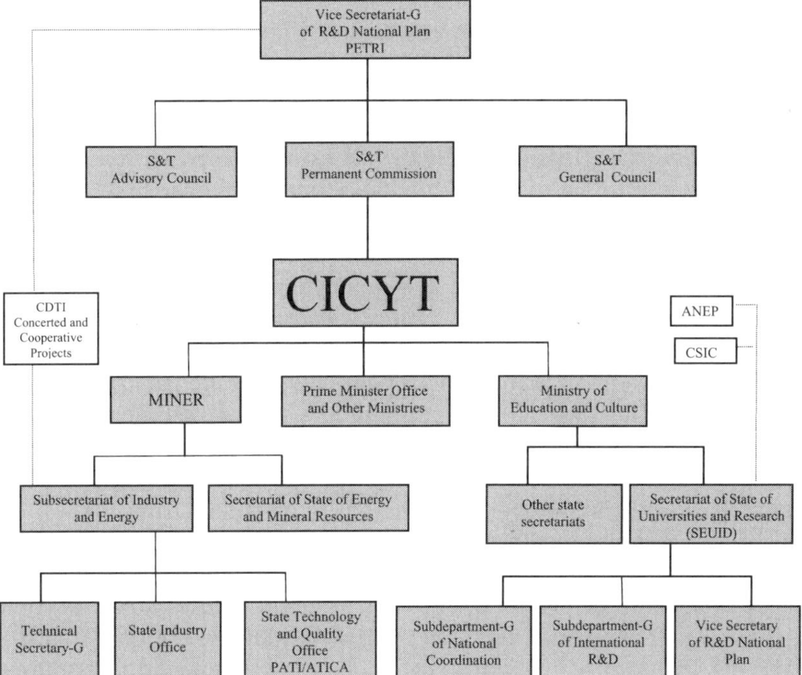

Figure 12.1 S&T policy organigram in Spain

National Plans set the objectives and priorities of domestic R&D policies and allocate resources among different fields of activity. They are financed by the National Fund and managed by several institutions. Their aim is to encompass the whole innovation process from basic scientific research to development by industry.

National Plans (NPs) are organized around several types of activity. They can be designed to finance projects undertaken by research teams, including equipment and scientific and technical infrastructures as well as the organization of meetings and conferences, and the travel expenditure of the main researchers. Some other lines are designed to promote cooperation either among firms or between firms and public research centres (Coordinated and Cooperative Projects). In some cases, NPs encourage the development of large projects related to new products or processes that involve several technologies (Integrated Programmes). In addition, NPs encourage public centres to initiate research activities whose results can be easily transferred and developed by firms (PETRI). These three types of projects lead, in most cases, to research joint ventures involving a mix of public institutions and private firms.

The main reason behind the creation of PETRI is that many public research centres focus entirely on basic research. This means that the projects' results still require development before they can be readily used by industry; thus PETRI finances complementary research to facilitate adoption by economic agents. Accordingly the research group involved in each project is asked to have previous contacts with firms. The latter must be willing to participate in the design and development of the project, and committed to use the results of the project for industrial applications. This ensures a certain demand for the new product or process.

In general, NPs follow some priority lines, leading research groups towards specific areas of interest. NPs include National Programmes, Specific Ministry Programmes and programmes that are coordinated with Regional Administrative Units. The latter may propose specific projects of their interest to be included in the plan and co-finance them. As a general rule, the sectorial priorities of the NPs closely mirror those of the EU's Framework Programmes.

The LFCICT also redefines the role of the CDTI, to which it assigns new tasks related to the control, supervision and diffusion of the results, as well as the direct management of some of the projects. Besides, since 1989, the *Oficina de Transferencia de Tecnología* (Technology Transfer Office – OTRI/OTT) has been integrated in every University, public administration, industrial association and research institution. The aim is to promote cooperation between firms and public research institutions, and foster the transfer of knowledge generated by public research to the productive sector of the economy. Moreover, the OTRI also encourage the exchange of researchers between research centres and firms.

After the First National Plan (1988–91), two more pieces of legislation were approved in order to reinforce the S&T national policy: first, the *Ley de Deducción por Inversion en I + D* (R&D Investment Tax Allowance Act) and, second, *Procedimiento para la Concesión de Subvenciones Públicas* (Procedure for Awarding Public Subsidies). The Second National Plan aimed to achieve better efficiency in the use of public resources. While the structure and contents of the third EU Framework Programme – approved in April 1990 – were taken into account in the design of the Second National Plan, the latter has maintained the same principles, objectives, and types of activity of the First Plan. The Third National Plan (1996–1999) included several novelties. First, it is more explicitly oriented towards applied research. In particular, it aims to improve the transfer of knowledge and results from the scientific to the productive sectors. It is expected that, in the future, R&D will focus more on finding solutions to specific socio-economic problems, while at the same time maintaining some attention to basic research. Second, one of its stated objectives is to improve the coordination of R&D activities, both nationally and internationally. Third, much emphasis is put on the distribution of existing technological knowledge across the economic fabric.

Several strategies were designed to fulfil these objectives. Given the interactive character of innovation systems, the Programme for the Promotion of the Science and Technological-Industrial System (PACTI) was created in order to identify and develop a set of actions aimed at maximizing interactions between the different communities involved in R&D. More precisely, they focus on developing networks between companies, innovation centres and the OTRIs. PACTI also aims to spur awareness of R&D developments by creating technology watch agencies (which provide information on existing activities and major technological trends), and to facilitate the integration of research personnel into companies.

While the broad outline Fourth National Plan (2000–2003) is similar to that of previous ones, there are some noteworthy innovations. The general philosophy of the National Plan is now more focused. As mentioned above, the Spanish NSI is clearly diffusion oriented, and the Fourth Plan aims to further the penetration of new technologies into the economic fabric. This is to be achieved through greater interaction between all the actors (both public, semi-public, and private) of the Spanish NSI. The emphasis is no longer restricted to 'R&D' *stricto sensu*, and the terminology used by Spanish authorities now includes innovation (R&D&I). In the same line, the new National Plan puts emphasis on projects that have a more direct potential to generate economic value, with emphasis being put on projects that are close to the market. In 2000, the *Programa de Fomento de la Investigación Técnica* (PROFIT) was specifically launched with a view to foster private sector innovative activities that have clearly identifiable applications. The rules regulating PROFIT are explicit: save for space and aeronautics, no funding is provided for basic research, and non-profit making entities cannot apply for funding (though they continue to benefit from traditional sources). Another characteristic of the Fourth Plan is the emphasis on the need to actively promote Spanish participation in international research projects, and in particular, EU financed ones. Much emphasis is put on the need to fully integrate Spanish actors into the European research area. The objectives of the Fourth Plan are summarized in Table 12.4. Public authorities' declared aim is to bring Spain in line with the rest of the EU in terms of R&D&I. In order to fulfil these objectives, important increase in public funding would have to be undertaken, and the private sector's involvement would have to increase substantially. It should also be noted that an interesting innovation is the declared aim of undertaking rigorous monitoring and ex-post evaluation of the NP's activities. A new law reforming the university system has just been approved by both chambers (*Ley Organica de Ordenación Universitaria*). A noteworthy feature is that private sponsors (firms) will have a direct say on spending decisions, and, it is hoped, will foster competition among universities. Last, the government has launched a series of fiscal incentives to R&D&I in the form of tax deductions that coincided with the launching of the Fourth NP.

Table 12.4   The Fourth National Plan: main quantitative targets (projections)

	2000	2001	2002	2003
R&D as % of GDP	1.17	1.23	1.26	1.29
Public sources (%)	35.6	35.1	34.9	34.7
Private sources (%)	64.4	64.9	65.1	65.3
R&D&I as % of GDP	1.83	1.92	1.96	2
Public sources (%)	22.8	22.6	22.5	22.4
Private sources (%)	77.2	77.4	77.5	77.6

Note: R&D&I Research and Development and Innovation.

Source: Comisión Interministerial de Ciencia y Tecnología (2000), 'National Plan for Scientific Research, Technological Development, and Innovation', vol. 1, Objectives and Structures.

SUPPORTING POLICIES

In conjunction with the National Plans, the MINER has developed an incentive system directed to R&D activities. Since 1990, this system is framed in the First and Second *Plan de Actuación Tecnológica Industrial* (Industrial and Technological Action Plan – PATI) and, since 1997, in the *Iniciativa de Apoyo a la Tecnología, la Seguridad y la Calidad Industrial* (Supporting Actions for Industrial Technology, Safety and Quality – ATYCA), which integrates previous quality and safety programmes.

These programmes are financed by the national budget. Their main objectives are to improve competitiveness through the incorporation and generation of advanced technologies in firms, and in particular, small and medium sized ones. Special attention is given to less favoured regions, and emphasis is put on close coordination with Spanish regional administrations.

S&T has recently received an increased amount of attention from the central government. The CICYT is now chaired by the Prime Minister (*Presidente del Gobierno* in 2003). Following an administrative reorganization, many of the programmes that were managed by MINER have transferred to the new ministry of Science and Technology (*Ministerio de Ciencia y Tecnología – MCYT*). In addition, the government has embarked on the reform of the Spanish university system. While the traditional attitude has been one of complacency, there is an increased recognition that the Spanish university system underperforms when compared to other developed countries. With a few notable exceptions, the scientific productivity of tenured university professors is abysmal, and the visibility of the Spanish S&T community on the international stage has been limited as a result. At the time of writing this chapter, the fundamental law that governs universities (*Ley Organica de Ordenación Universitaria*, which replaces the LRU) had been approved by both chambers of parliament. However, a strong opposition to this law has emerged from diverse corners, and in particular, from within the university itself. Whether this law is effectively applied or the government backtracks, the fundamental flaws in the Spanish university system will remain.

Finally, several Spanish Autonomous Communities have developed their own science and technology programmes. To that end, some Autonomous Communities have adopted legislation and put in place a regional technological infrastructure. Research and Technological Innovation Interdepartmental Commissions have been created in several Communities, such as Cataluña (1980), Aragón (1983), Valencia (1984), Madrid (1986), Andalucía (1987), Galicia (1987), and Navarra (1988). Moreover, these and some other communities have created advisory agencies in which regional institutions, firms, and scientists interact, and some of them have developed Regional Research Plans.

COLLABORATIVE PROJECTS

1. Legal Framework Applicable to Collaborative Projects in Spain

As a general rule, the operation of joint ventures, and research joint ventures in particular, is constrained by the relevant legislation on competition policy, company law, and intellectual property rights protection. In some instances, the conduct of national industrial policies may have a direct influence on the operation of a RJV. The next paragraphs review existing Spanish and European legislation on the areas identified above. The basic conclusion is that, prior to its entry into the EU, Spain had no relevant legislation, or it was obsolete. *De facto*, the legal regime applicable to RJVs in Spain consists in the translation (literally as well as metaphorically) of European law into the Spanish legal framework. It should also be noted that the absence of any case law in Spain pre-empts any policy evaluation.

Competition policy in Spain consists in the translation of Articles 81 (ex 85) and 82 (ex 86) of the Treaty of Rome, and the relevant Regulations (*Real Decreto 1882/1986*, August 29). The modalities of application of these treaty articles are established by EC regulations 17/62 and 1017/68, which have been translated into national law. These two regulations define the Commission's competencies as well as those of national authorities responsible for the implementation of competition policy. In the case of Spain, the *Tribunal de Defensa de la Competencia* (Antitrust Court) is responsible for applying competition policy. This Commission is thus endowed with substantial powers of search (that is, inspectors authorized by it have the right to search premises and have access to confidential documents). In addition to the *Real Decreto* of 1986, the *Ley 16/1989* (17 July) translates the provisions of the so-called Merger Regulation of 1989 into the Spanish legal framework.

The other piece of relevant legislation regards the protection of intellectual property rights,[4] and can be summarized as follows. The *Ley de Patentes* (Patents Act) of 1986 replaces a 1929 Law that was deemed to be inadequate. It translates the 1973 Munich Convention on European Patents, and the 1975 Luxembourg agreement on a European Community patent. *De facto*, Spain has not generated many patentable innovations; rather, it has 'adopted' innovations developed abroad.[5] Thus, the main policy issue pertains to effective protection of patents developed elsewhere. As a normal consequence of entry into the EC, a process of legal harmonization was initiated. Not so long ago (1996), in the pharmaceutical industry, the transition from a system of ineffective IPR protection to the EU system generated frictions between Spain and its European partners.[6] By now, the Spanish legal system has been, for the most part, brought into line with that of the rest of Europe, and it mainly consists of transposed EU legislation (for example, legislation on genetically modified products adopted in 1994 that embraces Directives 90/219/EEC and 90/220/EEC). *A fortiori*, other pieces of secondary European Law (*'droit derivé'*) that may affect the operation of RJVs are applicable in Spain.[7]

2. The National Plans: Implementation of Collaborative Projects

After the approval in 1986 of the LFCICT, it took two years to draw up the First Plan for the period 1988 to 1991. The budget for the period 1988 to 1991 was 693.3 million euros (1 euro = 166.386 Ptas). The Second Plan, for the period 1992 to 95, was endowed with a total budget of 504.9 million euros. Table 12.5 gives the annual breakdown for the period 1988 to 1999.

*Table 12.5   Budget of the National Plans (million euros)**

YEAR	BUDGET (million euros)
1988	124.7
1989	164.8
1990	199.6
1991	203.9
1992	117
1993	122.1
1994	131.6
1995	134.2
1996	*139.8*
1997	*137.8*
1998	*149.0*
1999	*144.4*
Total First Plan (1988–91)	693.3
Total Second Plan (1992–95)	504.9
Total Third Plan (1996–1999)	*571.1*

Note: * The 1988–1991 period includes the Programa Sectorial de Promoción General del Conocimiento del Ministerio de Educación y Ciencia (Local Programme for the Promotion of General Knowledge financed by the Ministry of Education and Science). Since 1991, it also includes the Programa de Formación y Perfeccionamiento de Personal Investigador del Ministerio de Educación y Ciencia (Researchers Training and Improvement Programme financed by the Ministry of Education and Science), and the I+D Agrario y Alimentario del Ministerio de Agricultura, Pesca y Alimentación (Food and Agricultural R&D Programme financed by the Ministry of Agriculture, Fishing and Food), both included in the National Plan.

Source: Comisión Interministerial de Ciencia y Tecnología, CICYT (1997), 'Memoria de Actividades del Plan Nacional de I+D de 1988 a 1991', Comisión Interministerial de Ciencia y Tecnología, CICYT (1997), 'Memoria de Actividades del Plan Nacional de I+D en 1995', Comisión Interministerial de Ciencia y Tecnología, CICYT, 'Memoria de Actividades del Plan Nacional de I+D. Año 1996', Comisión Interministerial de Ciencia y Tecnología, CICYT, 'Memoria de Actividades del Plan Nacional de I+D. Año 1997', Comisión Interministerial de Ciencia y Tecnología, CICYT, 'Memoria de Actividades de I+D+I Año 1998', and Comisión Interministerial de Ciencia y Tecnología, CICYT, 'Memoria de Actividades de I+D+I Año 1999'.

*Table 12.6   Distribution of expenditures by types of activities and by
scientific areas*

A. By type of activity	First plan (1988–1991)	Second plan (1992–1995)	Third plan (1996–1999)*
Research projects and special actions	38%	43%	51.7%
Infrastructure	15%	13%	12.5%
Coordinated projects and co-operative projects	20%	17%	17.7%
Other activities	4%	5%	7.1%
Training of researchers	23%	21%	12.0%
B. By technical and scientific areas			
Production and communication technologies	42%	41%	44.3%
Social and cultural studies and horizontal and special programmes	19%	10%	7.0%
Quality of life and natural resources	35%	47%	45.2%
Other actions	3%	2%	3.4%

Note: * As of 1998, 'infrastrucure' projects have been relabelled FEDER projects.

Source: Comisión Interministerial de Ciencia y Tecnología, CICYT (1997), 'Memoria de
Actividades del Plan Nacional de I+D de 1988 a 1991', Comisión Interministerial de
Ciencia y Tecnología, CICYT (1997), 'Memoria de Actividades del Plan Nacional de I+D
en 1995', Comisión Interministerial de Ciencia y Tecnología, CICYT, 'Memoria de
Actividades del Plan Nacional de I+D. Año 1996', Comisión Interministerial de Ciencia y
Tecnología, CICYT, 'Memoria de Actividades del Plan Nacional de I+D. Año 1997',
Comisión Interministerial de Ciencia y Tecnología, CICYT, 'Memoria de Actividades de
I+D+I Año 1998', and Comisión Interministerial de Ciencia y Tecnología, CICYT,
'Memoria de Actividades de I+D+I Año 1999'.

Table 12.6 shows the distribution of the expenditures by activities and by
technical and scientific areas. By type of programme, the largest expenditure is on research projects and special actions, while the sectoral
breakdown indicates that production and communication technologies
have received most funds over the entire period (1988–1999). It is worth
noting that 'Quality of Life' and natural resources projects have seen
their share increase substantially at the expense of 'social and cultural
studies and horizontal and special programmes'. By and large, the
Spanish plans closely mirror the priority areas of the EU's Framework
Programmes.

During the three first years (1989 to 1991) of the PETRI programme, 401
applications were received for a budget of 28.9 million euros. Of these, 155

were accepted and granted a total contribution of 6.1 million euros, clearly indicating difficulties in the absorption of available funds. In the Second National Plan we can observe an increase in the figures: 246 applications were accepted and granted a total of 9.4 million euros.

Additionally, Tables 12.7 and 12.8 present the distribution of coordinated projects, where firms and public research centres co-operate, by area and firms' size. First, most of the resources have gone to production and communication technologies. Second, even if small firms have played an important role in the development of the projects, large firms have been the main beneficiaries (despite the fact that approximately 80 per cent of Spanish firms have less than 50 employees).

With respect to the PATI/ATYCA programmes, Table 12.9 indicates that the volume of direct subsidies has reached the amount of 306.5 million euros for the period 1997–1999, to which we need to add preferential credits conceded by the CDTI. These credits are typically associated with subsidized financial packages, such as 0 per cent interest charged on loans.

In 1998, the average subsidy provided to 418 projects by the CDTI was 0.41 million euros. For large firms (more than 500 employees), the average subsidy stood at 0.58 million euros, distributed among 55 projects. Finally, in 1998, support by the CDTI to 66 collaborative and cooperative projects stood at a low 0.002 million euros per project.

CONCLUSION

The principal characteristics of the Spanish innovation system can be summarized as follows. First, it is still in its infancy, as coherent policies were only developed in the 1980s. Second, the conduct of S&T policy is fairly decentralized in Spain, with various ministries and different layers of government enjoying direct compentencies. Third, Spanish S&T policy has been greatly influenced by entry into the EU. This is reflected in the legal framework as well as the sectoral priorities chosen by Spanish authorities. Fourth, the formal performance of the Spanish NSI is rather weak. Fifth, the weight of the public sector is well above the EU average. Despite these weaknesses, the recent performance of the Spanish economy would tend to indicate that the gap with the rest of the EU is somehow being closed.

Table 12.7   Distribution of coordinated and cooperative projects by areas

First National Plan (1988–1991)

Coordinated and cooperative projects	No. of projects	Total Budget (Mill. euros)	No. of agreements with PRCs*
Food, agriculture and natural resources	117	21.2	166
Quality of life	56	21.4	127
Production and Comm. Technologies	270	94.7	315
TOTAL	443	137.3	608

Second National Plan (1992–1995)

Coordinated and cooperative projects	No. of projects	Total Budget (Mill. euros)	No. of agreements with PRCs*
Food, agriculture and natural resources	104	46.3	132
Quality of life	43	35.3	101
Production and Comm. Technologies	237	154.6	305
TOTAL	384	236.2	538

Third National Plan (1996–1999)

Coordinated and cooperative projects	No. of projects	Total Budget (Mill. euros)	No. of agreements with PRCs*
Food, agriculture and natural resources	77	45.9	112
Quality of life	37	34.0	84
Production and Comm. Technologies	149	110.6	182
TOTAL	263	190.5	378

Note: *PRCs stand for Public Research Centres.

Source: Comisión Interministerial de Ciencia y Tecnología, CICYT (1997), 'Memoria de Actividades del Plan Nacional de I+D de 1988 a 1991', Comisión Interministerial de Ciencia y Tecnología, CICYT (1997), 'Memoria de Actividades del Plan Nacional de I+D en 1995', Comisión Interministerial de Ciencia y Tecnología, CICYT, 'Memoria de Actividades del Plan Nacional de I+D. Año 1996', Comisión Interministerial de Ciencia y Tecnología, CICYT, 'Memoria de Actividades del Plan Nacional de I+D. Año 1997', Comisión Interministerial de Ciencia y Tecnología, CICYT, 'Memoria de Actividades de I+D+I Año 1998', and Comisión Interministerial de Ciencia y Tecnología, CICYT, 'Memoria de Actividades de I+D+I Año 1999'.

Table 12.8　Distribution of coordinated and cooperative projects by firms size

First National Plan (1988–1991)	
No. of employees	No. of projects
1–50	152
51–250	111
251–1000	84
>1,000	96
TOTAL	443

Second National Plan (1992–1995)	
No. of employees	No. of projects
1–50	117
51–250	110
251–1000	125
>1.000	32
TOTAL	384

Third National Plan (1996–1999)	
No. of employees	No. of projects
1–50	86
51–250	98
251–1000	38
>1,000	42
TOTAL	264

Source:　Comisión Interministerial de Ciencia y Tecnología, CICYT (1997), 'Memoria de Actividades del Plan Nacional de I+D de 1988 a 1991', Comisión Interministerial de Ciencia y Tecnología, CICYT (1997), 'Memoria de Actividades del Plan Nacional de I+D en 1995', Comisión Interministerial de Ciencia y Tecnología, CICYT, 'Memoria de Actividades del Plan Nacional de I+D. Año 1996', Comisión Interministerial de Ciencia y Tecnología, CICYT, 'Memoria de Actividades del Plan Nacional de I+D. Año 1997', Comisión Interministerial de Ciencia y Tecnología, CICYT, 'Memoria de Actividades de I+D+I Año 1998', and Comisión Interministerial de Ciencia y Tecnología, CICYT, 'Memoria de Actividades de I+D+I Año 1999'.

Table 12.9   Budget of ATYCA projects, 1997–1999

	1997	1998	1999
Million euros	110.8	111.2	84.5

Source: Comisión Interministerial de Ciencia y Tecnología, CICYT, 'Memoria de Actividades de I+D+I Año 1998', and Comisión Interministerial de Ciencia y Tecnología, CICYT, 'Memoria de Actividades de I+D+I Año 1999'.

NOTES

1. We would like to thank Tomás Gamero, Ana Juara, Txema Lopez Raquel Vegas Sánchez and Luis Wong for research assistance during the preparation of this chapter. Financial support from the EU Commission, as part of the TSER 'STEP to RJV' project, is gratefully acknowledged.
2. *Consejo General de la Ciencia y la Tecnología* (Science and Technology General Council).
3. *Consejo Asesor para la Ciencia y la Tecnología* (Science and Technology Advisory Council).
4. In Spanish, 'intellectual property' only refers to works of art. The broader notion that encompasses patentable products is referred to as 'industrial property', and the relevant legislation is the Patents Act.
5. The main justification for adopting a *Ley de Patentes* (B.O.E, 7900, 26/03/86) consists in claims that the adoption of a patent law may enhance 'industrial national competitiveness'. Apart from these somewhat vague statements, the imperative is clearly to adapt Spanish legislation to the EU's legal framework.
6. More precisely, a single market for pharmaceuticals was put in place only recently, well after the 31 December 1992 deadline. French and German pharmaceutical industries complained that Spanish based producers were exporting drugs that had not been submitted to EU IPR rules, and thus requested that barriers to trade be re-introduced as long as Spanish exports escaped IPRs. Eventually, the matter was settled as the volume of Spanish exports falling into that category was small (and close to their expiry dates) and that new output is subject to IPR protection. This example is just an illustration of the problems posed by the transition from an inadequate system of patent protection to the European system.
7. In that respect, Regulation 2349/84 on patent licences, and Regulation 418/85 on R&D agreements, and their respective extensions, are the most relevant pieces of legislation. Another piece of legislation, Regulation 417/84/EEC, could also potentially affect the operation of a RJV. The latter pertains to the operation of 'specialization' agreements.

REFERENCES

Abramovitz, M. (1986), 'Catching up, forging ahead and falling behind', *Journal of Economic History*, **46**(2), 385–406.

Buesa, M. and J. Molero (1990), 'Crisis y transformación de la industria española: base productiva y comportamiento tecnológico', *Revista de Economía Política*, **0**(17), 119–54.

Comisión Interministerial de Ciencia y Tecnología (1996), *III Plan Nacional de I+D*, Madrid: Secretaria de Estado de la Comunicación.

Comisión Interministerial de Ciencia y Tecnología (1997a), *Memoria de Actividades del Plan Nacional de I+D de 1989 a 1991*, Madrid: Secretaria de Estado de la Comunicación.
Comisión Interministerial de Ciencia y Tecnología (1997b), *Memoria de Actividades del Plan Nacional de I+D en 1995*, Madrid: Secretaria de Estado de la Comunicación.
Comisión Interministerial de Ciencia y Tecnología (2000), *National Plan for Scientific Research, Technological Development and Innovation*, Vol. 1, Objectives and Structures, Madrid: Secretaria de Estado de la Comunicación.
Ergas, H. (1987), 'The importance of technology policy', in Partha Dasgupta and Paul Stoneman (eds), *Economic Policy and Technological Performance*, Centre for Economic Policy Research series, Cambridge, New York and Sydney: Cambridge University Press, pp. 51–96.
Ergas, H. (1987), 'Does technology policy matter?', in B. R. Guile and H. Brooks (eds), *Technology and Global Industry: Companies and Nations in the World Economy*, series on technology and social priorities, Washington, DC: National Academy Press, pp. 191–245.
Instituto Nacional de Estadística, INE (1995, 1997), *Encuesta sobre actividades de Investigación y Desarrollo (I+D)*, Madrid: Instituto Nacional de Estadística.
Ministerio de Economía y Hacienda (1991, 1997), *Principales indicadores económicos*.
Mowery, D. and N. Rosenberg (1993), 'The US national innovation system', in R. Nelson (ed.), *National Innovation Systems: A Comparative Analysis*, Oxford, New York, Toronto and Melbourne: Oxford University Press, pp. 29–75.
Nelson, R. and S. Winter (1982), 'The Schumpeterian trade off revisited', *American Economic Review*, **72** (1), 114–32.
Neven, D., P. Papandropoulos and P. Seabright (1998), *Trawling for minnows: European competition policy and agreements between firms*, distributed by Brookings Institution, Washington, DC, London: Centre for Economic Policy Research, pp. xvii and 227.
OECD (1997), *Main Science and Technology Indicators*, Paris: Organisation for Economic Co-operation and Development.
OECD (2000), *S&T Policy Outlook 2000*, Paris: Organisation for Economic Co-operation and Development.
OECD (2001), *Main Science and Technology Indicators*, Paris: Organisation for Economic Co-operation and Development.

13. US policy towards RJVs[1]

Nicholas S. Vonortas

AN INTRODUCTION TO US TECHNOLOGY POLICY UNTIL 2001

For much of the post-war period, the economic policy of the United States (US) had, more or less, been synonymous to macroeconomic policy. The federal government had largely shied away from industrial policy and civilian technology policy.[2] Various presidents since Herbert Hoover, in the late 1920s, had expressed interest in technological advancement for economic growth and in the difficulties of industry segments – primarily small manufacturers – in producing and/or accessing new technologies. However, it was President William Clinton and Vice President Albert Gore who first issued an official document outlining an aggressive approach to technology policy, for the federal government, focusing directly on economic growth. Released only a few months after their arrival to the White House, this document proclaimed a radical departure from the post-war policies of the US, as is evident early on the first page:

> American technology policy must move in a new direction to build economic strength and spur economic growth. The traditional federal role in technology development has been limited to support of basic science and mission-oriented research in the Defense Department, NASA, and other agencies. This strategy was appropriate for a previous generation but not for today's profound challenges. We cannot rely on the serendipitous application of defense technology to the private sector. We must aim directly at these new challenges and focus our efforts on the new opportunities before us, recognizing that government can play a key role in helping private firms develop and profit from innovations. (White House, 1993a, p. 1)

The 'old' orientation of US science and technology policy had stood on two pillars. First, a very active basic science policy, based on the consensus built around the suggestions of Vannevar Bush's report to the US president at the closing of World War II (Bush, 1945 [1990]). Second, the development of advanced technology by several federal agencies in pursuit of their statutory missions (Ergas, 1987). The most important of these missions has been national defence spearheaded by large R&D expenditures by the Department of Defense – until recently accounting for more than the expenses of all other government agencies combined – and extensive military procurement.

According to Branscomb (1993), since World War II, US policy had been based on the following principles:

1. Basic science is a public good. Investments in science lead to new technologies and, occasionally, new industries; however, the market fails to support basic research to the socially optimal level. Recognizing the importance of basic science the government entered into a 'social contract' with scientists, accepting to support scientific research at a much grander scale than ever before while permitting the direction and quality of this research to be determined on the basis of scientific meritocracy (peer review).
2. Federal agencies must aggressively pursue the development of new technology for specific 'missions' in activities with extensive public good characteristics, including national defence, nuclear energy, space exploration, and public health.
3. The federal government must refrain from 'picking winners' through R&D investments directed to technologies for commercial exploitation and specific firms. It is the private sector's responsibility to try to benefit from government-supported science (and education) and from mission technology spin-offs.
4. A further role of the federal government is to create the appropriate regulatory environment to enable efficient markets and to occasionally steer private sector investment in desired directions (e.g., toward environmentally benign technologies). Science and technology can be used to support the struggle against communism.

This was essentially a supply-side approach. The mechanism through which government investments in R&D would assist industrial innovation was that of a 'linear' ('pipeline') model according to which scientific discoveries (and mission technology spin-offs) inevitably lead to new commercial technologies. The selection of technologies for development and the timing of commercial innovation is left entirely to market forces.

In contrast, the 'new' policy orientation of the early 1990s has had the following objectives:

1. Strengthening America's industrial competitiveness and creating jobs;
2. Creating a business environment where technical innovation can flourish and where investment is attracted to new ideas;

3.   Ensuring the coordinated management of technology all across the government;
4.   Forging a closer working partnership among industry, federal and state governments, workers, and universities;
5.   Redirecting the focus of national efforts toward technologies crucial to today's businesses and a growing economy, such as information and communication, flexible manufacturing, and environmental technologies; and,
6.   Reaffirming our commitment to basic science, the foundation on which all technical progress is ultimately built.' (White House, 1993a, p. 1)

Several of these objectives pointed at a radical shift in the traditional policies of the US federal government. Particularly striking were objectives one, three and five, calling for an aggressive federal technology policy to improve the international economic competitiveness of the country, to coordinate management across agencies, and to aim for technologies explicitly for economic growth (Vonortas, 1995). Objectives two and four also called for an enhanced government role in creating the necessary infrastructure and social capital to attract and efficiently utilize private investment in areas of technology of strategic economic importance. Objective six simply continued earlier policies. With the possible exception of the third, all above objectives remain on the agenda of the Administration.

The basic principles of the new US S&T policy orientation in the 1990s have been succinctly characterized by Branscomb (1993) to be the following:

1.   The government must partly shift its priorities from large government missions toward assisting the technological prowess and international competitiveness of the private sector. National defence cannot anymore be driving technologies in many cutting-edge fields. Government agencies are encouraged to buy off-the-shelf, state-of-the-art technologies from the private sector. Agencies with significant S&T budgets should try to develop, to the extent possible, dual-use technologies.
2.   The government must try to balance the supply and demand sides of its technology policy. That is, in addition to the creation of new technologies, significant weight must be placed on technology dissemination. The government must pay attention to the ability of firms to locate, access, adapt, and use new technologies.
3.   State governments must increase their role in the national technology policy. At a minimum, they must be prepared to assist smaller firms, attract capital, and diffusing innovation-related knowledge (e.g., manufacturing extension services).

4. An increased dialogue with industry is necessary to assist the government in making decisions with respect to civilian technologies. Specific technology policy goals can be frequently pursued through public/private cooperative R&D undertakings.
5. A more relaxed antitrust environment allows firms to enter multiple strategic alliances to allay the pressures from increased international competition and to assist them in responding to the demands of rapidly changing technologies. Multi-firm research joint ventures for precompetitive and infrastructural R&D must be favoured.
6. An increasingly stringent enforcement of intellectual property rights by the court system promotes the creation and rapid commercialization of new technological knowledge for the competitiveness of American industry. Intellectual property matters can be linked with the efforts of the US Trade Representative office to ensure a 'level playing field' for American companies in foreign markets.
7. The system of national laboratories should increase their interaction with the private sector in order to expedite the transfer of innovation-related knowledge and facilitate large-scale, heavy facility-dependent R&D.
8. The research universities must also interact more with the private sector. This will both create an alternative source of funds for the universities and will speed up the commercialization of good science to benefit industry.
9. Large science projects should be increasingly funded and undertaken cooperatively with other countries.

Almost all policy principles listed above are more or less related directly to cooperative R&D. It is reflected in the large number of programmes that were set in place during 1993 and 1994 to implement the new policy principles and the existing initiatives relating to civilian technologies that were given a significant boost. Well-known examples of new or enhanced programmes include the Advanced Technology Program (ATP), the Technology Reinvestment Program (TRP), the Environmental Technology Initiative (ETI), the Manufacturing Extension Partnership (MEP), the Partnership for a New Generation of Vehicles (PNGV), and the Small Business Innovation and Research (SBIR) programme. Information technologies, advanced manufacturing technologies, and environmental technologies were considered areas of strategic importance, needy of government intervention due to significant infrastructure requirements and frequent market failure. The National Information Infrastructure (NII) initiative was put in place. The Defense Advanced Research Projects Agency (DARPA) was renamed the Advanced Research Projects Agency (ARPA) and focused on dual use technologies. Government laboratories (many of them part of the Department of Energy's research system) were strongly induced to set up Cooperative R&D Agreements (CRADAs) with industry. Manufacturing R&D was promoted through collaborative agreements in the private sector, made possible by an increasingly relaxed antitrust regulatory system.

AN INTRODUCTION TO POLICIES FOR RESEARCH JOINT VENTURES

The first Clinton Administration arrived with a grand vision that turned technology policy into a front-runner (White House, 1993b). Although it set out to implement a serious policy shift, however, neither the justifications of this shift nor the specific instruments to achieving the main policy objectives were entirely new. The 'new' policy orientation reflected issues and solutions debated for years in the United States.[3] President Jimmy Carter's science advisor had considered several similar ideas in the late 1970s. The science advisor to President George Bush (Clinton's predecessor) was also more sympathetic to an active government role in civilian technology policy.[4]

One such recommendation was that a more balanced supply-side/demand-side technology policy is much more appropriate for the US today than, say, twenty years ago. The obvious justification relates to the change in society's perception of high technology (Branscomb and Florida, 1998). The traditional perception of high tech – still reflected in our indicators – has been research-intensive manufacturing industries, like computers and aircraft. The penetration of technologies like information technology, biotechnology, and advanced materials throughout the economy has, however, changed the basic meaning of high tech. Rather than referring to the output of R&D-intensive industries, high tech now refers to a style of work applicable to just about every business. We can have high tech steel production and low tech steel production; high tech machine tools and low tech machine tools; high tech banking services and low tech banking services; high tech entertainment services and low tech entertainment services; and so forth.

This change is said to have revolutionized the features of a successful technology policy. Distributed knowledge, skill and entrepreneurship, together with new forms of collaboration between firms, universities and the government, can now result in more effective products and services. Importantly for both firm and worker income, they can result in significantly differentiated products and services. In other words, technology policy must be more user-centred and demand-based than ever before.

The S&T policy community in the US had observed such changes since the late 1970s, slowly but steadily moving towards a position of extensive S&T policy modifications. The arguments often drew strength from the signs of declining American competitiveness in vital industries such as consumer electronics, cars, machine tools, and computers from the mid-1970s to the mid-1990s. The signs were strong enough to even move the Reagan Administration, in principle hostile to anything that can be labelled micro-economic management. At least two major steps were taken during its time. One was the discontinuation of the long-term policies of the United States related to competition and intellectual property rights. Another was the initiation of an extensive public debate on economic competitiveness, exemplified by the set-up of the President's Commission on Industrial Competitiveness and its report in the mid-1980s (PCIC, 1985).

The activities around the first step culminated in two concrete actions. First, there was a radical change in the philosophy of antitrust (competition) regulations, starting with the new 'Merger Guidelines' issued by the Antitrust Division of the Department of Justice and the Federal Trade Commission in 1982.[5] Second was the creation of the 11th Circuit Court in the District of Columbia, the first court dedicated to the adjudication of issues related to intellectual property, also in 1982. Essentially, the long-term US policy was being reversed, from strict enforcement of antimonopoly regulations (based on a '*per se*' approach) and fairly lax enforcement of intellectual property rights laws, to more relaxed enforcement of anti-monopoly regulations (based on a 'rule of reason' approach) and much stricter enforcement of intellectual property rights laws (Vonortas, 1997a).

These actions were in line with the Administration's philosophy that, besides the big 'missions' like national defence, the role of the government is limited to the general economic and regulatory environment in which businesses operate. Three successive Republican Administrations in the 1980s became increasingly convinced that the world had changed for American business and that this necessitated policy changes. They were willing to take the initiative to help strengthen what the S&T policy community was claiming to be the foundation of the competitiveness of American business: its ability to create and deploy technological innovations. Often nudged by the Democratic Party-dominated Congress, these administrations were willing to push for the aforementioned changes in antitrust and intellectual property rights policies, introduce a R&E tax credit, maintain the government's support of basic research, and go along with supporting R&D in small businesses through the SBIR programme (requiring all agencies with R&D budget to allocate part of it to small businesses). They were, however, much less willing to offer the direct assistance to civilian technology development that many S&T experts had hoped for.

The public debate on competitiveness culminated in the passing of the Omnibus Trade and Competitiveness Act in 1988 by the American Congress. This was an important piece of legislation, which the Bush Administration was basically forced to accept. Among many other provisions, it radically changed the nature of a little known agency known as the National Bureau of Standards (NBS). It renamed NBS into National Institute of Standards and Technology (NIST) and transformed it into a much more formidable agency enveloping, in addition to its long-standing laboratories for industrial standards, the newly established Advanced Technology Program, Manufacturing Extension Program and Baldridge Quality Award.

The Clinton Administration reinforced the policies of its predecessors and added some new, more interventionist policy instruments. It also added a new strong vision of a more balanced supply-side/demand-side technology-cum-innovation policy. Overall, it gave a strong signal to American industry of a government seriously concerned with technology for economic growth.

COMPETITION POLICY REGARDING COLLABORATIVE R&D

The National Cooperative Research Act

Since its foundation around the turn of the century, US antitrust policy has been primarily concerned with the preservation of competition in industry.[6] Antitrust law has been utilized frequently to fend off damaging cartels, domineering mergers, and various forms of restraints to free market operations raised by dominant firms, such as vertical market foreclosure and other vertical restraints. Inter-firm cooperative agreements (officially defined as joint ventures) have traditionally been treated as partial mergers, that is, an intermediate stage between arm's length market transactions and mergers.

In the 1970s and early 1980s, horizontal mergers with substantial market share came close to being ruled outright (*per se*) illegal, the only exception being cases where one of the firms was on the brink of failure. The hostility extended to horizontal joint ventures – that is, joint ventures among competitors – with substantial market share, including joint ventures focusing on R&D. The prevalent view was that research joint ventures might easily facilitate collaboration among member firms in activities beyond those covered by the explicit agreement (Mason, 1946). To the extent they did, they were raising unwanted barriers for others and were thus undesirable.

The first set of merger guidelines of 1968 on which this restrictive view of JVs was built were, however, extensively revised in the early 1980s. A new set of merger guidelines were issued by the Antitrust Division of the Department of Justice and the Federal Trade Commission in 1982, and were subsequently revised again in 1984. The new guidelines introduced significant changes in the interpretation of the law and they were used by the Reagan Administration to develop new concepts and policies. These changes reflected a build-up of 'antistructural' views since the 1970s that rendered doubtful the mainstream consensus stressing that market structure is a significant indicator of the degree of market power. The antistructural views, instead, were based on beliefs that any type of market structure allows significant variability in firm behaviour and that the entry potential in a market is more important as a predictor of firm behaviour than internal market conditions, even when there is high market dominance (Mueller, 1993).

The Horizontal Merger Guidelines were revised once more in 1992 without, however, reversing the course set during the 1980s. According to this set of guidelines, 'market share and market concentration data provide only the starting point in analysing the competitive effects of mergers' (quoted by Ordover and Willig, 1993, p. 144). Instead of being automatically challenged, a merger lying outside the 'concentration safe region' would be placed under scrutiny to determine whether anticompetitive effects are likely involving a comprehensive examination of the specific market circumstances.[7] Specific market conditions need to be related to one of the anticompetitive effects of concern identified in the guidelines, and explicitly assessed. The most recent amendment of the Horizontal Merger Guidelines in 1997 remained on the same course.

The merger guidelines outline the two agencies' approach to horizontal mergers and acquisitions, and certain competitor collaborations. More importantly, however, the merger guidelines have provided the necessary background for seriously questioning the adequacy of the traditional economic reasoning over whether, why, and when inter-firm collaboration promotes or inhibits competition on the basis of static welfare arguments. Concern over the long-term viability and expansion of American high technology industries during the last couple of decades dictated the introduction of dynamic considerations of market evolution, in addition to the preservation of maximum possible competition, in shaping antitrust policy. Suddenly, organizational forms other than the stand-alone business firm were being contemplated as potentially effective for promoting industrial competitiveness and growth. Inter-firm cooperation, a typical loser in the earlier system of antitrust regulations (largely based on static economic arguments), has been a major beneficiary of such developments. *Per se* rules of the anticompetitive effects of many forms of cooperative agreements have been replaced by a 'rule-of-reason' standard, emphasizing judgment on the merits and drawbacks of individual agreements on the basis of overall economic reasonableness. Dynamic factors (creating competitive advantage) have joined static ones (degree of existing competition) in determining what is good and what is bad.

More recently, the Federal Trade Commission and the US Department of Justice have issued a new set of 'Antitrust Guidelines for Collaborations among Competitors' (April, 2000). These guidelines, specific for horizontal cooperative agreements, come as a supplement to the Horizontal Merger Guidelines and are intended to give guidelines to business people in a year when '. . . the increasing varieties and use of competitor collaborations have yielded requests for improved clarity regarding their treatment under the antitrust laws'. With few exceptions, the rule-of-reason approach is adopted. The mildness of this set of guidelines is evident right from p. 1 where it is declared that '[S]uch collaborations often are not only benign but procompetitive. Indeed, in the last two decades, the federal antitrust agencies have brought relatively few civil cases against competitor collaborations.' Although Congress has protected certain kinds of cooperation from antitrust liability (see below), it is considered that relatively few collaborations have actually sought protection. The Guidelines for Collaborations cover production collaborations, marketing collaborations, buying collaborations, and R&D collaborations.

Cooperation in R&D has played a leading role in shaping the argumentation for more lenient antitrust legislation for inter-firm cooperation during this time period. RJVs have, thus, featured prominently on the antitrust policy agenda. By evoking the dynamic efficiencies in technological change, economists proposed in the early 1980s that cooperation in R&D could, in fact, enhance the participants' competitive advantage. Calls for a more accommodative treatment of RJVs quickly proliferated.

Policy makers responded in 1984 with the enactment of the National Cooperative Research Act (NCRA), intended to sanction inter-firm cooperation in research of generic interest. The rationale for allowing collaboration in the 'earlier' (precompetitive) stages of R&D relied on traditional arguments emphasizing the insufficient incentives of individual firms to undertake basic and precompetitive research at socially optimal levels due to: difficulties in appropriating the output of such research; difficulties in exchanging generic knowledge through the market while assuring a fair rate of return for the investor; the existence of economies of scope in generic research that no single firm can capture adequately; and high levels of uncertainty for the final result. 'Downstream' activities, on the other hand, including product/process development, production and marketing were considered to fall squarely in the domain of private firm operations. Such activities continued to be deemed inappropriate for collaboration.

NCRA required RJVs to be registered with the US Attorney General (Department of Justice) and the Federal Trade Commission in return for preferential antitrust treatment. Even if challenged and convicted in court for limiting competition, a registered RJV would be only liable for the actual damages determined by the court instead of treble damages as the law allows in such cases. Registration of RJVs under the provisions of NCRA started on 1 January 1985.

Extension: The National Cooperative Research and Production Act

NCRA's limited reach to precompetitive research was subsequently challenged in favour of widespread modifications to its provisions in order to include downstream activities such as product development, prototyping and production (for example, US Senate, 1991). Criticism of the NCRA essentially came from two sides, both claiming to perceive some kind of a problem for American firms in commercializing innovations and keeping up with frequent product/process improvements. The driving argument of the first group – the 'traditionalists – was that firm incentives to collaborate in precompetitive research (which the NCRA tried to promote) were being hampered by subsequent restrictions concerning the collective exploitation of the results of this research. Theoretical analysis showed, for example, that the anticipation of head-on competition in development and production between potential co-venturers lowers their *ex ante* incentive to co-operate in research because they expect the surplus to flow to consumers (Katz and Ordover, 1990). It was thus argued that '. . . to the extent that unbridled downstream competition dissipates rents from successful R&D efforts, it may be necessary to allow RJV participants some restraints on ex post competition' (Ordover and Baumol, 1988, p. 30). Such restraints could boost incentives for more research upstream and speed the transfer of innovations to the market.

While traditionalist claims may indeed be true, the analysis they have depended on is far from conclusive. The arguments depended extensively on theoretical models, where R&D leads to innovations in the absence of any direct reference to how new technologies materialize in different industries, and how the process of technological advance affects the incentives for, and the outcomes of, collaborating. There was little or no reference to the technological conditions under which a possible extension of NCRA's provisions might work and when they might not. The actual process of technological advance was essentially dismissed as an argument.

The concern of the second group of proponents of extending NCRA –

the 'nontraditionalists' – was exactly the dismissal of the process of technological innovation from the economic arguments that supported the original NCRA. Being the product of a basically linear model of innovation, they argued, the NCRA was an ineffective policy tool. By differentiating between various types of research for which cooperation is or is not permissible, the NCRA implicitly contended that there is a clear demarcation between basic and precompetitive research on one hand and development research on the other, and that the former precedes the latter. Instead, Jorde and Teece (1990) solicited an alternative model (the simultaneous model of technological innovation) to refuse the existence of any clear distinction between precompetitive research, development research, and production activities in terms of when each activity occurs and how information flows between activities. '[T]he simultaneous model of innovation', they wrote, 'recognises the existence of tight linkages and feedback mechanisms which must operate quickly and efficiently, including links between firms, within firms, and sometimes between firms and other organisations like universities' (Jorde and Teece, 1990, p. 77). Under those circumstances, vertical as well as horizontal linkages assume important roles in leveraging the in-house technical capabilities of a firm.[8]

The opposition to broadening the coverage of NCRA basically concentrated on fears that antitrust policy was becoming too relaxed, thus, endangering further loss of the country's international competitiveness by allowing extensive restrictions to competition. It was argued that existing merger guidelines were already very lenient for joint activities involving firms with considerable combined market share (Harris and Mowery, 1990). There were also fears that increasing cooperation and concentration of market power would adversely affect smaller firms.[9] The proposed extensions were said to increase the chances for collusion while ignoring the real weakness of American firms, which is their slow adoption of new technologies developed internally or externally (Rosenberg and Steinmueller, 1988).

Ultimately, favour went with the proponents of change; the challenge was sustained. Amendments to the NCRA were turned into public law known as the National Cooperative Research and Production Act (NCRPA) in 1993. The prerequisites for collaboration in production were determined to be that, first, the joint venture participants had also cooperated earlier in R&D and, second, they would not exclude independent activities in the same field.

About nine hundred RJVs, with several thousands of business participants, have registered under the provisions of the NCRA and the NCRPA during the first 16 years (1985 to 2000). The response to the legislation is considered low, given the fact that inter-firm strategic technical alliances have exploded at the same time. What's more, an increasing rate of registrations until 1995 has turned into a rapidly decreasing rate in the second half of the 1990s. Recent studies have shown that the registered RJVs have tended to focus on high technology areas, led by information technology and followed by new materials technologies and, in some distance, biotechnology (Vonortas, 1997a; 1997b).

INTELLECTUAL PROPERTY PROTECTION

The United States intellectual property protection system is arguably one of the oldest and the best developed in the world (Wallerstein et al., 1993). This system has been greatly reinforced since the early 1980s, starting with the creation of the 11th Circuit Court of Appeals specializing in intellectual property rights issues in the District of Columbia in 1982.[10] Intellectual property law does not single out RJVs in any way from other stand-alone organizations that legally protect their intellectual property or try to access the intellectual property of someone else.

It is contract law where one should look for evidence of special arrangements in the case of RJVs in order to protect both the intellectual property of individual members as well as the intellectual property that is created by the RJV. There are no generally applicable rules governing the sharing of intellectual property among the members of a joint venture or among the joint venture and third parties. Contracts pertaining to intellectual property in RJVs are built on the basis of prior case experience. Even government programmes that subsidize RJVs, while usually strongly suggesting the use of appropriate legal protection of the resulting intellectual property, leave it to the RJV participants to determine exactly how.

For our purpose, it is interesting to briefly examine the intersection of antitrust (competition) law and intellectual property protection. Similarly to any other organization that acquires, creates, uses and diffuses intellectual property, RJVs are considered benign, procompetitive, and welfare-enhancing but also potentially able to use intellectual property as a means to acquire market power. The US Department of Justice and the Federal Trade Commission have, in fact, released a set of 'Antitrust Guidelines for the Licensing of Intellectual Property' (6 April, 1995). These Guidelines state the Agencies' antitrust enforcement policy with respect to the licensing of intellectual property protected by patent, copyright and trade secret law, and of know-how.[11] The release was in recognition that intellectual property laws and antitrust laws share the goal of promoting innovation and enhancing consumer welfare.

The Intellectual Property Guidelines do not single out RJVs for special treatment in any way. In addition, the guidelines indicate that the two agencies apply the same general antitrust principles to conduct involving intellectual property that they apply to conduct involving any other form of tangible or intangible property. While it is recognized that intellectual property has certain special characteristics, it is also considered that these can be sufficiently taken into account by standard antitrust analysis. Activities that allow intellectual property to be combined more efficiently with other complementary factors of production, including contacts, selling of intellectual property, and joint ventures are generally considered procompetitive. Licensing, cross-licensing, or other means of transferring intellectual property are typically thought to confer procompetitive benefits and be welfare enhancing by allowing access.

Nonetheless antitrust concerns might arise, as for example in the case where an arrangement effectively merges the R&D activities of two or more of only a few entities that could plausibly engage in R&D in the relevant field, thus, harming competition for development of new goods and services (a plausible scenario in an RJV). Three kinds of markets might be adversely affected by intellectual property licensing restraints and are examined by the agencies: (a) (extant) goods markets, related to the licensed intellectual property; (b) technology markets, consisting of the intellectual property that is licensed (when rights to the intellectual property are marketed separately from the products in which they are used); and (c) innovation markets, consisting of the R&D directed to particular new or improved goods or processes, and the close substitutes for that R&D. In the vast majority of intellectual property cases, restraints are evaluated under the rule of reason. This involves an inquiry into whether the restraint is likely to have anticompetitive effects and, if so, whether the restraint is reasonably necessary to achieve procompetitive benefits that outweigh those anticompetitive effects. Application of the rule of reason generally requires a comprehensive inquiry into market conditions.

No such inquiry is initiated for intellectual property arrangement restraints that affect product, technology, and innovation markets falling within the antitrust 'safety zones' defined by the guidelines. Absent extraordinary circumstances, the antitrust authorities will abstain from challenging a restraint if, one, the restraint is not facially anticompetitive and, two, the licensor and the licensees collectively account for no more than 20 per cent of the relevant goods market significantly affected by the restraint. Also, absent extraordinary circumstances, the authorities will abstain from challenging a restraint that may affect competition in a technology market if (a) the restraint is not facially anticompetitive and (b) there are four or more independently controlled technologies in addition to the technologies controlled by the parties in the IP arrangement that may be substitutable for the exchanged technology at a comparable cost to the user. Finally, absent extraordinary circumstances, the authorities will abstain from challenging a restraint that may affect competition in an innovation market if the restraint is not facially anticompetitive and four or more independently controlled entities in addition to the parties in the IP arrangement possess the required specialized assets or characteristics and the incentive to engage in R&D that is a close substitute of the R&D activities of the parties in the IP agreement.

CONCLUDING REMARKS

A dramatic change has occurred in the way policy analysts and decision-makers in capitalist economies perceive the advantages and disadvantages of inter-firm cooperation. Rather than organizational mechanisms to assist declining industries and weakened firms, inter-firm cooperative agreements are now viewed as veritable competitive mechanisms, right at the strategy core of most companies in high technology industries. A voluminous economic and business literature has shown that large numbers of firms regularly use strategic technical alliances to access, create, and diffuse technological knowledge. Research joint ventures – being just one kind of strategic technical alliances – now feature prominently on the policy agenda of every developed country government.

The US government has decidedly followed this trend since the early 1980s. While there have been serious disagreements between the two major political parties during this time period, concerning the appropriate role of the government in providing incentives to the private sector to cooperate in R&D, few in either camp seem to doubt the value of RJVs.

Abiding with the doctrine on non-market interference, the Republican Administrations of the 1980s set the stage for a radical shift in market environment affecting business strategy and behaviour, including the undertaking of R&D, by introducing extensive changes in antitrust and intellectual property-rights law and enforcement. On one hand, a series of annotated merger guidelines issued by the Department of Justice and the Federal Trade Commission have promoted a new attitude towards 'partial mergers' (joint ventures). The competitive effects of joint ventures is now judged on a 'rule-of-reason' basis, requiring that the possible anticompetitive effects are juxtaposed to their potential for current and future (dynamic) procompetitive and consumer welfare-enhancing effects. Starting in the early 1980s, this shift opened the door for the National Cooperative Research Act of 1984 to offer antitrust protection to RJVs undertaking research of generic interest, a clear signal that cooperative research was now becoming a desirable activity. Its follow-up, the National Cooperative Research and Production Act of 1993, extended protection to any type of inter-firm collaboration as long as it is based on cooperative R&D.

On the other hand, the establishment of a new Circuit Court for IPR matters that took a much stricter approach to infringement gave a clear signal that private intellectual property is a very valuable resource, much recognized by society and well protected in court. This gave additional incentives for collaboration by allaying the fears of prospective RJV partners regarding involuntary loss of own knowledge to other RJV members and by better enabling the RJV and its partners to better exploit the returns from R&D collaboration. In addition, a series of legislative actions in the past twenty years have created the legal framework for promoting industry-university-government cooperation in science and technology and for allowing industry and universities to benefit financially from the results of the research undertaken with or for the government (excepting national defence items). Instrumental pieces of this legislation that paved the road in the 1980s for the greater government-industry partnership in the 1990s have been the Stevenson-Wydler Technology Innovation Act (1980), the Bayh-Dole University and Small Business Act (1980), the Small Business Innovation Development Act (1982), the Federal Technology Transfer Act (1986) and the National Competitiveness Technology Transfer Act (1989). The National Cooperative Research Act (1984) and the National Cooperative Research and Production Act (1993) should be added to this list too.

The Democratic Administrations that took office early in the 1990s built on this system. In addition to reinforcing the legal environment favouring the establishment of RJVs, they pushed forward a series of programmes actively promoting collaboration in R&D through subsidies or other incentives. The objective was now to use government resources to 'channel' private sector R&D activity in certain technological areas with significant potential for widespread economic returns. Government resources were limited; RJVs were used as a mechanism to leverage these resources with the resources of industry. The ATP, the TRP, and the PNGV are only a few, well-known examples of such efforts. CRADAs involving government laboratories and industry also expanded rapidly.

Unfortunately for the Administration, an extensively renewed 104th Congress in 1994 quickly got busy unravelling its technology policy objectives and strongly pushed in reverse. The 105th Congress, sworn in office in 1996, continued in the same direction, as has, more or less, also been the case with the 106th Congress starting in 1998 and until the time of this writing. The extended set of programmes that were pushed forward in the first 4-year term of the Clinton Administration did not survive intact. Some were eliminated (TRP for example), others were weakened or neutralized (for example, ATP), and still others lost their direction under a weakened Administration and became ineffective, even non-operational (such as PNGV). The blow was severe and, together with the continuing conservatism of the legislature concerning the appropriate role of the government in science and technology (US Congress, 1998), it seems to have curtailed the enthusiasm of the Administration for active technology-cum-innovation policy.

The extraordinary circumstances in which the current (Bush-Cheney) Administration has governed have not helped the situation either. Clearly, the focus has shifted once again to security matters and, if anything, the US government policies seem to lean towards the older supply-side approach (see the first section of this chapter), emphasizing missions, basic research, and public health.

Even so, the general policy orientation towards legislative leniency regarding inter-firm collaboration and a strong partnership between industry, universities, and government has remained intact. Government policy has largely adapted to and, even more, has acquired a clear supporting attitude towards the continuing drive of the private sector to engage in complex webs of strategic technology alliances.

NOTES

1. This chapter draws extensively on Vonortas (1995, 1997a, and 2000).
2. With exceptions, of course, particularly at times of widely perceived national emergencies like the response to the oil price increases in the 1970s. In addition, one must consider the policies at the state level which have often been much more microeconomic in nature and much more explicitly concerned with issues related to industry, investment, and technology (Rycroft, 1990).
3. A significant number of high-visibility reports were produced in the late 1980s and early 1990s stressing the need for radical policy change. See various reports by committees organized under the aegis of the National Academy of Sciences, National Academy of Engineering, and the Institute of Medicine – for instance, Committee on Science, Engineering and Public Policy (1992, 1993); and Committee on Technology Policy Options in a Global Economy (1993). See also National Science Board (1992), Council on Competitiveness (1991), and Competitiveness Policy Council (1993).
4. During the tenure of President Bush in the late 1980s, an Industrial Technology Division was established in the Office of Science and Technology Policy (OSTP) of the White House. In addition, the dormant Federal Coordinating Council for Science, Engineering and Technology (FCCSET) was revived and given authority to identify programme areas of interest across all major S&T agencies. However, the effort to back up the identified 'critical technologies' of high performance computing and communication, biotechnology, advanced materials, and advanced manufacturing with real budgets did not get very far. An OSTP document of the time entitled 'US Technology Policy' did not have much success either.
5. Subsequent versions of these guidelines have followed in the same direction. See the next section.

6.   The Sherman Act of 1890 was the first federal antitrust law in the US and is generally
     accepted as setting in place the foundations of US antitrust policy. (By the time the
     Sherman Act was passed, twelve states had passed their own antitrust laws.) The major
     follow-up legislation establishing merger control provisions were the Clayton Act
     of 1914, the Celler-Kefauver Act of 1950, and the Hart-Scott-Rodino Premerger
     Notification Act of 1976. See Scherer (1994) for an overview.
7.   The expression 'concentration safe region' denotes the borders of acceptable market
     competition. A merger that falls within this region is not contestable. Another falling
     outside it, contestable *per se* with the old rules, may not be contestable under the rule-
     of-reason.
8.   Such views permeate the contemporary applied literature on inter-firm strategic alli-
     ances. See, for example, Culpan (1993), Gomes-Casseres (1996), Gulati (1998), Teece
     (1992).
9.   See, for example, the testimony of Michael Porter (US Senate, 1991).
10. Studies show that, up to 1982, about one third of all legal claims against patent infringe-
     ment were successful in court. This share has increased to about three quarters since
     1982.
11. The term 'licensing' is used generically for technology transfer; it incorporates licensing,
     cross-licensing and other means of transferring of intellectual property.

REFERENCES

Branscomb, L. M. (ed.) (1993), *Empowering Technology*, Cambridge, MA: The
     MIT Press.
Branscomb, L. M. and R. Florida (1998), 'Challenges in technology policy in a
     changing world economy', in L. M. Branscomb and J. H. Keller (eds), *Investing
     in Innovation: Creating a Research and Innovation Policy that Works*, Cambridge,
     MA: The MIT Press.
Bush, V. (1945), *Science – The Endless Frontier: A Report to the President on a
     Program for Postwar Scientific Research*, 40th anniversary publication (1990) by
     the National Science Foundation.
Committee on Science, Engineering, and Public Policy (1992), *The Government Role
     in Civilian Technology: Building a New Alliance*, Washington, DC: National
     Academy Press.
Committee on Science, Engineering, and Public Policy (1993), *Science, Technology,
     and the Federal Government: National Goals for a New Era*, Washington, DC:
     National Academy Press.
Committee on Technology Policy Options in a Global Economy (1993), *Mastering
     a New Role: Shaping Technology Policy Options in a Global Economy*,
     Washington, DC: National Academy Press.
Competitiveness Policy Council (1993), 'Technology policy for a competitive
     America', report to the US president, Washington, D.C.
Council on Competitiveness (1991), *Gaining New Ground: Technology Priorities for
     America's Future*, Washington, DC: Council on Competitiveness.
Culpan, R. (ed.) (1993), *Multinational Strategic Alliances*, New York: International
     Business Press.
Ergas, H. (1987), 'Does technology policy matter?', in B. Guile and H. Brooks (eds),
     Technology and Global Industry, Washington, DC: National Academy Press.
Federal Trade Commission and US Department of Justice (2000), *Antitrust
     Guidelines for Collaborations among Competitors*, Washington, DC, April.

Gomes-Casseres, B. (1996), *The Alliance Revolution: The New Shape of Business Rivalry*, Cambridge, MA: Harvard University Press.

Gulati, R. (1998), 'Alliances and networks', *Strategic Management Journal*, **19**, 293–317.

Harris, R. G. and D. C. Mowery (1990), 'New plans for joint ventures', *The American Enterprise*, September/October, 52–5.

Jorde, T. M. and D. J. Teece (1990), 'Innovation and cooperation: implications for competition and antitrust', *Journal of Economic Perspectives*, **4**(3), 75–96.

Katz, M. L. and J. A. Ordover (1990), 'R&D cooperation and competition', *Brookings Papers on Economic Activity: Microeconomics*, 137–91.

Mason, E. S. (1946), *Controlling World Trade: Cartels and Commodity Agreements*, New York: McGraw-Hill.

Mueller, D. C. (1993), 'US merger policy and the 1992 Merger Guidelines', *Review of Industrial Organization*, **8**(2), 151–62.

National Science Board (1992), *The Competitive Strength of US Science and Technology: Strategic Issues*, Washington, DC: National Science Foundation.

Ordover, J. A. and W. J. Baumol (1988), 'Antitrust policy for high-technology industries', *Oxford Review of Economic Policy*, **4**, 13–35.

Ordover, J. A. and R. D. Willig (1993), 'Economics and the 1992 merger guidelines: A brief survey', *Review of Industrial Organization*, **8**(2), 139–50.

United States President's Commission on Industrial Competitiveness (1985), *The Report of the President's Commission on Industrial Technology*, Washington, DC: GPO.

Rosenberg, N., and D. E. Steinmueller (1988), 'Why are Americans such poor imitators?', *AEA Papers and Proceedings*, 229–34.

Rycroft, R. (1990), 'The internationalization of U.S. intergovernmental relations in science and technology policy', *Technology and Society*, **12**, 217–33.

Scherer, F. M. (1994), *Competition Policies for an Integrated World Economy*, Washington, DC: The Brookings Institution.

Teece, D. J. (1992), 'Competition, cooperation, and innovation: organizational arrangements for regimes of rapid technological progress', *Journal of Economic Behavior and Organization*, **18**, 1–25.

United States Congress (1998), 'Unlocking our future: toward a new national science policy', report to the House Committee on Science, September.

United States President's Commission on Industrial Competitiveness (PCIC) (1985), *The Report of the President's Commission on Industrial Technology*, Washington, DC: GPO.

United States Senate (1991), 'The National Cooperative Research Act Extension of 1991', Bill No. 479.

Vonortas, N. S. (1995), 'New directions for US science and technology policy: the view from the R&D assessment front', *Science and Public Policy*, **22**(1), 19–28.

Vonortas, N. S. (1997a), *Cooperation in Research and Development*, Norwell, MA and Dordrecht, Netherlands: Kluwer Academic Publishers.

Vonortas, N. S. (1997b), 'Research joint ventures in the United States', *Research Policy*, **26**, 577–95.

Vonortas, N. S. (2000), 'Technology policy in the United States and the European Union: shifting orientation towards technology users', *Science and Public Policy*, **27**(2), 97–108.

Wallerstein, M. B., M. E. Mogee and R. A. Schoen (eds) (1993), *Global Dimensions of Intellectual Property Rights in Science and Technology*, Washington, DC: National Academy Press.
White House (1993a), 'Technology for America's economic growth, a new direction to build economic strength', report issued by the US president, February, Washington, DC.
White House (1993b), 'Technology for economic growth: President's progress report', report issued by the US president, November, Washington, DC.

14. Policies for cooperative R&D

Yannis Caloghirou, Nicholas S. Vonortas and Stavros Ioannides

Since the early 1980s, the governments of industrialized countries have made a strong effort to promote cooperative industrial research. The chapters in this part of the book point out significant convergence of key policy areas in Europe during the past 10 to 15 years that directly affect the incentives of firms to engage in cooperative R&D. Such convergence has been reflected in science, technology, and innovation policies, competition policies, and intellectual property rights policies. Important tendencies in this direction across the continent include:

- Increasing awareness of the competitiveness issue and its relation to innovation.
- Increasing awareness of innovation as a process involving both a technology-producing and a technology-using side.
- Increasing awareness of systems of innovation, firmly based on interconnections and interaction between economic agents of different kinds.
- Greater attention to the potential of R&D cooperation to serve as a mechanism that promotes such interaction and contributes to increasing the technological prowess of firms and regions.
- Emphasis on university-industry and public research institute-industry cooperation.
- Assistance to small and medium sized enterprises (SMEs), placing special emphasis on small entrants into emerging high technology markets.
- Awareness of the importance of the institutional, physical, regulatory, and financial infrastructure to support emerging technologies and increasing realization of the importance of adequate competition and IPR policies to promote cooperative R&D.

By and large, however, the story told in these chapters – and in other papers available to the editors dealing with the policies of countries such as

Ireland, Sweden, and Japan – is one of continuing divergence. There have been extensive differences between the approaches of individual EU member states and between Europe, Japan and the United States. Table 14.1 below attempts to summarize the major features of policies towards cooperative RTD in the countries examined in this study (Caloghirou, Vonortas and Ioannides, 2002). Six criteria are listed in the first column. The first criterion (C1) is whether RTD cooperation was initiated predominantly at the policy level in a top-down mode or in a bottom-up mode. The second criterion (C2) is whether the essence of a national policy is to structure the development of national S&T competence or, rather, to adapt to standards imported from outside the respective country. The third criterion (C3) is whether national S&T policy merely enables cooperation in RTD or actively promotes it. The fourth criterion (C4) concerns the primary policy mechanism towards RTD cooperation: funding or institutional regulation. The fifth criterion (C5) is whether competition policy aims actively to promote RJVs or is passively adapting to standards imported from abroad. Finally, the sixth criterion (C6) is whether IPR arrangements are specifically targeting the intellectual property problems that arise in the context of cooperative RTD or whether they are of general character. We are adopting a binary system of assessment; the figure in each box is meant to signify the predominant quality of the policy of the respective country according to the specific criterion. As it is evident from Table 14.1, there are some instances where it is not possible to single out the dominant feature for a specific country.

The effort to promote cooperative RTD is well entrenched in Europe. However, national policy approaches have ranged widely, from almost complete indifference to the issue until recently (Ireland), to decreasing and refocusing attention (UK), to lukewarm policies (Greece and Italy), to established, wide-ranging network systems (Sweden), to highly determined programmes to assist cooperative industrial RTD (France and Spain). The level and type of support has varied widely as have the specific policies and programmes, their technological focus and the numbers and kinds of participating economic agents. Amidst this variation, the analysis underlying the chapters in this part suggests that the European Commission's policies have played a boosting and cohesive role that sets them apart from the policies adopted by the US and even Japan.

Japan has been, and continues to be an active supporter of cooperative RTD (notice the difference from the US with reference to C1, C3 and C4 in Table 14.1). Government-sponsored RJVs seem to have made the transition since the 1980s, from being primarily mechanisms assisting whole sectors to catch up with world practice, to being mechanisms creating a richer and more effective technological superstructure for a large group of

Table 14.1   Policies towards cooperative R&D

Characteristic	EU	FR	IT	UK	S	EL	IR	ES	J	US
C1										
RTD co-operation policy: top-down (TD) or bottom-up (BU)	TD	TD	TD	TD-BU	TD	TD	TD	TD	TD	BU
C2										
The essence of policy: structuring (S) or adaptive (A)	S	S	S-A	S	S	A	A	S-A	S	S
C3										
Is policy merely enabling (E) or actively promoting (P) cooperation in RTD?	P	P	E-P	E-P	P	E	E-P	E-P	P	E
C4										
Primary policy mechnism for coop. RTD: funding (F) or regulation (R)	F	F	F	F-R	F-R	F	F	F	F-R	R
C5										
Is competition policy actively (A) promoting RJV or passively (P) adapting?	A	P	P	P	P	P	P	P	A	A
C6										
Is IPR policy specifically targeting (T) RJVs or is it general (G) in nature?	T	G	G	G	T	T	G	G	T	T

Source: Caloghirou, Vonortas and Ioannides (2002).

high technology sectors. In contrast to Japan, in the US cooperative RTD has been a bottom-up process, which the administration had to accommodate through its S&T policies. Even though it is has not always been obvious, in retrospect the US seems to have followed a rational approach to the issue. It first changed its institutional structure and relevant legal system. It then moved forward to put in place specific programmes to actively promote cooperative RTD. Therefore, although responding to a process that it had not initiated, US policy has attempted to actively structure the environment for cooperative RTD activity (hence the assessment with reference to C2, C5 and C6 in Table 14.1).

The EU approach appears to have been the reverse of the American approach, but equally rational on the face of the specific situation of the region. Confronted with a large collection of significantly varied nationally-based S&T policies, the Commission first moved to put in place its own supra-national programmes for cooperative RTD before trying to harmonize policies across its member states.[1] It has hoped that a series of well established and funded Framework Programmes for RTD would increase the chances for bringing European research organizations together, thus increasing the effectiveness and cohesiveness of capabilities existing in Europe. Our analysis suggests that this policy has been especially successful in the case of 'cohesion' countries, where it has provided a valuable framework for national policies towards RJVs to adapt to. (Notice the assessment of the policies of Greece, Ireland and Spain with reference to C2, C3, C4 and C5 in Table 14.1.) At the same time, however, there is some evidence of harmonization, as our assessments of the quality of S&T policies in France, UK, Italy and Sweden (especially in criteria C2, C4 and C5) seem to reflect. Thus, even in countries with experience in cooperative RTD, it appears that the establishment of a EU framework has led to some harmonization of relevant policies. EU policies have clearly influenced policies at the national level and, in certain cases, shaped them to the extent of straightforward translation.

NOTE

1. In fact, the first FWP was initiated in 1984 before the legal basis for Community S&T programmes was in place. The legal basis for S&T policy was provided in 1987 by the Single European Act and in 1992 by the Treaty of Maastricht, which amended the Treaty of Rome. See also Peterson and Sharp (1998).

REFERENCES

Caloghirou, Y., N. S. Vonortas and S. Ioannides (2002), 'Science and technology policies towards research joint ventures', *Science and Public Policy*, **29**(2), 82–94.
Peterson, J. and M. Sharp (1998), *Technology Policy in the European Union*, New York: St. Martin's Press.

15. Policy implications

Yannis Caloghirou and Nicholas S. Vonortas

Since the early 1980s, most industrial country governments have promoted cooperative industrial R&D aggressively. The European Union has been a front-runner, turning cooperative R&D into a cornerstone of the Framework Programmes in RTD, *de facto* the most important piece of the Union's science and technology policy. The direct or indirect support of cooperative R&D has also gained a lot of ground in member states, including both those with significant experience in science, technology and industrial innovation policy and those without.

We believe that the research results reported in the various chapters of this book justify the following implications for policy decision-makers and analysts.

1. It is time to take stock of the widespread cooperative R&D in Europe.
Support for cooperative R&D in high-technology industrial activities is widespread in Europe. This compounds the already widespread practice of strategic technical alliances under private initiative. The process has created high expectations for increased competitiveness that has proved very difficult to show quantitatively until now. New policy expectations for cooperative R&D have also been introduced in the form of achieving social and economic cohesion among the EU's many different member countries and regions. The proclaimed structure of the sixth Framework Programme on RTD, based on the formation of 'networks of excellence' and on 'integrated projects', is a clear signal of the need for appraisal of past achievements by employing multi-faceted methodologies able to systematically analyse large amounts of empirical information and combine them with in-depth case studies.

2. Policy analysts need to consider long lists of benefits and costs to cooperative R&D.
Cooperative R&D creates private and social benefits (and costs). Private benefits (and costs) accrue to participating organizations. Potential private benefits include:

- R&D cost sharing;
- Reduction of R&D duplication;
- Risk sharing, uncertainty reduction;
- Spillover internalization;
- Continuity of R&D effort, access to finance;
- Access of complementary resources and skills;
- Research synergies;
- Effective deployment of extant resources and further development of resource bases;
- Strategic flexibility, market access and the creation of investment 'options';
- Promotion of technical standards;
- Market power, co-opting competition;
- University and research institute research better attuned with private sector interests.

Examples of private costs are the actual cost of the activity, loss of control over a technology, transaction costs to ensure compliance and smooth collaboration, and so on.

Cooperative R&D also creates social benefits (and costs) that accrue to non-participating organizations and the rest of society. Social benefits may be the result of:

- Knowledge spillovers to non-participants;
- Increased competitiveness;
- Increased levels of competition;
- Favourable changes in investment behaviour;
- Technology standards;
- Economic convergence.

Social costs may be the result of collusion and anticompetitive behaviour, lessened innovative effort, waste of taxpayers' money, creating dependencies on public funds, and so on.

There are also direct and indirect benefits and costs from R&D cooperation. Direct benefits and costs are those linked directly to a cooperative R&D activity for example, the introduction of a new innovation, or the transaction costs involved in this activity. Indirect benefits and costs are the unintended by-products that often turn out to be very significant. For example, engaging in a RJV may not only result in the introduction of a new product, but also the maintenance of certain capabilities internally that will allow the firm's presence in that technological area for time to come. Or, increased competitiveness in a particular industry segment may also boost the chances of client industries. It may also have other socio-economic benefits like employment and regional upgrading. The latter might be an interesting issue for future investigation.

Policy analysts should try to account for as many as possible of these in cost-benefit appraisals. Unfortunately, it is the private, and direct, benefits and costs that are relatively easier to determine within some acceptable range of accuracy. Social, and indirect, benefits and costs are much harder. It is, of course, the latter that policy makers are primarily interested in.

3. The recently introduced European approach of appraising the socio-economic effects of policy seems appropriate in the case of cooperative R&D.

As a result of the fact that RJVs create direct and indirect, private and social benefits and costs, the analysis of the incentives of firms and other organizations to participate and the impacts of these RJVs necessitates a multi-faceted and interdisciplinary approach. A strong case can be made for both objective and subjective measures of performance. Essentially, this means that the socio-economic appraisal of incentives and impacts is the most reasonable way to proceed.

4. Benefits (and costs) of cooperative R&D cannot be appraised solely on the basis of objective measures of performance – such as financial data for firms. Subjective measures of performance are at least as necessary.

Experts have struggled with thorny issues regarding both methodology and measurement of the outcomes of collaboration. The long-standing debate on whether financial or other objective measures of performance, such as partnership survival, duration and stability, should be preferred over subjective measures of performance has been at the forefront of attention. Much of the problem resides in the controversy concerning the measurement of organizational performance in general. Difficulties get compounded in the case of hybrid organizational forms where, not surprisingly, there is no consensus concerning both the definition and measurement of performance. There is no clear definition of partnership success. There is disagreement on whether objective measures (such as profitability, growth and duration) or subjective measures of success are more appropriate in appraising success. Objective measures are more widely available. However, objective measures may not adequately reflect the extent to which a partnership achieved its short- and long-term objectives, which are often diverse. Even when subjective measures can be constructed, there is difficulty in assigning values to individual measures of success for the partnership as a whole. Various partners usually have different expectations from the same partnership, thus making several authors argue against generalizing from one partner's evaluation. 'Triangulation' of partner evaluations has thus been suggested.

When queried, firms often tend to rank their objectives to participate in collaborative R&D quite differently than standard theory would anticipate. In fact, they rank 'soft' objectives pretty highly, of the kind that economic theory has had problems to appraise them. For example, highly ranked objectives by firms in this study include: (a) establishment of new relationships; (b) access to complementary resources and skills; (c) technological learning; (d) keeping up with major technological developments. Such objectives are difficult to quantify accurately.

All in all, problems in combining objective and subjective measures of partnership performance abound. It is beyond doubt, however, that the use of subjective measures of performance is unavoidable if we are to reasonably approximate the true extent of the diverse benefits and costs involved in cooperative R&D agreements (and strategic alliances more generally).

5. **The most frequent participants in RJVs are large firms whereas the majority of participating firms are SMEs. Firms participating in RJVs tend to operate in a business environment characterized by technology and product-features based competition.**

6. **There is a fixed cost involved in collaboration. Government programmes can assist in creating the preconditions for newcomers, especially smaller firms, to be successfully integrated into RJVs.**

The parties willing to enter a transaction must be able to create a mechanism to provide the necessary incentives to perform to expected standards. The way RJVs may achieve such a mechanism is by creating a 'mutual hostage' situation through the commitment of resources by all partners. To the extent that the agreement is one of a kind for the specific partners, the RJV will require significant commitments of specialized resources by each and every one of them. Smaller firms, often lacking reputation and market credibility when trying to enter their first RJV, will need to compensate with a significant resource commitment. On the contrary, the presence of multi-market and multiproject contact between partners (firms 'meeting' each other in many markets and many partnerships) may easily create the necessary preconditions for mutual forbearance between partners, freeing them from the burden of significant resource commitment. Such conditions require diversified and larger firms with presence in various present and future markets. The implication is that firms that lack significant resources need them the most in order to be accepted in RJVs. Cooperative R&D programmes could be tailored to assist SMEs to create the necessary 'capital' in their first steps to collaboration.

There is also a fixed cost involved in R&D activity. This is especially important for the 'cohesion' countries that often lack significant resources for initiating research activities. Funded cooperative agreements offer the possibility for achieving a critical mass of R&D, not only because of sub-sidizing this fixed cost but also because actors from Southern Europe become networked with other organizations and establish channels for knowledge transfer and for keeping up with technological developments. The urgency of this factor increases with the anticipated expansion of the European Union to the east and south in the near future.

7.   Benefits obtained from collaborative R&D increase with the internal (independent) capabilities and research activities of firms. Put differently, collaborative R&D is a complement to, rather than a substitute of, internal R&D.

Evidence in this study strongly confirms earlier results indicating that knowledge in the public domain does not benefit everyone equally. Two conditions are required: (a) a willingness to learn; and (b) an ability to learn. Earlier work has shown that, in addition to creating new knowledge, R&D is useful for maintaining/increasing the ability to learn from others. Translated in the context of RJVs, internal R&D, perhaps even parallel R&D projects, increase the benefits from R&D undertaken cooperatively. Active monitoring (willingness to learn) also works in the same direction.

By offering the possibility to achieve a critical mass of R&D resources, subsidized cooperative R&D projects assist partners to improve their capa-bilities, at least in doing R&D. Considering the positive correlation between capabilities of the firm and benefits obtained from the R&D undertaken through cooperation, it could be that the first time participation in a subsi-dized RJV may become a positive factor for continuation in successful future R&D cooperative programmes.

8.   Ability to learn enhances the benefits from cooperative R&D.

In an effort to account for the apparently differential benefits that some partners in RJVs are able to obtain compared to others, we related each of three broad categories of benefits (product development, process and knowledge base) to a long list of learning mechanisms. The mechanism of undertaking internal, independent, and related R&D was strongly corre-lated with all three types of benefits. Benefits to the knowledge base corre-lated with all other learning mechanisms. This is also the case with product development benefits (with only one exception), particularly so with devel-oping formal and informal relationships with users and/or suppliers. Process development benefit was positively correlated with learning by imi-tating other firms. In all cases, ability to learn was important for reaping benefits from cooperative R&D. The lesson for public policy is that innovation involves complex processes that require attention not only to 'technology push' factors – the traditional focus of technology policy – but also to 'technology pull' factors (technology user).

9. **Trust is a major factor in inter-organizational collaboration. Mutual trust among prospective partners lowers transaction costs and increases the desirability of a RJV. Tailoring government programmes to 'underwrite' trust can prove a real booster for R&D cooperation, particularly for firms with lesser amounts of market reputation and goodwill (such as new technology-based firms (NTBFs)).**

Trust between partners plays a critical role in cooperation. By lowering transaction costs, trust makes partnerships more desirable. Trust-building, however, is a process dependent on reputation and prior interaction. It is not accidental that this and other studies have found a strong, positive relationship between prior engagements in collaborative R&D activities and tendency to do it again. The reason is that frequent RJV participants use their reputation as good, trustworthy partners for lowering their direct resource commitment in later deals and in enticing new partners. It is also not accidental that firm size has a strong, positive relationship with RJV participation – the effect comes through reputation. Governments may have a critical role to play in assisting newcomers (especially SMEs) to create the necessary 'reputation capital' and obtain the necessary resources in order to be accepted to the club.

10. **There is a great need to better understand the factors that determine the specific pairs of cooperating firms. We still lack standardized indicators of prospective pairs of collaborators forming in particular technological fields. Such indicators would greatly help in designing public programmes.**

The material presented here has pointed out some of the variables that could be used to create standardized indicators of likely pairs of collaborators. Such essential variables match the characteristics of pairs of firms that have ended up collaborating in the past, trying to extrapolate future collaboration patterns. They include the sector(s) of the firms in the pair, the relationship between their products, and the extent to which the firms are symmetric. Several other characteristics could also be tested. A particularly useful exercise may be to test the extent to which the defined relationships between characteristics hold as firms tie up more and more often within individual technological areas. Being able to anticipate more accurately the likely participants to RJVs, should promote better delivery of public programmes to the targeted populations.

11. The design and governance of government programmes supporting cooperative R&D is important in determining the effects on industry.

The different design and governance of Framework Programmes and EUREKA have resulted in different sets of RJVs and differential effects on industry. While the evidence in this book is far from conclusive, there was evidence nonetheless of relatively different features between the two sets of RJVs and pairs of collaborating firms with differential objectives. Similar arguments could also be made for cooperative R&D supported by national programmes. Such findings concur with those in other literature and underline the importance of the design and governance of a programme for achieving its objectives. Indirectly, they also underline the importance of using differential approaches to appraise programmes with different objectives.

12. Is public funding necessary? This perennial question of government policy was answered positively with respect to the formation of RJVs.

A total of 456 firms answered the question in the RJV survey relating to alternatives that would be open to them, if public funding for the specific RJV had not materialized. Almost two-thirds reported that they would not have undertaken the specific research without government funding. For between two-thirds and three-quarters of the respondents, the specific cooperative R&D related to their core business activity.

Standing on its own, this information may be significantly discounted because it is based on the subjective evaluations of the respondents to the survey. It gets additional weight when combined with the discussion on points 4 and 5 above. Public funding may be more important for some kinds of firms than others. The funding also receives additional credibility when there is evidence that the R&D supported by public funds has latent public good characteristics. Public funding is more important for some kinds of research than others. Attention to SMEs and focus on precompetitive research would seem to fit the bill.

Government funding is not only important for its resource aspect, however. Confirming earlier work in the United States, case studies showed that larger, more sophisticated firms frequently participate in publicly underwritten cooperative R&D programmes not for the money as such but for the ability to reach partners considered valuable. In other words, public programmes may create the institutional framework that makes collaboration possible. One way this can happen is through the implicit guarantee of acceptable behaviour by all partners in the presence of the public authority as an arbitrator. Such a guarantee could, for example, allay the fears of smaller firms that may feel intimidated to collaborate with much larger counterparts, being afraid of losing control of critical knowledge to them.

Another way this can happen is by making available the minimum necessary resources for enticing smaller, valued partners to participate in the RJV.

The case study analysis revealed a specific aspect of the policy initiatives supporting R&D cooperation, that of creating a context fostering research entrepreneurship, by:

1. increasing financial resources directed to R&D cooperation and supporting the development of physical infrastructure,
2. developing human resources as they motivated, especially, academics to undertake initiatives that were closer to the market needs, providing a context in which researchers could develop new ideas and obtain experience through repeated participation and
3. developing social capital through established trust and formal and informal ties.

It is thus expected that policy initiatives for supporting R&D cooperation have more long-term effects because they establish a common understanding for further collaboration, improve social capital and create communities of interaction that allow knowledge diffusion and creation.

13. Framework Programmes on RTD have contributed in the formation of networks in several technology fields involving for-profit companies as well as non-profit research organizations. Network formation should be an effective mechanism for transforming the European knowledge-base and for promoting economic cohesion.

14. Improving research links between universities and public research institutes and industry has become a policy priority in Europe. RJVs are an appropriate vehicle for such interaction.
When it comes to research, there is a difficult trade-off in the relationship between industry and universities. On the one hand, they do not usually see each other as direct competitors and consider that they have complementary capabilities and resources. On the other hand, the extensive differences in the incentive systems of the two kinds of organizations make collaboration difficult. Complementarities induce cooperation: knowledge and experiences are exchanged more easily among non-competing organizations. While there is never going to be a perfect match as long as the incentive systems remain so different, industry and universities already collaborate extensively on R&Ds and more of it is expected in the future.

**15.   Firms often react to the opportunities (constraints) provided (imposed)
by the institutional set-up and regulations (environmental, technical
standards, and so on). Policy affecting institutions and regulations will
have an impact on cooperative R&D.**

Firms try to adapt to their environment. One mechanism of adaptation is
cooperation – strategic alliances are indeed said to increase the flexibility of
the private sector. Earlier research in the United States has shown that, in
at least one broad field (environmental technologies), RJVs have formed in
reaction to (or anticipation of) regulatory changes. The case studies conducted in this project also found evidence to that effect.

**16.   Firms realize the value of complementary resources, strengths and
needs for reaping benefits from cooperative R&D.**

The frequency of collaboration between firms with complementary resources,
strengths and needs was underlined in this study as it has been before. An
important reason tends to be the complexity of the product under development that requires complementary capabilities. Cooperation among firms
operating in different, but related, sectors (such as telecommunications services and semiconductors) with different strategies and corporate cultures
also facilitates the exchange of assets, skills and experiences. In addition, it
has long been understood that interaction between technology users and producers increases innovation efficiency. Moreover, firms that are not direct
competitors will exchange information much more willingly than if they were.
And so forth. The lesson for policy analysts is that they should look for such
complementarities in designing and implementing cooperative R&D programmes as they are a major determinant of the success of collaboration.

That is not to say that competitors do not ever cooperate. Rather, it is to
say that they will tend to cooperate in the limited set of circumstances that
economic theory has predicted, including the establishment of technical
standards and the undertaking of research that is subject to severe problems of appropriability. Standards and knowledge appropriability problems would, then, provide more appropriate foci for programmes aiming at
horizontal cooperation between firms.

**17.   Firms do not appreciate cumbersome reporting requirements to public
authorities and frequent policy changes.**

Not surprisingly, several case studies showed complicated proposal submission procedures, cumbersome reporting requirements, and frequent policy
changes to discourage collaboration (under government auspices). This is
in full agreement with findings in other regions, including the United States.

18. Widespread collaboration in R&D can also have a downside in that it may promote anticompetitive behaviour. Competition policy authorities must be vigilant.

Several parts of this study indicated that RJVs are largely the domain of large firms. While this may partially reflect exogenous preferences and/or capture, the finding of repeated participation by large firms and their core role in networking corroborates with several similar findings in other available literature looking at the structure of different sets of RJVs than those examined here. The underlying reasons can be many but they certainly include the existence of high fixed costs, learning (how to cooperate) costs, and transaction costs in setting up collaborative agreements. RJVs were also found to take place in more concentrated industries. While cooperative R&D agreements enjoy block exemption from antitrust consideration in the European Union, we feel that competition authorities would do well to keep an open eye.

A potential source of anticompetitive behaviour, which this study did not explore systematically but some recent literature has called attention to, is the combination of multimarket and multiproject contact. The idea is straightforward. Multimarket contact – referring to the fact that large, diversified firms often 'meet' (compete) in many markets – increases the possibilities of anticompetitive behaviour, as both the benefits from collusion and the ability to enforce collusion increase with the number of markets in which two firms 'meet'. Multiproject contact – referring to firms 'meeting' (collaborating with) each other multiple times through RJVs and other technical alliances – could also raise the chances for anticompetitive behaviour. The argument is similar: both the benefits from collusion and the ability to enforce collusion increase with the number of future markets in which two firms expect to 'meet'. Importantly, however, whereas multimarket contact refers to existing markets, multiproject contact refers to future markets (those to be opened as a result of current R&D). Compounded, multimarket and multiproject contact can have deleterious effects on competition.

It is our understanding that the possibilities of multimarket and multiproject contact have not been picked up by competition authorities around the world. This is partly a matter of availability of adequate information, given that the analysis necessitates having the picture of the whole nexus of collaborative agreements of individual firms. Such a picture is what the STEP TO RJVs Databank may help provide.

The above policy implications are of special relevance at the present juncture, where European S&T policy is embarking upon two important and interrelated undertakings: the sixth FWP and the creation of a ERA. The 20 years of transnational, collaborative industrial research in Europe, the experience gained and the lessons learned, are of paramount importance for both undertakings. The new instruments introduced by the sixth FWP, Integrated Projects and Networks of Excellence, would be unthinkable without the rich networking effects that the implementation of the past five FWPs has promoted. On the other hand, the idea of a ERA would be mere utopia, had European RTD actors not grown accustomed to the construction of transnational Europe-wide relationships.

Even more importantly, one should not forget that both undertakings must be viewed in terms of their wider implications for the grand strategy that the EU is currently pursuing: Lisbon 2000. In the Lisbon summit, in June 2000, European leaders set for themselves the ambitious goal of transforming Europe into the most competitive knowledge-based economy in the world by the year 2010. To this end, the role of both S&T policy and of collaboration in R&D is, of course, crucial. The contributions collected in the present volume have perhaps shed some light on past experiences as well as on the policy choices facing decision makers and policy analysts.

Index